T0226233

Nonsequential and Distributed Programming with Go

Christian Maurer

Nonsequential and Distributed Programming with Go

Synchronization of Concurrent Processes:
Communication—Cooperation—
Competition

 Springer

Christian Maurer
Institut für Informatik
Freie Universität Berlin
Berlin, Germany

ISBN 978-3-658-29781-7   ISBN 978-3-658-29782-4   (eBook)
https://doi.org/10.1007/978-3-658-29782-4

Responsible Editor: Sybille Thelen
This Springer imprint is published by the registered company Springer Fachmedien Wiesbaden GmbH part of
Springer Nature.
The registered company address is: Abraham-Lincoln-Str. 46, 65189 Wiesbaden, Germany

Dedicated to my golden angel

Preface

First of all, we have to explain, why—by not following the "mainstream"—

"Nonsequential Programming"

was chosen as title of this book instead of

"Concurrent Programming".

In the German language, there exist two words for "concurrent":

- *nebenläufig* and
- *nichtsequentiell.*

The first word is the exact translation of "concurrent"[1] , the second is simply the negation of *sequentiell*, i.e. *"nichtsequentiell"* is just "not *sequentiell*".

So, strictly speaking, "concurrent programming" means, that several developers are working together to write a program, but makes no sense for a book title; whereas "nonsequential programming" means the development of nonsequential programs, which is our topic. *Processes* with access to shared resources may run *concurrently* on one or more computers; *algorithms,* however, cannot be *concurrent*—they are either *sequential* or not. This is probably the reason, why in all German universities lectures on this topic are named "Nichtsequentielle Programmierung".

This is why we prefer to use the German word for "nonsequential" in the context of "programs" and "programming", as in our opinion that adjective is much better suited for this purpose, and stick to the German term in so far, as we use the spelling "nonsequential" instead of "non-sequential". Furthermore,

▶ we will generally use the abbreviation "NSP" for "nonsequential programming".

---

[1] Latin: *concurrere = cum + currere*; *cum* = (together) with, *currere* = run, go, walk

Basic techniques of nonsequential programming are either the subject of a separate lecture in the bachelor's program of computer science studies or are part of lectures on areas, in which nonsequential algorithms play an essential role.

This book systematically develops basic concepts for the synchronization of concurrent processes and for their *communication*[2] —even in the distributed case:

- locks,
- semaphores,
- fairness and deadlocks,
- monitors,
- message passing,
- network-wide message passing.
- exploration of networks,
- traversal in networks and
- selection of a leader in them.

The algorithms are formulated in Go (see https://golang.org). Among other things, this language is characterized by the following features:

- a C-like syntax (see https://golang.org/ref/spec)—but with significant influence from Wirth's languages (see https://golang.org/doc/fac#history),
- the trend towards *concise language* and freedom from language stuttering of the kind " foo.Foo* myFoo = new(foo.Foo)",
- garbage collection,
- the "rebellion" against cumbersome type systems such as e.g. in C++ or Java, and consequently
- a very expressive *type system* with *static type check when compiling a source text, dynamic type adjustment at runtime* as well as a *rigid dependency analysis,*
- but *without* type hierarchy ("types just are, they don't have to announce their relationships")—so *lighter* than in typical OO languages,
- "orthogonality of the concepts" ("methods can be implemented for any type; structures represent data while "interfaces" represent abstraction.") and
- the installation of various constructs for NSP, including message passing—inspired by Hoare's CSP calculus—as well as support for parallel, multicore and networked computing.

---

[2]Latin: *communicare* = to communicate, to share, to discuss

More information can be found in the net at the beginning of the *Frequently Asked Questions* by Go (https://golang.org/doc/faq).

To run the programs from the book, the installation of Go version 1.9 (or higher) is assumed.

Basic knowledge of Go is certainly helpful for understanding the basic concepts, but not necessary because of the simple syntax.

However, familiarizing yourself with Go is *significantly* (!) easier than, for example, acquiring the knowledge in Java required to understand algorithms in comparable depth.

If you don't want to do this, you can understand the Go source texts "meta-linguistically"—such as the language-independent representations of algorithms in the textbooks of Andrews, Ben-Ari, Herrtwich/Hommel, Raynal or Taubenfeld .

At "switching points"—*locks, semaphores, monitors* and *network-wide message passing*—some basic approaches to programming in C and Java are also presented.

Knowledge of imperative representations of *abstract data objects,* of the principles of *"information-hiding"* and the basic concepts of *object-oriented programming* are however required; some important information—as far as it is needed for this book—can be found in Chap. 2 about packages, interfaces and abstract data types.

The content structure is inductive:

The growing distance from the machine is associated with increasing abstraction, which corresponds very naturally to the historical development of NSP: locks—semaphores—monitors—message passing. This structure can already be described as *traditional,* as it can also be found in most other textbooks.

Reading is therefore essentially only meaningful sequentially, i.e. in the order of the chapters.

Focusing on Go would have offered an alternative order of the contents, starting with the highest level of abstraction, the passing of messages via channels—a core concept of this language—which is particularly recommended by its developers as the means of choice for synchronization (see Sect. 1.9 on process states in the introduction and Chap. 11 about messages). This path is deliberately not followed here, however, in order to be able to use the book in environments in which other languages are favoured.

A fundamental principle of the book consists in the fact that *the same classic examples* are taken up *again and again,* which facilitates the comparison between the presented concepts and language tools.

The readers are *strongly* recommended,

- to work through these examples carefully in order to gain deeper insight into the similarities and differences between the concepts,
- to perceive the suggestions for their own activities, i.e. to take up as many suggestions for exercises as possible,
- to go *ad fontes* (original papers are fundamental sources, because they provide deeper insights into the systematics of the development of NSP),

- and—either—to install Go and *get all examples and programs running*—or—to implement the algorithms in their preferred programming language, in order to acquire practical programming competence.

Compared to the third edition, some bugs have been fixed and minor enhancements added.

The *essential* difference to the 3rd edition, however, is that—due to a change in the Go system—adjustments were required: The previous basic assumption that a value assignment of a constant or variable to a variable of an elementary type is atomic is now only valid in Go if the computer used has only one processor or if `runtime.GOMAXPROCS(1)` was called.

Therefore, the value assignments to shared variables used in the entry and exit protocols to protect critical sections now *principally* need to be replaced by an atomic instruction—realized with an indivisible machine instruction.

For some of the algorithms given in the book test runs can be carried out in which their sequence is visualized dynamically. The corresponding program files, some of which use C-library-routines and header files in /usr/include, are included in the source texts of this book.

I would like to thank Mrs. Dipl.-Inf. Sybille Thelen from Springer-Verlag very much; she also supported the publication of this edition very kindly again.

In June 2018 she informed me, that *Springer Nature* had selected my book among some others to create in cooperation with *DeepL* an English version. I was very happy about that idea and immediately agreed. In the middle of December 2019 I got the result, but I after having read the first pages of it was a bit disappointed on quite a lot of mistakes in the computer aided translation. The were some really funny ones as, e.g., "castle" and "lure" for lock, "trial" and "lawsuit" for process, "net curtain" for "store", "voltage tree" and "current beam" for spanning tree, "beacon" for signal, "embassy" for message and "episode" for sequence and, furthermore, lots of things like the remarkable statement "Any deterministic algorithm is deterministic, but not *any* deterministic algorithm is necessary deterministic." But there were also several of really annoying errors such as grammar mistakes, rather strange orders of words in sentences and many wrong translations that completely distorted contents. However, this experience implies, that I will *never* sit in an AI-controlled car.

I have to thank the book production teams of Springer Nature, Heidelberg, and of Scientific Publishing Services Ltd., Chennai: They have improved my corrections of the DeepL-translation. I would also like to thank Mrs. Ivonne Eling for organizing things in the background and Mr. Stefan Schmidt for several suggestions.

Finally, an important hint: Despite constant and thorough comparison of all source texts reproduced in the book in the course of their development, it cannot be ruled out with *absolute* certainty, that there are inconsistencies somewhere. (Hints to discovered discrepancies or errors are of course very gratefully accepted!)

All source texts are is available on the *pages of the book in the worldwide web:* https://maurer-berlin.eu/nspbook/4.

Berlin   Christian Maurer
January 25th and November 20th 2020

Contents

List of Figures

List of Tables

Introduction

1

Abstarct

In this chapter, central concepts of concurrent programming are defined and conceptual differences to sequential programming are worked out. It is shown that the magnitudes of the number of possible sequences of concurrent programs exceed any human imagination. Afterwards, notations for concurrent instructions are introduced and the process concept is introduced informally. Some examples demonstrate the extreme vulnerability to errors that can result from conflicts when multiple processes access shared resources. They make clear that programs without synchronization of these accesses are completely unusable or even arbitrarily harmful. After explaining what is meant by atomic (indivisible) instructions, the interplay between the concept of indivisibility and that of critical sections is explained and, based on this, lock synchronization is defined as a first concept for avoiding access conflicts. The chapter concludes with the development of the process concept and the presentation of the transitions between process states. They serve the understanding of abstract terms and allow insight into inner processes in the computer.

1.1 Definition of Terms

Before dealing with concurrent programming, it is necessary to distinguish some properties of algorithms from each other in order to clarify this concept.

At first a remark on a word common to mathematicians:

▶ "iff" means "if and only if".

© Springer Fachmedien Wiesbaden GmbH, part of Springer Nature 2021
C. Maurer, *Nonsequential and Distributed Programming with Go*,
https://doi.org/10.1007/978-3-658-29782-4_1

An algorithm is called

- *determined,* if it returns the same result values for the same input values, i.e., its *results* are *reproducible,*
- *deterministic,* if the *order* in which the statements are processed is clearly defined, i.e., if its *progress* is reproducible;
- *sequential,* if its individual steps are executed one after the other in the order defined by the sequence of statements in its text (whereby, of course, *all* constructs of *imperative* programming for generating statements—starting with atomic—are permitted: *sequence, case distinction* and *repetition,*
- *nonsequential,* iff it is *not sequential,* so the *linear* order of its individual steps is replaced bye a *nonlinear* order;
- *parallel,* if it is broken down into several parts, each of which is designed for processing on its *own processor,*
- *distributed,* if it is broken down into several parts, each of which is designed for processing on its one *own computer,* i.e., *without* recourse to *shared memory*

The following relationships exist between these terms:

▶ Any deterministic algorithm is determined, but not *any* determined algorithm is necessarily deterministic.

The first statement follows immediately from the definitions. A simple example of the invalidity of the reversal are two assignments of constants to two different variables—the result is independent of their order.

▶ Any deterministic algorithm is sequential, but not any sequential algorithm is necessarily deterministic.

The sequence of a deterministic algorithm is simply the sequence of the steps of its well-defined sequence.

▶ Any deterministic algorithm is sequential, but not *any* sequential algorithm is necessarily deterministic.

The sequence of a deterministic algorithm is simply the succession of the steps of its well-defined progress.

Counterexamples of the reverse are the guarded alternative and iterative instructions of DIJKSTRA in [4] and ANDREWS in [1]—the narrow "ring" around the central area of deterministic algorithms in Fig. 1.1. However, we do not go into this in detail, because our topic is (determined) nonsequential algorithms—the gray area in this illustration.

▶ Any algorithm designed to run on multicore processors is nonsequential.

In this case, there cannot be a linear sequence of the individual steps, because the algorithm contains parts that are executed by different processors overlapping in time or simultaneously.

We will not go into parallel algorithms in detail; most of them are more likely to be special subjects in mathematics than in computer science—far outside the framework set for this book—the development of *basic* concurrent programming techniques.

Distributed algorithms have become by far the largest part of NSP due to their size and importance; they represent an independent subject area.

In the following chapters about network-wide message passing, heartbeat algorithms, traversal algorithms, and leader election algorithms, we provide a small insight into this area. Now we turn to the logical consequence of the first two points:

▶ Any concurrent algorithm is nondeterministic, but may well be deterministic.

By *nonsequential* execution of a *concurrent algorithm* we understand that—beyond the fixed sequence of the steps of its sequential components—*no assumptions at all are made about the order of its execution,* which means that *any conceivable shape of concurrency* is permissible, i.e., any design that is arbitrarily interlocked in terms of time, if only *one*

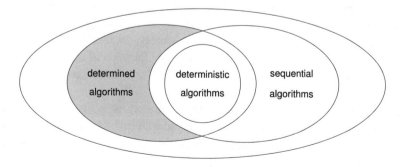

Fig. 1.1 Rough division of the universe of algorithms

processor is present, or any arbitrarily overlapping parallel execution on systems with *several* processors.

In the development of nonsequential algorithms, i.e., algorithms in which nondeterminism is not only permitted but even desired by the concurrent execution of instruction sequences, the demand for *determinacy* is, of course, *unavoidable*.

To construct correct algorithms, it is necessary to analyze all possible effects of the interaction between their individual steps; for example, if they operate on shared data or are mutually dependent on conditions influenced by concurrent instruction sequences.

This is essentially done by controlling competing accesses by means of *synchronization*[1], i.e., by limiting their arbitrariness in time and by taking measures to coordinate them among themselves.

The aim is to exclude nonsensical processes that lead to *nonreproducibility* of the result and destruction of the data when accessing them. In Sect. 1.6, we will get to know some typical examples of such conflicts, which one can get in the programming of concurrent systems and which indicate a core of the problems of concurrency.

So, the paradigm of NSP can be strikingly expressed as follows:

▶ Nonsequential algorithms in connection with suitable methods for synchronization are determined.

Its central theme is, therefore:

- to find suitable synchronization schemes for certain types of problems,
- to classify them, and
- to specify and implement suitable algorithms for their solution.

1.2   Motivation and Applications

Computers are used for the input and output of data by means of peripheral devices, such as keyboard, mouse, graphics tablet, microphones, cameras, measuring devices, sticks, optical memories, disks, diskettes, tapes, network cards, screens, printers, plotters, loudspeakers, projectors, control devices, ... The management and allocation of main memory and the coordination of access to such devices—summarized under the term *operating resources*—is the concern of the construction of *operating systems*.

These resources work in complex interdependencies and usually have to be synchronized. The key goal is to prevent data from being destroyed with simultaneous access by multiple users or devices because they can become inconsistent if competing operations are not carefully coordinated.

---

[1] ancient Greek: $\sigma\acute{\upsilon}\nu$ = (together) with, $\chi\varrho\acute{o}\nu o\varsigma$ = time, duration; $\chi\varrho o\nu\acute{\iota}\zeta\varepsilon\iota\nu$ = to spend time, to take long, to hesitate

(Please try to imagine the unsynchronized access to some of the mentioned resources using suitable examples—with a little imagination you will quickly end up with scenarios with slapstick character.)

The risks inevitably associated with the management of the *operating resources* entail that almost all the questions raised outside the paradigm of NSP cannot even be formulated, let alone answered.

There are further fields of application on a larger scale:

For many computation-intensive problems, where very large amounts of data are processed using complex numerical methods, such as in weather forecast, parallel algorithms, where the system load is skillfully distributed over several processors, are, of course, clearly superior to sequential solutions in terms of efficiency (and mostly only *feasible in this way* within reasonable time).

Furthermore, large—sometimes global—projects are increasingly being automated, for which the computing capacity of individual machines is far from sufficient, or where data have to be managed that are spread across many locations. This requires the interconnection of several—sometimes very many and extremely different—*computers* in a network and their coordination. The basis for this is programming techniques, that allow to access other machines from one computer.

For obvious reasons, some systems, e.g., for controlling road, rail or air traffic or production processes, make extremely tight time-critical demands up to sharply defined machine requirements such as *reactions in real time*.

One of the central tasks of *database systems* is to ensure the atomicity of access to the managed data, isolating the data when accessed, and finally ensuring their consistency and durability. For this purpose, many concurrent complex execution sequences, so-called *transactions,* have to be synchronized while accessing possibly shared databases.

With these remarks, those fields of computer science are outlined, from which, on the on hand, the techniques of concurrent programming have emerged, which, on the other hand, they both presuppose and further develop:

- *operating systems,*
- *parallel algorithms,*
- *network programming,*
- *distributed systems,*
- *real-time programming*, and
- *database transactions.*

The following postulate applies to all these cases:

▶ The architecture of a program should reflect the structure of the task, which is performed using computers.

However, this structure is not necessarily sequential; consequently, the paradigm of sequentiality often represents a restriction on the design of a program, which is out of the question.

A concise aphorism from LÖHR's lectures on NSP may be quoted:

▶ Nonsequential environmental behaviour induces nonsequential program structures.

There are innumerable inherently massively concurrent systems whose common characteristic is the management of enormous amounts of data for a large number of users and whose solution is, therefore, without the use of (sometimes very) many computers no longer imaginable at all, such as for

- worldwide search, information, and documentation,
- communication mediation and live transmission,
- administration of personnel and life work data,
- account management and execution of financial transactions,
- accounting and merchandise management,
- booking, ordering and purchasing in the worldwide web,
- service and damage recording and invoicing,
- preparation of expert reports, expert opinions, forecasts,
- computer aided medical diagnostics and therapy,
- computer support for risky operations,
- development, design, and manufacturing,
- machine, plant, and production control,
- control of road vehicles, trains, ships, and airplanes,
- production of simulations and animations,
- observation and control of automated processes,
- monitoring of security-sensitive areas,
- registration of substances and equipment subject to authorization,
- social networking between persons or groups of people,
- participation in online games and betting,
- modeling of climatic and maritime processes,
- geographical mapping and visualization,
- navigation in road, rail, and air traffic,
- early warning of disasters, and
- control in satellite and space technology.

1.3   The (Non-)Sense of Testing

The necessity of a drastic restriction of the possible execution sequences of concurrent programs with the aim of controlling their construction and their comprehensibility becomes clear through the following considerations.

For this reason alone, the design of correct concurrent algorithms receives an unusual quality compared to sequential algorithms, simply because the number of all possible execution sequences *combinatorially explodes*:

With p sequences of $n_1, n_2, \ldots, n_p$ atomic statements, that is, those whose progress cannot be interrupted,

$$a(n_1, n_2, \ldots, n_p) = \frac{\left(\sum_{i=1}^{p} n_i\right)!}{\prod_{i=1}^{p} n_i!} = \frac{(n_1 + n_2 + \cdots + n_p)!}{n_1! \cdot n_2! \cdot \ldots \cdot n_p!}.$$

execution sequences are possible.

There is a total of

$$n_1 + n_2 + \cdots + n_p$$

statements, and consequently, we have

$$(n_1 + n_2 + \cdots + n_p)!$$

permutations of *all* statements; since for each individual sequence only *one*, namely its original sequential order, is permissible, this number has to be divided for each i ($1 \leq i \leq p$) by the number

$$n_i!$$

of the permutations of its statements.

Of course, this result can also be developed recursively. Functional programming is, of course, an option for the formulation—e.g., in Haskell:

```haskell
a :: [Int] -> Int

a (0:ns) = a ns
a (n:ns) = (n + sum ns) * a ((n-1):ns) `div` n
a []     = 1
```

Because

$$a(0, n_2, \ldots, n_p) = \frac{(n_2 + \cdots + n_p)!}{n_2! \cdot \ldots \cdot n_p!} = a(n_2, \ldots, n_p)$$

and

$$\frac{n_1 + n_2 + \cdots + n_p}{n_1} \cdot a(n_1 - 1, n_2, \ldots, n_p) = a(n_1, n_2, \ldots, n_p)$$

it supplies the above formula.

The meaning of the formula, however, can only be grasped through concrete numerical examples that very clearly illustrate the paradigm of the "combinatorial explosion":

- With 2 sequences of 3 instructions each, there are only 20 possibilities.
  (You should convince yourself of this by listing all possible cases,
  e.g., recursively with $a(0, k) = a(k, 0) = 1$ and
  $a(n + 1, k) = a(n, k) + a(n + 1, k - 1) = (n + 1 + k) * a(n, k)/(n + 1)$.).
- With 4 sequences of 4 instructions each more than 60 million.
- With 6 sequences of 5 instructions, 90 trillion already.
  (With the printouts on DIN A4 paper—double-sided, one instruction per line—you could wrap the earth almost a hundred times.).
- With 8 sequences of 6 instructions each more than 170 sextillion.
  (The printout would need paper of the volume of more than 6000 times our solar sphere.)

These numbers, which at first glance seem completely crazy, are by no means exaggerated: Look—e.g., with the Unix command top—how many processes are running on your computer immediately after the boot process. (On a computer running Linux there are at least about 12 dozen.)

And because of the fact that the approach of an amount of 3 to 6 atomic statements for a *critical section*—a sequential program section defined by certain properties—is absolutely realistic, you will find lots of examples in this book.

(Don't be discouraged by the terms *atomic instruction, process*, and *critical section*; each of these notions will be explained precisely in their own sections in this Introduction.)

A fundamental conclusion to be drawn from this observation is that any attempt to verify the correctness of nonsequential algorithms by *testing,* which already in the sequential algorithm is only used for the proof of the *presence* (sic!) of *errors,* in NSP is not only extremely questionable, but a crude malpractice:

▶ Even if a program runs smoothly without any problems countless times, you can *by no means* conclude that it is error-free.

1.4   Examples of Concurrent Algorithms

We want to demonstrate some basic ideas with three very simple examples of parallel algorithms. A possible field of application for concurrency is *nonlinear recursion,* for example the following implementation of *mergesort:*

```
func mergesort (a []int, e chan int) {
  if len(a) > 1 {
    m := len(a)/2
```

```
    c, d := make(chan int), make(chan int)
    go mergesort (a[:m], c)
    go mergesort (a[m:], d)
    <-c
    <-d
    merge (a, m)
  }
  e <- 0
}
```

in which a sequence to be sorted is divided into two "halves", which are sorted in parallel, and then with the *merge* algorithm

```
func merge (a []int, m int) {
  n := len(a)
  b := make([]int, len(a))
  for j, i, k := 0, 0, m; j < n; j++ {
    if i < m && k < n {
      if a[i] < a[k] {
        b[j] = a[i]; i++
      } else {
        b[j] = a[k]; k++
      }
    } else if i < m {
      b[j] = a[i]; i++
    } else if k < n {
      b[j] = a[k]; k++
    }
  }
  copy (a, b)
}
```

and merged into an ordered sequence.

The algorithms are used in the following program:

```
package main

func merge (a []int, m int) {
  ... as above

func mergesort (a []int, e chan int) {
  ... as above

func main() {
  done := make(chan int)
  is := []int{7,9,1,4,0,6,8,2,5,3}
  go mergesort (is, done)
  <-done
  for _, i := range is { print(i, " ") }
  println()
```

}

Basically, of course, the practicability has to be questioned. With larger input sequences, unreasonable numbers of branched processes can result. In the example presented here, the role of the *channels* of type `chan int` generated by the statements `make(chan int)` is not yet clear; also, it remains unclear what the *sending* and *receiving* of *messages* have to do with the statements `c <-` and `<-c` for a channel `c`.

At the moment, only so much should be said that this is a *core idea* of the language Go for synchronization. Readers are asked to accept this for the time being until we justify in Sect. 1.9 on *process states,* why it is necessary to inform a calling process via a *message* about the termination of its diverted message and discuss in Chap. 11 about messages passing the syntactic aspects for that.

As a second example, we show a procedure in which certain parts can be computed independently of each other—for example, the multiplication of 3×3-matrices, representing linear maps $\mathbb{R}^3 \to \mathbb{R}^3$ with respect to given bases; the calculation of their product corresponds to the composition of the corresponding maps.

The product $(c_{ik}) = (a_{ij}) \cdot (b_{jk})$ $(0 \leq i, j, k < 3)$ of two matrices is defined as follows: the number $c_{ik} = \sum_{j=0}^{2} a_{ij} b_{jk}$ in its i-th row and k-th column is the scalar product of the i-th row of (a_{ij}) and the k-th column of (b_{jk}).

For that we need the scalar product:

```
type vector [3] float64

func scalarproduct (v, w vector, p *float64, d chan float64) {
   for j := 0; j < 3; j++ {
     *p += v[j] * w[j]
   }
   d <- 0
}
```

The values of the product matrix can be calculated concurrently:

```
type matrix [3] vector

func column (a matrix, k float64) (s vector) {
   for j := 0; j < 3; j++ {
     s[j] = a[j][k]
   }
   return s
}

func product (a, b matrix) (p matrix) {
   done := make (chan int)
   for i := 0; i < 3; i++ {
     for k := 0; k < 3; k++ {
       go scalarproduct (a[i], column(b, k), &p[i][k], done)
```

```
      }
    }
    for j := 0; j < 9; j++ {
      <-done
    }
    return p
}
```

In a program, this is used as follows:

```
package main

... types and functions as above

func main() {
  a := matrix { vector{1,2,3}, vector{4,5,6}, vector{7,8,9} }
  b := matrix { vector{9,8,7}, vector{6,5,4}, vector{3,2,1} }
  c := product (a, b)
  for i := 0; i < 3; i++ {
    for k := 0; k < 3; k++ {
      print(c[i][k], " ")
    }
    println()
  }
}
```

The third example is only hinted at, leaving its coding as an exercise: We call two trees *equivalent,* if they have the same number of nodes, the contents of which (in preorder) match pairwise. To test this, it makes sense to create three processes, two of which traverse a tree and write the leaves in a sequence, while the third immediately starts traversing these sequences simultaneously and checking their elements for equality in pairs.

1.5   Concurrency and the Informal Notion of a Process

For the construct *sequence* from two sequential statements or statement sequences A and B we use the notation

    A; B

with separation by a semicolon, if they stand behind each other, and omit the semicolon, if—as is usual in multiline program texts—they are standing

    A
    B

one below the other.

For the notation of the *concurrency* of A and B an appropriate simple construct is needed. By

```
A || B
```

we designate a *nonsequential statement* with the following semantics:

The instruction sequences A and B are executed concurrently; the end of the statement A || B is achieved, *iff* both A and A are finished.

The order of A and B doesn't matter, of course:

```
A || B
```

and

```
B || A
```

have the *same effect*.

This construct is naturally expandable to finitely many instruction sequences

```
A || B || ... || X
```

In the literature, similar metalanguage notations can be found, e.g., in [3] by DIJKSTRA

parbegin A; B **parend**

in [1] by ANDREWS

co A // B **oc**

and in [5] by HERRTWICH/HOMMEL

conc A || B **end conc**

A typical small concurrent program, for example, consisting of a sequential statement sequence A for the input of data, a nonsequential statement B || C for completing two parts of a task and a final sequential statement sequence D for processing the partial results and output of the result then looks like this:

```
A
B || C
D
```

Apart from Pascal-FC by BURNS/DAVIES (see [2]) there are hardly any programming languages that have such a construct. Instead, you will find calls to the *branch* of a statement sequence and *wait* for it to end.

In accordance with Unix system calls, which in their semantics roughly correspond to what is to be expressed here, we use the identifiers fork and wait with the following semantics:

- The statement fork A branches off the statement sequence A and executes it concurrently to the subsequent statement sequence;
- the statement wait A delays the call of the subsequent statement until A is finished, if this wasn't already the case at the time of calling wait A.

This means that the sequence

```
fork  C
B
wait  C
```

is equivalent to the construct

```
B  ||  C
```

and our little program above is now—syntactically—close to common programming languages:

```
A
fork  C
B
wait  C
D
```

These concepts are inseparably linked to a central concept of NSP, that of the *process*.

At the moment, it is going to be defined only informally. First of all, it should be noted that in this book, however, we do not refer to *operating system processes*, which as *"virtual computers"*

- run in a separate address space and use all resources managed by the operating system separately,

but leave those *"heavy weight processes"* to the subject *operating systems*.

With the view to cooperating and competing, we confine ourselves to the *virtual processors,* the *threads within* operating system processes (also called *lightweight processes,* which

- are executed in the same address space as the branching process and, therefore, have access to the same data.

▶ It is, therefore, generally agreed, that the concept of *process* is used as a synonym for a *lightweight process.*

Now to the definition: A process is

- *Static*:
  the source code of an elementary statement (a value assignment or the call of a function without return value) or of a statement sequence in a nonsequential program, which is called

  - in Pascal-FC by starting a `process` procedure with a call between `cobegin` and `coend` (for details see [2]),
  - in C by creating a thread with `pthread_create`,
  - in Modula-2 by the start of a coroutine with `NEWPROCESS` (for details see [8], Chapter 30),
  - in Java by implementing the interface `Runnable` and the start of a new thread, and
  - in Go by branching off a *goroutine* with `go`.
- *Dynamic*:
  a part of a program in its execution on a processor—from the call of its first statement to the completion of its last statement, i.e., the actual effects of this sequence of statements in the form of *state changes* in the computer.

Section 1.9 on *process states* at the end of this Introduction is dedicated to a more detailed description.

In this book, whenever we speak about a *process,* it can be seen from the respective context, whether it is a static or a dynamic process.

Each process represents a sequential program section that conceptually runs on its own processor. For the realization of these *logical processors* there are the following possibilities:

- They share only *one real* processor, assigned to them by the *process management* according to a certain strategy, e.g., according to the *round robin* procedure.
- For the duration of its execution, each process receives its *own processor,* i.e., the processes run in *parallel.*
- Hybrid forms from these two methods are used, since the number of processes can vary greatly from case to case, whereas the number of real processors is a static quantity in a computer system.

Since the paradigm of NSP *principally* makes no statement about this, what we already postulated in the first section, should be emphasized again:

▶ All algorithms must be designed completely independently of such considerations!

1.6   Conflicts When Addressing Shared Data

In the simplest case, the interaction between processes takes place via shared variables. To investigate the problems of accessing them, let's look at a very simple example where two processes independently increase a counter with the initial value 0 by 1 each.

The counter values during the program run are written on the screen.

```
package main
import ("math/rand"; "time")

var (
   counter uint
   done chan bool
)

func v() {
   time.Sleep (Duration(rand.Int63n (1e5)))
}

func inc (n *uint) {
   accu := *n // "LDA n"
   v()
   accu++      // "INA"
   v()
   *n = accu  // "STA n"
   println(*n)
   v()
}

func count (p uint) {
   const N = 5
   for n := uint(0); n < N; n++ {
     inc (&counter)
   }
   done <- true
}

func main() {
   done = make (chan bool)
   go count (0); go count (1)
   <-done; <-done
   println("counter ==", counter)
}
```

However, calls to this program usually provide a final counter value between 5 and 9, but not the expected 10. If the time delays v() are omitted, the final value is (always?) 10.

The purpose of their installation is merely to give the other process the opportunity to interrupt the current one here and, thus, to ensure nonsensical results.

The same purpose is served by decomposing the statement n++ into the three steps

```
accu := *n
accu++
*n = accu
```

—we'll take a closer look.

Some advice first:

It is definitely worth "playing around" with this small, faulty program. You should increase the number of processes involved, increase the constant N by powers of 10, or arrange
for unsymmetrical delays, e.g., by parameterizing it with the process number p. You will
then get quite different results.

Accordingly, you will notice that the system always (?) continues counting correctly to
the end, if the loop body in the function count simply consists of the statement "n++".

To figure out what's happening here, we imagine the statement n++ in a fictitious
assembler language with the commands

- LDA and STA to load and store values of memory cells into and out of the accumulator
  and,
- INA to increase the value in the accumulator,

as a sequence of these three machine instructions, as is shown (with the literal " ; " as an
introduction to a comment) in Tab. 1.1.

In the case of a nondeterministic process, an execution sequence (of the 20 possible
ones—see Sect. 1.3) such as in Tab. 1.2 is not excluded.

In this case, both processes increase the original value of the counter independently by 1
and then store this increased value, which results in a *lost increase*. That's exactly what we
have provoked with the "detour" above,

Tab. 1.1 Fictitious assembler language

Machine instruction	Comment
LDA X	; load the content of the memory cell
	; X into the accu
INA	; increase the accu by 1
STA X	; store the content of the accu
	; into the memory cell X

Tab. 1.2 Possible sequence of executions

Process 1	Process 2
	LDA X
LDA X	
INA	
	INA
	STA X
STA X	

```
accu := *n
accu++
*n = accu
```

Obviously, such (or similar) interlocking between statements from the two processes involved is the cause of the disaster!

With these difficulties we encountered a central problem of NSP:

▶ *Unsynchronized* access to shared data by several processes can falsify them or cause their
loss, therefore, making programs *totally unusable.*

To remedy this, it is necessary to avoid such temporal interferences between reading data
and changing their values.

The second example shows how destructive concurrent access to more complex data
objects can be. We overwrite the string `012345678901234567889012345` character
by character with `abcdefghijklmnopqrstuvwxyz` and copy them concurrently into
a second variable—for the same reasons as above, with delays that cause the writing and
reading processes to overtake each other several times:

```go
package main
import ("strings"; "time")

var (
  a, b string
  done = make(chan int)
)

func pause() {
  time.Sleep (1e6)
}

func write() {
  for n := 0; n < len(a); n++ {
    switch n {
    case 5, 11, 14, 22:
      pause()
    }
    a = strings.Replace (a, string(byte(n)
                            string(byte(n) + 'a'), 1)
  }
  done <- 0
}

func read() {
  for n := 0; n < len(a); n++ {
    switch n {
    case 3, 10, 17, 23:
```

```
      pause()
    }
    b += string(a[n])
  }
  done <- 0
}

func main () {
  a = "012345678901234567889012345"
  go write()
  go read()
  <-done
  <-done
  println(b)
}
```

A program run delivers neither the original nor the copy, which should hardly surprise you after the previous example, but e.g., the hopeless confusion `012defghijk123456 rstuv2345`. Dynamic data structures are just as insecure when faced with such errors:

Given is a doubly linked list with the node structure

```
type node struct {
  content interface{}
  next, prev *node
}
```

Let `A` be a reference to a node in this list. Suppose process 1 wants to insert a new node behind this one and process 2 wants to remove the node behind it. Let `B` be the reference to a new node that process 1 has just created to insert it.

Then the execution sequence shown in Tab. 1.3 is possible.

The consequence is that while traversing in the direction `next`, both the new node and the one to be removed are traversed, but in the opposite direction neither of the two are reversed. The processes not only missed their respective targets, but left the list in an inconsistent state—totally unacceptable. If dynamic data objects are more intertwined

Tab. 1.3 Possible execution sequence

Process 1	Process 2
B.next = A.next	
B.prev = A	
	A.next = A.next.next
B.next.prev = B	
	A.next.prev = A
A.next = B	

internally by references, as is the case, e.g., with trees or graphs, even much greater chaos can result.

Obviously, all the errors presented have the same cause. Statements that were changing data—inevitably accepting intermediate inconsistency of data structures—were interrupted by other concurrent statements that also wanted to work with these data. As a result, they could no longer complete their tasks by restoring the consistency of the data structure, which in turn meant that the other statements did not have defined prerequisites for their operations.

The consequence in all cases was the—at least partial—destruction of data, which leads to the total unusability of the program.

As an exercise it is suggested to think about which results are possible if three processes concurrently increase a counter with the initial value 0 by 1, 2 or 4.

1.7   Atomic Statements

This insight leads to the demand for statements, that are *not interruptible,* hence the following notion:

A *statement sequence* is called *atomic* (also: *indivisible*) if it cannot be interrupted by concurrent statements.

The state transitions of the computer during the execution of an atomic statement sequence are "not visible" to other concurrent processes; they appear to them like a statement implemented by a single indivisible machine instruction.

For atomic statements, we use the notation used in [1] with *indivisibility brackets.*

For a statement sequence A

$$<A>$$

signifies the *indivisible* execution of A. This construction is suitable for the specification of *mutual exclusion,* which we will discuss in the following section.

The indivisibility of a statement sequence A can be easily expressed by

$$A=<A>.$$

With this notation, we can also create a general construct for the *specification* of simple *synchronization* algorithms:

For a statement sequence A and a Boolean expression B, the *conditional atomic instruction*

```
<await B; A>
```

is defined by the fact that the calling process is blocked until the condition B is fulfilled, and then the statement sequence A is executed atomically, where B guaranteed as a prerequisite for A is assured.

If A is the empty statement, we get the statement for the *conditional synchronization*

<await B>.

As good as this construct is for the *specification of algorithms* for synchronization at a high level of abstraction, so difficult it is, of course, in general to *implement*.

At the lowest level, atomic statements are instructions from the instruction set of a processor, whose execution cannot be interrupted by other instructions—not even by another processor in the same computer.

The processors of Intel® or AMD® have the instruction LOCK (for details see the *manuals* of the processors), which as a prefix before certain operations ensures that, in a system with several processors, the processor allocated to the calling process has exclusive read and write access to the *working memory,* i.e., access to the memory that cannot be interrupted by other processors. As a prefix before one of the permitted operations, this instruction has the effect that the subsequent operation is performed atomically. These include some addition and subtraction commands, logical operators and certain comparison and exchange operations.

In the first part of the following chapter, we will solve some simple synchronization problems using indivisible machine instructions from the latter command group.

The *construction* of atomic statement sequences on *higher language levels* is a topic of NSP that will occupy us throughout.

1.8   Critical Sections and Lock Synchronization

In order to be able to formulate approaches to the solution of the problems presented, first of all those parts of program texts are characterized that can cause loss or inconsistency of data, when called by several processes with access to those data.

A *critical section* is

- a *sequential* statement sequence within a *concurrent* statement sequence, in which several processes access the *same* data,

where the case

- that in at least *one* of the concurrent sequential statement sequences involved a *write* access might occur

cannot be excluded.

This term is closely related to the *indivisibility*. Critical sections in which the same data is accessed

- must be from the point of view of the concurrent processes involved in accessing the data *atomic*—i.e., *not interruptible* by other instruction sequences, so
- must run under *mutual exclusion*, i.e., that the accesses to shared data from critical sections, which are executed concurrently by *different* statement sequences, run *without intertwining* each other.

These requirements also serve to define critical sections

- in [1] as sections of *programs* that have access to shared objects,
- in [2] as a *program piece* that appears indivisible from the point of view of the other processes, and
- in [5] as *statement sequences* whose execution requires mutual exclusion.

By *lock synchronization* we understand measures to avoid data loss or inconsistencies, which can arise when several processes access shared data.

It is defined by the following four properties:

- *Mutual exclusion*:
  There is at most *one* process in the critical section at any time.
- *Absence of unnecessary delay*:
  If processes want to enter a critical section, one of them will immediately succeed if no process is in the critical section.
- *Absence of deadlock*:
  If several processes want to enter a critical section, there must be no *waiting cycle* among them, i.e., among them there must not be n processes $(n > 1)$ $P_1, P_2, ..., P_n$, such that P_1 is waiting for P_2, P_2 for P_3, ...and P_n for P_1.
- *Fairness* (also called *absence of starvation*):
  No process that is trying to enter the critical section will be permanently prevented from entering. Each of them will *eventually* succeed.

One way of guaranteeing mutual exclusion is that each process, before entering a critical section, runs through an *entry protocol* that permits the entrance to exactly *one* of them; dually, when leaving the critical section, it has to announce this in an *exit protocol* to allow another one to enter.

The first two points run like a "red thread" through the whole book; the last two are treated in their own chapters.

1.9   Process States

To conclude the Introduction, we now want to clarify the concept of "*process*".

The dynamics of a process is defined by the transitions of its states; its static aspect is defined only by the statement sequences it executes.

We distinguish the following states of processes:

- *nonexistent*,
- *generated* or *executable*, differentiated between
    - *ready*, i.e., waiting for the allocation of a processor, and
    - *active*, in possession of a processor, i.e., executing,
- *blocked*, while waiting for a certain event, e.g., for
    - the termination of another process,
    - the end of a period, in which it is delayed,
    - the release of a *semaphore*,
    - permission to enter a *monitor* or the occurrence of a *condition* in a monitor,
    - the reception of a *message* on a *channel* or the receipt of a sent message,
- *terminated*.

Between the individual states of a process there are the following transitions, which are shown in Fig. 1.2.

- *Nonexistent → ready*
    through the creation of the process in the sense of our `fork` construct, specifying the static process to be executed by it in the form of a statement sequence or function.
- *Ready ⇄ active*
    by its activation or deactivation, i.e., the allocation of a processor or by its withdrawal.
- *Active → blocked*
    by calling a statement to *wait*, for example, for

Fig. 1.2 State transitions

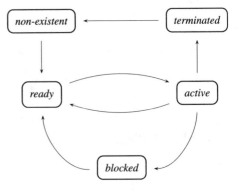

  - the completion of another process,
  - the expiry of a certain period of time,
  - the ability to enter a *critical section*, in which another process is in progress, by unlocking a *lock,* the release of a *semaphore* or a *signal* to enter a *monitor,*
  - a *condition* in a monitor to become true,
  - the arrival of a *message* or the receipt of a sent *message,*
  - the result of a *service* of a remote computer currently busy with other processes,

  which means that the process can only continue when the transition
- *blocked → ready*

  is enabled by an external *event*, e.g., because
  - of the termination of the process it's been waiting for,
  - the scheduled time has expired,
  - another process has left a critical section and unlocked the lock, has released the semaphore or has signaled the possibility to enter the monitor,
  - another process has caused an expected condition to be satisfied,
  - it received the receipt of a sent message or an expected message,
  - a called service of a remote computer was made available to it.
- *Active → terminated*

  after processing its static process if that terminates, or by an operating system process forcibly terminating it, because it could not have continued working sensibly due to a fundamental error that was not caught.
- *Terminated → nonexistent*

  by releasing all the resources it uses.

Here again—as already in Sect. 1.3—your patience must be asked for.

   The terms *lock, semaphore, signal, monitor, condition, message* and *service* used above are to be understood here only cumulatively in anticipation of the detailed discussions in the corresponding chapters.

1.9.1   Process Transitions in C, Java, and Go

We now go into more detail about the individual transitions and their implementation in C, Java, and Go.

nonexistent → ready
This transition is the realization of our construct `fork` B for a statement sequence B.

Implementation in C
In C, a process is branched off from the running process with a call to the function

`pthread_create`. For its specification we give here an excerpt from the *manpage* of the Linux Programmer's Manual again:

```
NAME
pthread_create – initialize a mutex
SYNOPSIS
#include <pthread.h>
int pthread_create(pthread_t *thread,
                   const pthread_attr_t *attr,
                   void *(*start_routine) (void *),
                   void *arg);
```
Compile and link with -pthread.
DESCRIPTION
The `pthread_create()` function starts a new thread in the calling process. The new thread starts execution by invoking `start_routine()`; `arg` is passed as the sole argument of `start_routine()` ...
If `attr` is NULL, then the thread is created with default attributes.
Before returning, a successful call to `pthread_create()` stores the ID of the new thread in the buffer pointed to by thread; this identifier is used to refer to the thread in subsequent calls to other pthread functions.
RETURN VALUE
On success, `pthread_create()` returns 0; on error, it returns an error number, and the contents of `*thread` are undefined.

Therefore, this function is to be given pointers to

- the process `thread` to be branched off,
- an attribute structure `attr` (NULL for the standard attributes),
- a function `f` with the prototype `void *f (void *x)`, as well as
- the object `arg` to be processed by it (respectively, NULL)

The type `pthread_t` of the process variables is defined in `/usr/include/bits/pthreadtypes.h` as `unsigned long int`; it thus realizes natural numbers as *handles* to the processes. The process variables, however, must not be directly accessed, because they are *variables* of an abstract data type.

In simple cases, i.e., without a variable for an object to be processed by B, the incarnation of `fork` B in C looks like this:

```
pthread_t p;
pthread_create (&p, NULL, &f, NULL);

void *f (void *x) { B; return NULL; }
```

Implementation in Java
In Java the branching of a process is syntactically a bit more complex:

- The static process forms—as a statement sequence or arbitrarily parameterized method call—the body of the run method of an implementation of the Runnable interface,
- of which a copy has to be generated,
- which in turn is passed to the constructor as a parameter to create an example of the class Thread.
- Finally, with the method start() of this thread the dynamic process is made ready. (For details see java.long.Runnable and java.long.Thread.)

All in all, as an incarnation of fork B in Java we, in principle, get the following:

```
Runnable r = new Runnable() { public void run() { ... }};
Thread t = new Thread (r);
t.start();
```

where for ... either the static process B or the call of a static method with the body B has to be inserted.

Implementation in Go

It's a little easier in Go:

A lightweight process, called *goroutine*, is called by the current process using the go statement (for details see https://golang.org/ref/spec#Go_statements).

The implementation of fork B in Go is, therefore, simply the call

```
go f()
```

with a function or method call f(), whose body consists of the statement sequence B. The call of f may be given arbitrary parameters.

Also anonymous functions can be passed to the go statement (similar to anonymous classes in Java):

```
go func() { B }()
```

where B is the statement sequence of the static process.

If there is a parameter list in brackets behind f or func, then the corresponding actual parameters have to be passed in the corresponding brackets.

A major difference to C and Java remains to be noted:

▶ There is no explicit data type for processes in Go.

Here, we pick up the promise from Sect. 1.4 of examples of nonsequential algorithms:

In all these cases, the process that creates another process in this way, immediately continues with its execution—concurrently to the process created. A *common* end to *both* processes is, therefore, only possible, if the branching process "waits" until the branched process has terminated.

How its termination leads to the branching process being "awakened" again is described in the sections *active → blocked* and *blocked → ready*.

ready ⇄ active:
The processes involved have no influence on the control of the concurrency progress by distributing the available processor resources among the ready processes, i.e., deactivating active and activating ready processes.

These "*context switches*" for heavyweight processes are one of the core tasks of the operating system and are carried out for lightweight processes using special libraries. They are an essential part of the "*scheduling*" of the sequence control in the computer.

The run time system uses the system clock as follows: Always after a certain period of time has elapsed, it withdraws the processor from an active process ("*preemption*") and allocates it to a higher-level operating system process, the "*dispatcher*", which has the task to allocate the existing processors to other processes, the virtual processors.

The reader who reflects about this, may stumble regarding threatening *antinomies*. The *dispatcher* is a *process* that allocates a processor to *processes*.

- So himself, too?
- And who withdraws the processor from him?
- Which process controls the system clock, and who allocates the processor to it?

(What about those ancient stories of the barber, who barbes all those men, who do not barbe themselves; or the Cretan, who claimed that all Cretans were lying …)

A consistent solution to this problem is basically quite simple—you will certainly find it yourself. You can check your ideas by consulting the relevant literature, [7] or [6].

For this purpose, certain attributes of a process, such as

- a *handle* as an identity token—usually a natural number,
- its *state*, and
- its *pointers* to other processes

are summarized in a *process control block*, a data structure that is a fundamental part of every implementation of process management.

In a single-processor system, in the simplest case fairness is guaranteed by the fact that the scheduler manages the processes in the *ready list*, a circularly linked list, by cyclically running through it and giving an order to the dispatcher to activate exactly *one* of the processes at a time (*round robin* procedure).

For multiprocessor systems this is more difficult; scheduling algorithms can fill entire chapters in textbooks on operating systems.

active → blocked
This is about the implementation of the construct

```
wait  C
```

for a statement sequence C.

The end of the nonsequential statement B || C, consisting of a statement sequence B and a concurrent statement sequence C is reached, iff both statement sequences have reached their end.

A statement sequence D following a statement sequence B must, therefore, be blocked until the branched process that executes C has terminated, provided that was not already the case, when B was finished (see Fig. 1.3).

C

In the programming language C, this is done with the function `pthread_join` by calling

```
pthread_join(t, &r)
```

for `void *r`, when `t` is the process of type `pthread_t` that was branched off for the execution of B with `pthread_create(&t, ...)`. Here is an excerpt from the corresponding *manpage*:

> NAME
> `pthread_join` – join with a terminated thread
> SYNOPSIS
> `#include <pthread.h>`
> `int pthread_join(pthread_t thread, void **retval);`
> Compile and link with `-pthread`.
> DESCRIPTION
> The `pthread_join()` function waits for the thread specified by `thread` to terminate.
> If that thread has already terminated, then `pthread_join()` returns immediately. The
> thread specified by `thread` must be joinable.
> If `retval` is not NULL, then `pthread_join()` copies the exit status of the target thread
> (i.e., the value that the target thread supplied to `pthread_exit(3)`) into the location
> pointed to by `*retval`. If the target thread was canceled, then PTHREAD_CANCELED is
> placed in `*retval`.
> RETURN VALUE
> On success, `pthread_create()` returns 0; on error, it returns an error number.

This blocks the calling process until exactly the point in time, when `t` terminates, and then immediately returns to the status *ready*.

If `t` has already ended at the time of the call, the call is, of course, effect free (see Fig. 1.4): D is executed immediately after the end of B, because C was finished before.

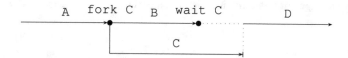

Fig. 1.3   D is blocked until C has terminated

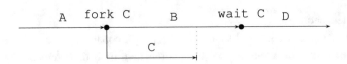

Fig. 1.4 D can start immediately after the end of B

Java

The procedure in Java is very similar:

The class Thread has the method join, to be placed in a try/catch block, because the waiting thread may have terminated during this time, triggering a corresponding exception.

We achieve the desired purpose with the instruction

```
try {
  t.join();
catch(InterruptedException e) {...}
```

where t is the process that was branched off with the call of the method start(), and . . . the code to handle the exception.

Go

In Go, on the other hand, there can be no comparable solution, because there are no process variables.

The Go authors favour another technique, due to their motto from the "*Frequently Asked Questions*" (https://golang.org/doc/faq/):

▶ *Do not communicate by sharing memory. Instead, share memory by communicating.*

Go places this concept at the centre of the treatment of concurrency—we will treat this in detail in Chap. 11 on *message passing*.

In anticipation of this, we will only briefly mention the basic terms we need for our purpose of *sending* and *receiving* of *messages* via *channels*.

Go has the type constructor

```
chan
```

for the construction of an abstract data type "*channel*" of objects of an arbitrary type for the exchange of messages of this type; it assigns to any type T the channel type chan T.

The basic operations for a channel `var c chan t` for messages of the type `t` are

- Its initialization:
  `c = make(chan t).`
- The *receive operation* `<-c`:
  `<-c` is an expression of type `t`, its value is the value stored on the channel `c`.
  For example, for `var x t` the statement `x = <-c` is the assignment of the value of
  the received message to `x`.
- The *send operation* `c <-`:
  an expression `y` of type `t` is sent by the statement `c <- y`.

After a send operation a process is *blocked,* until the message was *received* by another
process, and after a receive operation, as long as a message has arrived. (With that we have
state transitions *active → blocked → ready.*) Using this concept, the `wait` construct in Go
is realized as follows.

For each process that is branched off, a channel is set up, on which it sends a message at
the end of its statements—usually with irrelevant content—and thus informs about its end.

If the branching process executes a receive operation on this channel, it has the consequence that it is blocked, until this message has arrived. If it has branched off several
processes, it has to wait for a corresponding number of messages, so it is blocked until they
are all finished.

The state transitions *active → blocked* mentioned above are central subjects of Chap. 4
on *semaphores* and Chap. 9 on *monitors;* the above briefly mentioned notion of *message
passing via channels* is presented in detail in Chaps. 11 and 13 on message passing.

blocked → ready

A process is unblocked, when the one it has been waiting for has terminated. In C and in
Java this is done by the above incarnations of `wait`.

In Go, this effect is achieved by unblocking a process, that has called a receive operation
on a channel when a message has arrived on that channel, i.e., when it has actually received
it.

For the various other possible transitions *blocked → ready* –as at the end of the previous
point—reference is made in the later chapters.

active → terminated

Either a process terminates and goes into the state *terminated,* or not, so remains active until
the end of the operating system process containing it.

In C, a branched process can be terminated by calling `pthread_exit`; in Go, by
calling the function `Goexit()` from the file `panic.go` in the package `runtime`.

terminated → nonexistent

We do not deal with this transition, because at the end of the comprehensive operating system process, this is done by the runtime system, whereby all resources occupied by the process are released.

1.9.2   Example in C, Java, and Go

Finally, we summarize our small program fragment from Sect. 1.5 on *concurrency and the informal notion of a process* in the three languages.

For A, B, C, and D, quite banal statement sequences are inserted in order "to see" the concurrency of the two processes with the instruction sequences B and C when "trying out" the programs. (For the C-program, the `pthread` library must be linked in!)

C

```c
#include <stdio.h>
#include <pthread.h>

const int N = 10000;

void *c (void *x) {
   int i; for (i = 0; i < N; i++) { printf ("-"); };
   return NULL;
}

void main () {
   pthread_t p;
   printf ("begin\n");                               // A
   pthread_create (&p, NULL, &c, NULL);              // fork C
   int i; for (i = 0; i < N; i++) { printf ("."); }  // B
   pthread_join (p, NULL);                           // wait C
   printf ("\nend\n");                               // D
}
```

Java

```java
class Beispiel {
   static final int N = 10000;
   static Runnable c = new Runnable() {
                       public void run() {
                           for (int i = 0; i < N; i++) {
                               System.out.print ("-");
                           }
```

```
                         }
                       };

    public static void main(String[] arg) {
      Thread p;
      System.out.println("begin");                              // A
      p = new Thread(c); p.start();                             // fork C
      for (int i = 0; i < N; i++)
      { System.out.print("."); }                                // B
      try { p.join(); } catch(InterruptedException e) {}       // wait C
      System.out.println("\nend");                              // D
      System.exit(0);
    }
}
```

Go

```
package main

const N = 10000
var done = make (chan int)

func c() {
  for i := 0; i < N; i++ {
    print ("-")
  }
  done <- 0
}

func main() {
  println ("begin")           // A
  go c()                       // fork C
  for i := 0; i < N; i++ {
    print (".")               // B
  }
  <-done                       // wait C
  println ("\nend")            // D
}
```

References

1. Andrews, G.R.: Concurrent Programming. Principles and Practice, Addison-Wesley, Menlo Park (1991)
2. Burns, A., Davies, G.: Concurrent Programming. Addison-Wesley, Harlow (1993)

3. Dijkstra, E.W.: Solution of a problem in concurrent programming control. Commun. ACM. **8**, S. 569 (1965). https://doi.org/10.1145/365559.365617

4. Dijkstra, E.W.: Guarded commands, nondeterminacy and formal derivation of programs. Commun. ACM. **18** S. 453–457 (1975) https://doi.org/10.1145/360933.360975 https://www.cs.utexas.edu/users/EWD/ewd04xx/EWD418.PDF

5. Herrtwich, R.G., Hommel, G.: Nebenläufige Programme (Kooperation und Konkurrenz). Springer, Berlin (1994, 1989). https://doi.org/10.1007/978-3-642-57931-8

6. Maurer, Ch.: Die Unlösbarkeit des Halteproblems und sein Bezug zu klassischen Antinomien. epubli-Verlag (2012) https://www.epubli.de/shop/buch/Unlösbarkeit-des-Halteproblems-und-sein-Bezug-zu-den-klassischen-Antinomien-Christian-Maurer-9783844227857/18908

7. Tanenbaum, A.S.: Moderne Betriebssysteme. Pearson Studium, München (2003)

8. Wirth, N.: Programming in Modula, Bd. 2, Springer, Berlin (1982)

Packages, Interfaces, and Abstract Data Types

2

Abstarct

This chapter deals with the important programming principles indicated in the Preface, which are independent of NSP. It only serves to illustrate some aspects of the programming techniques used in this book. Essentially, this is about how fundamental software-engineering principles can be implemented in Go. Some basic packages from the source texts of this book, the nUniversum, are introduced and some examples are given—the interface `object` and the abstract data types "queue" and "bounded buffer". They serve to explain in detail the realization of some software principles.

2.1   The Role of Packages

For the construction of *packages* and on their differentiation from others, a very simple point of view is justifiable, based on the postulate of *software engineering* for *information hiding*, and is, therefore, strongly recommended:

▶   A package can define *exactly one* abstract data type or abstract data object.

Abstract means that the implementation of the data type is not visible, but is only accessed via its specification. It follows that:

▶   Specification and implementation within a package are to be separated textually cleanly, i.e., split into different text files.

PARNAS taught us these principles in his ground-breaking papers [2, 3] on software engineering already in the early 1970s.

© Springer Fachmedien Wiesbaden GmbH, part of Springer Nature 2021
C. Maurer, *Nonsequential and Distributed Programming with Go*,
https://doi.org/10.1007/978-3-658-29782-4_2

Thereby, we can make extensive use of the fact that in Go interfaces can be passed on to other interfaces—simply by means of the `import` clause; we will come to talk about that in detail.

Important for these principles is the hint to the fact, that in Go identifiers are exported by a package, *if and only if* they begin with an uppercase letter; identifiers starting a lowercase letter and, on the other hand, cannot be accessed from outside the package (see https://golang.org/ref/spec → Exported Identifiers).

The specification of an abstract data type has the syntactic form of an *interface*, that starts with the type declaration.

Afterwards

- the names of used interfaces as well as
- the syntax of exported methods.

can follow.

The first of these two cases shows that this may be interpreted as a *recursive* definition, which represents a very powerful aspect of Go. This mechanism of "*inheritance on the level of specification*" is in my opinion *much* more significant than on the level of implementation, because it saves mountains of source code lines when used skillfully.

Different implementations of an abstract data type in a package realize different design decisions that offer alternatives for clients, e.g., regarding runtime considerations or memory efficiency.

In principle, *constructors* do not belong syntactically to a specification, because this—in contradiction to the object-oriented approach—would limit the possible variety of implementations.

But with a simple "trick" one can get around that:

A constructor function is included in the specification, which in turn calls a function from the implementation—inaccessible from the outside, because it starts with a lower case letter—and thus hides the details of its construction. This ensures that clients are informed about the syntax and semantics of the constructors without having to look into the source code of the implementation (which is a frequently observed but extremely critical violation of the principle of "information hiding").

If a package contains more than one implementation, the constructor functions should contain notes—in the form of comments—about the semantic differences between the corresponding implementations, so that a client can select the constructor that fits his application purposes.

A package can also contain an abstract data object, which makes sense, for example, when accessing the hardware—a computer usually has only *one* keyboard, *one* mouse, and *one* screen.

However, it is also possible to construct abstract data objects using abstract data types. For this purpose—only in the implementation—a data type is defined and a single copy is generated from it.

In this case, the specification no longer specifies an interface type, but only the access functions to the object "behind the scenes", which is just the idea of an *abstract* data object; conveniently, how it was done above with the constructors: The access function in the specification calls a function from the implementation (for example, with the same name but a leading lowercase letter).

With the aim of a drastic shortening of the text in specifications throughout the book we make the following agreement:

▶ In all specifications in this book. *principally* the calling object is designed with x.

However, packages can also play a different role:

2.1.1   Packages Only as Interfaces

The *recursive* aspect of the interfaces mentioned in the above section naturally suggests that the package concept also makes sense *without* specifying an abstract data type or an abstract data object—simply as a "*pattern*" for use in other interfaces.

▶ A package can also define only an interface, *without* specifying a data type.

Section 2.3.3 below gives a nice example of this, that of "objects".

2.1.1.1 On the Naming of Identifiers

Finally, I would like to draw your attention to one of my "whims" and ask my readers to forgive me for this:

The names of packages are—with the aim of limiting the text length of the import clauses—usually very short, e.g., seq for sequences, buf for buffers, sem for semaphores and nchan for network channels. This is essentially motivated by the brevity of the names of many Go packages (e.g., cmd, fmt, io, math, net, os).

The same applies to some names of methods, e.g., Ins to insert, Del to remove (delete), Num for number, Val for value and Trav to traverse.

If you do not like this, replace the names of these identifiers with your own creations.

2.2   All Source Codes from This Book in the nUniverse Package

All source texts for the many examples in this book is "packaged" in packages, which in turn are included in the nUniverse package nU (where "n" stands for "nano").

These packages are those parts of the μUniverse (see [1]) that are used in this book.

▶   This package is available on the book page of the worldwide web: https://maurer-berlin.eu/nspbook/4.

It is stored there as a compressed tar file named nu.tgz, that has to be unpacked in your personal Go home directory $HOME/go/src/ with the command tar xfzv nu.tgz.

The installation of all packages and programs from the nUniverse is done calling the shell script install.sh

```
#!/bin/sh

for f in $(ls *.go); do
  go install $f
done
```

—contained in the source texts of this book—that creates the subdirectory $HOME/go/src/nU.

2.3   The Package Object

In various places in this book we need a number of basic types and interfaces, which actually have nothing to do with NSP *directly*, but will prove to be extremely useful or even necessary in miscellaneous contexts.

We gather such things in a package, which we present here. In later chapters, more interfaces and functions will be added, which should, of course, be placed textually in different files in this package in order to structure things a bit.

2.3.1   Any

Let's start with the definition of a basic data type, behind which *all* data types can "hide" themselves, the *empty interface*. It gets its own name for abbreviation purposes.

For reasons that become clear in the following section, we put it in the package, which is there defined:

```
package obj

type Any interface{}
```

2.3.2   Interfaces for Describing Objects

First we present four interfaces:

```
Equaler
Comparer
Clearer
Coder
```

The motivation and basis for their construction is the significance that the following Java interfaces have for many classes—in particular partly also for the class `Object`:

```
java/lang/Cloneable.java
java/lang/Comparable.java
java/util/Collection.java
java/io/Serializable.java
```

2.3.2.1 Equaler

Most objects in computer science can be compared with others to see if they are the same, and they can be copied. The following interface serves this purpose:

```
package obj

type Equaler interface {

// Returns true, iff x has the same type as y
// and is identical with x.
  Eq (y Any) bool

// Returns a copy of x, i.e., x.Eq(x.Clone()).
  Clone() Any

// If y has the same type as x, then x.Eq(y).
// y is not modified.
  Copy (y Any)
}

// Pre: a and b are atomic or implement Equaler.
// Returns true, iff a and b are equal.
func Eq (a, b Any) bool { return eq(a,b) }

// Pre: a is atomic or implements Equaler.
// Returns a copy of a.
func Clone (a Any) Any { return clone(a) }
```

The implementation of the functions `Eq` and `Clone` are not shown here; we refer to the source texts of this book.

2.3.2.2 Comparer

In many cases, objects can also be arranged by *order*, for which it is necessary to compare their size. This makes it possible, for example, to sort sequences of them.

```
package obj


type Comparer interface {

// Pre: y has the same type as x.
// Returns true, if x is smaller than y.
  Less (y Any) bool
}


// Pre: a and b are atomic or implement Equaler.
// Returns true, iff less (a, b).
func Less (a, b Any) bool { return less(a,b) }
```

2.3.2.3 Clearer

Objects can be empty, and they can be deleted with the effect of being empty. What "empty" means depends on the semantics of the type of the calling objects. If it is a set or a sequence, the meaning is clear; otherwise, it is, for example, an object with an undefined value, represented by a text of spaces only.

```
package obj


type Clearer interface {

// Returns true, iff x is empty.
  Empty() bool

// x is empty.
  Clr()
```

2.3.2.4 Coder

Objects can be serialized into byte sequences (connected in memory), e.g., to store them persistently on an external memory or to transport them as "data packets" over the network. The appropriate type for such byte sequences is slices of bytes ([]byte), to which we assign the name *stream*:

```
package obj


type (
  Stream = []byte
  AnyStream = []Any
  UintStream = []uint
```

)

Such *"type aliases"* have been included in the Go specification since version 1.9. *Coding* and *decoding* of objects must, of course, be reversibly unique, i.e., these functions are inverse to each other.

```go
package obj

type Coder interface {

// Returns the number of bytes that are necessary
// to code x reversibly uniquely.
  Codelen() uint

// x.Eq (x.Decode (x.Encode()))
  Encode() Stream

// Pre: s is the result of a call of y.Encode()
//      for an object y with the same type of x.
// x.Eq(y) and the slices x.Encode() and s are identical.
  Decode (s Stream)
}

// Returns codelen(int(0)) (== codelen(uint(0))).
func C0() uint { return c0 }

// Pre: a is atomic or implements Object.
// Returns the code length of a.
func Codelen (a Any) uint { return codelen(a) }

// Pre: a is atomic or implements Object.
// Returns a as coded stream.
func Encode (a Any) Stream { return encode(a) }

// Pre: a is atomic or implements Object.
//      s is a coded stream.
// Returns the object, that is coded in this stream.
func Decode (a Any, s Stream) Any { return decode(a,bs) }
```

We don't go into further detail on the implementation of the functions `codelen`, `encode`, and `decode`, but refer to the tools from the packages `asn1`, `json`, and `gob` from the Go package `encoding` or our simple constructions in the packages of nU.

Only an excerpt from the function `codelen`, which returns, among other things, the result of `C0()` —depending on the address width of the computer used—which we'll need later,

```go
var c0 uint

func init() {
```

```
switch runtime.GOARCH {
case "amd64":
  c0 = 8
case "i386":
  c0 = 4
}
}

func codelen (a Any) uint {
  switch a.(type) {
  ...
  case int, uint:
    return c0
  ...
}
```

2.3.3   The Interface of the Package

Subjects such as *genericity* or *parametric polymorphism* are not dealt with in this book, because—as we will see–things are *much* easier in Go. The specification of the data type, which is represented in this section, makes a decisive contribution to this.

Strongly influenced by the ideas that surround the root of the class hierarchy in Java, the class "*Object*", it makes sense to define an interface in Go that defines "objects".

Every "reasonable" object should—for the reasons given in the respective interface— implement all four interfaces mentioned above. Excluded from this requirement are, of course, "atomic objects", i.e., variables of simple data types (see func Atomic).

```
package obj

type Object interface {

  Equaler
  Comparer
  Clearer
  Coder
}

// Returns true, iff a is one of the types
// [u]int{8|16|32}, float[32|64], complex[64|128],
// string or stream (we consider both these types
// also as "atomic")
func Atomic (a Any) bool { return atomic(a) }

// Returns true, iff the type of a implements Object.
func IsObject (a Any) bool { return isObject(a) }
```

Since it makes sense to package nonatomic variables into abstract data types, this "classification" in the form of

- atomic variables, and
- objccts

is quite stringent.

All the interfaces, methods, and functions developed so far will help us a lot in later parts of this book, which deal with net-wide message passing and distributed algorithms, to transport not only atomic variables, but also "variables", which are of type `Object` as messages through the network.

2.3.4   Queues as Abstract Data Type

The following examples are intended to illustrate the principles presented around a standard structure, which plays a fundamental role in computer science: *queues* according to the FIFO principle *"first-in-first-out"*.

The corresponding data type `Buffer` is constructed as a package called `nU/buf`. It is specified as an interface, which, in addition to the name of the data type, exports some methods and defines a constructor according to the principle described in Sect. 2.1.

Thus, all implementation details are consequently hidden, which fulfills the postulate mentioned there.

```
package buf
import . "nU/obj"

type Buffer interface {

// Returns true, iff x is empty,
// i.e., if it does not contain objects.
  Empty() bool

// Returns the number of objects in x.
  Num() int

// a is inserted in x as last object.
  Ins (a Any)

// Returns the pattern object of x, if x is empty,
// otherwise the first object in x,
// and this object is removed from x.
  Get() Any
}
```

```
// Pre: a is atomic or implements Equaler.
// Returns an empty buffer for objects
// of the type of a with patternobject a.
func New (a Any) Buffer { return new_(a) }
```

You can also find other names for this data type and its methods, for example, `Queue` for `Buffer`, `Enqueue` for `Ins` and `Dequeue` for `Get`.

A possible implementation is based on the construct of the "*slices*" in Go (see https://golang.org/ref/spec#Slice_types and https://blog.golang.org/go-slices-usage-and-internals), which can be perceived as dynamic fields ("*arrays*"):

```
package buf
import . "nU/obj"

type buffer struct {
  Any "pattern object"
  s []Any
}

func new_(a Any) Buffer {
  x := new(buffer)
  x.Any = Clone(a)
  x.s = make([]Any, 0)
  return x
}

func (x *buffer) Empty() bool {
  return len(x.s) == 0
}

func (x *buffer) Num() int {
  return len(x.s)
}

func (x *buffer) Ins (a Any) {
  x.s = append(x.s, a)
}

func (x *buffer) Get() Any {
  if x.Empty() {
    return x.Any
  }
  a := x.s[0]
  x.s = x.s[1:]
  return a
}
```

However, other implementations are also possible; for example, with an abstract data type `Sequence` for (finite) sequences of objects of a certain type, specified by

```
package seq
import . "nU/obj"

type Sequence interface {

// Returns true, iff x does not contain any object.
  Empty() bool

// Returns the number of objects in x.
  Num() int

// a is inserted in x as last object.
  InsLast (a Any)

// If x is empty, nothing has changed.
// Otherwise, the first object of x is removed from x.
  DelFirst()

// Returns the pattern object of x, if x is empty,
// otherwise the first object from x.
  GetFirst() Any
}

// Pre: a is atomic or implements Equaler.
// Returns an empty sequence with patter object a.
func New (a Any) Sequence { return new_(a) }
```

A really useful data type of this kind would, of course, have to provide a number of other methods. However, we limit ourselves here to the ones that are required for the following alternative implementation of queues:

```
package buf
import (. "nU/obj", "nU/seq")

type bufferSeq struct {
  Any "pattern object"
  seq.Sequence
}

func newS (a Any) Buffer {
  x := new(bufferSeq)
  x.Any = Clone(a)
  x.Sequence = seq.New(a)
  return x
}

func (x *bufferSeq) Ins (a Any) {
  x.InsLast (a)
}
```

```
func (x *bufferSeq) Get() Any {
  if x.Empty() {
    return x.Any
  }
  defer x.DelFirst()
  return x.GetFirst()
}
```

To be able to use this alternative, the interface has to include the constructor function

```
func NewS (a Any) Buffer { return news(a) }
```

(with references of the kind mentioned above).

What is remarkable about this implementation is first of all that the methods `Empty` and `Num` don't show up. This is exactly one of the brilliant aspects of the Go authors' design, which saves unnecessary lines of code. Due to the fact that interfaces can be "*inherited*" (in this case, by importing of `seq`), this is not necessary—simply the methods of the interface with the same names are used.

The same applies to the methods used `InsLast`, `DelFirst` and `GetFirst` from the package `nU/seq`; the respective prefix `x.Sequence` can be omitted, because there can be no confusion with methods of the same name of the data type `Buffer`—also in this case, simply the methods from the data type `Sequence` are called.

However, care must be taken in such considerations. If, e.g., the method `Num` also belongs to the data type `Sequence`, this method would have to be implemented in `Buffer` as follows:

```
func (x *BufferSeq) Num() int {
  return x.Sequence.Num()
}
```

Why? (Hint: nonterminating recursion).

2.3.5   A Queue as an Abstract Data Object

If—for whatever reason—only *one* queue is used, the following specification of an abstract data object (to be supplemented with comments as above) is appropriate:

```
package buf1 // Zugriffe auf eine FIFO-Warteschlange
import ("nU/obj", "nU/buf")

func Empty() bool { return empty() }
func Num() int { return num() }
func Ins (a Any) { insert(a) }
func Get() Any { return get() }
```

The implementations are then based on an abstract data type buffer as above. The functions empty, num, insert and get in the implementation are then based on an abstract data type Buffer as above.

2.3.6   Bounded Buffers

Another important application in computer science is a data type that is usually referred to as a *bounded buffer*—nothing but FIFO queues with a limited recording capacity. This means that no more objects can be included in a *full* buffer.

In order for this precondition to be met by a client, a method must, of course, be provided to indicate, whether the buffer is full.

This makes the specification very simple:

```
package bbuf
import (. "nU/obj"; "nU/buf")

type BoundedBuffer interface {
  buf.Buffer

// Returns true, iff x is filled up to its capacity border.
// ! Full() is the precondition for a call of Ins(a).
  Full() bool
}

// Pre: a is atomic or implements Equaler; n > 0.
// Returns an empty buffer of capacity n
// for objects of the type of a.
func New (a Any, n uint) BoundedBuffer { return new_(a,n) }
```

The brevity of this specification clearly demonstrates the elegance of the above principle. Since this structure will be used in later chapters, the "classical" implementation in the form of a *ring buffers* is also shown:

```
package bbuf
import . "nU/obj"

type boundedBuffer struct {
  Any "pattern object"
  int "number of objects in the buffer"
  cap, in, out uint
  content AnyStream
}

func new_(a Any, n uint) BoundedBuffer {
  x := new(boundedBuffer)
  x.Any = Clone(a)
  x.cap = n
```

```
  x.content = make(AnyStream, x.cap)
  return x
}

func (x *boundedBuffer) Empty() bool {
  return x.int == 0
}

func (x *boundedBuffer) Num() int {
  return x.int
}

func (x *boundedBuffer) Full() bool {
  return x.int == int(x.cap - 1)
}

func (x *boundedBuffer) Ins (a Any) {
  if x.Full() { return }
  CheckTypeEq (a, x.Any)
  x.content[x.in] = Clone (a)
  x.in = (x.in + 1)
  x.int++
}

func (x *boundedBuffer) Get() Any {
  if x.Empty() {
    return x.Any
  }
  a := Clone (x.content[x.out])
  x.content[x.out] = Clone (x.Any)
  x.out = (x.out + 1) % x.cap
  x.int--
  return a
}
```

2.4   On the Problem of References

You may be surprised that in the implementations presented here, Clone(a) is always used instead of a. For example, suppose we'd just handed over a while inserting. If in this case, the object to be appended has the form

```
  *a
```

i.e., if it is a *reference* to an object, then that is no longer secure in the queue, because the object can be accessed from outside and changed, as the following example shows:

```
package main
import "nU/buf"

func main() {
  a, b := new(int), 1
  *a = b
  buffer := buf.New(0)
  buffer.Ins(a) // it looks as if 1 is in the queue,
  c := a // but:
  *c = 2 // with this access it is changed
  println(*buffer.Get().(*int)) // writes 2, not 1
}
```

Consequently, instead of

```
*a
```

a *reference to a copy* of the object referenced by a has to be handed over—and if this object itself is a reference, then …

With the handover of *a copy*, such errors are generally avoided. This also explains why the prerequisites for the constructors require, that the "pattern object" implement the type *Equaler*, if it is not atomic,

References

1. Maurer, C.: Das μUniversum. https://maurer-berlin.eu/mU
2. Parnas, D.L.: A Technique for Software Module Specification with Examples. Commun. ACM **15**, 330–336 (1972). https://doi.org/10.1145/355602.361309
3. Parnas, D.L.: On the Criteria To Be Used in Decomposing Systems into Modules. Commun. ACM **15**, 1053–1058 (1972). https://doi.org/10.1145/361598.361623

Locks

3

Abstract

This is the first chapter dealing with the construction of certain algorithms for synchronizing concurrent processes—the entry and exit protocols to protect critical sections. The effect of an entry protocol can be intuitively imagined in this way: A process closes access to a critical section as it passes through a door to it in order to reopen the door after leaving the critical section in the exit protocol. Therefore, the implementations of these protocols are called *lock algorithms* and the corresponding data types are called *locks*. After the specification of locks, they are implemented using machine instructions—oriented to common processors—and these procedures are evaluated. Afterwards, possibilities are presented, to implement entry and exit protocols for entering critical sections with elementary methods of sequential programming by accessing shared variables. Many of these solutions are "classical algorithms", which have shaped research for years. However, a number of disadvantages and limitations—both conceptual and practical—also emerge.

3.1 Specification of Locks

Under a *lock* (or a *lock variable*) we understand an *abstract data object* `locked` of type `bool`, which can be accessed by means of two operations, `Lock` and `Unlock`, to lock and unlock a critical section. Here is the specification:

```
Lock: <await !locked; locked = true>
Unlock: <locked = false>
```

with the initial value `locked == false`.

© Springer Fachmedien Wiesbaden GmbH, part of Springer Nature 2021
C. Maurer, *Nonsequential and Distributed Programming with Go*,
https://doi.org/10.1007/978-3-658-29782-4_3

If several processes start the operation Lock, *one* of them will succeed in executing it: It assigns—not interruptable by calls of Lock or Unlock of other processes— true to locked, so that all other processes will have to wait until it has executed Unlock and, therefore, enables exactly *one* of the waiting processes to terminate its call of Lock, i.e., to enter the critical section. This secures the mutual exclusion.

The *absence of deadlocks* follows from the indivisibility of Lock.

Unnecessary delays cannot happen, since one of the processes that has called Lock executes this function as soon as it becomes active.

It is only about *fairness* that nothing has been said.

A first attempt to formulate the specification describes the state changes locked:

```
// Manages an abstract data object locked of type bool
// with the initial value false. The functions Lock and
// Unlock are atomic, i.e., they cannot be interrupted
// by calls of Lock and Unlock of other processes.

// locked == true. The calling process is blocked on locked,
// iff locked was already true at the time of the call.
   lock()

// If at the time of the call, there were processes blocked on
// locked, exactly one of them is deblocked and locked == true;
// otherwise locked == false.
   unlock()
```

But for the following reason this is suboptimal. Specifications should be *orthogonal* to implementations, i.e., *completely* independent of them. They have to describe the *status after termination of the call* of a function, i.e., to make static statements about "what" is done instead of dynamic statements about "how" that is done, which is ultimately a diffuse anticipation of implementation details, i.e., a serious violation of the software technical imperative of the "*information hiding*" principle.

This requirement is met by the following formulation of the specification:

```
// Ensures the access to a critical section.
// The functions Lock and Unlock are not interruptable
// by calls of Lock or Unlock of other processes.

// Pre: The calling process is outside the critical section.
// It is now the only one in the critical section.
   Lock()

// Pre: The calling process is in the critical section.
// Now it is not any more in the critical section.
   Unlock()
```

The fairness problem mentioned above could be included here by an explicit guarantee of the specification of Lock, that the call terminates in finite time.

3.2   Locks in C, Java, and Go

Obviously the specification of locks can be expanded to an *abstract data type*. This does not only *principally* make sense due to general *software-technical* considerations but is ultimately a question of practicability:

The concept is only usable if it establishes the possibility, to protect *several* critical sections in a larger system *independently of each other* by *various* locks.

3.2.1   Locks in C

In C the glibc ("*GNU C Library*") provides the type `pthread_mutex_t` with the function `pthread_mutex_init` for the initialization of a variable of this type (for details, see /usr/include/bits/pthreadtypes.h).

To specify this function, here is an excerpt from the *manpage*:

NAME
   `pthread_mutex_init` – initialize a mutex
SYNOPSIS
   #include <pthread.h>
   `int pthread_mutex_init(pthread_mutex_t *restrict mutex,`
       `const pthread_mutexattr_t *restrict attr);`
DESCRIPTION
   The `pthread_mutex_init()` function shall initialize the mutex referenced by `mutex` with attributes specified by `attr`. If `attr` is NULL, the default mutex attributes are used; the effect shall be the same as passing the address of a default mutex attributes object. Upon successful initialization, the state of the `mutex` becomes initialized and unlocked.
RETURN VALUE
   If successful, the `pthread_mutex_init()` function shall return zero; otherwise an error number shall be returned to indicate the error.

The following functions are available for locking and unlocking critical sections:

   `pthread_mutex_lock` and `pthread_mutex_unlock`.

For their specification here is another excerpt from the *manpage*:

NAME
   `pthread_mutex_lock, pthread_mutex_unlock` – lock and unlock a mutex
SYNOPSIS
   #include <pthread.h>
   `int pthread_mutex_lock(pthread_mutex_t *mutex);`
   `int pthread_mutex_unlock(pthread_mutex_t *mutex);`

DESCRIPTION

The mutex object referenced by `mutex` shall be locked by calling `pthread_mutex_-lock()`. If the mutex is already locked, the calling thread shall block until the mutex becomes available. This operation shall return with the mutex object referenced by `mutex` in the locked state with the calling thread as its owner.

The `pthread_mutex_unlock()` function shall release the mutex object referenced by `mutex`. The manner in which a mutex is released is dependent upon the mutex's type attribute. If there are threads blocked on the mutex object referenced by `mutex` when `pthread_mutex_unlock()` is called, resulting in the mutex becoming available, the scheduling policy shall determine which thread shall acquire the mutex.

RETURN VALUE

If successful, the `pthread_mutex_lock()` and `pthread_mutex_unlock()` functions shall return zero; otherwise, an error number shall be returned to indicate the error.

3.2.2   Locks in Java

In Java, mutual exclusion could originally only be achieved by modifying the methods containing a critical section with the keyword `synchronized`. With a class method, this causes the class to be locked, before the method is executed, with an instance method, this causes the class instance to be locked.

Since version 1.5 of Java, this is more straightforward: There is now the—here only excerpted—interface `Lock`

```
package java.util.concurrent.locks;
import java.util.concurrent.TimeUnit;

public interface Lock {
  /**
   * Acquires the lock.
   *
   * If the lock is not available then the current thread
   * becomes disabled for thread scheduling purposes and
   * lies dormant until the lock has been acquired.
   */
  void lock();
  /**
   * Releases the lock.
  void unlock();
```

in `java.util.concurrent.locks`, which provides the class `ReentrantLock` as an implementation of it.

3.2.3   Locks in Go

In the Go library, there is the package `sync` with an interface. Here is an excerpt from it:

```
package sync
```

```
// A Locker represents an object
// that can be locked and unlocked.
type Locker interface {
  Lock()
  Unlock()
}
```

It also provides an implementation of the specification for this abstract data type:

```
// A Mutex is a mutual exclusion lock.
// Mutexes can be created as part of other structures;
// the zero value for a Mutex is an unlocked mutex.
// A Mutex must not be copied after first use.
type Mutex struct ...

// Lock locks m. If the lock is already in use, the
// calling goroutine blocks until the mutex is available.
func (m *Mutex) Lock() {
  ...

// Unlock unlocks m. It is a runtime error
// if m is not locked on entry to Unlock.
// A locked Mutex is not associated with a particular
goroutine.
// It is allowed for one goroutine to lock a Mutex and then
// arrange for another goroutine to unlock it.
func (m *Mutex) Unlock() {
  ...
```

Processes have to use `Lock()` and `Unlock()`, to ensure mutual exclusion of the accesses to shared data in critical sections, *generally* in pairs as follows:

```
var mutex sync.Mutex
...
mutex.Lock()    // entry protocol
...             // statements within the critical section
mutex.Unlock()  // exit protocol
```

The complicated implementations of the presented locks are based on, among other things, operations of the lowest level:

3.3   Locks Based on Indivisible Machine Instructions

A basic way to implement locks is to use instructions from a processor.

The errors observed above arose, because it was not ensured that a process could read a state and then change it without being interrupted by concurrent processes. In this section we will present some atomic machine instructions that can be used to prevent this.

3.3.1 Test and Set

The reasons for the conflicts when accessing shared data were impermissible interlockings in the course of concurrent processes. The interruptions causing that can be avoided with the function `TestAndSet`, which returns the value of a Boolean variable and assigns— indivisibly from that— `true` to its value:

```
// *a = true. Returns the value of *a at the time of the call.
func TestAndSet (a *bool) bool
```

We place this function—as well as all other indivisible functions from this section—in the package `nU/atomic` of the nUniverse `nU`, the source texts of this book (see 2.2).

Using this, the implementation of a lock is, therefore, quite simple:

```
var locked bool

func Lock() {
  for TestAndSet (&locked) {
    Nothing()
  }
}

func Unlock() {
  locked = false
}
```

The function `Nothing` is *in principle* the "empty" statement.

```
func Nothing() { }
```

But: In Go it is *indispensably* necessary to allow the scheduler to switch within busy queues to another goroutine, so that the programs that use such queues do not get stuck in them. Setting such interrupt points can be done with a call to `Sleep` from the package `time` (`time.Sleep(1)` is enough); an alternative is an explicit hint to the scheduler that it can switch. Exactly *that* is accomplished with the call of the function `Gosched()` from the Go package `runtime` (see https://golang.org/pkg/runtime/#Gosched).

So we implement the function `Nothing()` as follows:

```
func Nothing() {
  runtime.Gosched()
}
```

We place this function in our package `nU/obj` (see Sect. 2.3).

Locking the critical section within the loop in the function `count` with the protocol calls

```
Lock()              // Eintrittsprotokoll
accu := counter     // "LDA counter"
v()
accu++              // "INA"
v()
counter = accu      // "STA counter"
Unlock()            // Austrittsprotokoll
```

leads to a correct counter increase until the end.

The Motorola® processor family 680x0 provides the instruction TAS with a similar specification. Here is the specification from [16]:

> Tests and sets the byte operand addressed by the effective address field. The instruction tests the current value of the operand and sets the N and Z condition bits appropriately. TAS also sets the high-order bit of the operand. The operation uses a locked or read-modify-write transfer sequence. This instruction supports use of a flag or semaphore to coordinate several processors.

For AMD® and Intel® processors TestAndSet can be realized with the instruction XCHG. Here is an excerpt from the specification of XCHG from [1]:

> Exchanges the contents of the two operands. The operands can be two general-purpose registers orregister and a memory location. If either operand references memory, the processor locks automatically, whether or not the LOCK prefix is used and independently of the value of IOPL.

and from [10]:

> Exchanges the contents of the destination (first) and source (second) operands. The operands can be two general-purpose registers or a register and a memory location. If a memory operand is referenced, the processor's locking protocol is automatically implemented for the duration of the exchange operation, regardless of the presence or absence of the LOCK prefix or of the value of the IOPL. (See the LOCK prefix description in this chapter for more information on the locking protocol.) This instruction is useful for implementing semaphores or similar data structures for process synchronization. (See „Bus Locking" in Chap. 8 of the Intel® 64 and IA-32 Architectures Software Developer's Manual, Volume 3A, for more information on bus locking.)

It can be made uninterruptible with the machine instruction LOCK. Here an excerpt from the specification of LOCK from [1]:

> The LOCK prefix causes certain kinds of memory read-modify-write instructions to occur atomically....The prefix is intended to give the processor exclusive use of shared memory in a multiprocessor system...
>
> The LOCK prefix can only be used with ...CMPXCHG, ..., DEC, ..., XADD, XCHG ...

and from [10]:

> Causes the processor's LOCK# signal to be asserted during execution of the accompanying instruction (turns the instruction into an atomic instruction). In a multiprocessor environment, the LOCK# signal ensures that the processor has exclusive use of any shared memory while the signal is asserted...
>
> The LOCK prefix can be prepended only to the following instructions and only to those forms of the instructions where the destination operand is a memory operand: ...CMPXCHG, ..., DEC, INC, ..., XADD, and XCHG.

For the specifications of all machine instructions given here, we refer to the manuals for software developers of AMD [1] and Intel [10] and to https://golang.org/doc/asm.

`TestAndSet` is implemented in the Go assembler-language for 64-bit-AMD® and Intel® processors as follows:

```
TEXT  ·TestAndSet(SB),NOSPLIT,$0
MOVQ  a+0(FP),  BP    // BP = &a
MOVL  $1,  AX         // AX = 1
LOCK                  // lock the bus
XCHGL AX,  0(BP)      // AX = *a || *a = 1 (= true)
MOVL AX,  ret+8(FP)   // AX is return value
RET
```

and for 32-bit processors like this:

```
TEXT  ·TestAndSet(SB),NOSPLIT,$0
MOVL  a+0(FP),  BP
MOVL  $1,  AX
LOCK
XCHGL AX,  0(BP)
MOVL AX,  ret+4(FP)
RET
```

We place this function—as well as those from the following sections—in the package `nU/atomic`.

Don't get confused by the fact that we have not implemented the interface `Locker`, that is, an abstract data type with the methods `Lock` and `Unlock`, but only constructed an abstract data object, i.e., `Lock` and `Unlock` as functions.

An implementation of `Locker` is, of course, a bit more complex; we will come back to this in Sect. 3.6. Here is just a simple example. For this purpose—e.g., in a package `lock`—the definition of a type as a carrier for the methods `Lock` and `Unlock` is needed, as well as the export of a constructor—a function for constructing copies of the class.

This leads to an extension of the above source code like this:

```
package lock
import "nU/atomic"

type tas struct {
  bool "locked"
}

func newTAS() Locker {
  return new(tas)
}

func (x *tas) Lock() {
  for TestAndSet (&x.bool) {
    Nothing()
  }
}
```

```
func (x *tas) Unlock() {
  x.bool = false
}
```

For the sake of simplicity, we will not use this syntactic ballast in the following, since it does not contribute anything essential to the actual ideas at issue here.

If you don't want to get to the bottom of assembler programming, you can simply make use of the fact that a Go package exports a very useful function:

3.3.2   Compare and Swap

A generalization of the above construction is the function `Compare And Swap`. This is an indivisible machine instruction for the comparison of two variable values and the alteration of a value depending on that:

```
// Returns true, if at the time of the all *n == k.
// In this case now *n == m, otherwise *n is not changed.
func CompareAndSwap (n *uint, k, m uint) bool
```

A look at the implementation of the function `CompareAndSwapUint64` from `sync/atomic`—the assembler source code `runtime/internal/atomic/asm_amd64.s`

```
TEXT runtime/internal/atomic·Cas64(SB), NOSPLIT, $0-25
   MOVQ ptr+0(FP), BX
   MOVQ old+8(FP), AX
   MOVQ new+16(FP), CX
   LOCK
   CMPXCHGQ CX, 0(BX)
   SETEQ ret+24(FP)
   RET
```

shows us that the implementations for the AMD® and Intel® processors—even with the 32-bit version in `asm_386.s`— rely on the instruction `CMPXCHG`.

To this end, here are excerpts from the specifications from [1]:

Compares the value in the AL, AX, EAX, or RAX register with the value in a register or a memory location (first operand). If the two values are equal, the instruction copies the value in the second operand to the first operand and sets the ZF flag in the rFLAGS register to 1. Otherwise, it copies the value in the first operand to the AL, AX, EAX, or RAX register and clears the ZF flag to 0. The OF, SF, AF, PF, and CF flags are set to reflect the results of the compare. When the first operand is a memory operand, CMPXCHG always does a read-modify-write on the memory operand. If the compared operands were unequal, CMPXCHG writes the same value to the memory operand that was read. The forms of the CMPXCHG instruction that write to memory support the LOCK prefix.

and from [10]:

Compares the value in the AL, AX, EAX, or RAX register with the first operand (destination operand). If the two values are equal, the second operand (source operand) is loaded into the destination operand. Otherwise, the destination operand is loaded into the AL, AX, EAX or RAX register....

This instruction can be used with a LOCK prefix to allow the instruction to be executed atomically.

Together with an analogue implementation for 32-bit computers, this function can also be used for the data type `uint`.

With this we have a lock in almost exactly the same way as above, which makes it clear that `Test And Set` is basically a special case of `CompareAndSwap`:

```
var n uint

func Lock() {
  for ! CompareAndSwap (&n, 0, 1) {
    Nothing()
  }
}

func Unlock() {
  n = 0
}
```

3.3.3 Exchange

Also the atomic function

```
// *n = k. Returns the value of *n before the allr.
func Exchange (n *uint, k uint) uint
```

—implemented by

```
TEXT  ·Exchange(SB),NOSPLIT,$0
  MOVQ n+0(FP), BX
  MOVQ k+8(FP), AX
  XCHGQ AX, 0(BX)
  MOVQ AX, ret+16(FP)
  RET
```

for 64-bit processors and

```
TEXT  ·Exchange(SB),NOSPLIT,$0
  MOVL n+0(FP), BX
  MOVL k+4(FP), AX
  XCHGL AX, 0(BX)
  MOVL AX, ret+8(FP)
  RET
```

for 32-bit processors with the Intel®/AMD® instruction XCHG—which exchanges two Boolean variables indivisibly with each other. It can be used to implement a lock according to the following intuitive idea:

All processes possess their own invalid tag. Furthermore, globally exactly one valid tag is available, which enables the process, which owns it, to enter the critical section.

If processes continuously exchange their tag indivisibly for the globally available one, always *exactly one* of them will possess the valid tag. It will return it after its exit from the critical section by exchanging it for the globally available (invalid) tag:

```
var valid uint

func Lock() {
  local := uint(1)
  for Exchange (&valid, local) == 1 {
    Nothing()
  }
}

func Unlock() {
  valid = 0
}
```

3.3.4 Decrement

Other instructions can also be used to construct entry and exit protocols. A further example is the function Decrement for decrementing an integer variable, which—inseparably from that—sets the negative flag:

```
// Pre: n - 1 is in the range of int64 or int32 resp.
//      (depending on the computer).
// *n is decremented by 1.
// Returns true, iff now *n < 0.
func Decrement (n *int) bool
```

This can be used to construct protocols:

```
var n int = 1

func Lock() {
  for Decrement(&n) {
    Nothing()
  }
}

func Unlock() {
  n = 1
}
```

At assembler level, an atomic `Decrement` for 64-bit processors is realized as follows:

```
TEXT  ·Decrement(SB),NOSPLIT,$0
  MOVQ  n+0(FP),  BP
  LOCK
  DECQ  0(BP)
  SETMI  ret+8(FP)
  RET
```

The implementation for 32-bit processors is left as an exercise; based on the previous examples this should be very easy.

3.3.5 Fetch and Increment

As a last example of an efficient tool for the development of algorithms for synchronization, we present `FetchAndIncrement`, a function for indivisibly reading and incrementing a natural number variable:

```
// Pre: *n + 1 is in the range of uint.
// Returns the old value of k.
// *n is now incremented by 1.
func FetchAndAdd (n *uint) uint
```

This function is used in Sect. 3.5.6 for the construction of a high level lock for several processes.

At the assembler level, the instruction behind this is XADD. Also, from [1]:

Exchanges the contents of a register (second operand) with the contents of a register or memory location (first operand), computes the sum of the two values, and stores the result in the first operand location. The forms of the XADD instruction that write to memory support the LOCK prefix.

and from [10]:

Exchanges the first operand (destination operand) with the second operand (source operand), then loads the sum of the two values into the destination operand. The destination operand can be a register or a memory location; the source operand is a register...

This instruction can be used with a LOCK prefix to allow the instruction to be executed atomically.

Here is the implementation for a 64-bit processor:

```
TEXT  ·FetchAndIncrement(SB),NOSPLIT,$0
  MOVQ  n+0(FP),  BP
  MOVQ  $1,  AX
  LOCK
  XADDQ  AX,  0(BP)
```

```
MOVQ AX,  ret+8(FP)
RET
```

—and for a 32-bit processor?

3.3.6   The Counter Problem

Functions implemented using indivisible machine instructions can, of course, also be used for other simple synchronization problems, such as our counter problem from Sect. 1.6.

Using the function

```
func Add (*n uint, k uint)
```

—for 64-bit processors implemented by

```
TEXT  ·Add(SB),NOSPLIT,$0
   MOVQ n+0(FP),  BP
   MOVQ k+8(FP),  AX
   LOCK
   XADDQ AX,  0(BP)
   RET
```

in the function `count` in the first `main` package from Sect. 1.6 returns each call of the program for a count variable `var counter uint` returns

```
const
   N = ...

func count (p uint) {
   for n := 0; n < N; n++ {
      Add (&counter, 1)
   }
   done <- true
}
```

the expected result—even for large numbers of processes and large N.

3.3.7   Evaluation of the Use of Machine Instructions

The techniques presented as examples for using machine instructions to implement indivisible instruction sequences are on the one hand historically significant, because they represented very important methods in the beginnings of NSP and later strongly influenced the technical development of processors.

On the other hand, they have by no means lost their significance today; they are used in the Linux kernel (e.g., you can find `cmpxchg` in header-files in the directory `/usr/src/linux/kernel/locking/`).

Indisputable *advantages* of these implementations are

- *good comprehensibility*:
  these are very simple algorithms, the correctness of which is immediately obvious or can be proven elementarily;
- *easy generalizability* to $n > 2$ processes:
  they allow directly not only two, but several processes to be synchronized;
- *high efficiency*:
  the implementations consist of very short statement sequences, so the execution of the protocols is very efficient.

However, there are also a number of serious *drawbacks*:

- *hardware dependency*:
  a program can only be run on a computer with *that* processor, for which it was written; as a result, there are
- *problems with portability*:
  solvable only by conditional compilation or compiler options, whereby—depending on the processor of the target machine— different instruction sequences are generated or used at machine level, or by encapsulation in more or less identical high-level language calls, behind which implementations for various common processors are hidden, such as in the `sync/atomic` package in Go;
- *waste of resources* through *busy waiting*:
  active processes wait to enter a critical section, i.e., they consume processor time without making any progress in their algorithm.

The first two disadvantages are controllable with the methods indicated; the last point, on the other hand, represents a *serious drawback*: When n processes apply concurrently for entry into a critical section, then, in principle, $\frac{n-1}{n}$ of the processor time is not used, which is, of course, completely unacceptable.

The implementation of locks by the use of such machine-oriented (*"low level"*) constructions is, therefore, *not* suitable as a measure for synchronization. Exceptions are routines in the operating system kernel that ensure that the times of busy waiting are insignificant or negligible.

Except from the next chapter, in the following ones more powerful concepts of higher levels of abstraction are developed—among other things to avoid busy waiting— which is why we will not go into this further now but will at first eliminate the first two disadvantages in the following sections with elementary high-level language methods.

Finally, a fundamentally different procedure should be mentioned, to achieve indivisibility of instruction sequences at machine level, even if this does not play a role in our context:

The suppression of *interrupts* for single-processor computers or by corresponding further measures for multiprocessor computers. However, such measures only make sense if the critical sections to be protected are short; otherwise the vitality of the system will be severely restricted. In addition, the suppression and readmittance of interrupts by user programs is generally not permitted, partly because suppressed interrupts could also be abused.

3.4   Lock Algorithms for 2 Processes at High-Level Language Level

Before we try to develop such algorithms, we have to consider a particularity in Go, which was already mentioned in the Preface:

3.4.1   On the Indivisibility of Value Assignments

As noted in the Preface, for computers with multiple processors, it is not ensured that value assignments $y = x$ to a variable y of an elementary type are indivisible, if x is a constant or a variable of an assignment-compatible type. Unfortunately, there is no corresponding information in the Go specification. Only at beginning of the Go document "The Go Memory Model" (see https://golang.org/ref/mem) you will find the following advice:

> Programs that modify data being simultaneously accessed by multiple routines must serialize such access.

> To serialize access, protect the data with channel operations or other synchronization primitives such as those in the sync and sync/atomic packages.

Therefore, the value assignments to the shared variables used in the entry and exit protocols to protect critical sections now need to be *principally* replaced by an indivisible instruction—realized with an indivisible machine instruction.

For this reason, we add a function to our `nU/atomic` package, which ensures this:

```
// *n = k. The execution of this function
// cannot be interrupted by other processes.
func Store (n *uint, k uint)
```

We implement them for 64-bit computers as follows:

```
TEXT  ·Store(SB),NOSPLIT,$0
   MOVQ  n+0(FP), BX
   MOVQ  k+8(FP), AX
   LOCK
   XCHGQ AX,  0(BX)
   RET
```

and correspondingly for 32-bit computers:

```
TEXT  ·Store(SB),NOSPLIT,$0
   MOVL  n+0(FP), BX
   MOVL  k+4(FP), AX
   LOCK
   XCHGL AX,  0(BX)
   RET
```

The LOCK statements are, in fact, superfluous, because in [10] one finds the remark:

> The XCHG instruction always asserts the LOCK# signal regardless of the presence or absence
> of the LOCK prefix.

Similarly in [1] with the specification of XCHG:

> If either operand references memory, the processor locks automatically, …

In the following lock algorithms, shared two-valent (i.e., basically Boolean) variables are
replaced by variables of the type uint with values < 2, to be able to assign values to them
with this function.

3.4.2   Approaches to the Development of a Correct Algorithm

In order to find a purely high-level construction of a lock for the protection of critical sections,
we introduce a state variable for synchronization, which logs whether there is a process that
wants to enter the critical section (iff interested == 1):

```
var interested uint // interested < 2

func Lock() {
  for interested == 1 {
    Nothing()
  }
  v()
  Store (&interested, 1)
}

func Unlock() {
  Store (&interested, 0)
}
```

Program runs, however, show that this approach is completely useless (the installation
of the function v() for delay serves this proof):

At the end incorrect counter values result.

Due to the preliminary considerations from the Introduction, the cause of the errors should
be clear:

The principle of *indivisibility* of an inquiry of a state and its modification is not respected;
it is, therefore, not a correct implementation of the specification of a lock, but merely a naive
attempt to implement the await construct with busy waiting.

For example, a chronological sequence as in Table 3.1 is possible, which proves that
mutual exclusion is not guaranteed.

Apparently, it is impossible to implement Lock atomically with only *one* variable,
because it is read and overwritten concurrently by several processes. So we limit ourselves
to two processes and give each of them *its own* variable, which must be modified only *by
itself*, and consequently, also their own protocol to each of them:

Table 3.1 Mutual exclusion not guaranteed

process	statement	comment
0	`interested == 1 ?`	no
1	`interested == 1 ?`	no
1	`Store (&interested, 1)`	entry into the critical section
0	`Store (&interested, 1)`	entry into the critical section

```
var interested [2]uint

func Lock (p uint) { // p < 2
  for interested[1-p] == 1 {
    Nothing()
  }
  interested[p] = 1
}

func Unlock (p uint) { // p < 2
  interested[p] = 0
}
```

However, this is not yet sufficient for mutual exclusion because, as in the first approach, there can be an interference between the (guaranteed) postcondition `interested[0]` of `Lock(0)` and the (desired) postcondition `!interested[0]` of `Lock(1)`.

In order to avoid that *before* a process announces that it wants to enter the critical section, the other process rushes through the loop and can no longer be prevented from entering the critical section, each process must document its willingness to enter *before* it checks the status of the other process:

```
func Lock (p uint) { // p < 2
  interested[p] = 1
  for interested[1-p] == 1 {
    Nothing()
  }
}
```

With this approach, mutual exclusion is ensured, because before process 0 enters the critical section, it has executed the statement `interested[0] = true`. Therefore, process 1 cannot leave the loop in its entry protocol `Lock(1)`. after it has declared its willingness to enter. Because of the symmetry of the protocols, the same applies vice versa; the concurrent entry of both processes into the critical section is excluded.

A typical test run of this approach, however, unfortunately ends with a sobering "crash": The program does not terminate. The reason for this is that the two processes *got stuck* as follows: One of them was *after* its declaration of willingness to enter, *before* it entered the loop interrupted by the other one, which then also declared its willingness to enter,

Now both wait in their loop for the other process to give up its willingness to enter, which is not possible because it cannot leave its loop.

Strictly speaking, this is not a *deadlock*, but "only" a "*livelock*": Both processes only execute useless instructions but are still *active*. The effect, however, is the same as with a deadlock, so the distinction between them is basically meaningless.

Also the somewhat more elaborate next attempt with the installation of an inquiry in the loop respecting the other one

```
func Lock (p uint) { // p < 2
  for interested[p] == 0 {
    interested[p] = 1
    if interested[1-p] {
      interested[p] = 0
    }
  }
}
```

is characterized by a "classic" form of "*livelock*", in which two people block each other in front of a door—both wanting to give way to the other.

We counteract the risk of a deadlock by introducing an additional variable to favour one of the two processes:

```
var favoured uint // < 2

func Lock (p uint) { // p < 2
  for favoured == 1-p {
    Nothing()
  }
}

func Unlock (p uint) { // p < 2
  Store (&favoured, 1-p)
}
```

This simple protocol satisfies important lock synchronization conditions: because the variable favoured always has exactly *one* of the two possible values 0 or 1, the invariant

$$! \ (\text{favoured} == 0 \ \&\& \ \text{favoured} == 1)$$

for mutual exclusion is guaranteed; and because exactly one of the loops in the two entry protocols terminates immediately after the call, deadlocks are also excluded.

What makes this approach completely useless, however, is the presence of massive mutual *delay*:

Both processes can only enter the critical section *strictly alternating*—even with a slight temporal asymmetry in the course of the two processes, this can have the effect that one of them is only busy waiting for the other to run through the critical section instead to progress in its instructions.

Imagine you want to enter the zoological garden in Berlin through the lion-gate opposite the station "Zoologischer Garten", but in front of you there is already a very long queue of tourists from twenty-seven buses—whereas in front of the elephant-gate next to the aquarium only three people are waiting to enter. If do not live near the zoo like the author, have a look at Google Maps on https://www.google.com/maps?ll=52.50770,13.33800&t=k&z=18; the lion-gate is in the west, the elephant-gate in the south.

3.4.3   Algorithm of Peterson

A skillful combination of the ideas from the previous approaches, however, leads to a fairly simple solution, proposed by PETERSON—even with a generalization to several processes, the "*tiebreaker*" algorithm—published in [17].

```
var (
   interested [2]uint  // < 2
   favoured uint       // < 2
)

func Lock (p uint) { // p < 2
   Store (&interested[p], 1)
   Store (&favoured, 1-p)
   for interested[1-p] == 1 && favoured == 1-p {
     Nothing ()
   }
}

func Unlock (p uint) { // p < 2
   Store (&interested[p], 0)
}
```

We will now prove that it is a correct implementation of lock synchronization for two processes.

Mutual Exclusion

When a process enters the critical section, the following states of the other process play a role because of their interruptibility:

(a) It is outside its critical section and has not yet declared its willingness to enter.
(b) It has declared that but has not yet set the variable to favour the first process.
(c) It has set this variable and is in front of or in its loop.
(d) It has left its loop and has access to the critical section.

For increased readability in the following for p == 0, 1 we use the Boolean expressions

$$i_p \text{ for interested}[p] == 1$$

and

$$f_p \text{ for favoured} == p .$$

In doing so, because of the above invariant we have

$$f_p = \neg f_{1-p} \, .$$

When process 0 is in state (d) at the time of its entry into the critical section, we have

$$i_0 \wedge (\neg i_1 \vee f_0) \, .$$

Before also process 1 can assume state (d), it must have passed through the states (b) and (c), having set

$$i_1 \wedge f_0 \, .$$

As long as process 0 has not left the critical section and thus has set $\neg i_0$, process 1 cannot enter it, because its loop exit condition

$$\neg i_0 \vee f_1 = \neg (i_0 \wedge f_0)$$

is just the negation of the state following (d)

$$i_0 \wedge (\mathit{false} \vee f_0) = i_0 \wedge f_0$$

in which process 1 has changed to state (b).

For reasons of symmetry, it is, therefore, impossible for both processes to be in the critical section at the same time.

Absence of Unnecessary Delay

If only one process, e.g., 0, is willing to enter, its entry is possible because of $\neg i_0$, so it satisfies the exit condition for its loop.

If *both* processes want to enter the critical section, the entry is ensured to *one* of them, because the disjunction of the exit conditions in the loops of the entry protocols

$$\neg (i_1 \wedge f_1) \vee \neg (i_0 \wedge f_0) = \neg i_1 \vee \neg i_0 \vee f_0 \vee \neg f_0 = \mathit{true} \, .$$

is valid, since $f_1 = \neg f_0$.

A short time delay, such as in the execution sequence in Table 3.2, does not play a role here, because it does not represent an unnecessary delay.

On the other hand, if, e.g., process 0 is in the critical section, and therefore process 1 has to wait in the loop of its entry protocol, this loop terminates, after process 0 has gone through its exit protocol.

The effect $\neg i_0$ of this protocol has the consequence that the exit condition

$$\neg (i_0 \wedge f_0) = \neg i_0 \vee f_1$$

for the loop is satisfied.

Table 3.2 Short time delay

process 0	process 1
	`Store (&interested[1], 1)`

`Store (&interested[0], 1)`
`Store (&favoured, 1)`
process "is waiting"	

	`Store (&favoured, 0)` process hangs in its loop
process enters the critical section	

For reasons of symmetry, it follows that each process can enter the critical section as soon as the other has released it.

Absence of Deadlocks

A deadlock is only possible, if with satisfaction of the preconditions i_0 and i_1 for entry into the loops in both entry protocols, neither of them terminates, that is, if

$$(i_1 \wedge f_1) \wedge (i_0 \wedge f_0)$$

which is not possible, because $f_1 = \neg f_0$, i.e., $\neg(f_0 \wedge f_1)$.

Fairness

As the example given above shows, it is possible that a process that has declared its willingness overtakes another process in its waiting loop, which had announced its willingness to enter earlier. But this does not matter, because in its exit protocol it creates the precondition that the waiting loop of the other terminates; therefore this process will enter the critical section at the next context switch. Consequently, no process can overtake the other more than once.

For practice purposes, you should compare this proof with the assertional proof of DIJKSTRA in [5].

The following question is posed as a further exercise: Is the algorithm also correct, if the first two statements in the `Lock` protocol are exchanged?

3.4.4 Algorithm of Kessels

KESSELS modified PETERSON's algorithm in [11]. His basic idea was to reduce the accesses to shared variables. He replaced the shared variable `favoured` with read *and* write access by *both* processes by a variable `turn [2]uint` with the semantics

- `favoured == 0,` iff `turn[0] != turn[1]` and
- `favoured == 1,` iff `turn[0] == turn[1],`

where process p only overwrites "its" variable `turn[p]`.

Therefore, we have the following entry protocol for process 0:

```
Store (&interested[0], 1)
Store (&turn[0], turn[1])
for interested[1] && turn[0] == turn[1] {
  Nothing()
}
```

and for process 1:

```
Store (&interested[1], 1)
Store (&turn[1], 1 - turn[0])
for interested[0] && turn[1] != turn[0] {
  Nothing()
}
```

—summarized:

```
func Lock (p uint) { // p < 2
  Store (&interested[p], 1)
  Store (&turn[p], (p + turn[1-p]) % 2)
  for interested[1-p] == 1 && turn[p] == (p + turn[1-p]) % 2 {
    Nothing()
  }
}
```

The proof that this algorithm also fulfills all requirements for lock synchronization is left as an exercise. It can be proven similarly to the correctness proof of the algorithm of PETERSON. (A detailed proof can be found in the paper of KESSELS.)

3.4.5 Algorithm of Dekker

PETERSON found his elegant solution almost two decades after DEKKER's first solution (see [4]). Here we present the algorithm first of all almost literally in the "*spaghetti*" style that was common at the time of DIJKSTRA's publication in [3]—but translated to Go:

```
func Lock (p uint) { // p < 2
  A:
  Store (&interested[p], 1)
  L:
  if interested[1-p] == 1 {
    if favoured == p {
      goto L
    }
    Store (&interested[p], 0)
    B:
    if favoured == 1-p {
```

```
      goto B
   }
   goto A
}
}
```

```
func Unlock (p uint) { // p < 2
  Store (&favoured, 1-p)
  Store (&interested[p], 0)
}
```

If you despair of the attempt to understand this historical piece of source code, perhaps DIJKSTRA's remark in his paper [4] will comfort you: "*The solution for two processes was complicated, ...*" (The continuation of this quotation can be found in Sect. 3.5.2 on DIJKSTRA's generalization of this algorithm.)

But before you angrily rip the page with the above text of Lock() out of the book, you should translate it into a structured form without first looking into the following "sample solution":

```
func Lock (p uint) { // p < 2
  Store (&interested[p], 1)
  for interested[1-p] == 1 {
    if favoured != p {
      Store (&interested[p], 0)
      for favoured != p {
        Nothing()
      }
      Store (&interested[p], 1)
    }
    Nothing()
  }
}
```

The proof of the correctness of the algorithm is left as an exercise. We just indicate the basic idea here:

$i_0 \wedge \neg i_1 \wedge f_0$ is the precondition, that process 0 can enter the critical section, which in case he wants to enter is equivalent to the fact that process 1 is not willing to enter or is rotating in its inner loop, because f_0 is valid, and can only leave that loop, if process 0 has left the critical section, from which $f_1 = \neg f_0$ results.

If *both* processes are willing to enter, only the favoured one can enter the critical section, because in the case $i_0 \wedge i_1$ only the favoured process fulfils the exit condition of its inner loop and the other has previously withdrawn his willingness to enter, with the result that the favoured process satisfies the exit condition of its outer loop.

The algorithm is fair, too:

For example, if process i is hanging in its inner loop, the other process 1-i executes the statement favoured = i when leaving the critical section. After that process i assigns true to interested[i] and now waits for interested[1-i] to again become false, and no longer executes the statements in the inner loop. If the other process wants to enter the critical section again, this happens in its outer loop, before it gets stuck in its inner loop. This has the consequence that process `i` eventually leaves the outer loop and can enter the critical section.

What remains remarkable is that it took about fifteen years—at a time of very active research in the field—until someone managed to simplify DEKKER's complicated idea ...

3.4.6 Algorithm of Doran and Thomas

It is left as an exercise to prove the correctness of the following variant of the entry protocol of DORAN and THOMAS in [6]:

```
func Lock (p uint) { // p < 2
  Store (&interested[p], 1)
  if favoured == 1 - p {
    Store (&interested[p], 0)
    for favoured != p {
      Nothing()
    }
    Store (&interested[p], 1)
  }
  for interested[1-p] {
    Nothing()
  }
}
```

and—with the additional variable `var afterYou [2]uint`—

```
func Lock (p uint) {
  Store (&interested[p], 1)
  if interested[1-p] == 1 {
    Store (&afterYou[p], 1)
    for interested[1-p] == 1 &&
        (favoured != p || afterYou[1-p] == 0) {
      Nothing()
    }
    Store (&afterYou[p], 0)
  }
}
```

```
func Unlock (p uint) {
  Store (&favoured, 1 - p)
  Store (&interested[p], 0)
}
```

Table 3.3 Possible execution sequence in Hyman's algorithm

process	statement	comment
0	`Store` `(&interested[0], 1)`	
0	`favoured != 0 ?`	yes, so into the outer loop
0	`interested[1] ?`	no, so out of the inner loop
1	`Store` `(&interested[1], 1)`	
1	`favoured != 1 ?`	no, so not into the outer loop, hence process 1 enters the critical section
0	`Store (&favoured, 1)`	process 0 also enters the critical section!

3.4.7   Algorithm of Hyman

In [9], HYMAN gave a "simplification" of Dekker's algorithm. Here we reproduce its "
Lock"-part—freed from the gruesome style of unstructured "spaghetti programming" in
the original:

```
func Lock (p uint) { // p < 2
  Store (&interested[p], 1)
  for favoured != p {
    for interested[1-p] == 1 {
      Nothing ()
    }
    Store (&favoured, p)
  }
}
```

This entry protocol is, however, *false*:

It doesn't guarantee mutual exclusion. This can be seen, for example, in the possible execution sequence in Table 3.3 with `favoured == 1` and `interested[1] == false`
at the beginning.

3.5   Lock Algorithms for Several Processes

A self-evident attempt of a direct generalization of the entry protocol in PETERSON's algorithm to three processes would be the following:

```
func Lock (p uint) { // p < 3
  interested[i] = true
  j, k := (p + 1) % 3, (p + 2) % 3
```

```
favoured = j
 for interested[j] && favoured == j || interested[k] &&
favoured == k {
    Nothing()
 }
}
```

The possible execution sequence in Table 3.4 shows, however, that this has not been thoroughly figured out.

In this process, processes 0 and 2 are not mutually excluded. Consequently, more subtle considerations are needed to solve the problem.

Table 3.4 There is no mutual exclusion

process	statement	comment
0	Store (&interested[0], 1)	
0	j, k = 1, 2	
0	Store (&favoured, 1)	
1	Store (&interested[1], 1)	
1	j, k = 2, 0	
2	Store (&interested[2], 1)	
2	j, k = 0, 1	
2	Store (&favoured, 0)	
0	interested[1] && favoured == 1 ?	no
0	interested[2] && favoured == 2 ?	no
0		process 0 enters the critical section
1	Store (&favoured, 2)	
2	interested[0] && favoured == 0 ?	no
2	interested[1] && favoured == 1 ?	no
2		also process 2 enters the critical section

3.5.1 Tiebreaker Algorithm of Peterson

Although there were generalizations of DEKKER's algorithm before [17], at first we present PETERSON's solution, because the "*extremely simple structure*" (quote of the author) of his algorithm allows a simple generalization to $n > 2$ processes.

The basic idea for n processes is the following: On any one of $n - 1$ levels, whereby on the i-th level for $1 \leq i \leq n$ can be at most $n + 1 - i$ processes, at least one process has to wait, until on the $n - 1$-th level only one of the two processes remains, which is allowed to enter the critical section.

Since a process in the entry protocol cannot favour *the* other, because there are *several* others, it is logged (in a array `last` indexed by the levels) which process is the last one reaching a certain level (the processes thus declare, so to speak, their own subordination).

In addition, the Boolean variables `interested` are generalized to an array of natural numbers `accessed`, indexed by the process numbers, in which each process records the level it reached. At the beginning all processes are on level 0.

The outer loop represents the ascent from the 0th to the $(n - 1)$-th level, at which each ascending process logs that it has reached this level and that it was the last one to reach it; in the loop within a level, the calling process compares itself successively with all others, whereby in each case it has to wait, when the other has reached this level or a higher one, and it *self* is the last one on this level, i.e., it can only continue, if the other has not yet reached this level or if another process has arrived there later.

Thus a process has gone through all queues and can enter the critical section iff it is the only one or the first of two at the highest level. In the exit protocol, a process descends again to the level 0.

Conflicts with concurrent read and write accesses to the values of the field `accessed` and `last` do not exist, because the write accesses are implemented by the atomic instruction `Store` (see Sect. 3.4.1).

```
const N = ... // number of the processes involved
var accessed, last [N]int

func Lock (p uint) { // p < N
  for e := 1; e < N; e++ {
    Store (&accessed[p], e)
    Store (&last[e], p)
    for a := 0; a < N; a++ {
      if p != a {
        for e <= accessed[a] && p == last[e] {
          Nothing ()
        }
      }
    }
  }
}
```

```
func Unlock (p uint) {
  Store (&accessed[p], 0)
}
```

In case n==2, this is—with the corresponding renaming—of course, exactly the algorithm of PETERSON for two processes.

The proof that the algorithm meets all the conditions of lock synchronization is a simple generalization of the corresponding proof for PETERSON's algorithm in Sect. 3.4.3; it is left as an exercise.

Other multiprocess solutions developed later than DEKKER's algorithm, have only the basic idea in common with it, to skillfully nest two loops; in this respect, they ultimately represent new algorithms.

3.5.2 Algorithm of Dijkstra

Next is presented the oldest solution formulated in a high programming language, the *algorithm of* DIJKSTRA from [3], of which the author wrote in [4], "... *the solution for N processes was terribly complicated. The program pieces for "enter" and "exit" are quite small, but they are by far the most difficult pieces of program I ever made*".

Here is the original version in literal translation to Go—but with process numbers 0...N-1 instead of 1...N:

```
var (
  turn uint
  b, c [N]uint
)

func Lock (p uint) {
  b[p] = 0
L:
  if turn != p { // begin
    c[i] = 1
    if b[turn] == 1 {
      turn = p
      goto L
    }
  } // end
  c[i] = 0
  for j := 0; j < N; j++ { // begin
    if j != i && c[j] == 0 {
      goto L
    } // end
  }
}
```

```
func Unlock (p uint) {
  turn = N
  c[p], b[p] = 1, 1
}
```

The translation into a structured form will certainly be easy for you after training on the two-process version of DEKKER. Try it before you look at the following solution!

To adapt the source text to our other examples, the variables b, c [N]uint are replaced by interested, critical [N]bool with 0 = true and 1 = false:

```
var (
  favoured uint
  interested, critical [N]uint
)

func otherCritical (p uint) bool {
  for j := uint(0); j < N; j++ {
    if j != p {
      if critical[j] == 1 {
        return true
      }
    }
  }
  return false
}

func Lock (p uint) {
  Store (&interested[p], 1)
  for {
    for favoured != p {
      Store (&critical[p], 0)
      if interested[favoured] == 0 {
        Store (&favoured, i)
      }
    }
    Nothing ()
    Store (&critical[i], 1)
    Nothing ()
    if otherCritical (i) == 0 {
      break
    }
  }
}

func Unlock (p uint) {
  Store (&favoured, (p + 1) % N)
  Store (&interested[p], 0)
  Store (&critical[p], 0)
}
```

Those who follow this tricky algorithm will probably agree with DIJKSTRA: It does indeed take a lot of thought to be convinced by its correctness.

The mutual exclusion is guaranteed by the fact that for process i in the critical section

```
critical[p]  ==  1
```

is valid, which because of the termination condition is only possible, if all other processes are not yet critical, i.e., if for them

```
critical[j]  ==  0  //  j  !=  p
```

is valid.

After the entrance of a process into the critical section, the others cannot leave the outer loop, because it is the sole favoured process and remains critical until its exit.

In the inner loop, at least one of the processes will succeed in trying to favour itself. This also ensures freedom from unnecessary delays and deadlocks.

However, the algorithm does not guarantee fairness, because each process can be overtaken immediately after its exit from the loop in the entry protocol by the process, that is, the first to favour itself after the exit of a third process from the critical section.

3.5.3   Algorithm of Knuth

In [12] KNUTH published an algorithm that excludes this effect by replacing the Boolean state description of the processes with the field interested by a "trivalent logic" with the field flag. The following implementation by RAYNAL in [19] is easier to understand:

```
const  (passive = iota;  requesting;  active)

var  (
   favoured  =  uint(N)
   flag  [N]uint
)

func test (p uint) bool {
   for j := uint(0); j < N; j++ {
     if j != p {
       if flag[j] == active {
         return false
       }
     }
   }
   return true
}

func Lock (p uint) {
   for {
     Store (&flag[p], requesting)
     j := favoured
     for j != i {
       if flag[j] == passive {
         j = (j + N - 1) % N
       } else {
         j = favoured
```

```
        }
    }
    Nothing ()
    Store (&flag[p], active)
    if test (p) {
        break
    }
  }
  Store (&favoured, p)
}

func Unlock (p uint) {
  Store (&favoured, (p + N - 1) % N)
  Store (&flag[p], passive)
}
```

Mutual exclusion is ensured, because for `i != j` also `test(i) != test(j)` is valid. Freedom from unnecessary delays and deadlocks are secured for the same reason as in the algorithm of DIJKSTRA.

If the algorithm were *unfair*, there would be a process `i` that *never* could enter the critical section. But then there has to be at least *one* `j != i`, for which process `j` enters the critical section arbitrarily often and thus continuously prevents process `i` from entering.

This means that for process `j` in each execution of `Lock(j)`, for which `flag[i] != passive` is valid, the value of `favoured` in the line `j := favoured` must have been set by a process `k` with `i > k > j` in the descending cycle N-1, N-2, ..., 1, 0, N-1 because if such a process `k` would not exist, process `i` would not have been blocked.

If process `j` continuously overtakes process `i`, this effect must also occur continuously, i.e., process `k` always enters the critical section before process `j`. Consequently, there must be a process `n` with `i > n > k`, ..., and so on ...

However, because the number of processes involved is finite, process `i` must eventually be able to enter the critical section. This proves the fairness of the algorithm.

KNUTH leaves the proof that the waiting time can be $O(2^{N-1})$, as an exercise.

DE BRUIJN in [2] reduced this time to $O(N^2)$ by setting `favoured` initially to `uint(k)` for `k < n` instead of to `uint(N)`, omitting the last statement `favoured = i` in the entry protocol and replacing the first statement in the exit protocol by

```
func Lock (p uint) {
  if flag[turn] == passive || turn == p {
    turn = (turn + N - 1) % N
  }
}
```

by

```
  if flag[p] == 0 || favoured == p {
    favoured = (favoured + N - 1) % N
  }
```

3.5.4 Algorithm of Eisenberg and McGuire

In their algorithm in [7], EISENBERG and MCGUIRE even reduced the waiting time to $O(N)$.
This is their implementation, formulated by RAYNAL in [19], translated to Go:

```go
const (passive = iota; requesting; active)

var (
   favoured = uint(N)
   flag [N]uint
)

func Lock (p uint) {
   for {
      Store (&flag[p], requesting)
      j := favoured
      for j != p {
         if flag[j] == passive {
            j = (j + N - 1) % N
         } else {
            j = favoured
         }
      }
      Nothing()
      j = 0
      Store (&flag[p], active)
      for j < N && (j == 0 || flag[j] != active) {
         j++
      }
      if j <= N && (favoured == p || flag[favoured] == passive {
         break
      }
   }
   Store (&favoured, i)
}

func Unlock (p uint) {
   j := (favoured + 1) % N
   for j != favoured && (flag[j] == passive) {
      j = (j + 1) % N
   }
   Store (&favoured, j)
   Store (&flag[p], passive)
}
```

The proof of the correctness of this algorithm and the fact, that the waiting time is indeed
in $O(n)$, is left as an exercise. (Hint: For the solution, see [19].)

3.5.5 Algorithm of Habermann

Fairness is also guaranteed by HABERMANN's refinement of DIJKSTRA's algorithm (see [8]). It determines the order of the favouring by means of a cyclic order given by the process numbers:

```
var (
   favoured uint
   interested, critical [N]bool
)

func Lock (p uint) {
   for {
      Store (&interested[p], 1)
      for {
         Store (&critical[p], 0)
         f := favoured
         otherInterested := false
         for f != p {
            otherInterested += interested[f]
            if f + 1 < N {
               f++
            } else {
               f = 0
            }
         }
         if otherInterested == 0 {
            break
         }
         Nothing ()
      }
      Store (&critical[p], 1)
      otherCritical := 0
      for j := uint(0); j < N; j++ {
         if j != p {
            otherCritical += critical[j]
         }
      }
      if ! otherCritical {
         break
      }
      Nothing ()
   }
   Store (&favoured, p)
}

func Unlock (p uint) {
   f := p
   for {
      f = (f + 1) % N
      if interested[p] == 1 || f == p {
         break
      }
   }
```

```
}
Store (&favoured, f)
Store (&interested[p], 0)
Store (&critical[p], 0)
}
```

The insight into the functioning of this algorithm, which pursues DIJKSTRA's ideas, and the justification for its correctness is left as a demanding exercise. (Note: This algorithm is discussed in detail in [8]).

3.5.6   Ticket Algorithm

An alternative that is clearly more manageable in terms of its structure is the *ticket algorithm*.

It replicates a common procedure in public authorities and supermarkets: On arrival, customers draw consecutive numbers for the order in which they are served after their number has been called.

To implement the assignment of consecutive numbers, the function FetchAnd-Increment is suited, because this ensures that the numbers are assigned only once:

```
var number, turn uint

func Lock() {
  ticket := FetchAndIncrement (&number)
  for ticket != turn {
    Nothing()
  }
}

func Unlock() {
  FetchAndIncrement (&turn)
}
```

The indivisibility of unlock is dispensable, because in each case only *one* process can execute the exit protocol.

To ensure the mutual exclusion of the inner critical section

```
ticket[i] = number; number++
```

you could also use another lock algorithm, for example an implementation using TestAndSet or the tiebreaker algorithm. Then fairness is not guaranteed, but because of the brevity of this section, the delay in it can be neglected compared to that in the loop in the entry protocol.

An overflow of the sequential number is avoided by a small modification of the implementation of unlock:

```
FetchAndAdd (&turn, turn % M + 1)
```

where M must be selected as a constant with M > number of processes to guarantee the uniqueness of the numbers drawn.

The fairness of this algorithm is immediately apparent, because the condition `ticket == turn` to leave the loop is achieved in any case.

3.5.7   Bakery Algorithm of Lamport

A simplification of the DIJKSTRA algorithm that can be implemented without recourse to machine instructions, is the bakery algorithm from Lamport in [13].

Its basic idea is a variant of the ticket algorithm in which arriving customers do not receive a centrally assigned consecutive number, but set their number themselves: one larger than the largest number of the present customers.

However, since the concurrency of this assignment does not ensure that different processes actually receive different numbers, for equal numbers the customer with the lower `process identity` is favoured.

An essential feature of this algorithm is that each process involved accesses by writing only its own variables, and thus no write conflicts can occur.

```
var (
  number [N]uint
  draws  [N]bool
)

func max() uint {
  m := uint(0)
  for j := uint(0); j < N; j++ {
    if number[j] > m {
      m = number[j]
    }
  }
  return m
}

func less (j, k uint) bool {
  if number[j] < number[k] {
    return true
  }
  if number[j] == number[k] {
    return j < k
  }
  return false
}

func Lock (p uint) { // p < N
  draws[i] = true
  Store (&number[p], max() + 1)
  draws[p] = false
  for j := uint(0); j < N; j++ {
    for draws[j] {
      Nothing()
```

```
    }
    for number[j] > 0 && less(j, p) {
      Nothing()
    }
  }
}

func Unlock (p uint) {
  number[p] = 0
}
```

The following facts are immediately clear:

1. If the processes i and k "are in the bakery" (i.e., when they have assigned false to "their" draws but are still in the entry protocol or in the critical section), where process i entered the bakery before process k has assigned true to draws[k], then number[i] < number[k] is true.

Furthermore:

2. If process i is in the critical section and process k in the bakery, then we have less(i, k), which can be seen as follows:

For k != i let t_1 be the point in time at which process i in its last execution of the first for-loop has read the value of draws[k], and t_2 that point in time, at which it for j == k has begun his last execution of the second for-loop. Then $t_1 < t_2$ and at the time t_1 !draws[k] holds.

If for process k $t_3 < t_4 < t_5$ are the moments that follow the instructions draws[k] = true, number[k] = max()+1 and draws[k] = false, respectively; then either i) $t_1 < t_3$ or ii) $t_5 < t_1$.

In case i), 1. furnishes the proof of the assertion.

In case ii), we have $t_4 < t_5 < t_1 < t_2$, so $t_4 < t_2$. Because process i for j == k after the moment t_2 has not checked the condition of the second for-loop once more, it must (because of i != k) have left the loop with less(i, k).

Because of 2., at most *one* process in the critical section, and it follows from 1. and 2. that processes enter the critical section according to the FIFO principle.

A few years later LAMPORT simplified the entry protocol in [14]:

```
func Lock (p uint) {  // p < N
  number[p] = 1
  Store (&number[i], max() + 1)
  for j := uint(0); j < N; j++ {
    if j != p {
      for number[j] > 0 && less(j, p) {
        Nothing()
      }
    }
  }
}
```

The initial setting of the numbers to 1 is absolutely necessary to avoid the following disaster:

A process notices that all others have the number 0 and is then—before assigning 1 to its number—interrupted by another process that is willing to enter, which assigns 1 to its number and enters the critical section. If the first process continues thereafter, it can no longer be prevented from also entering the critical section.

This algorithm is also fair: The exit condition for the loop in its entry protocol states that the process is in possession of the smallest number and, therefore, cannot be overtaken by any other process.

It is left as an exercise to justify the correctness of the two versions and to find out the subtle difference between them, for which studying the original papers can be very helpful and is, therefore, strongly recommended.

3.5.8   Algorithm of Kessels for N Processes

In this section we present a *tournament algorithm*, the generalization of the algorithm of KESSELS, presented in Sect. 3.4.4.

It extends the solution of the binary problem by "nesting" these solutions in a *tournament tree* (as in "knockout"tournaments—hence the name).

The tournament tree is a binary tree; its leaves represent the participating processes and the other nodes represent binary decisions. In order to enter the critical section—i.e., to gain exclusive privilege over the other processes— a process must pass through the tree along a path from its leaf up to the root, where each edge on that path represents a binary decision entry protocol.

The exit protocol—the release of the privilege—is performed by reversing this path; each edge represents a binary exit protocol.

The fact that the nodes are left in reverse order is consistent with the total decision, captured as nested binary decisions; this is even necessary because it guarantees that at most two processes meet in each node.

The nodes are numbered in the same way as in *heaps*: The number of the parent node of n is n/2, its children have the numbers 2n and 2n+1, which means that the parent node as well as the children are directly accessible.

For the sake of simplicity, KESSELS limits the problem to a number of N processes, which is a power of two; thus the tournament tree is totally balanced. In this tree, process i has the leaf number N + i.

To find the path again in the exit protocol during backward processing, an array var e [N] uint is used, in which the node numbers are archived on the path upwards in the entry protocol. Thus the loops in both functions preserve the following invariant: Only exactly all nodes on the path from leaf N + i upwards are assigned to the process i.

Further details can be found in the explanations in [11].

```
const N = ... // number of involved processes (a power of 2)
var (
   interested, turn [N][2]uint
   edge [N]uint
)

func Lock (p uint) { // p < N
   for n := N + p; n > 1; n /= 2 {
      k, m := n / 2, n % 2
      Store (&interested[k][m], 1)
      Store (&turn[k][m], (turn[k][1-m] + m) % 2)
      for interested[k][1-m] == 1 &&
           turn[k][m] == (turn[k][1-m] + m) % 2 {
        Nothing ()
      }
      edge[k] = m
   }
}

func Unlock (p uint) { // p < N
   n := uint(1)
   for n < N {
      n = 2 * n + edge[n]
      Store (&interested[n/2][n%2], 0)
   }
}
```

3.5.9 Algorithm of Morris

If the implementation of locks is only constructed *weakly*, i.e., according to the specification in Sect. 3.1 without any statement about its fairness, it is not guaranteed that the standard solution

```
s.Lock()
... // critical section
s.Unlock()
```

for securing the mutual exclusion of a critical section with a lock s guarantees fairness for more than two processes involved, because with the call of s.Unlock() it is not defined *which one* of the processes blocked on s is unblocked. Therefore, in principle, it can happen that several processes, which constantly alternate with each other when entering the critical section, always overtake a certain other process blocked on s.

This risk is eliminated by the fact that the Lock and Unlock operations are implemented *strongly*, which means that such an effect is not possible. This can be achieved, for example, by a design in which blocked processes are always left in the critical section according to the FCFS principle ("first come, first served").

We present here the algorithm of MORRIS from [15], with which he refuted the conjecture that the problem could not be solved without such a strong implementation. His concept provides a "waiting room" in front of a critical section, protected by an—initially closed—lock `door`, protected by a lock `door0`.

Two counters, `n0` and `n`, document the number of processes blocked on `door0` and `door`, and the concurrent accesses to `n0` are protected by another lock `mutex` (see Figure 3.1).

The basic idea of the progress is a cycle with two phases:

First, processes can enter the waiting room as long as the "scramble" goes on; during this time, no one can enter the critical section. After that, no process comes into the waiting room, until all processes waiting there have successively executed their work in the critical section.

```
var (
    door0, door, mutex sync.Mutex
    n0, n uint
)

func init() {
    door.lock()
}

func Lock() {
    mutex.Lock()
    n0++
    mutex.Unlock()
    door0.Lock()
    n++
    mutex.Lock()
    n0--
    if n0 > 0 {
        mutex.Unlock()
        door0.Unlock()
    } else { // n0 == 0
        mutex.Unlock()
        door.Unlock()
    }
    door.Lock()
    n--
}

func Unlock() {
    if n > 0 {
        door.Unlock()
    } else { // n == 0
```

Fig. 3.1 Rooms and doors in the algorithm of Morris

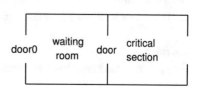

```
    door0.Unlock()
  }
}
```

This allows the cycle of events to start all over again.

In the following we briefly explain the correctness of the algorithm. As an exercise it is recommended to convert these plausibility considerations into a formal proof of correctness in the style of the proof of the correctness of PETERSON' algorithm. (Hint: For that you should study the very sophisticated considerations in [15]!) One of MORRIS's basic ideas about this is that the locks door0 and door form a "split binary semaphore". We return to this term in Sect. 5.1.1 of Chap. 5 on the *baton algorithm*.

Mutual Exclusion

The mutual exclusion is guaranteed by the lock door that is initially closed:

If a process is in the critical section, previously door.Unlock() was called, which requires n0 == 0—indivisibly from that being secured by the lock mutex. But this can only happen again, when the last process has come from the waiting room into the critical section, at its exit has called door0.Unlock(), because further processes arriving at the waiting room would lead to n0 > 0 and be blocked on door0.

Absence of Unnecessary Delay

Processes are prevented from entering the critical section, until the scramble in front of the waiting room is over, i.e., until a process entering there determines n0 == 0.

If the using system manages a lot of processes, which often require access to a certain critical section, this can slow down the throughput of the system considerably; however, this is only an academic problem, because the purpose of the construction of this algorithm is not efficiency, but the proof that the above-mentioned conjecture is wrong.

This delay has to be accepted, because making it possible to enter the critical section beforehand leads to the fact that fairness—the decisive content of this algorithm—is no longer guaranteed. For example, it can no longer be ensured that eventually the case n0 == 0 occurs. (You should think about a corresponding scenario with three processes.)

Absence of Deadlocks

Deadlocks at the lock mutex cannot occur, because each call of mutex.Lock() after an access to n0 is immediately followed by a call of mutex.Unlock().

When a process is deblocked by executing door.Lock(), it enters the critical section; if it leaves, then in the case of n0 > 0 it deblocks one of the processes blocked on door0, otherwise one of those blocked on door, if such exist.

Therefore deadlocks are excluded.

Fairness

Any process that wants to enter the critical section must first pass through the waiting room.

If p is the number of processes involved, it is deblocked after a call of `mutex.Lock()`, at the latest after $p - 1$ concurrent such calls, so that it increases n0. Either its subsequent call of `door0.Lock()` has the consequence, that it enters the waiting room immediately, or that n0 > 0 as long as it is blocked on door0. In this case, it belongs to the set of processes that can enter the waiting room before door0 because of n0 == 0 is closed.

In the second phase, it eventually lands as one of the n processes in the waiting room in the critical section, before it can be overtaken by any of the processes that after the closure of door0 again call `door0.Lock()`.

3.5.10 Algorithm of Szymanski

In [20], SZYMANSKI improved an algorithm of PETERSON in [18].

For the description of the process states, in the entry protocol his solution needs shared variables, represented by three fields of Boolean variables, which the author called "*process specific*". By this he means that a process *overwrites* only its own variables and only *reads* the values of the variables of the other processes.

In his paper, he points to a number of advantageous details that result from this: All state changes require only *one* write access to a bit (a Boolean variable).

In addition, his algorithm is in a sense "*strongly fair*", as no process can enter the critical section, if others are already waiting in their entry protocol, and it can be easily extended to be robust against two classes of errors:

- Crash and restart of a process—associated with resetting all its variables to their initial values.
- Read errors during write accesses ("*flickering bits*"): If a process overwrites the value of a shared variable with a new value, read accesses could return both old and new values.

His basic idea is the same as that in the algorithm of MORRIS from the previous section.

We follow closely [20] to explain how it works:

In the entrance protocol there is a waiting room with an entrance door and an exit door. Exactly *one* of these two doors is always open; initially this is the entrance door. Processes that have declared their willingness to enter at about the same time enter through it the waiting room and gather there.

After passing through the entrance door, each process checks whether there are any other processes that *also* that want to enter the critical section. If this is the case, it leaves the entrance door open and enters the waiting room; otherwise it closes the door and opens the exit door.

Then the processes from the waiting room enter—one after the other—the critical section; first always the process with the lowest process number. This ensures mutual exclusion.

All other processes that want to enter the critical section at this time must wait in front of the entrance door outside the waiting room.

In the long run no process remains in the waiting room, because in the set of processes that have entered it through the entrance door, there is always one that was the *last* to enter the waiting room, i.e., it does not have to wait for further processes but can then leave the waiting room immediately through the exit door.

When a process has left the waiting room through the exit door, the door remains open, until all processes in the waiting room have left the entry protocol. The last of these processes closes the exit door and reopens the entrance door.

The variable `flag [N]uint` describes its current state for each of the N processes. It can take values from 0 to 4, the meaning of which is explained in Table 3.5.

The possible state transitions are $0 \to 1$, $1 \to 3$, $3 \to 2$, $2 \to 4$ (functionally equivalent to $2 \to 3 \to 4$), $3 \to 4$, and $4 \to 0$. SZYMANSKI realizes these states with three fields of Boolean variables, `intent`, `doorIn`, and `doorOut`, which for each process encode the values of its state as indicated in Table 3.6.

We do not use this coding in our implementation, because it makes the algorithm a little less understandable.

The above-mentioned strong fairness *"linear wait"* is achieved by the fact that a process that has overtaken another when entering the critical section cannot pass through the entrance door until all the processes it has overtaken have left the critical section.

Table 3.5 States in the algorithm of SZYMANSKI

State	Meaning
0	process is outside the critical range
1	process wants to enter the critical section
2	process waits for other processes to pass the front door
3	process has entered the waiting room through the front door
4	process has left the waiting room through the exit door

Table 3.6 Coding of the status values

state	intent	doorIn	doorOut
0	false	false	false
1	true	false	false
2	false	true	false
3	true	true	false
4	true	true	true

The details of these considerations prove that the algorithm satisfies *all four* conditions of lock synchronization (see Sect. 1.8). They are left as an exercise (the "sample solutions" are in the original paper).

There is a small error in the original: The "and" (&&) in the exit condition (tag E0) must be replaced by an "or" (||).

Here at first the abstract formulation of the algorithm from [20] (with the tag prefixes P/ E for "*Prologue*"/"*Epilogue*"):

```
Lock (p uint) {
P10: flag[p] = 1
P11: wait until ∀j: flag[j] <= 2
P20: flag[p] = 3
P21: if ∃j: flag[j] == 1 {
        flag[p] = 2
P22:    wait until ∃j: flag[j] == 4
     }
P30: flag[p] = 4
P31: wait until ∀j < p: flag[j] <= 1
}

Unlock (p uint) {
E0: wait until ∀j > p: flag[j] <= 1 || flag[j] == 4
E1: flag[p] = 0
}
```

The first statement from the exit protocol can also be moved into the entry protocol after the statement P30. In the exit protocol, however, this increases efficiency, because a process can enter the critical section without having to wait for all other processes to leave the waiting room.

Here is the translation of the algorithm to Go with this modification, where the comments contain exactly the abstract formulation given above:

```
const (outsideCS = uint(iota); interested;
          waitingForOthers; inWaitingRoom; behindWaitingRoom)
var flag [N]uint

func allLeqWaitingForOthers() bool {
  for j := uint(0); j < N; j++ {
    if flag[j] >= inWaitingRoom {
      return false
    }
  }
  return true
}

func exists (i, k uint) bool {
  for j := uint(0); j < N; j++ {
    if flag[j] == k {
      return true
    }
  }
}
```

```
  return false
}

func allLeqInterested (i uint) bool {
  for j := uint(0); j < i; j++ {
    if flag[j] >= waitingForOthers {
      return false
    }
  }
  return true
}

func allOutsideWaitingRoom (i uint) bool {
  for j := i + 1; j < N; j++ {
    if flag[j] == waitingForOthers || flag[j] ==
inWaitingRoom {
      return false
    }
  }
  return true
}

func Lock (p uint) {
  Store (&x.flag[p], interested)
  for { // wait until ∀j: flag[j] <= waitingForOthers
    if allLeqWaitingForOthers (p) {
      break
    }
    Nothing()
  }
  Store (&x.flag[p], inWaitingRoom)
  if x.exists (p, interested) { // if exists j: flag[j] ==
interested {
    Store (&x.flag[p], waitingForOthers)
    for { // wait until ∃j: flag[j] == behindWaitingRoom
      if exists (p, behindWaitingRomm) {
        break
      }
      Nothing()
    }
  }
  Store (&x.flag[p], behindWaitingRoom)

  for { // wait until ∀j > p: flag[j] <= interested ||
                              flag[j] = behindWaitingRomm
    if allOutsideWaitingRoom (p) {
      break
    }
    Nothing()
  }
  for { // wait until ∀j < p: flag[j] <= interested
    if allLeqInterested (p) {
      break
```

```
      }
      Nothing ()
   }
}

func Unlock (p uint) {
   Store (&x.flag[p], outsideCS)
}
```

3.6   Locks as Abstract Data Types

Of course, it makes sense to construct all locks presented in this chapter as abstract data types, i.e., as interfaces and their implementations, as noted at the beginning of Sect. 3.2 and in the last part of Sect. 3.3.1.

Their interfaces are very similar to Go's (see Sect. 3.2.3). We place them in three packages. In which of these three our algorithms are "packaged" is clear from their names.

lock2

This package contains the locks for two processes.

```
package lock2
// functions for the protection of critical sections, that
   cannot
// be interrupted by calls of these functions of other
   processes.

type Locker2 interface {

// Pre: p < 2.
//      The calling process is outside the critical section.
// It is the only one in the critical section.
   Lock (p uint)

// Pre: p < 2. The calling process is in the critical section.
// Now it is outside the critical section.
   Unlock (p uint)
}

// Return new open locks for 2 processes.
func NewPeterson() Locker2 { return newPeterson() }
func NewKessels() Locker2 { return newKessels() }
func NewDekker() Locker2 { return newDekker() }
func NewDoranThomas() Locker2 { return newDoranThomas() }
```

Using the example of PETERSON's algorithm, we show the syntax of the implementations:

```
package lock2
import (. "nU/obj"; . "nU/atomic")

type peterson struct {
  interested [2]uint
  favoured uint "identity of the favoured process"
}

func newPeterson() Locker2 {
  return new(peterson)
}

func (x *peterson) Lock (p uint) {
  Store (&x.interested[p], 1)
  Store (&x.favoured, 1 - p)
  for x.interested[1-p] == 1 && x.favoured == 1-p {
    Nothing()
  }
}

func (x *peterson) Unlock (p uint) {
  Store (&x.interested[p], 0)
}
```

lock

In this package you will find the locks for n ($n \geq 2$) processes, in which the protocols do not require a process identity as a parameter.

```
package lock
// ... (as above)

type Locker interface {

// Pre: p < number of the processes determined by the
//   constructor.
// ... (as above)
  Lock()

// ... (as above)
  Unlock()
}

// Return new open locks.
func NewMutex() Locker { return newMutex() }
func NewTAS() Locker { return newTAS() }
func NewCAS() Locker { return newCAS() }
func NewXCHG() Locker { return newXCHG() }
func NewDEC() Locker { return newDEC() }
func NewUdding() Locker { return newUdding() }
func NewMorris() Locker { return newMorris() }
```

In Sect. 3.3.1 you can find the TAS version as an example of the syntax of the implementations.

lockn

This package contains the locks for n ($n \geq 2$) processes, for which the value of n is determined by the call of the constructor.

```
package lockn
// ... (as above)

type LockerN interface {

// ... (as above)
  Lock (p uint)

// ... (as above)
  Unlock (p uint)
}

// Each constructor returns a new open lock for n processes
(n > 1).
func NewTiebreaker (n uint)LockerN { return newTiebreaker(n) }
func NewDijkstra (n uint) LockerN { return newDijkstra(n) }
func NewKnuth (n uint) LockerN { return newKnuth(n) }
func NewHabermann (n uint) LockerN { return newHabermann(n) }
func NewTicket (n uint) LockerN { return newTicket(n) }
func NewBakery (n uint) LockerN { return newBakery(n) }
func NewBakery1 (n uint) LockerN { return newBakery1(n) }
func NewKessels (n uint) LockerN { return newKessels(n) }
func NewSzymanski (n uint) LockerN { return newSzymanski(n) }
```

References

1. Advanced Micro Devices Corporation, Inc.: AMD64 Architecture Programmer's Manual. (May 2018) https://developer.amd.com/resources/developer-guides-manuals/
2. De Bruijn, J.G.: Additional comments on a problem in concurrent programming control. Commun. ACM **10** (1967), 137–138. https://doi.org/10.1145/355606.361895
3. Dijkstra, E. W.: Cooperating Sequential Processes. Technical Report EWD-123, Technological University Eindhoven (1965) https://www.cs.utexas.edu/users/EWD/ewd01xx/EWD123.PDF
4. Dijkstra, E. W.: Hierarchical Ordering of sequential processes. Acta Informatica 1 (1971) 115–138 https://www.cs.utexas.edu/users/EWD/ewd03xx/EWD310.PDF
5. Dijkstra, E. W.: An Assertional Proof of a Program by G. L. Peterson. (1981) https://www.cs.utexas.edu/users/EWD/ewd07xx/EWD779.PDF
6. Doran, R.W., Thomas, L.K.: Variants of the software solution to mutual exclusion. Inf. Proc. Letters **10**, 206–208 (1980). https://doi.org/10.1016/0020-0190(80)90141-6
7. Eisenberg, M.A., McGuire, M.R.: Further comments on Dijkstra's concurrent programming control problem. Commun. ACM **15**, 999 (1972). https://doi.org/10.1145/355606.361895

8. Herrtwich, R. G., Hommel, G.: Nebenlä ufige Programme (Kooperation und Konkurrenz). Springer-Verlag Berlin Heidelberg New York (1994, 1989) doi: https://doi.org/10.1007/978-3-642-57931-8
9. Hyman, H.: Comments on a problem in concurrent programming control. Commun. ACM **9**, 45 (1966). https://doi.org/10.1145/365153.365167
10. Intel Corporation: Intel® 64 and IA-32 Architectures Software Developer Manuals (January 2019). https://software.intel.com/en-us/articles/intel-sdm
11. Kessels, J.L.W.: Arbitration without common modifiable variables. Acta Informatica **17**, 135–141 (1982). https://doi.org/10.1007/BF00288966
12. Knuth, D.E.: Additional comments on a problem in concurrent programming control. Commun. ACM **9**, 321–322 (1966). https://doi.org/10.1145/355592.365595
13. Lamport, L.: A new Solution of Dijkstra's Concurrent Programming Problem. Commun. ACM **17** (1974) 453–455 https://doi.org/10.1145/361082.361093 https://research.microsoft.com/en-us/um/people/lamport/pubs/bakery.pdf
14. Lamport, L.: A new Approach to Proving the Correctness of Multiprocess Programs. ACM Trans. Program. Lang. Syst. **1** (1979) 84–97 https://doi.org/10.1145/357062.357068 https://research.microsoft.com/en-us/um/people/lam-port/pubs/new-approach.pdf
15. Morris, J.M.: A starvation: free solution to the mutual exclusion problem. Inf. Proc. Letters **8**, 76–80 (1979). https://doi.org/10.1016/0020-0190(79)90147-9
16. Motorola Inc.: Programmers Reference Manual. Motorola https://www.nxp.com/files-static/archives/doc/ref_manual/M68000PRM.pdf
17. Peterson, G.L.: Myths about the Mutual Exclusion Problem. Inf. Proc. Letters **2**, 115–116 (1981). https://doi.org/10.1016/0020-0190(81)90106-X
18. Peterson, G.L.: A New Solution to Lamport's Concurrent Programming Problem Using Small Shared Variables. ACM Trans. Program. Lang. Syst. **5**, 56–65 (1983). https://doi.org/10.1145/357195.357199
19. Raynal, M.: Algorithms for Mutual Exclusion. MIT-Press (1986)
20. Szymanski, B. K.: A Simple Solution to Lamport's Concurrent Programming Problem with Linear Wait. In Lenfant, J. (ed.): ICS '88, New York. ACM (1988) 621–626 doi: https://doi.org/10.1145/55364.55425

Semaphores

4

Abstract

Although simple synchronization problems can be solved by using lock algorithms, their implementations have quite a number of disadvantages. The oldest idea to eliminate some of these disadvantages is the synchronization construct of *semaphores* by DIJKSTRAR. In this chapter his ideas are presented, and many applications are used to demonstrate how semaphores can be used. This chapter specifies binary and—in the context of bounded buffers—general semaphores and discusses the interrelations between them; afterwards DIJKSTRA's sleeping barber is awakened, and the pitfalls of constructing general semaphores from binary ones are pointed out. The readers–writers problem and some of its solutions with semaphores lead to the pattern of the baton algorithm. It also deals with some specific issues: additive semaphores, barrier synchronization, the left–right problem, DIJKSTRA's dining philosophers, the problem of the cigarette smokers, hints on the implementation of semaphores and the convoy phenomenon.

4.1 Disadvantages of the Implementation of Locks

The disadvantages indicated in the summary in detail are:

1) Busy waiting means a senseless consumption of the operating resource *processor*.
2) The protocols are machine dependent or quite complicated.
3) Processes are, if necessary, *themselves* responsible for their delay before entering a critical section, which severely compromises security.
4) In more complicated cases, the measures for the synchronization of the algorithms are scattered far across the source code of the program, which leads to complexity and, thus, makes it difficult to find errors.

© Springer Fachmedien Wiesbaden GmbH, part of Springer Nature 2021
C. Maurer, *Nonsequential and Distributed Programming with Go*,
https://doi.org/10.1007/978-3-658-29782-4_4

5) It is not possible to prevent unauthorized access to shared data *without synchronization*.
6) The termination of a process in the critical section before executing its exit protocol can have serious (possibly even destructive) effects on the program.

DIJKSTRA presented the disadvantages 1) and 2) with the introduction of semaphores in his groundbreaking paper [8]. He utilised them in the "*THE* Multiprogramming system" (see [9]); ultimately it was basic research for the design of operating systems.

Please note: In this chapter, we do *not* treat operating system semaphores which can, in principle, be used for heavyweight processes in the same way as the semaphores for lightweight processes discussed here, because they clearly belong to the topic of *operating systems*.

4.2   Dijkstra's Approach

The basic idea of DIJKSTRA to avoid disadvantage 1) is the following: A process that has to wait for a condition to continue its work announces that by calling an *entry-protocal*—in principle like at `Lock` for a lock.

If the condition is not fulfilled, e.g., if the critical section is occupied, then the process will not be delayed by the "voluntary" stay in an *active* waiting queue, but instead be blocked by the process management, which removes it in the protocol from the *ready list*. The consequence is that no processor is assigned to it until further notice, i.e., it causes no load in the system.

If another process fulfills the condition for which the first one is waiting, e.g., by leaving the critical section, it reports this to the process management by calling a release protocol—in principle, as with `Unlock`.

In this protocol, the process management inserts the blocked process in the ready list again, so that it can become active again when the scheduler distributes the processors.

DIJKSTRA's terminology is based on *railway* terminology:

A train may only enter a track block in front of it, if there is no other train inside that block. To do this, it "passes" an entry signal to secure the block, whereby the following happens:

It calls the operation P, which allows it to enter the block by the signal "Clear", if there is no train in it, and immediately sets the signal behind it to "Stop" again, thus preventing a following train to enter the block; otherwise it waits at the signal "Stop", until the train in front of it has left the block.

If the train has passed the block itself, it releases the entry signal by the operation V again, so that it shows "Clear", which enables a following train to enter.

DIJKSTRA's abbreviation P and V come from the Dutch "*passeren*" and "*vrijgeven*". By this disadvantage 2) is eliminated:

The complex synchronization algorithms disappear behind the facade of calling methods of a copy of the class that implements such *signals*; the machine-dependent parts are linked in from libraries of the programming language used.

However, it will turn out that this concept is not yet effective against the disadvantages 3) to 6). This requires more powerful constructs, which we will discuss in later chapters.

4.3 Binary Semaphores

The traditional specification of *binary semaphores* is

```
s.P: <await s; s = false>
s.V: <s = true>
```

with the initial value `s == true`.

A conceivable alternative to the fact that a V-operation executed on a semaphore s with the value `true` (i.e., one on which no processes are blocked) has no effect, would be either the creation of an exception or a blocking semantics:

```
s.V: <await !s; s = true>
```

However, these variants do not play a role for applications, because processes must execute P and V-operations always in pairs—in this order (or imagine a signalman who always stops a train leaving a block until there is a train waiting at the entry signal of this block …).

This means that the specification of binary semaphores is virtually identical to that of locks:

A call to `s.P()` assigns `false` to the value of the semaphore s and causes the state transition *active → blocked* of the calling process, if the value of s was already `false` before; a call from `s.V()` realizes the transition *blocked → ready* for a process blocked on s, if such exists, and in this case does not change the value `false` of s, otherwise it reassigns `true` to the value of s.

The only difference to locks is the "inverse logic": A critical section is secured by a lock `locked` is *locked*, iff `locked == true`; but a semaphore s signals with `s == true` that the section it has to secure is *free*, because a signal with `s == false` is traditionally associated with the semantics *Stop*.

▶ The realization of entry and exit protocols for lock synchronization of critical sections is, therefore, *the* standard application of binary semaphores.

4.3.1 Equivalence of Locks and Binary Semaphores

The consequence of the previous section is the following insight:

With a binary semaphore s we have an implementation of Lock and Unlock, that is insofar much better than those presented in the previous chapter, as no process temporarily blocked by the call of lock has to waste processor time by busy waiting:

```
func Lock() {
  s.P()
}

func Unlock() {
  s.V()
}
```

So also disadvantage 1) is eliminated.

Conclusion:

▶   As a synchronization concept, binary semaphores are just as expressive as locks.

Go uses the indivisible machine instructions CompareAndSwap32 (see Sects. 3.3.2) and AddInt32 to implement locks of type Mutex.

Even though binary semaphores are an adequate construct for mastering lock synchronization, they can be generalized in a very obvious way in order not only to decide, whether a process *is* in a critical section *or not*, but to count *how many* are in the section, if several processes are allowed to enter certain critical sections at the same time. Binary semaphores will prove to be special cases of this.

4.3.2 Algorithm of Udding

The *fairness* of binary semaphores—the guarantee that processes blocked on them will eventually be unblocked—can also be achieved, if they rely on *not* necessarily fair locks, which are called *"weak"* by UDDING in his paper [18].

We quote the author:

> A semaphore is called *weak*, if absence of individual starvation among processes blocked on that semaphore cannot be guaranteed. For weak semaphores, one assumption is made, however, viz. a process that executes a V-operation on a semaphore will not be the one to perform the next P-operation on that semaphore, if a process has been blocked on that semaphore. One of the waiting processes is allowed to pass the semaphore.

UDDING proved this in [18], emphasizing that such a solution does not have to "come out of the blue", as it—in his opinion—happened in [14] and [15], but can be systematically developed step by step. The quintessence of his considerations is briefly presented here.

The basic idea of his algorithm is—similar to the algorithm of MORRIS in Sect. 3.5.9—to assemble processes before they enter the critical section in a waiting room in front of a barrier—realized by a lock `door` with the initial value `locked`, and then to let them enter the critical section one by one.

A process must not return to this "assembly" after having left the critical section. Instead, it has to stay in front of an "entrance door", until all processes have passed from the waiting room to the critical section. The entrance door is not unlocked until the last process from the waiting room has entered and left the critical section.

UDDING takes the standard solution from [8] for a lock `door` that does not guarantee fairness, as a starting point:

```
door.Lock()
... // critical section
door.Unlock()
```

The problem with this is that if there are more than two processes, a process that executes a `Lock` operation can again land at an `Unlock` operation, before all processes waiting at `door` have been able to enter the critical section. So, no process must be allowed to arrive at `door` before all processes already waiting there have passed.

Usually for this purpose another lock `mutex` is used, which together with `door` represents a *split lock*—a pair of locks, whereby at most *one* of them can have the value `unlocked` (see "split binary semaphore" in Sect. 5.1.1 in the chapter on the *baton algorithm*).

If the first of the processes waiting in front of `door` is allowed to pass, the lock `mutex` has to prevent the arrival of further processes at `door`, until all processes waiting there have passed through. With the counters `n` for the number of processes waiting at `door` and `n1` for those ones waiting at `mutex`, he develops the following protocol in two well-founded steps:

```
func Lock() {
  mutex.Lock()
  n0++
  mutex.Unlock()
  mutex.Lock()
  n++
  n0--
  if n0 > 0 {
    mutex.Unlock()
  } else { // n0 == 0
    door.Unlock()
  }
  door.Lock()
  n--
}
```

```
func Unlock() {
  if n > 0 {
    door.Unlock()
  } else {
    mutex.Unlock()
  }
}
```

This version ensures mutual exclusion and prevents deadlocks. However, the first `mutex.Lock` is yet another place that can cause unfairness, whereby the question of priorities when waiting at the two `mutex.Lock`s plays a decisive role. Finally, he justifies the fact that the fairness of the entry protocol developed so far is achieved by the introduction of another lock `queue` with the initial value `locked`, in order to manage the processes blocked on the second `mutex.Lock` in a queue, and proves that this supplement can neither lead to unfairness nor to deadlocks.

His final entry protocol is thus:

```
func Lock() {
  mutex.Lock()
  n0++
  mutex.Unlock()
  queue.Lock()
  mutex.Lock()
  n++
  n0--
  if n0 > 0 {
    mutex.Unlock()
  } else {
    door.Unlock()
  }
  queue.Unlock()
  door.Lock()
  n--
}
```

4.4   Buffers in the Nonsequential Case

A typical application of computer science is the buffering of data generated by one or more processes and read concurrently by one or more other processes. Simple examples are "*event queues*" to process inputs by keyboard, mouse, etc., and a printer spooler to manage a shared printer for several users.

The classical paradigm is the model of *producers* that store objects in the buffer and *consumers* that take the objects from it.

Usually, buffers are *bounded* and work as *queues* according to the FIFO principle ("first in, first out").

We will now make a small excursion as a clean basis for discussing a *fundamental* difference between data types for purely sequential applications and those that allow— through appropriate synchronization measures—concurrent access to variables of their type by *several* processes.

With a view to reusability, it naturally makes sense to realize the construction of buffers as packages with separated specifications and implementations, according to the explanations in Chap. 2.

In the sequential case—for "single-user systems"—where synchronization does not play any role, it makes no sense to avoid an attempt to store an element in a full buffer or remove it from an empty one by blocking the calling process, because this would lead to the termination of the program.

The prerequisites that the buffer is not empty or not full form a "contract" between the users and the constructor of the package:

A client has to observe them for his accesses; the implementation can rely on them being observed. In order for a process to meet these prerequisites, the construction of the package has to provide the corresponding enquiries. Consequently, the specification for the sequential case is (see also Sect. 2.3.6):

```
package buf

type Buffer interface { // FIFO-buffer of bounded capacity

// Returns true, iff x does not contain any objects.
  Empty() bool

// Returns then number of elements contained in x.
  Num() uint

// Returns true, iff x is filled up to its capacity.
  Full() uint

// Pre: x is not full.
// a is inserted into x as last object.
  Ins (a Any)

// Pre: x is not empty.
// Returns the first object of x.
// This object is now removed from x.
  Get() Any
}


// Returns an empty buffer of capacity n.
func New (n uint) Buffer { return new_(n) }
```

With `Get` a consumer gets the "first" object from the buffer, a producer always puts his object with `Ins` as "last" into the buffer. If the buffer is empty, a consumer must not call `Get`; it is full, i.e., filled up to its capacity, a producer must not call `Ins`. The functions `Empty` and `Full` are used to check these prerequisites A possible implementation of this specification was shown in Sect. 2.3.6.

Our goal—that of NSP—is to extend the package `buf` in such a way that it can be used concurrently by consumers and producers without the typical errors of unsynchronized accesses, where wrong values are returned or the buffer gets into inconsistent states, i.e., its content is falsified or destroyed.

First, we limit ourselves to the case with only *one* producer and *one* consumer. We treat the synchronization of concurrent accesses of *several* producers and consumers at the end of this section.

Now, there is a substantial difference between the *sequential* case and the situation, in which *several* processes concurrently use the buffer, i.e., a *multiprocess capable* buffer:

It does not make sense to check whether a buffer is not full or not empty, so that an object can be placed in or removed from it, because the inquiry and the subsequent storage or removal would not be indivisible—in the meantime, other processes could have filled or emptied the buffer. Therefore, the functions `Empty`, `Num`, and `Full` from the package `buf` do not belong to our package to be created.

The prerequisites for `Ins` and `Get` are omitted; if the buffer is full, the producer has to wait, and if the buffer is empty, the consumer must be delayed accordingly. Consequently, for the concurrent situation, we need quite another specification:

```
package mbuf
import . "nU/obj"


type MBuffer interface { // multiprocess capable FIFO-buffers
                         // of bounded capacity

// The functions Ins and Get are atomic,
// i.e., they cannot be interrupted by calls
// of Ins and Get of other processes.
// x in the following always denotes the calling object.

// b is a last element inserted in x.
// The calling process was delayed, until
// that was possible, i.e., x was not full.
  Ins (a Any)

// Returns the first element of x.
// This element is now removed from x.
// The calling process was delayed, until
// that was possible, i.e., x was not empty.
  Get () Any
}
```

```
// Pre: a != nil, n > 0.
// Returns an empty buffer of capacity n
// for elements of the type of a.
func New (a Any, n uint) MBuffer { return new_(n) }
```

Indeed, an implementation is possible with busy waiting by just adding for each buffer location a Boolean value, to record if it is occupied:

```
package mbuf
import ("sync"; . "nU/obj"; "nU/buf")

type mbuffer struct {
  buf.Buffer
  occupied [n]bool
}

func new_(n uint) MBuffer {
  x := new(mbuffer)
  x.Buffer = buf.New (a, n)
  x.occupied = make([]bool, n)
  return x
}

func (x *mbuffer) Ins (a Any) {
  for occupied[in] {
    Nothing()
  }
  occupied[in] = true
  x.Buffer.Ins(a)
}

func (x *mbuffer) Get() Any {
  for ! occupied[out] {
    Nothing()
  }
  occupied[out] = false
  return x.Buffer.Get()
}
```

But that brings us back to the frowned upon *"busy waiting"*. Consequently, we have to investigate whether semaphores can be used to solve the problem.

4.5   General Semaphores

If we want to use the advantages of the semaphore concept, *binary* semaphores, however, are not sufficient for this. Since the producer may only enter the critical section *as often* as there are free spaces in the buffer, and the consumer as often as there are occupied spaces, the binary semaphores must be generalized such that they are able to "*count*", which means that their Boolean values are replaced by natural or integer numbers.

The number n_P of the completed P-operations on a semaphore s must never exceed the sum of its initial value n and the number n_V of the completed V-operations. This leads to the *semaphore invariant*

$$n_P \leq n + n_V$$

or—with n + nV − nP as value of a semaphore s—to

$$s \; >= \; 0$$

This invariant allows us to specify general semaphores.

4.5.1 Specification of General Semaphores

The specification for *general semaphores* (with the operation New for its initialization) is:

```
s.New(n): s = n
s.P: <await s > 0; s-->
s.V: <s++>
```

From this result, the binary semaphores—under the assumption justified at the beginning of the previous section that a V-operation is executed only after a corresponding P-operation—with the invariants

$$0 < n \leq 1 \quad \text{and} \quad n_V \leq n_P \leq n_V + 1$$

as a special case:

```
s.New: s = 1
s.P: <await s == 1; s = 0>
s.V: <s = 1>
```

Here is a first attempt to formulate the specification of an interface for semaphores—with colloquially formulated comments—in a version in which the blocking and unblocking of the processes involved is included in the specification:

```
package sem

// Natural numbers as entry protocols to critical sections
// for concurrent access to shared data by several processes

type Semaphore interface {

// The methods P and V are not interruptible
// by calls of P or V of other processes.

// The calling process was blocked on x,
// until its value was > 0.
// Now its value is decremented.
  P()

// If there are processes blocked on x at the time
// of the call, now exactly on of them is deblocked.
// The value of the x is now incremented.
  V()
}
// Returns a semaphore with the value n.
// No process is blocked on that semaphore.
func New(n uint) Semaphore { return new_(n) }
```

For the reasons given in Sect. 3.1, we prefer the following more abstract formulation to avoid contradictions to the principle of *"information hiding"* (func New as above):

```
type Semaphore interface {

// The calling process is among at most n-1 other
// processes in the critical section, where n is the
// initial value of the semaphore given to the constructor.
  P()

// The calling process is no longer in the critical section.
  V()
}
```

4.5.2   Development of a Correct Implementation

In order to develop a solution for the problem of the *bounded buffer*, we consider the numbers e_P and e_C of *entries* into the critical section of the producer and the consumer, respectively, and the numbers a_P and a_C of the exits.

Since a process cannot leave the critical section until it has entered it, and must have left it before it enters it again, we have the following:

$$a_X \leq e_X \leq a_X + 1 \tag{EA}$$

for $X = P, C$. For the number a of the elements in an initially empty buffer we have

$$a_P - e_C \leq a \leq e_P - a_C, \tag{PC}$$

because, on the one hand, the element produced are available in the buffer if they have not yet been taken from the consumer, and on the other hand, only *those* elements that the producer has stored in total can be in the buffer or consumed.

For a buffer of size n the two invariants

$$e_P \leq n + a_C \tag{P}$$

$$e_C \leq a_P \tag{C}$$

ensure that the producer does not produce if the buffer is full, and that the consumer does not consume if the buffer is empty.

With these sizes we have the following *inequalities*:

For the number a of the elements in a buffer of size n it holds that

$$0 \leq a \leq n.$$

Furthermore, the following inequalities always apply

$$0 \leq e_P - e_C \leq n,$$
$$0 \leq n + a_C - e_P \leq n \quad \text{and}$$
$$0 \leq a_P - e_C \leq n$$

and with a full buffer $e_P = n + a_C$ holds, and $e_C = a_P$ holds when it is empty.

Here are the proofs of our statements:

From (C) and (PC) follows $0 \leq a$, from (PC) and (P) we get $a \leq n$.

From (C) and (EA) follows $0 \leq a_P - e_C \leq e_P - e_C$, from (P) and (EA) follows $e_P \leq n + a_C \leq n + e_C$, hence $e_P - e_C \leq n$.

(P) is equivalent to $n + a_C - e_P \geq 0$; from $0 \leq a$ because of (PC) we get $0 \leq e_P - a_C$, so $a_C \leq e_P$, hence $n + a_C - e_P \leq n$.

(C) is equivalent to $a_P - e_C \geq 0$; from $a \leq n$ because of (PC) we get $a_P - e_C \leq n$.

The buffer is full, iff $a = n$; from (PC) and (P) in this case it follows, that $n \leq e_P - a_C \leq n$, hence $n = e_P - a_C$. If the buffer is empty (for $a = 0$), from (C) and (PC) follows $0 \leq a_P - e_C \leq 0$, hence $a_P - e_C = 0$.

From these results we can derive correct specifications of the entry and exit protocols of producer and consumer:

```
inP: <await eP < n + aC; eP++>
inC: <await eC < aP; eC++>
outP: <aP++>
outC: <aC++>
```

If the producer has gone through its entry protocol, e_P is incremented. Due to the indivisibility of the protocol this is equivalent to the decrement of the number

$$notFull = n + a_C - e_P$$

of free spaces in the buffer. Analogously, if the consumer has entered the critical section, e_C is incremented, i.e., the number of occupied spaces in the buffer

$$notEmpty = a_P - e_C$$

is decremented.

After the producer's exit, a_P, and consequently *notEmpty*, are incremented; correspondingly, after the consumer's exit a_C and, thus, *notFull* are incremented.

With the above values for *notFull* and *notEmpty*, the following entry and exit protocols result:

```
inP: <await notFull > 0; notFull-->
inC: <await nichtLeer > 0; notEmpty-->
outP: <notEmpty++>
ousC: <notFull++>
```

The comparison of these specifications with those of general semaphores shows that their use solves the problem completely.

In the constructor, *notFull* has to be initialized with the value n and *notEmpty* with the value 0, because at the beginning $a_C = e_P = a_P = e_C = 0$ holds.

All in all, these considerations prove that the following implementation is correct:

```
package mbbuf
import (. "nU/obj"; "nU/bbuf"; "nU/sem")

type mBuffer struct {
   bbuf.BoundedBuffer
   notEmpty, notFull sem.Semaphore
}

func new_(a Any, n uint) MBuffer {
   x := new(mBuffer)
   x.BoundedBuffer = bbuf.New (a, n)
```

```
  x.notEmpty, x.notFull = sem.New(0), sem.New(n)
  return x
}

func (x *mBuffer) Ins (a Any) {
  x.notFull.P()
  x.BoundedBuffer.Ins (a)
  x.notEmpty.V()
}

func (x *mBuffer) Get() Any {
  x.notEmpty.P()
  a := x.BoundedBuffer.Get()
  x.notFull.V()
  return a
}
```

With this solution, the mutual exclusion between producer and consumer can be dispensed with, because both always operate on different variables:

For `in != out` that is immediately clear, but the case `in == out` requires a justification: It is equivalent to $e_P \bmod n \equiv e_C \bmod n$, for which, according to the second inequality $0 \leq e_P - e_C \leq n$, there are only two possibilities: $e_P = n + e_C$ or $e_P = e_C$.

In the first case, because of (P) and (EA) $e_P \leq n + a_C \leq n + e_C = e_P$ holds, and, consequently, $n + a_C - e_P = 0$, which has the effect that the producer is blocked on the semaphore `notFull`; in the other case, (C) and (EA) result in $e_P = e_C \leq a_P \leq e_P$, so $e_C = a_P$, i.e., the consumer is blocked on the semaphore `notEmpty`. In both cases it is, therefore, impossible that a producer and a consumer access the same variable `buffer[in]`.

The situation is somewhat more difficult if the buffer will be used by *several* producers and consumers. In this case, the two groups must be excluded from each other in order to prevent, for example, that several producers concurrently access the same buffer space.

The accesses to a buffer space in the functions `Ins` and `Get` are critical, because this is associated with the modification of internal data of the buffer, which ensure its consistency. These accesses must be secured with two binary semaphores `ins` and `get`, i.e., the representation of the buffer must be supplemented.

This gives us an implementation of our package that can be used by any number of producers and consumers:

```
package mbbuf
import (. "nU/obj"; "nU/bbuf"; "nu/sem")

type mBuffer1 struct {
  bbuf.BoundedBuffer
  notEmpty, notFull, ins, get sem.Semaphore
}
```

```
func new1 (a Any, n uint) MBuffer {
  x := new(mBuffer1)
  x.BoundedBuffer = bbuf.New (a, n)
  x.notEmpty, x.notFull = sem.New(0), sem.New(n)
  x.ins, x.get = sem.New(1), sem.New(1)
  return x
}


func (x *mBuffer1) Ins (a Any) {
  x.notFull.P()
  x.ins.P()
  x.BoundedBuffer.Ins (a)
  x.ins.V()
  x.notEmpty.V()
}


func (x *mBuffer1) Get() Any {
  x.notEmpty.P()
  x.get.P()
  a := x.BoundedBuffer.Get()
  x.get.V()
  x.notFull.V()
  return a
}
```

With this implementation, for example, concurrent access by several producers to the same buffer space is no longer possible.

4.6   Unbounded Buffers and the Sleeping Barber

In the case of an *unbounded buffer*, i.e., a buffer that can store any amount of elements—limited only by the available storage space—it is not necessary to block a producer. So the semaphore `notFull` is superfluous.

A representation by a ring list in a static array is not possible; it must be replaced by a dynamic structure, for example, a linked list. In order to avoid inconsistencies, the mutual exclusion of *all* accesses among each other is required, for which *one* semaphore `mutex` suffices. This simplifies the synchronization for the implementation of an unbounded buffer when storing an element

```
mutex.Lock()
Ins (object)
mutex.Unlock()
notEmpty.V()
```

and when removing an element

```
notEmpty.P()
mutex.Lock()
object = Get()
mutex.Unlock()
```

We restrict ourselves to *one* consumer and show as in [8] that binary semaphores are sufficient for the synchronization, whereby we use DIJKSTRA's metaphor of the *sleeping barber* (and— as he does—refrain from synchronizing the participants during shaving, which requires another pair of semaphores).

A barber has a shop with a separate waiting room (see Fig. 4.1). From the outside, a sliding door leads to the waiting room; the same sliding door leads from the waiting room to the shop with the barber's chair. Either the entrance to the waiting room or the passage to the shop is open. The door is so small that only one customer can pass at a time.

When the barber has finished a haircut, he lets the customer out, opens the door to the waiting room, and checks to see whether any customers are still waiting. If so, he invites the next customer, otherwise he sits down on a chair in the waiting room and falls asleep.

New customers, who find other customers in the waiting room, wait there for the barber, otherwise they look into the shop. When the barber is working, they stay in the waiting room; when he sleeps, they wake him up.

The key point is that the general semaphore notEmpty is replaced by a binary semaphore customerWaiting (initially false) and a variable n as counter for the number of waiting customers (initially 0), and that the mutual exclusion when accessing the counter is secured with a binary semaphore mutex.

To avoid a typical error, which we will discuss afterwards, an additional variable k is needed, which saves a copy of the counter value:

```
func wait() {
  takeSeatInWaitingRoom()
  mutex.Lock()
  n++
  if n == 1 {
    customerWaiting.Unlock()
```

Fig. 4.1 The shop of the barber

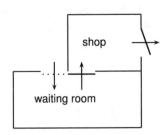

```
  }
  mutex.Unlock()
}

func barber() {
  sleepInBarbersChair()
  if k == 0 {
    customerWaiting.Lock()
  }
  mutex.Lock()
  n--
  k = n
  mutex.Unlock()
  haveSeatInBarbersChair()
}
```

To block the barber when no customer is waiting (n == 0), he must check the copy k of the number n in order to avoid that n was changed by customers after he unlocked mutex which may, for example, lead to the error situation developed in Table 4.1,

This problem does not occur with the above algorithm, because the barber uses the old value of n saved in k to decide whether he has to execute the Lock statement.

However, it can be made a little more efficient: If customers find the waiting room empty (n == 0), they must check whether or not the barber is busy to be blocked in the first case. A pair of Lock/Unlock statements is superfluous in this case and can be omitted.

If no more customers are waiting, the barber sits down on a chair in the waiting room and falls asleep.

Newly arriving customers will find other customers in the waiting room (n > 0) or not (n <= 0). In the second case, the waiting room is either empty (n == 0), then they know without looking that the barber is busy and wait for him to invite one of them; or the barber is sleeping (n == -1), and then they wake him up.

```
func wait() {
  ...
  mutex.Lock()
  takeSeatInWaitingRoom()
  n++
  if n == 0 {
    mutex.Unlock() // *
    customerWaiting.Unlock()
  } else {
    mutex.Unlock()
  }
  ...
}

func barber() {
  ...
  mutex.Lock()
```

Table 4.1 Barber error

wait()	barber()	n	customerWaiting
initial	blocked	0	false
mutex.Lock()		1	
n++			
customerWaiting.Unlock()	deblocked		false
mutex.Unlock()			
	mutex.Lock()		0
	n--		
	mutex.Unlock()		
mutex.Lock()		1	
n++			
customerWaiting.Unlock()			true
mutex.Unlock()			
	if n == 0 {	1	true (!)
	mutex.Lock()		
	n--		
	mutex.Unlock()		0
	if n == 0 {	0	
	customerWaiting.Lock()		true
	mutex.Lock()	0	
	n--	-1	false
	mutex.Unlock()		
	not blocked!		(!)

```
n--
if n == -1 {
  mutex.Unlock()
  customerWaiting.Lock();
  mutex.Lock() // *
}
haveSeatInBarbersChair()
mutex.Unlock()
...
```

For further simplification, the operations marked with " *" can also be omitted; a customer then hands over the critical section directly to the barber when he wakes him up.

We will generalize this approach in the following section by showing that general semaphores are basically superfluous, because they can be simulated with binary semaphores.

The source texts of this book contain the file `barber.go`—a program to animate the sleeping barber.

4.7   Construction of General Semaphores from Binary Semaphores

Binary semaphores can be reproduced by general ones—with the exception of the idempotence of the binary V-operations because they do not operate effect free on *general* semaphores with the value 1 but rather increment the value to 2, and, hence, violate the invariant.

This is normally irrelevant, however, because binary V-operations are used to abandon exclusive critical sections, which is not repeated without prior execution of a P-operation.

Since, on the one hand. we have "unmasked" *binary semaphores* as special cases of *general semaphores* and, on the other hand, can also use *locks* for them, which is a grey area anyway for the reasons outlined above, because the difference lies only in the implementation—blocking by removing from the ready list versus by busy waiting—we make the following agreement:

▶   For binary semaphores we *either* use locks *or* general semaphores (with 1 and 0 for true and false, respectively).

In this section, we will use the Go-typical locks from the package `sync` for binary semaphores; the start value 0 we can get simply by a `Lock` operation.

The aim of this section is to provide the announced proof that general semaphores can be implemented with binary semaphores.

In connection with the insight from Sect. 4.3.1 that binary semaphores are basically locks, this results in the following:

▶   Everything that can be synchronized using semaphores can, in principle, also be done with locks and vice versa.

4.7.1   Representation

The representation of general semaphores is clear. An integer value is needed "to count", a binary semaphore s to block processes when the critical exclusion must not be entered, and a binary semaphore mutex to protect the accesses to the value:

```
type semaphore struct {
   int "value of the semaphore"
   s, mutex sync.Mutex
}
```

4.7.2   Naive (Wrong) Approach

The following first attempt with a straightforward approach contains—as will be shown on closer examination—a subtle error, which cannot appear in the example of the sleeping barber, because there is only *one* producer:

```
func New (n uint) Semaphore {
   x := new(semaphore)
   x.int = int(n)
   x.s.Lock()
   return x
}

func (x *semaphore) P() {
   x.mutex.Lock()
   x.int--
   if x.int < 0 {
     x.mutex.Unlock()
// *
     x.s.Lock()
   } else {
     x.mutex.Unlock()
   }
}

func (x *semaphore) V() {
   x.mutex.Lock()
```

```
x.int++
if x.int <= 0 {
  x.s.Unlock()
}
x.mutex.Unlock()
}
```

If several P-operations are interrupted at position U, and then V-operations are performed, their effect is lost from the second one. This can be seen in the execution example shown in Table 4.2

In Go, this execution sequence cannot occur: The x.mutex.Unlock() executed at the call of the second Unlock operation directly after the x.mutex.Unlock() in the Unlock operation before would lead to a runtime error: "unlock of unlocked mutex".

This language-specific peculiarity of Go, however, does not change the fundamental statement that this attempt is also useless.

Table 4.2 V-operation lost

process	statement	x.int	x.s	comment
	New(2)	2	false	initially
1	P	1	false	1 in critical section
2	P	0	false	2 is blocked
3	P until *	-1	false	
4	P until *	-2	false	
1	V	-1	true	2 in critical section
2	V	0	true (!)	the critical section is free
3	P after *	0	false	3 in critical section
4	P after *	0	false	4 blocked
3	V	1	false	the critical section is free, but process 4 is blocked!

4.7.3   Correction and Consequence

The error from the previous section can be corrected, following the last idea in the simplification of the sleeping barber. The direct transfer of the access to x protected by x.mutex makes sure that a V-operation enforces the termination of an interrupted P-operation:

```
func (x *semaphore) P() {
  x.mutex.Lock()
  x.int--
  if x.int < 0 {
    x.mutex.Unlock()
    x.s.Lock()
  }
  x.mutex.Unlock()
}

func (x *semaphore) V() {
  x.mutex.Lock()
  x.int++
  if x.int <= 0 {
    x.s.Unlock()
  } else {
    x.mutex.Unlock()
  }
}
```

But this is also not yet optimal, because it severely restricts the liveliness of the system. To avoid that one could add a counter n of type int to the representation of semaphore, with which the Unlock operations on the semaphore s for blocking are counted to trigger an additional Unlock operation if necessary:

```
func (x *semaphore) P() {
  ...
  if x.int < 0 {
    x.mutex.Unlock()
    x.s.Lock()
    x.mutex.Lock()
    x.n--
    if x.n > 0 {
      x.s.Unlock()
    }
  }
  ...
}

func (x *semaphore) V() {
  ...
  if x.int <= 0 {
    x.n++
```

```
      x.s.Unlock()
  }
  ...
}
```

Both problems can be avoided by the addition of a further lock `seq` of type `sync.Mutex` in the representation of `semaphore`, with the help of which the `Lock/Unlock` operations in the first solution are "encapsulated" as follows:

```
func (x *semaphore) P() {
  x.seq.Lock()
  ...
  x.seq.Unlock()
}
```

This leads to the mutual exclusion of the P-operations, which is why then always only *one* process can arrive at *. Consequently, the problem from the first approach does not arise.

With this correct solution, the announced goal of this section has already been achieved:

▶ Locks and general semaphores are conceptually equivalent means of expression for synchronization.

4.7.4 The Algorithm of Barz

However, there have been many more attempts to improve this algorithm. In [3], BARZ systematically developed and discussed several successive versions. But here we limit ourselves to the reproduction of his last version, which only needs two semaphores:

```
func New (n uint) Semaphore {
  x := new(semaphore)
  x.int = int(n)
  if x.int == 0 {
    x.s.Lock()
  }
  return x
}

func (x *semaphore) P() {
  x.s.Lock()
  x.mutex.Lock()
  x.int--
  if x.int > 0 {
    x.s.Unlock()
  }
  x.mutex.Unlock()
}
```

```
func (x *semaphore) V() {
  x.mutex.Lock()
  x.int++
  if x.int == 1 {
    x.s.Unlock()
  }
  x.mutex.Unlock()
}
```

It is not quite easy to see that this solution is optimal. A detailed explanation of its correctness can also be found in [4]. BEN- ARI also notes that "... *so many incorrect algorithms have been proposed for this problem*".

The subtlety of the errors and the great variety of their corrections make it clear once again:

▶   It is extremely difficult to construct nonsequential programs in which processes can be interrupted at any point. A lot of care must be taken to ensure the correctness of the algorithms.

In addition, the considerations show that general semaphores—*despite* their equivalence to binary ones—are, indeed, an adequate language tool for certain problem classes.

4.8   Semaphores in C, Java, and Go

4.8.1   Semaphores in C

For C, semaphores are provided by the same library in which the `pthreads` are constructed: Their type is called `sem_t` (see /usr/include/pthreads.h). A semaphore is initialized with the function

`sem_init`

with a natural number as the value. Here is an excerpt from the *manpage* of the Linux programmer's manual:

NAME
    `sem_init` – initialize an unnamed semaphore
SYNOPSIS
    #include <semaphore.h>
    int sem_init(sem_t *sem, int pshared, unsigned int value);
    Link with -pthread.
DESCRIPTION
    `sem_init()` initializes the unnamed semaphore at the address pointed to by `sem`. The
    value argument specifies the initial value for the semaphore. The pshared argument ...

For the `P` and the `V`-operation, there are the functions

sem_wait and sem_post,

described in the *manpages*

NAME
    sem_wait, ...– lock a semaphore
SYNOPSIS
    `#include <semaphore.h>`
    `int sem_post(sem_t *sem);`
    Link with -pthread.
DESCRIPTION
    sem_wait() decrements (locks) the semaphore pointed to by `sem`. If the semaphore's value is greater than zero, then the decrement proceeds, and the function returns, immediately. If the semaphore currently has the value zero, then the call blocks until either it becomes possible to perform the decrement (i.e., the semaphore value rises above zero), or a signal handler interrupts the call.

and

NAME
    sem_post, ... – unlock a semaphore
SYNOPSIS
    `#include <semaphore.h>`
    `int sem_wait(sem_t *sem);`
    Link with -pthread.
DESCRIPTION
    sem_post() increments (unlocks) the semaphore pointed to by `sem`. If the semaphore's value consequently becomes greater than zero, then another process or thread blocked in a `sem_wait call` will be woken up and proceed to lock the semaphore.

4.8.2   Semaphores in Java

In the package `java.util.concurrent` Java offers the class `Semaphore` with two constructors, with which fairness can be controlled, and the methods

acquire and release

for the `P` and the `V`-operation.

For this purpose, here is an excerpt from the file `Semaphore.java`:

```
package java.util.concurrent;
import java.util.Collection;
import java.util.concurrent.locks.AbstractQueuedSynchronizer;
```

```
public class Semaphore implements java.io.Serializable {
  /**
   * Creates a Semaphore with the given number of
   * permits and nonfair fairness setting.
   * @param permits the initial number of permits available.
   * This value may be negative, in which case releases
   * must occur before any acquires will be granted.
   */
  public Semaphore(int permits) {
      sync = new NonfairSync(permits);
  }
  /**
   * Acquires a permit from this semaphore, blocking until one
   * is available, or the thread is interrupted.
   * Acquires a permit, if one is available and returns im-
   * mediately, reducing the number of available permits by one.
   * If no permit is available, then the current thread becomes
   * disabled for thread scheduling purposes and lies dormant
   * until one of two things happens:
   * - Some other thread invokes the release method for this
   *   semaphore, and the current thread is next to be assigned
   *   a permit; or
   * - some other thread interrupts the current thread.
   */
  public void acquire() throws InterruptedException {
      sync.acquireSharedInterruptibly(1);
  }
  /**
   * Releases a permit, returning it to the semaphore.
   * Releases a permit, increasing the number of available
   * permits by one. If any threads are trying to acquire a
   * permit, then one is selected and given the permit that
   * was just released. That thread is (re)enabled for thread
   * scheduling purposes.
   */
  public void release() {
      sync.releaseShared(1);
  }
```

You can also pass negative numbers as values to the constructors, which requires the call of correspondingly many V-operations, until a P-operation permits access to the critical section.

4.8.3 Semaphores in Go

In Go, there is no type `Semaphore`.

Before Go 1, the package `runtime` contained the functions `Semacquire` and `Semrelease`, which are now only available internally in `runtime` but are no longer exported. Their implementations use instructions from the package `runtime/internal /atomic`. Since Go 1, therefore, for the implementation of semaphores one has to resort to one of the many other methods presented in this book—preferably to `sync.Mutex` and to *message passing*.

4.9 Additive Semaphores

General semaphores can be generalized even further; e.g., to the effect that the `P` and V-operations do not change the semaphore values by `1` but by a given natural number.

Semaphores according to specification

```
s.P(n): <await a >= n; s -= n>
s.V(n): <s += n>
```

are called *additive semaphores*. A naive approach is the attempt of an implementation with the representation

```
type addSem struct {
  sem.Semaphore
}
```

and the functions

```
func (x *addSem) P (n uint) {
  for i := uint(0); i < n; i++ {
    x.s.P()
  }
}

func (x *addSem) V (n uint) {
  for i := uint(0); i < n; i++ {
    x.s.V()
  }
}
```

But this is wrong. Why? (Hint: Risk of deadlocks!)

A correct solution is much more complicated.

We consider only the case that the parameters are bounded by a constant `M`. In this case, it is a good idea—in addition to the total value of the semaphore—to introduce for each value <= `M` of a parameter a semaphore `b` and the number `nB` of processes blocked on `b` that are responsible for the processes with this requirement—both in an array. Furthermore, a binary semaphore `mutex` is needed to protect access to these components:

```
import ("sync"; "nU/sem")
const M = ...

type addSemaphore struct {
  uint "number of processes allowed to enter the critical section"
  sync.Mutex
  b [M]sync.Mutex
  nB [M]int // number of processes blocked by b
}

func New (n uint) AddSemaphore {
  x := new(addSemaphore)
  x.uint = n
  for i := uint(0); i < M; i++ {
    x.b[i] = sem.New(0)
  }
  return x
}
```

An implementation of P and V and a discussion of it is given in [12]:

```
func (x *addSemaphore) P (n uint) { // n <= M
    x.uint -= n
    x.Mutex.Unlock()
  } else {
    x.nB[n]++
    x.Mutex.Unlock()
    x.b[n].P()
  }
}
```

Processes can only be unblocked by V-operations, if the value of the semaphore counter is large enough:

```
func (x *addSemaphore) V (n uint) {
    for i := uint(1); i < x.uint; i++ {
    for j := x.nB[i]; j > 1; j-- {
      if x.uint >= i {
        x.nB[i]--
        x.uint -= i
        x.b[i].V()
      } else {
        return
    }
  }
  x.Mutex.Unlock()
}
```

4.9.1   Multiple Semaphores

For the sake of completeness, a further generalization of general semaphores should be mentioned. *Multiple semaphores* are semaphores with n-tuples of values ($n \geq 1$), on which associated P-operations block, if any of the n values are negative, and their V-operations indivisibly increment all n values, that is, according to the specification

```
P(S[1], ..., S[n]):⟨await S[1] > 0 && ... && S[n] > 0;
  S[1]--; ...; S[n]--⟩
V(S[1], ..., S[n]):<S[1]++; ...; S[n]++>
```

4.10   Barrier Synchronization

Complex iteration methods for the calculation of numerical values give rise to the design of parallel algorithms, if the times for the calculations are to be shortened by the use of several processors. If each step of the iteration is distributed to parallel processes, the calculation can only be continued when all results of the partial calculations of the processors involved are available.

Therefore, the following synchronization problem arises. Before the next step is distributed among the participating processes, we must wait until every process has accomplished its task. The corresponding synchronization point is called a *barrier*. A barrier can only be passed after it has been reached by all processes. We want to show how this problem can be solved with the help of semaphores without going into applications here.

The implementation of

```
type Barrier interface {

// The calling process was blocked, until all
// participating processes have called Wait.
  Wait()
}

// Pre: m > 1.
// Returns a new barrier for m processes.
func New(m uint) Barrier { return new_(m) }
```

consists of the number of processes involved, a semaphore to block them until all have reached the barrier, a counter n for protocol purposes, and a mutex for access protection to these data with the appropriate initialization:

```
type barrier struct {
  uint "number of the participating processes"
  n uint // number of blocked processes
  sem.Semaphore
```

```
  sync.Mutex
}

func new_(m uint) Barrier {
  x := new(barrier)
  x.uint = m
  x.Semaphore = sem.New(0)
  return x
}
```

The barrier is realized by the function `Wait`, which blocks the first `m-1` processes to then unblock them all again at the last one as follows: This process—by passing the mutual exclusion—unblocks the penultimate one, whereby it counts backwards; that process again unblocks one of the remaining ones, etc., until finally the last one no longer unblocks another one but gives up the mutual exclusion.

The trivial case `M == 1` is effect free.

The details of the functionality of the following implementation are easily comprehensible by taking a close look:

```
func (x *barrier) Wait {
  x.Mutex.Lock()
  x.n++
  if x.n == x.uint {
    if x.n == 1 {
      x.Mutex.Unlock()
    } else {
      x.n--
      x.Semaphore.V()
    }
  } else {
    x.Mutex.Unlock()
    x.Semaphore.P()
    x.n--
    if x.n == 0 {
      x.Mutex.Unlock()
    } else {
      x.Semaphore.V()
    }
  }
}
```

Synchronization is achieved by the fact that after completion of its tasks each process calls `Wait`.

4.11 Shortest Job Next

As a further application we show the solution of the problem of the *allocation of resources* according to the principle to prefer the process having requested the resource with the shortest time needed ("shortest job next"). To do this, an abstract data type `pqu.PrioQueue` with obvious access operations is used, in which pairs of time requirement and process identity with lexicographical order are inserted.

We leave the study of this subtle algorithm and its generalization to several resources as an exercise and represent it here only briefly due to [1]:

```
import ("sync"; "nU/pqu")

const N = ... // number of the participating processes

type pair struct {
  time, proc uint
}

var (
  q = pqu.New (pair {0, 0})
  free bool = true
  mutex sync.Mutex
  m []sync.Mutex = make([]sync.Mutex, N)
)

func Request (time, p uint) { // p = process identity
  mutex.Lock()
  if ! free {
    q.Ins (pair {time, p})
    mutex.Unlock()
    m[p].Lock()
  }
  free = false
  mutex.Unlock()
}

func Release() {
  mutex.Lock()
  free = true
  if q.Empty() {
    mutex.Unlock()
  } else {
    m[q.Get().(pair).proc].Unlock()
  }
}

func init() {
  for _, mp := range m {
```

```
   mp.Lock()
  }
}
```

4.12 The Readers–Writers Problem

In general, access to shared data is characterized by mutual exclusion, i.e., by the invariant

$$n_P \leq 1$$

where n_P is the number of processes allowed to work concurrently in a critical section.

When processes access the shared data only *reading* or only *writing*, this restriction can be weakened. If n_R denotes the number of active readers and n_W the number of active writers (i.e., of the processes that are in the critical section for reading or writing), it is sufficient to postulate the invariant

$$(n_W = 0) \vee (n_W = 1) \wedge (n_R = 0)$$

i.e., either *deny* entry to writers and admit *arbitrarily many* readers or allow only *one* writer and *no* readers to enter the critical section at the same time. With $m_R = \min(1, n_R)$, this can be described by

$$m_R + n_W \leq 1$$

because $m_R + n_W = 1$ is because of $m_R \leq 1$ equivalent to

$$(n_W = 0) \vee (m_R = 0) \wedge (n_W = 1)$$

and $m_R = 0$ to $n_R = 0$.

4.12.1 The First Readers–Writers Problem

We now present a synchronization of readers and writers with semaphores, which will, however, show a lack of fairness. This solution was retrospectively named the "*first readers–writers problem*".

With a semaphore `rw` with the value 1 - (mR + nW), i.e., 1 for nR == 0 and nW == 0 and 0 otherwise, the entry/exit protocol for the writers is obvious:

```
func WriterIn() {
  rw.Lock()
}

func WriterOut() {
  rw.Unlock()
}
```

The first reader (nR == 1) is in competition with the writers and may have to be blocked until an active writer has left the critical section and has assigned 1 to the semaphore rw in its exit protocol. Further readers can then (i.e., if nR > 1) enter the critical section without delay; the last reader must release it again.

Reading and changing the variable nR is protected by a binary semaphore mutex, which is also initialized with 1:

```
func ReaderIn() {
  mutex.Lock()
  nR++
  if nR == 1 {
    rw.Lock()
  }
  mutex.Unlock()
}

func ReaderOut() {
  mutex.Lock()
  nR--
  if nR == 0 {
    rw.Unlock()
  }
  mutex.Unlock()
}
```

The disadvantage of this algorithm is its lack of *fairness*.

Readers have an advantage:

They do not have to wait unless a writer is in the critical section. They can even overtake writers waiting for other readers to leave the critical section. On the other hand, it can happen that the entrance for writers is always impossible, because readers are constantly entering the critical section before them.

4.12.2 The Second Readers–Writers Problem

Alternatively, priority can be given to the writers. As soon as a writer is blocked because the critical section is occupied by active readers, they are allowed to finish their work, but other readers applying for entry are blocked until the waiting writer has had access. The solution of this *second readers–writers problem* is more elaborate.

The following algorithm was published by COURTOIS, HEYMANS, and PARNAS in their paper [7]. They presented the readers–writers problem and the solution of its two variants:

The number bW of writers waiting for the critical section is recorded by them; the access to bW is protected by a further semaphore mutexW. Each reader applying for the critical section will be blocked individually on a semaphore r if necessary, by "sequentializing" its inclusion into the set of applicants for the critical section with an additional semaphore r1. This gives the writers the opportunity to overtake waiting readers.

All semaphores involved must have the initial value 1. The exit of readers is unchanged (with mutexR instead of mutex).

```
func ReaderIn() {
   r1.Lock()
   r.Lock()
   mutexR.Lock()
   nR++
   if nR == 1 {
      rw.Lock()
   }
   mutexR.Unlock()
   r.Unlock()
   r1.Unlock()
}

func WriterIn() {
   mutexW.Lock()
   bW++
   if bW == 1 {
      r.Lock()
   }
   mutexW.Unlock()
   rw.Lock()
}

func WriterOut() {
   rw.Unlock()
   mutexW.Lock()
   bW--
   if bW == 0 {
      r.Unlock()
   }
   mutexW.Unlock()
}
```

The above-mentioned paper ends with the remark "We are grateful to A.N. Habermann …for having shown us an error in an earlier version of this report."—reminding us of DIJKSTRA's sigh (see Sects. 3.4.5 and 3.5.2).

4.12.3 Priority Adjustment

In [13], KANG and LEE compiled a whole series of further strategies for prioritizing readers or writers. In one of their algorithms, called the "*Counter-based Adaptive Priority*", the "age" of the readers and the "weight factor" for the writers are dynamically adapted to the arrivals of readers and writers. These numbers are used to decide which one has the higher priority and is, therefore, allowed to enter the critical section:

The priorities are defined as the product `wW * bW` from the weight factor of the writers and the number of blocked writers, and/or the sum `aR + bR` of the age of the readers and the number of blocked readers. A reader must also wait when entering if there are blocked writers, so that the writers cannot starve. Further explanations are given as comments in the following source code.

```
import ("sync"; "nU/sem")

var (
  nR, nW,
  bR, bW, // numbers of blocked readers and writers
  aR uint // age of readers
  wW uint = 1 // weight factor for the writers
  mutex sync.Mutex
  r, w sem.Semaphore = sem.New(0), sem.New(0)
)

func ReaderIn() {
  mutex.Lock()
  if nW + bW == 0 { // If there is no active or blocked writer,
    wW++            // the weight factor for the writers is incremented
    nR++            // and the reader can enter the critical section,
    mutex.Unlock()
  } else {
    bR++            // otherwise the reader is blocked.
    mutex.Unlock()
    r.P()
  }
}

func ReaderOut() {
  mutex.Lock()
  nR--
  if wW * bW < aR + bR {   // If the writers have a smaller
    if bW > 0 {            // priority than the readers,
      wW += bR             // and there are blocked writers,
    }                      // the weight factor of the writers
    for bR > 0 {           // is incremented
      nR++                 // and all blocked readers
      bR--                 // are unblocked,
      r.V()
    }
  } else {                 // otherwise at the last reader's
    if nR == 0 && bW > 0 { // exit, if writers are blocked,
      if bR > 0 {          // the age of the readers is set
```

```
      aR = bR              // to the number of blocked readers
    }
    if bW == 0 {           // if there are no blocked writers,
      wW = 1               // their weight factor is reset
    }
    nW++                   // and a writer is unblocked.
    bW--
    w.V()
  }
}

mutex.Unlock()
}


func WriterIn() {
  mutex.Lock()
  if nR + nW + bR + bW == 0 { // If neither readers nor writers
    nW++                      // are active or blocked, the writer
    mutex.Unlock()            // is permitted to enter
  } else {                    // enter the critical section.
    bW++                      // otherwise is is blocked.
    mutex.Unlock()
    w.P()
  }
}


func WriterOut() {
  mutex.Lock()
  nW--
  if wW * bW < aR + bR {   // If the writers have a smaller priority
    aR = 0                 // than the readers, the age of the readers
    if bW > 0 {            // is set to 0
      wW = bR
    }
    for bR > 0 {           // the weight factor for
      nR++                 // the writers incremented and
      bR--                 // all blocked readers unblocked.
      r.V()
    }
  } else {                 // otherwise,
    if bW > 0 {            // if there are blocked writers,
      if bR > 0 {          // the age of the readers is incremented
        aR += bR           // if there are blocked readers,
      }
      if bW == 0 {         // and if this was the last writer, the
        wW = 1             // weight factor for the writers is reset
      }
      nW++                 // and ond of the writers is unblocked.
      bW--
```

```
      w.V()
    }
  }
  mutex.Unlock()
}
```

4.12.4 Implementation with Additive Semaphores

With additive semaphores, the readers–writers problem can be solved particularly easily (albeit under the restrictive condition that the number of concurrent readers is limited) with an additive semaphore s, initialized to this maximal number maxR:

```
func ReaderIn() { s.P(1) }
func ReaderOut() { s.V(1) }
func WriterIn() { s.P(maxR) }
func WriterOut() { s.V(maxR) }
```

This brevity is, of course, brought about by the fact that the actual problem solution is located more deeply: in the implementation of additive semaphores by means of general ones.

4.12.5 Efficient Implementation in Go

In Go there is a particularly good support of the problem. In the file rwmutex.go of the package sync, the Go library provides an efficient implementation of mutual exclusion to the readers–writers problem, which makes an implementation trivial:

```
var rwMutex sync.RWMutex

func ReaderIn() { rwMutex.RLock() }
func ReaderOut() { rwMutex.RUnlock() }
func WriterIn() { rwMutex.Lock() }
func WriterOut() { rwMutex.Unlock() }
```

4.12.6 The Readers–Writers Problem as an Abstract Data Type

Analogously to Sect. 3.6 on locks as abstract data types, the readers–writers problem can be packed into an appropriate package.

Its specification looks as follows:

```
package rw

type ReaderWriter interface {

// Pre: The calling process is neither an active reader
```

```
//       nor an active writer.
// It is an active reader; there are no active writers.
// If there was an active writer at the time of the call,
// it was blocked, until this was not the case.
  ReaderIn ()


// Pre: The calling process is an active reader.
// Now it is no longer an active reader.
  ReaderOut ()


// Pre: The calling process is neither an active reader.
//       nor an active writer.
// It is an active writer and there are no other active
// readers or writers. It there were active readers
// or an active writer at the time of the call,
// it was blocked, until this was not the case.
  WriterIn ()


// Pre: The calling process is an active writer.
// Now it is no longer an active writer.
  WriterOut ()
}


func New1 () ReaderWriter { return new1 () }
func New2 () ReaderWriter { return new2 () }
func NewSemaphore () ReaderWriter { return newS () }
func NewAddSemaphore (m uint) ReaderWriter { return newAS (m) }
func NewGo () ReaderWriter { return newG () }
```

4.13   The left–right Problem

The following is a somewhat simpler problem.

In order to allow collision-free traffic in both directions on a single-lane road (or the use of a shared enclosure for lions and zebras in a zoo, see [12]), it must be ensured that vehicles either only travel in one direction (to the left, see Fig. 4.2—reminiscent of the cover of the second edition of this book) or only in the other (to the right) (or lions and zebras never meet in the enclosure).

With n_L or n_R for the number of active drivers to the left and to the right, the invariant—simpler than in the readers–writers problem—is

$$(n_L = 0) \vee (n_R = 0).$$

Fig. 4.2 Oncoming rail traffic

An elementary solution is given by the protocols for the readers in the first readers–writers problem (`RightIn`/ `RightOut` dual to it, i.e. by exchanging L and R):

```
func LeftIn() {
  mutexL.Lock()
  nL++
  if nL == 1 {
    lr.Lock()
  }
  mutexL.Unlock()
}

func LeftOut() {
  mutexL.Lock()
  nL--
  if nL == 0 {
    lr.Unlock()
  }
  mutexL.Unlock()
}
```

In accordance with the nomenclature of the readers–writers problem, this solution is the *first left–right problem.* Of course, it guarantees fairness just as little as in the first readers–writers problem, because uninterrupted traffic to the left does not allow vehicles to travel to the right, and vice versa.

Fair algorithms will be developed in the next two chapters using techniques that make this much easier than solving the second readers–writers problem in Sect. 4.12.2.

Finally, a simple exercise: Specify the left–right problem as abstract data type (`package lr`). (Hint: Sect. 4.12.6.)

4.14   The Dining Philosophers

In [10], DIJKSTRA discussed the following problem. Five philosophers indulge in their favourite activity: they philosophize. In-between they dine at a round table, which is covered with five plates and five forks—one each between two plates (see Fig. 4.3). They are constantly provided with a bowl of entangled spaghetti bolognese (this is, of course, also possible with female philosophers, chop suey, and chopsticks).

Since every philosopher uses a plate and the two forks to the left and right of the plate to eat, philosophers sitting next to each other cannot eat at the same time. Every philosopher, therefore, periodically goes through the cycle

```
philosophize
Lock()
dine
Unlock()
```

where `dine` is the critical section, because of the access to the shared forks or chopsticks for which `Lock()` and `Unlock()` represent the entry or exit protocol.

Fig. 4.3 The table of Plato, Socrates, Aristoteles, Cicero, and Heraklith

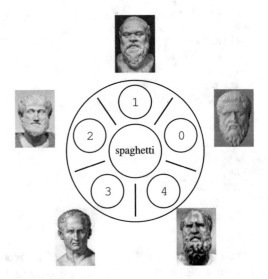

The construction of synchronization algorithms having the aim that no philosopher starves to death raises several problems that are characteristic for NSP. This has led to the problem being one of the "classic" topics in virtually every textbook (e.g., [2, 4, 5, 12]).

We place our solutions in the package nU/phil, whose interface extends that of the locks for *n* processes in Sect. 3.6 extended:

```
package phil
import . "nU/lockn"

type Philos interface {

  LockerN
}


func NewNaive() Philos { return new_() }
```

In the following, we develop various implementations of this package, the constructors of which, of course, have to be included in the specification (as in Sect. 3.6 of the chapter on locks).

The philosophers' decision to have a common meal can lead to a *deadlock* if everyone grabs the fork on the right at the same time and does not lay it down again before he can get hold of the fork on the left as well.

If each fork is represented by a binary semaphore and the fork to the right of the plate is numbered like the plate, this is reflected with the help functions

```
func left (p uint) {
  return (p+4) % 5
}
func right (p uint) {
  return (p+1) % 5
}
```

in the entry and exit protocol for the pth philosopher:

```
package phil
import "sync"

type naive struct {
  fork []sync.Mutex
}


func new_() Philos {
  x := new(naive)
  x.fork = make([]sync.Mutex, 5)
  return x
}


func (x *naive) Lock (p uint) {
  x.fork[p].Lock()
```

```
  x.fork[left(p)].Lock()
}

func (x *naive) Unlock (p uint) {
  x.fork[p].Unlock()
  x.fork[left(p)].Unlock()
}
```

In this case, the philosophers starve to death because they did not carry out the picking up of *both* forks as an *indivisible* action. The simplest—but at the same time the most restrictive—solution is that always only at most *four* philosophers can sit at the table to dine. This is achieved by an additional synchronization with a general semaphore with the initial value 4:

```
package phil
import ("sync"; "nU/sem")

type bounded struct {
  sem.Semaphore "takeSeat"
  fork []sync.Mutex
}

func newB() Philos {
  x := new(bounded)
  x.Semaphore = sem.New (5 - 1)
  x.fork = make([]sync.Mutex, 5)
  return x
}

func (x *bounded) Lock (p uint) {
  x.Semaphore.P()
  x.fork[left (p)].Lock()
  x.fork[p].Lock()
}

func (x *bounded) Unlock (p uint) {
  x.fork[p].Unlock()
  x.fork[left (p)].Unlock()
  x.Semaphore.V()
}
```

An alternative is to break the *symmetry* of the solution that can lead to a deadlock: All philosophers with odd seat numbers always first take up the fork to their left, the others first take up the fork on their right (this also works if only *one* of them does that).

```
package phil
import "sync"

type unsymmetric struct {
```

```
    fork [] sync.Mutex
}

func newU () Philos {
  x := new(unsymmetric)
  x.fork = make([]sync.Mutex, 5)
  return x
}

func (x *unsymmetric) Lock (p uint) {
  if p % 2 == 1 { // or just simply: if p == 0 {
    x.fork[left (p)].Lock()
    x.fork[p].Lock()
  } else {
    x.fork[p].Lock()
    x.fork[left (p)].Lock()
  }
}

func (x *unsymmetric) Unlock (p uint) {
  x.fork[p].Unlock()
  x.fork[left (p)].Unlock()
}
```

As an alternative, we present the approach of DIJKSTRA, that the philosophers always grab *both* forks at the same time. For this purpose, each philosopher is assigned his state (philosophizing, hungry, or dining)

```
const (thinking = iota, hungry, dining)
var status [5]int
```

and a lock `plate` to block him if the required forks are not available. Furthermore, a lock

```
var m sync.Mutex
```

is used to protect the changes of state. A hungry philosopher can pick up both forks and get into the state *dining* if none of his neighbours are dining; otherwise, he will be blocked until his neighbours have finished dining.

```
package phil
import "sync"

type semaphoreUnfair struct {
  plate []sync.Mutex
}

func (x *semaphoreUnfair) test (p uint) {
  if status[p] == hungry &&
     status[left(p)] != dining && status[right(p)] != dining {
    status[p] = dining
```

```
      x.plate[p].Unlock()
  }
}

func newSU() Philos {
  x := new(semaphoreUnfair)
  x.plate = make([]sync.Mutex, NPhilos)
  for p := uint(0); p < NPhilos; p++ {
    x.plate[p].Lock()
  }
  return x
}

func (x *semaphoreUnfair) Lock (p uint) {
  status[p] = hungry
  m.Lock()
  x.test (p)
  m.Unlock()
  x.plate[p].Lock()
  status[p] = dining
}

func (x *semaphoreUnfair) Unlock (p uint) {
  status[p] = thinking
  m.Lock()
  x.test (left (p))
  x.test (right (p))
  m.Unlock()
}
```

This solution is free of deadlocks, but not fair. A philosopher can starve to death if his two neighbours alternate as follows: One of them is still eating while the other sits down at the table, grabs both forks, and starts dining.

Fairness can be combined with another state `starving` to prioritize hungry philosophers with dining neighbours, where the function `test` is extended:

```
package phil
import "sync"

type semaphoreFair struct {
  plate []sync.Mutex
}

func (x *semaphoreFair) test (p uint) {
  if status[p] == hungry &&
    (status[left(p)] == dining && status[right(p)] == thinking ||
      status[left(p)] == thinking && status[right(p)] == dining) {
    status[p] = starving
  }
```

```
if (status[p] == hungry || status[p] == starving) &&
  ! (status[left(p)] == dining || status[left(p)] == starving) &&
  ! (status[right(p)] == dining || status[right(p)] == starving) {
  status[p] = dining
  x.plate[p].Unlock()
 }
}
```

```
func newSF() Philos {
  x := new(semaphoreFair)
  x.plate = make([]sync.Mutex, NPhilos)
  for p := uint(0); p < NPhilos; p++ {
    x.plate[p].Lock()
  }
  return x
}
```

```
func (x *semaphoreFair) Lock (p uint) {
  status[p] = hungry
  m.Lock()
  x.test (p)
  m.Unlock()
  x.plate[p].Lock()
  status[p] = dining
}
```

```
func (x *semaphoreFair) Unlock (p uint) {
  status[p] = thinking
  m.Lock()
  x.test (left(p))
  x.test (right(p))
  m.Unlock()
}
```

With multiple semaphores, the problem of the dining philosophers can be solved extremely easily:

```
func Lock (p uint) {
  P(S[left(p)], S[right(p)]
}
```

```
func Unlock (p uint) {
  V(S[left(p)], S[right(p)]
}
```

Among the source texts of this book is the file philosophen.go—a program to animate the problem of the dining philosophers.

In [6], CHANDY and MISRA deal with the *drinking philosophers* for conflict resolution in distributed systems. They regard graphs with processes as *nodes* and conflict possibilities between them (e.g., shared resources) as *edges*. The dining philosophers are their special case of a circular graph with five nodes (i.e., exactly *one* resource per edge), in which all processes want to use *both* incidental resources.

4.15   The Problem of the Cigarette Smokers

Three smokers sit at a table in a pub and want to smoke. One of them has a large supply of cigarette paper, the second of tobacco, and the third of matches; but none of the three give anything to the others.

The smokers call the landlady; she comes and puts two different utensils on the table. The smoker who lacks these utensils grabs them, produces a cigarette, and starts smoking. When he has finished, the process repeats itself: The smokers call the landlady; she comes, and …

PATIL posed this problem in [17]. He wanted to show that DIJKSTRA's semaphores were not expressive enough to solve synchronization problems under certain restrictions.

PARNAS took up the topic in [16] and contradicted PATIL on some points. We do not go into the subtle confrontation here, but merely show a naive solution as well as that of PARNAS.

To solve the problem we need a function for the landlady (*"the agent"*)— to lay two randomly chosen utensils on the table, in order to enable *that* smoker who lacks them to smoke, as well as two functions for smokers—to wait for the missing utensils and to call the landlady again. With this we have the following specification:

```
package smoke

type Smokers interface {

// Pre: u < 3.
// The calling process has made available
// the utensils complementary to u.
// It was blocked, until all smokers have finished smoking.
   Agent (u uint)

// Pre: u < 3.
// The utensils complementary to u are no longer available,
// but in exclusive possession of the calling smoker,
// that now is smoking.
// He was blocked, until this was possible.
   SmokerIn (u uint)

// The calling smoker finished smoking.
   SmokerOut ()
}
```

```
// Returns agent and smokers with risk of deadlock.
func NewNaive() Smokers { return new_() }

// Returns agent and smokers due to Parnas.
func NewParnas() Smokers { return newP() }
```

How to use this package is clear:

```
package main
import ("math/rand"; . "nU/smok")

var (
  x Smokers = NewNaive() // or NewParnas()
  done = make(chan bool) // s.u.
)

func agent() {
  for {
    x.Agent (uint(rand.Uint32()) % 3)
    // agent lays two randomly chosen utensils on the table
  }
}

func smoker (u uint) {
  for {
    x.SmokerOut() // request for new utensils
  }
}

func main() {
  go agent()
  for u := uint(0); u < 3; u++ {
    go smoker(u)
  }
  <-done // to avoid immediate termination of the program
}
```

The conditions for smoking or laying down new utensils are that the missing utensils are on the table or that the smoker has finished smoking. A smoker takes the utensils that the landlady has laid down there for smoking from the table.

Here is a naive solution with the risk of a deadlock: For example, if the landlady brings tobacco and cigarette paper, the smoker with the matches could grab the tobacco, but before he grabs the cigarette paper, the smoker with the tobacco stock grabs it. Neither of them can smoke now; consequently, the landlady is no longer called ...

```
package smok
import "sync"

type naive struct {
```

```
    smokerOut  sync.Mutex
    avail  [3]sync.Mutex
}

func  new_()  Smokers  {
  x  :=  new (naive)
  for  u  :=  uint(0);  u  <  3;  u++  {
    x.avail[u].Lock()
  }
  return  x
}

func  (x  *naive)  Agent  (u  uint)  {
  x.smokerOut.Lock()
  x.avail[(u+1)  %  3].Unlock()
  x.avail[(u+2)  %  3].Unlock()
}

func  (x  *naive)  SmokerIn  (u  uint)  {
  x.avail[(u+1)  %  3].Lock()
  x.avail[(u+2)  %  3].Lock()
}

func  (x  *naive)  SmokerOut()  {
  x.smokerOut.Unlock()
}
```

Here is the solution from PARNAS using helper processes:

```
package  smok
import  "sync"

type  parnas  struct  {
  avail  [3]bool
  mutex,  agent  sync.Mutex
  supplied,  smoke  [3]sync.Mutex
}

func  (x  *parnas)  help  (u  uint)  {
  var  first  bool
  for  {
    x.supplied[u].Lock()
    x.mutex.Lock()
    u1,  u2  :=  (u+1)  %  3,  (u+2)  %  3
    first  =  true
    if  x.avail[u1]  {
      first  =  false
      x.avail[u1]  =  false
      x.smoke[u2].Unlock()
    }
```

```
  if x.avail[u2] {
    first = false
    x.avail[u2] = false
    x.smoke[u1].Unlock() }
  if first {
    x.avail[u] = true
  }
  x.mutex.Unlock()
}
}


func newP() Smokers {
  x := new(parnas)
  for u := uint(0); u < 3; u++ {
    x.supplied[u].Lock()
    x.smoke[u].Lock()
  }
  for u := uint(0); u < 3; u++ {
    go x.help(u)
  }
  return x
}

func (x *parnas) Agent (u uint) {
  x.agent.Lock()
  x.supplied[(u+1) % 3].Unlock()
  x.supplied[(u+2) % 3].Unlock()
}

func (x *parnas) SmokerIn (u uint) {
  x.smoke[u].Lock()
}

func (x *parnas) SmokerOut() {
  x.agent.Unlock()
}
```

Among the source texts of this book is the file `smokers.go`—a program to animate the problem of the cigarette smokers.

4.16 Implementation of Semaphores

A semaphore consists of the combination of an integer value and a queue, into which those processes that are blocked on the semaphore are inserted. So, in principle, we have the representation

```
type semaphore struct {
```

```
int "value of the semaphore"
Buffer
}
```

where objects of the type `Buffer` are implemented as linked ring lists—preferably of the same type as the *ready list*.

When a semaphore s is initialized, the value of the passed parameter, which has to be >= 0, is copied to s.int, and an empty queue is generated for s.

If an active process calls a P-operation on a semaphore s, there are two possibilities:

- s.int > 0 or
- s.int <= 0.

In both cases, s.int is decremented. Of course, this has to happen atomically, because P and V-operations, which can be called concurrently by other processes, access the same data structure, i.e., could change s.int. In the second case, in addition, the following happens:

The calling process no longer runs through the rest of the time slice available to it, but is *immediately deactivated*, i.e., transferred from the state *active* to the state *blocked*. The processor is taken from it, and it is removed from the ready list and appended at the end of the waiting queue of s. Then the next process from the ready list changes from the state *ready* to the state *active*, i.e., the released processor is passed to it.

For the same reason as when changing the value of s, all operations that move the processes between the lists must also be implemented indivisibly.

When a process calls a V-operation on this semaphore, we also have to distinguish two cases:

- s.int < 0 or
- s.int >= 0.

In both cases, s.int is incremented atomically.

It is immediately clear that in the first case, the absolute amount of s.int is identical with the number of processes blocked on s. In this case, the first process in the waiting queue of s is removed from it and appended to the end of the ready list, i.e., transferred from the state *blocked* back to the state *ready*. In neither case is there process switching.

The realization of indivisibility is achieved in all common systems by recourse to *indivisible machine instructions*.

This implementation with FIFO queues ensures that each of the blocked processes is eventually unblocked again. For n>0 the n-th process in the waiting queue of s is ready again after exactly n V-operations on s.

A blocked process can, therefore—completely independently of the process scheduling strategy—never be overtaken by a process that was later blocked on the same semaphore, i.e., the implementation of semaphore operations is *strongly* fair (see Chap. 7).

However, we would like to point out once again that DIJKSTRA did *not* include this into the specification of semaphores; in his paper [8] he leaves open *which* process is unblocked with a V-operation: "*Which one …is left unspecified …*". The reason for this was probably considerations of the following type.

4.16.1 The Convoy Phenomenon

Although the implementation of semaphore queues according to the FIFO principle is obvious and seems advantageous, there are situations in which this principle can have a negative effect on the throughput of a concurrent system. For example, it can happen that processes that occupy resources for a longer period of time or have a low priority periodically hinder faster or higher prioritized processes over a longer period of time (see [11]).

An illustrative example is the poor utilization of a road, when a convoy with a slow vehicle (e.g., a Citroën 2CV) at the front and faster vehicles (Porsches, Mercedes SLs, Maseratis, etc.) behind always maintains the same order when overtaking other slow vehicles under difficult conditions (heavy oncoming traffic or the like). The same traffic jam is formed during each overtaking.

There are three ways to counter the convoy phenomenon:

- For a V-operation in which a process is to be unblocked, not the *oldest* process is moved from the waiting queue into the ready list, but—randomly—*any one* of them.
- If a P-operation has to lead to the blocking of the calling process, it is not appended behind the *end* of the waiting queue of the semaphore in question, but to some other *fortuitous* position.
- The order of the processes in the waiting queue of a semaphore—if it is not empty during a V-operation—is broken up by assigning 0 to s.int and removing *all* processes from the queue. This is achieved by the fact that the body of the P-operation is surrounded by a loop, which means that then exactly one of these processes becomes ready, and the others are blocked again.

The stochastic aspects, which in all cases come into play through the process management, let us, on average, expect a high degree of fairness.

References

1. Andrews, G.R.: Concurrent Programming. Principles and Practice. Addison-Wesley, Menlo Park (1991)
2. Andrews, G.R.: Foundations of Multithreaded. Parallel and Distributed Programming. Addison-Wesley, Reading (2000)

3. Barz, H.W.: Implementing semaphores by binary semaphores. ACM SIGPLAN Notices **18**, 39–45 (1983). https://doi.org/10.1145/948101.948103
4. Ben-Ari, M.: Principles of Concurrent and Distributed Programming. 2nd ed. Addison-Wesley, Harlow (2006)
5. Burns, A., Davies, G.: Concurrent Programming. Addison-Wesley, Harlow (1993)
6. Chandy, K.M., Misra, J.: The drinking philosophers problem. ACM Trans. Program. Lang. Syst. 6 (1984) 632–646 https://doi.org/10.1145/1780.1804 https://www.cs.utexas.edu/users/misra/scannedPdf.dir/DrinkingPhil.pdf
7. Courtois, P.J., Heymans, F., Parnas, D.L.: Concurrent control with "Readers" and "Writers", Commun. ACM **14**, 667–668 (1971). https://doi.org/10.1145/362759.362813
8. Dijkstra, E. W.: Cooperating sequential processes. Technical Report EWD-123, Technological University Eindhoven (1965) https://www.cs.utexas.edu/users/EWD/ewd01xx/EWD123.PDF
9. Dijkstra, E.W.: The structure of the "THE"-multiprogramming system. Commun. ACM **11**, 341–346 (1968). https://www.cs.utexas.edu/users/EWD/ewd01xx/EWD196.PDF
10. Dijkstra, E.W.: Hierarchical ordering of sequential processes. Acta Informatica **1** 115–138 (1971) https://www.cs.utexas.edu/users/EWD/ewd03xx/EWD310.PDF
11. Gray, J., Reuter, A.: Transaction Processing. Concepts and Techniques. Morgan Kaufmann, San Francisco (1992)
12. Herrtwich, R.G., Hommel, G.: Nebenläufige Programme (Kooperation und Konkurrenz). Springer, Berlin (1994, 1989). https://doi.org/10.1007/978-3-642-57931-8
13. Kang, S., Lee, H.: Analysis and solution of non-preemptive policies for scheduling readers and writers. ACM SIGOPS Oper. Syst. Rev. **32**, 30–50 (1998). https://doi.org/10.1145/281258.281268
14. Martin, A.J., Burch, J.R.: Fair mutual exclusion with unfair P and V operations. Inf. Proc. Lett. **21**, 97–100 (1985). https://doi.org/10.1016/0020-0190(85)90041-9
15. Morris, J.M.: A starvation: free solution to the mutual exclusion problem. Inf. Proc. Lett. **8**, 76–80 (1979). https://doi.org/10.1016/0020-0190(79)90147-9
16. Parnas, D.L.: On a solution to the cigarette smoker's problem without conditional statements. Commun. ACM **18**, 181–183 (1975). https://doi.org/10.1145/360680.360709
17. Patil, S.S.: Limitations and capabilities of Dijkstra's semaphore primitives for coordination among processes. MIT Computations Structures Group, Project MAC **57** (1971)
18. Udding, J.T.: Absence of individual starvation using weak semaphores. Inf. Proc. Lett. **23**, 159–162 (1986). https://doi.org/10.1016/0020-0190(86)90117-1

The Baton Algorithm

5

Abstract

In this chapter, we present a skillful construction to solve many problems that require condition synchronization. For several disjoint process classes, with this it is achieved that only processes from the *same* class may work concurrently, processes from *different* classes, on the other hand, only under mutual exclusion.

5.1 Development of the Problem

Given N classes of processes P_0, P_1, ..., P_{N-1} and a *critical section*, characterized by the following properties

- For each $k < N$, there is a bound m_k ($1 \leq mk \leq \infty$), so that at most m_k processes from *one* class P_k can enter *commonly* the critical section (for $m_k = \infty$ with ∞ realized as $2^{32} - 1$); this means that quasi any number of processes from P_k may enter).
- But there must *never* be two processes from *different* classes P_k and P_i in it; for any two processes $p \in P_k$ and $q \in P_i$ with $i \neq k$, the *mutual exclusion* of p and q must be secured.

For each $k < N$, let n_k in the following denote the number of processes from the class P_k that are in the critical section. Then we can formulate for all $k < N$ a Boolean expression as an entry condition for the processes from P_k:

$$c_k = \forall i (i \neq k \implies n_i = 0) \land (n_k < m_k).$$

The readers–writers problem (see Sect. 4.12) is a special case of this. Its invariant is

$$(n_W = 0) \vee (n_R = 0) \wedge (n_W = 1).$$

We set $N = 2$, $R = 0$ as an index for the readers and $W = 1$ for the writers, (i.e., $P_0 =$ readers and $P_1 =$ writers), $m_R = \infty$, and $m_W = 1$.

Since n_R is incremented at the entry of a reader, and n_W is incremented at the entry of a writer, the entry condition for a reader is

$$(n_W = 0) \wedge (n_R < \infty) = (n_W = 0) \qquad\qquad (c_R)$$

and that for a writer

$$(n_R = 0) \wedge (n_W < m_W) = (n_R = 0) \wedge (n_W = 0). \qquad\qquad (c_W)$$

Another example of this is the *left–right problem* (see Sect. 4.13).

If $m_L = m_R = \infty$, i.e., that in each case quasi any number of processes from *one* class may drive concurrently in the critical section, the conditions are as follows

$$n_R = 0 \quad \text{and, resp.,} \quad n_L = 0.$$

The algorithms presented in Sects. 4.12 and 4.13 can be refined to eliminate their inherent unfairness—running traffic in one direction brings oncoming traffic to a standstill (or—if the zebras do not leave the enclosure, it is taboo for the lions).

However, this is associated with complex extensions of the protocols (see the solution of the second readers–writers problem in Sect. 4.12.2 or the solution with dynamically adjusted priorities in Sect. 4.12.3).

In Sect. 5.3, we give a more complex example and in Chap. 6, we do this much more elegantly with *universal critical sections*.

5.1.1   The Baton of Andrews

Instead, a systematic approach by ANDREWS (from his books [1] and [2]) to solving such problems will be presented, the elegance of which is based on *simplification through clever generalization*.

Its basic idea is to block and unblock processes on arbitrary conditions, whose specialization provides the protocols and allow to change the strategy to privilege certain classes of processes by easily manageable local interventions.

For each condition c_k $(k < N)$, a binary semaphore s[k] with the initial value false is required to block the processes waiting for it; in the following, let nB[k] be the number of processes blocked on s[k] or to be blocked on it.

For the entrance, a further binary semaphore e, the „*baton*", is introduced, initialized with true: It has two tasks; on the one hand, to secure the mutual exclusion of the protocols and, on the other hand, to pass on the control, if no process P_k is waiting for its condition c_k, i.e., is blocked on s[k].

In principle, the processes of the class P_k have the protocols

```
func in() {
  e.Lock()
  if ! c[k] {
    nB[k]++
    e.Unlock() // *
    s[k].Lock()
  }
  ... // entry statements
  vall()
}

func out() {
  e.Lock()
  ... // exit statements
  vall()
}
```

where the data defining the conditions c[k] may only be changed in the entry or exit statements.

The common part of these protocols is the function

```
func vall() {
  if c[0] && nB[0] > 0 {
    nB[0]--; s[0].Unlock()
  } else if c[1] && nB[1] > 0 {
    nB[1]--; s[1].Unlock()
  } else if ...
    ...
  } else if c[n-1] && nB[N-1] > 0 {
    nB[N-1]--; s[n-1].Unlock()
  } else {
    e.Unlock()
  }
}
```

For their first N branchings, however, a language concept would be more appropriate for the problem that does not enforce the priority given by the textual order, but allows a nondeterministic selection among them (we consider this in the construction of *universal critical sections* in Sect. 6.1.2).

The progress of these protocols can be imagined as *passing the baton*, which explains the name of this technique. They have the following properties:

- The semaphores form a *split binary semaphore*: `s[0] + ... + s[N-1] <= 1`, i.e., at most *one* of the semaphores involved has the value `true` (consequently, at any time at most *one* process is in possession of the „baton").
- The mutual exclusion of the protocols is ensured because every possible statement sequence starts with `e.P()` and ends with exactly one V-operation.
- An interruption at point * is harmless: Always only *one* V-operation on `s[k]` can interfere, because further processes are blocked on `e` at this time.
- For each process, its condition `c[k]` is guaranteed when the statements of the protocol are executed, because it is exactly *then blocked* when the condition is *not fulfilled*, and exactly again *then unblocked* when it is *fulfilled*, where the condition `c[k]` is true again, because access to the protocols is protected by `e` at that time, and, therefore, no other process can change `c[k]` in the meantime.
- *Deadlocks* cannot occur, because at *any* exit, one of the processes blocked on `s[k]` is deblocked, if there is one.
- Only when there are no more blocked processes, although their condition is fulfilled, is another process allowed to enter its protocol. Thus, this technique allows a finely granulated control of the protocols, because it can be intervened at the earliest possible time.

5.2   The Readers–Writers Problem

For the first readers–writers problem, we found the conditions in the previous chapter (see Sect. 4.12); for the two process classes *reader* and *writer*, they are

$$n_W = 0 \qquad\qquad (c_L)$$

and

$$(n_R = 0) \wedge (n_W = 0). \qquad\qquad (c_W)$$

By using these conditions, whereby we denote the semaphores by `sR` and `sW` and do not need an array for `nB`, but simply use counting variables `var bR, bW uint`, the following protocols result:

```
func ReaderIn() {
  e.Lock()
  if nW > 0 {
    bR++
    e.Unlock()
    sR.Lock()  }
  nR++
  val1()
}
```

```
func ReaderOut() {
  e.Lock()
  nR--
  vall()
}

func WriterIn() {
  e.Lock()
  if nR > 0 || nW > 0 {
    bW++
    e.Unlock()
    sW.Lock()  }
  nW++
  vall()
}

func WriterOut() {
  e.Lock()
  nW--
  vall()
}
```

with the following function called in all protocols at the end

```
func vall() {
  if nW == 0 && bR > 0 {
    bR--
    sR.Unlock()
  } else if nR == 0 && nW == 0 && bW > 0 {
    bW--
    sW.Unlock()
  } else {
    e.Unlock()
  }
}
```

This function can be partially simplified, because some of the conditions are met on a case-by-case basis anyway.

At the beginning of the statement sequence in vall we have

- in the entry protocol of readers $nR > 0$ and $nW == 0$,
- in their exit protocol $nW == 0$ and $bR == 0$,
- for the writers at entry $nR == 0$ and $nW == 1$, and
- at their exit $nR == 0$ and $nW == 0$.

The fact that in the second point $bR == 0$ is valid follows, because at this point all blocked readers are successively unblocked to terminate their entry protocol, because all other processes are blocked on the semaphore e in their protocols, until the last unblocked reader releases it again in its `vall`.

By inserting a correspondingly shortened `vall`, the following statements result at the end of the respective protocols:

```
func ReaderIn() {
   ...
   if bR > 0 {
      bR--
      sR.Unlock()
   } else {
      e.Unlock()
   }
}

func ReaderOut() {
   ...
   if nR == 0 && bW > 0 {
      bW--
      sW.Unlock()
   } else {
      e.Unlock()
   }
}

func WriterIn() {
   ...
   e.Unlock()
}

func WriterOut() {
   ...
   if bR > 0 {
      bR--
      sR.Unlock()
   } else if bW > 0 {
      bW--
      sW.Unlock()
   } else {
      e.Unlock()
   }
}
```

The baton technique can be used to determine the order in which the processes involved enter the critical section. In addition, strategies for alternative priorities are also easily implementable, simply by changing the conditions in certain protocols.

As a simple example we show a solution of the second readers–writers problem, which is now absolutely trivial (compare it with the complicated solution in Sect. 4.12.2). The entry condition for a reader is

$$(n_W = 0) \land (b_W = 0).$$

Accordingly, with the protocol

```
func ReaderIn() {
  e.Lock()
  if nW > 0 || bW > 0 {
    . . .
}
```

newly arriving readers are blocked, if a writer is blocked; and with

```
func WriterOut() {
  e.Lock()
  nW--
  if bR > 0 && bW == 0 {
    . . .
}
```

writers are preferred, if a writer leaves the critical section.

With the baton technique, even largely fair strategies can be easily implemented (of course, only if the semaphores used are fair).

For example, with a Boolean variable `last_R`, the conditions

$$c_R = (n_W = 0) \land ((b_W = 0) \lor \neg last\,R)$$

and

$$c_W = (n_R = 0) \land (n_W = 0) \land ((b_R = 0) \lor \neg last\,R)$$

guarantee a change between readers and writers when the others are waiting. `last_R` is *set* when readers enter and *deleted* by writers; i.e., it is recorded whether a reader or a writer was the last in the critical section:

```
func ReaderIn() {
  e.Lock()
  if nW > 0 || bW > 0 && lastR {
    . . .
  lastR = true;
    . . .
}

Gfunc WriterIn() {
  e.Lock()
  if nR > 0 || nW > 0 || bR > 0 && ! lastR {
    bW++
    e.Unlock()
    sW.Lock()
  }
  lastR = false
```

```
   . . .
}

func WriterOut() {
   . . .
   if (bW == 0 || ! lastR) && bR > 0 {
     bR--
     sR.Unlock()
   } else if bR == 0 || lastR && bW > 0 {
     . . .
   . . .
}
```

5.3   The Second Left–Right Problem

We will now fulfill the promise made at the end of Sect. 4.13 to develop a more elaborate variant of the left–right problem that avoids emergency braking to avoid head-on collisions (or to ensure that the zoo does not always have to refresh its zebra population).

Fairness can be achieved in analogy to the step from the first to the second readers–writers problem, e.g., by interrupting the sequence of processes of one class on entry as soon as a process of the other class wants to enter, which can be seen from the fact that it is blocked in its entry protocol.

With the method `Blocked`, the number of blocked processes is safely callable within the entry protocols (see the remark in their specification).

With

- n_L and n_R for the number of active drivers to the left and to the right, b_L and b_R for the number of blocked drivers,
- m_L and m_R for the maximum number of processes that may pass through one after the other without interruption, provided that no one is waiting in the opposite direction, and
- d_L and d_R for the number of processes that have entered the critical section in sequence without being prevented by oncoming traffic,

the entry conditions are

$$c_L = (n_R = 0) \wedge ((d_L <= m_L) \vee (b_R = 0))$$

and

$$c_R = (n_L = 0) \wedge ((d_R <= m_R) \vee (b_L = 0)).$$

With the enrichment of the entry statements by the increase of d_L and d_R, respectively, and the resetting of the corresponding numbers d_R and d_L, respectively, of oncoming traffic to

0, we obtain the protocols by inserting the entry and exit conditions and the entry and exit statements:

```
func LeftIn() {
    e.Lock()
    if nR > 0 || dL >= mL && bR == 0 {
        nL++
        e.Unlock()
        sL.Lock()
    }
    nL++
    dL++
    dR = 0
    vall()
}

func LeftOut() {
    e.Lock()
    nL--
    vall()
}

func vall() {
    if nR == 0 && (dL < mL || bR > 0 && bL > 0 {
        bL--
        sL.Unlock()
    } else {
        if nL == 0 && (dR < mR || bL == 0) && bR > 0 {
            bR--
            sR.Unlock()
        } else {
            e.Unlock()
        }
    }
}
```

and the functions `RightIn` and `RightOut`. dual to `LeftIn` and `LeftOut`

In conclusion, it should be noted that for $m_L < \infty$ and $m_R = 1$ as a special case, we just get a solution of the second readers–writers problem.

References

1. Andrews, G. R.: Concurrent Programming, Principles and Practice. Addison-Wesley Menlo Park (1991). ISBN: 978-0-805-30086-4
2. Andrews, G.R.: Foundations of Multithreaded, Parallel and Distributed Programming. Addison-Wesley. Reading (2000). ISBN: 978-0-201-35752-3

Universal Critical Sections

6

Abstract

The baton algorithm in the previous chapter contains a "pattern for programming". This raises the question of whether it is possible to generate program code "automatically" by using this pattern as a "recipe" for constructing nonsequential algorithms. In this chapter, it is shown that this is, indeed, the case. The considerations result in the development of a universal synchronization concept, for the simple solution of problems that require condition synchronization.

With this we achieve a level of abstraction with which certain types of synchronization problems can be reduced to their conceptual core. The actual synchronization measures disappear behind the interface of an abstract data type, resulting in a *substantial* simplification of the implementations.

6.1   Basic Idea and Construction

An analysis of the solution of the first readers–writers problem using the baton technique leads to the construction of the "universal synchronization object" developed in this chapter The problem is completely described by its invariant

$$(n_W = 0) \lor (n_R = 0) \land (n_W = 1) .$$

As was shown in the previous chapter, the baton algorithm provides its synchronization. The values of the variables used to describe the invariants are changed in the entry and exit statements. The entry conditions and these statement sequences—and, thus, the entire synchronization—are shown in Table 6.1.

The entries in the left column of Table 6.1 are functions with a Boolean result, those in the other columns are statements. The entries in each column of the table can be combined

© Springer Fachmedien Wiesbaden GmbH, part of Springer Nature 2021
C. Maurer, *Nonsequential and Distributed Programming with Go,*
https://doi.org/10.1007/978-3-658-29782-4_6

Table 6.1 Synchronization of the readers–writers problems

Process class	Entry condition	Entry statements	Exit statements
Reader	nW == 0	nR++	nR- -
Writer	nR i= 0 && nW == 0	nW = 1	nW = 0

to a function that represents the spectrum of functions for *all* classes and is parameterized by the classes in the form of natural numbers. To such a *function spectrum* the process class is consequently passed as a parameter.

For this purpose, we expand our "help package" nU/obj by the types of the spectra of the entry conditions and the entry and exit statements:

```
package obj
import "runtime"

type (
  CondSpectrum func (uint) bool
  NFuncSpectrum func (uint) uint
  StmtSpectrum func (uint)
)

func NothingSp (i uint) { Nothing() }
```

The fact that value-returning functions are used for the entry statements is merely a precaution for more advanced applications; the function values are for the moment insignificant and are not used.

Before we develop the planned abstract data type, we present the functions that translate the synchronization table of the first readers–writers problem:

```
const (reader = iota; writer)
var nR, nW uint

func c (i uint) bool {
  if i == reader {
    return nW == 0
  }
  return nR == 0 && nW == 0
}

func e (i uint) uint {
  if i == reader {
    nR++
    return nR
  } else {
    nW = 1
  }
  return nW
}

func l (i uint) {
```

```
if i == reader {
  nR--
} else {
  nW = 0
  }
}
```

6.1.1   Specification

A *universal critical section* is a conditional critical section to ensure the consistency of shared resources accessed by at least two classes of processes. It may be concurrently entered by several processes of *one* class, but by processes of *different* classes only under mutual exclusion. The process classes are identified by natural numbers (starting with 0).

Mutual exclusion is guaranteed by entry conditions and by operations that control the conditions—depending on the respective process class. They are bundled in functions of the type CondSpectrum and StmtSpectrum, which have to be constructed by the clients.

When an instance of this class is created—i.e., at the initialization of a variable of this abstract data type—the content of the *synchronization table* is "transmitted" to it by passing the names of the preconstructed condition, function, and statement spectra as parameters to the constructor. The names of the preconstructed condition, function, and statement spectra are passed as parameters to the constructor. The functions for entering and leaving a critical section, Enter and Leave, are not interruptible by calls of these functions by other processes.

After the preparations from the previous section, the abstract data type can now be constructed, in which the actual synchronization measures are embedded behind the scenes of a suitable interface.

Here is the specification of the *universal critical sections*, encapsulated in the package cs:

```
package cs
import . "nU/obj"

type CriticalSection interface {

// Pre: i < number of classes of x. The function is called
//      within the entry conditions of x (see remark).
// Returns true, iff at the time of the call at least one
// process of the k-th class of x is blocked.
// Remark: The value might have changed immediately after the call;
//         consequently it can only be used, if the indivisibilty
//         of the call from later operations is ensured.
//         This is the case when the precondition is fulfilled.
Blocked (i uint) bool

// Pre: i < number of classes of x.
//      The calling process is not in x.
// It is now in the i-th class of x, i.e., it was blocked,
// until c(i) was fulfilled, and now e(i) is executed
// (where c is the entry condition of x
// and e the function at the entry of x).
```

```
// Returns the value of e(i).
Enter (i uint) uint

// Pre: i < number of classes of x.
//      The calling process is in the i-th class of x.
// It now is not any longer in x, i.e., l(i) is executed
// (where l is the operation at the exit from x and
// i the class of x, in which the calling process was before).
Leave (i uint)
}

// Pre: n > 1. c, e and l are defined for all i < n.
// Returns a new critical section with n classes
// to be used by concurrent processes.
// x has the entry condition c(i) and the
// operations e(i) and l(i) to enter the i-th class
// of x resp. to leave it.
// All entry conditions of x are fulfilled.
// No process is in x.
   func New (n uint, c CondSpectrum, e NFuncSpectrum,
             l StmtSpectrum) CriticalSection {
     return new_(n,c,e,l)
   }
```

6.1.2   Implementation

For the implementation, a package `perm` with the specification

```
package perm

type Permutation interface {

// x is randomly permuted.
  Permute()

// Pre: i <= size of x.
// Returns the i-th number of x.
  F (i uint) uint
}

// Pre: n > 1.
// Returns a new random permutation of size n,
// i.e., a permutation of the numbers 0, 1, ..., n-1.
func New (n uint) Permutation { return new_(n) }
```

is used to realize what was proposed in Sect. 5.1.1 after the source code of `vall`. (Its implementation is only of secondary interest here and is, therefore, skipped; it is included in the source texts of this book.)

The representation of the corresponding type is

```
import ("sync"; . "nU/obj"; "nU/perm")

type criticalSection struct {
  uint
```

```
      sync.Mutex
      s []sync.Mutex
      ns []uint
      CondSpectrum
      NFuncSpectrum
      StmtSpectrum
      perm.Permutation "random permutation"
}
```

Thereby

- uint is the number of process classes involved,
- Mutex the "baton"-lock,
- s the number of locks on which processes are blocked if the entry condition is not fulfilled (initially all open),
- ns the number of processes blocked on these locks,
- CondSpectrum the spectrum of the entry conditions,
- NFuncSpectrum the function spectrum to manipulate the internal variables in the entry protocols,
- StmtSpectrum the statement spectrum to manipulate the internal variables in the exit protocols, and
- Permutation a permutation for the nondeterministic selection in vAll.

This makes the implementation of the constructor obvious:

```
func new_(n uint, c CondSpectrum, e NFuncSpectrum,
               l StmtSpectrum) CriticalSection {
  x := new(criticalSection)
  x.uint = n
  x.s = make ([]sync.Mutex, x.uint)
  x.ns = make ([]uint, x.uint)
  for k := uint(0); k < x.uint; k++ {
    x.s[k].Lock()
  }
  x.CondSpectrum = c
  x.NFuncSpectrum = e
  x.StmtSpectrum = l
  x.Permutation = perm.New (x.uint)
  return x
}
```

Also, the implementation of the functions is basically quite easy. It simply consists of the translation of the metalinguistically given baton algorithm in Sect. 5.1.1 into program text:

```
func (x *criticalSection) vAll() {
  x.Permutation.Permute()
  for i := uint(0); i < x.uint; i++ {
    k := x.Permutation.F (i)
    if x.CondSpectrum (k) && x.ns[k] > 0 {
      x.ns[k]--
      x.s[k].Unlock()
      return
    }
```

```
  }
  x.Mutex.Unlock()
}

func (x *criticalSection) Blocked (i uint) bool {
  return x.ns[i] > 0
}

func (x *criticalSection) Enter (i uint) uint {
  x.Mutex.Lock()
  if ! x.CondSpectrum (i) {
    x.ns[i]++
    x.Mutex.Unlock()
    x.s[i].Lock()
  }
  defer x.vAll()
  return x.NFuncSpectrum (i)
}

func (x *criticalSection) Leave (i uint) {
  x.Mutex.Lock()
  x.StmtSpectrum (i)
  x.vAll()
}
```

Strictly speaking, exception handling is missing, if for i a value greater than or equal to the number of process classes is passed. One could think about

- the creation of a panic,
- the return of a Boolean value— false if i was too big, or
- the return of a value of type error.

But since this is an issue that has nothing to do with NSP, this problem is not pursued further here.

6.2   Semaphores

The—probably most trivial—application of universal critical sections is the implementation of general semaphores:

```
package sem
import "nU/cs"

type semaphoreCS struct {
  cs.CriticalSection
}

func newCS (n uint) Semaphore {
  val := n
  x := new(semaphoreCS)
  c := func (i uint) bool {
        return val > 0
```

```
        }
f  := func (i uint) uint {
        val--
        return val
      }
l  := func (i uint) {
        val++
      }
x.CriticalSection = cs.New (1, c, f, l)
return x
}


func (x *semaphoreCS) P() { x.Enter (0) }
func (x *semaphoreCS) V() { x.Leave (0) }
```

This implementation should be immediately understandable so that nothing needs to be explained.

6.3   The Sleeping Barber

Also the barber can serve his customers with a universal critical section (see Table 6.2).
   This is easily translated into Go code:

```
import (. "nU/obj"; "nU/cs")

type barberCS struct {
  cs.CriticalSection
}
const (customer = iota; barber)

func newCS() Barber {
  var n uint
  c := func (i uint) bool {
        if i == customer {
            return true
        }
        return n > 0
      }
  e := func (i uint) uint {
        if i == customer {
          n++
        } else {
          n--
        }
      }
```

Table 6.2 Synchronization of the barber's problems

Process class	Entry conditions	Entry statements	Exit statements
Customer	true	n++	Nothing()
Barber	n > 0	n--	Nothing()

```
                 return n
            }
  x := new(barberCS)
  x.CriticalSection = cs.New (2, c, e, NothingSp)
  return x
}
```

```
func (x *barberCS) Customer() { x.Enter (customer) }
func (x *barberCS) Barber() { x.Enter (barber) }
```

Also this example shows the potency of the concept.

6.4   The Readers–Writers Problem

As the next application we show an elegant solution of the first readers–writers problem.
An instance of the class is generated, given the preconstructed spectra c, f, and l for
synchronization; the protocols then are simply calls of Enter and Leave:

```
package rw
import . "nU/cs"

const (reader = iota; writer)

var (
  nR, nW uint
  x cs.CriticalSection
)

... // source text of the functions c, e and l

func ReaderIn() { x.Enter (reader) }
func ReaderOut() { x.Leave (reader) }
func WriterIn() { x.Enter (writer) }
func WriterOut() { x.Leave (writer) }

func main() { x = New (2, c, e, 1) }
```

This can easily be modified to a solution of the second readers–writers problem; only the
entry condition for the readers has to be changed:

```
func c (i uint) bool
  if i == reader {
    return nW == 0 && ! Blocked(writer)
  }
  return nR == 0 && nW == 0
}
```

A comparison of this easily understandable solution with the rather complicated idea of
COURTOIS, HEYMANS, and PARNAS (see Sect. 4.12.2) clearly shows the power of the concept
of universal critical sections.

Of course, it makes sense to generalize this construct to an abstract data type, so that it
can also be used in a system in which *several* critical readers–writers sections are required.
For this, the interface from Sect. 4.12.6 is supplemented by the constructor

```go
func NewCS() ReaderWriter { return newCS() }
```

The implementation looks a bit different from that above, because the spectra have to be included in the representation.

In Go, *inner functions* are helpful here:

```go
package rw
import "nU/cs"

type criticalSection struct {
  cs.CriticalSection
}

func newCS() ReaderWriter {
  var nR, nW uint
  x := new(criticalSection1)
  c := func (i uint) bool {
        if i == reader {
          return nW == 0
        }
        return nR == 0 && nW == 0
      }
  e := func (i uint) uint {
        if i == reader {
          nR++
          return nR
        }
        nW = 1
        return nW
      }
  l := func (i uint) {
        if i == reader {
          nR--
        } else {
          nW = 0
        }
      }
  x.CriticalSection = cs.New (2, c, e, l)
  return x
}

func (x *criticalSection1) ReaderIn() { x.Enter (reader) }
func (x *criticalSection1) ReaderOut() { x.Leave (reader) }
func (x *criticalSection1) WriterIn() { x.Enter (writer) }
func (x *criticalSection1) WriterOut() { x.Leave (writer) }
```

It is also very easy to develop this further into even *fairer* variants; but this is left as an exercise. (You can find such implementations in the source texts for this book in the package nU/rw.)

6.5   The Left–Right Problem

We now show the solution to the second left–right problem. Its synchronization results from the invariants in Sect. 4.13 and is summarized in Table 6.3. bL and bR denote the number of processes that are blocked in their entry protocol, because there was "oncoming traffic" at the time of their entry.

The translation of these tables into program text is trivial:

```
package lr
import "nU/cs"

type criticalSection2 struct {
  cs.CriticalSection
}

func newCS2() LeftRight {
  var nL, nR uint
  x := new(criticalSection2)
  c := func (i uint) bool {
        if i == left {
           return nR == 0 && (! x.Blocked (right) || nL == 0)
        }
        return nL == 0 && (! x.Blocked (left) || nR == 0)
     }
  e := func (i uint) uint {
        if i == left {
           nL++
           return nL
        }
        nR++
        return nR
     }
  l := func (i uint) {
        if i == left {
           nL--
        } else {
           nR--
        }
     }
  x.CriticalSection = cs.New (2, c, e, l)
  return x
}

func (x *criticalSection2) LeftIn()  { x.Enter (left)  }
func (x *criticalSection2) LeftOut() { x.Leave (left)  }
func (x *criticalSection2) RightIn() { x.Enter (right) }
func (x *criticalSection2) RightOut() { x.Leave (right) }
```

Table 6.3 Synchronization of the second left–right problem

Process class	Entry conditions	Entry statements	Exit statements
Left	nR == 0 && (bL == 0 || nL == 0)	nL++	nL- -
Right	nL == 0 && (bR == 0 || nR == 0)	nR++	nR- -

You could try to implement this example in the style of the classic solution of the second readers–writers problem from [1] with a bunch of scattered semaphores—have lots of fun with this! But perhaps you will also encounter something similar to what the authors of this solution did, who thank HABERMANN at the end of their paper (see Sect. 4.12.2) ...

The decisive advantage of the construction of universal critical sections has already been mentioned. Its basic idea to create with a general formulation of the algorithms for synchronization and, hence, for their separation from the application a *reusable pattern*, will also prove useful in other contexts.

The use of such *universal classes* makes applications free from all technical details of synchronization:

▶   The real intellectual achievement is only to work out the invariants of the problem to be solved.

The translation into corresponding function spectra, and their transfer to a copy of the classes at its generation, on the other hand, is a rather purely mechanical process, which may be accompanied by suitable "tools".

The following fact should also be noted:

▶   The concept of universal critical sections is independent of the programming language used.

It can also be implemented in other languages (e.g., in C, Modula-2, or Java), which justifies calling it a *universal* construction. We will introduce two further universal synchronization classes in Chap. 10 on *universal monitors* and in Chap. 14 on *universal far monitors*, which also drastically simplify the treatment of various classical synchronization problems.

6.6   Universal Critical Resources

A further application of the universal critical sections will be presented here. Objects that synchronize access to critical sections (such as operating system resources or shared data) for

- p process classes $P_0, P_1, ..., P_{p-1}$ $(p > 1)$,
- r resources $R_0, R_1, ..., R_{r-1}$ $(r > 0)$, and
- $p \cdot r$ numbers $m(k, n)$ $(k < p, n < r)$,

so that each resource of processes of *different* classes can only be used under mutual exclusion and the resource R_n $(n < r)$ concurrently only from at most $m(k, n)$ processes of the class P_k $(k < p)$.

Examples are:

- the *readers–writers* problem:

  $p = 2$, P_0 = readers and P_1 = writers; $r = 1$ (R_0 = shared data), $m(0, 0) = \infty$ and $m(1, 0) = 1$;

- the *left–right* problem:

  $p = 2$, P_0 = drivers to the left and P_1 = drivers to the right; $r = 1$ (R_0 = common lane) and $m(0, 0) = m(1, 0) = \infty$;

- the *bounded left–right* problem:

  the same as in the previous example with barriers with bounds $m(0, 0)$, $m(1, 0) < \infty$;

- the *bowling* problem:

  p = number of the participating clubs (v = players of the club $v < p$); r = number of the available bowling lanes R_b = bowling lane No. $b < r$), $m(v, b)$ = maximal number of players of club v on the lane b.

By abuse of mathematical language we denote by "∞" a very large natural number (e.g., $2^{64} - 1$), which is practically referred to as "infinite" (in the package `math` of the Go library there is `const MaxUint64`).

The specification of the problem is

```
package cr

type CriticalResource interface {

// Pre: m[i][r] is defined for all i < number of classes
//      and for all r < number of resources.
// The resource r of x can be accessed
// by at most m[i][r] processes of class i.
  Limit (m [][]uint)

// Pre: i < number of classes of x. The calling process
//      has no access to a resource of x.
// Returns the number of the resources that
// can now be accessed by the calling process.
// It was blocked, until that was possible.
  Enter (i uint) uint

// Pre: i < number of classes of x. The calling process
//      has access on a resource of x.
// It now has not any longer the access.
  Leave (i uint)
}

// Returns a new critical resource with k classes and r resources.
func New (k, r uint) CriticalResource { return new_(k, r) }
```

The implementation is quite simple by means of universal critical sections:

```
package cr
import ("unsafe"; "math"; "nU/cs")

type status struct {
  max []uint // indexed by the process classes
  number, class uint
}

func max() uint {
  if unsafe.Sizeof(int(0)) == 32 { return math.MaxUint32 }
  return math.MaxUint64
}

func new_(nc, nr uint) CriticalResource {
  x := new (criticalResource)
  x.nC, x.nR = nc, nr
  x.stat = make ([]status, x.nC)
  for r := uint(0); r < x.nR; r++ {
    x.stat[r].max = make ([]uint, x.nC)
    for c := uint(0); c < x.nC; c++ {
      x.stat[r].max[c] = max()
    }
  }
  c := func (i uint) bool {
        var b bool
        for r := uint(0); r < x.nR; r++ {
          b = b ||
              x.stat[r].number == 0 ||
              x.stat[r].class == i &&
              x.stat[r].number < x.stat[r].max[i]
        }
        return b
      }
  e := func (i uint) uint {
        for r := uint(0); r < x.nR; r++ {
          if x.stat[r].number == 0 || x.stat[r].class == i {
            x.stat[r].class = i
            x.stat[r].number++
            return r
          }
        }
        panic("")
      }
  l := func (i uint) {
        for r := uint(0); r < x.nR; r++ {
          if x.stat[r].class == i && x.stat[r].number > 0 {
            x.stat[r].number--
          }
        }
      }
  x.CriticalSection = cs.New (x.nC, c, e, l)
  return x
}

func (x *criticalResource) Limit (m [][]uint) {
  for c := uint(0); c < x.nC; c++ {
```

```
   for  r  :=  uint (0);  r  <  x.nR;  r++  {
     x.stat [r].max[c]  =  m[c][r]
   }
 }
}

func  (x  *criticalResource)  Enter  (i  uint)  uint  {
  return  x.CriticalSection.Enter  (i)
}

func  (x  *criticalResource)  Leave  (i  uint)  {
  x.CriticalSection.Leave  (i)
}
```

Again, I wish you a lot of fun with the attempt to implement this specification *without* recourse to universal critical sections!

It is clear that an implementation of the bounded left–right problem, for example, is also quite simple with recourse to the universal critical resources:

```
package  lr
import  "nU/cr"

type  criticalResource  struct  {
  cr.CriticalResource
}

func  newCR  (mL,  mR  uint)  LeftRight  {
  const  nc  =  2
  x  :=  &criticalResource  {  cr.New  (nc,  1)  }
  m  :=  make ([][]uint,  nc)
  for  i  :=  uint (0);  i  <  nc;  i++  {  m[i]  =  make ([]uint,  1)  }
  m[0][0],  m[1][0]  =  mL,  mR
  x.Limit  (m)
  return  x
}

func  (x  *criticalResource)  LeftIn ()  {  x.Enter  (left)  }
func  (x  *criticalResource)  LeftOut ()  {  x.Leave  (left)  }
func  (x  *criticalResource)  RightIn ()  {  x.Enter  (right)  }
func  (x  *criticalResource)  RightOut ()  {  x.Leave  (right)  }
```

6.7   The Dining Philosophers

Their problem can also be solved very easily with universal critical sections. Therefore, we extend the specification from Sect. 4.14 by the constructor

```
func  NewCriticalSection()  Philos  {  return  newCS()  }
```

The core of the synchronization is shown, e.g., in Table 6.4.

An alternative is given with var nForks [5]uint for the number of forks (initially all $==$ 2) in Table 6.5

Table 6.4 Synchronization of the philosophers with states

Process class	Entry conditions	Entry statements	Exit statements
p	`stat[left(p)] != dining`	`stat[p] =`	`stat[p] =`
	`&& stat[right(p)] != dining`	`dining`	`satisfied`

Table 6.5 Synchronization of the philosophers with forks

Process class	Entry conditions	Entry statements	Exit statements
p	`nForks[p] == 2`	`nForks[left(p)]--`	`nForks[left(p)]++`
		`nForks[right(p)]--`	`nForks[right(p)]++`

Thus, the three associated function spectra, whose names are passed as parameters to the constructor of a universal critical section, can be constructed immediately, making the implementation of the entry and exit protocols and the constructor trivial:

```go
package phil
import . "nU/cs"

type criticalSection struct {
  CriticalSection
}

func newCS() LockerN {
  nForks := make([]uint, NPhilos)
  for i := uint(0); i < NPhilos; i++ {
    nForks[i] = 2
  }
  c := func (i uint) bool {
        return nForks[i] == 2
      }
  f := func (i uint) uint {
        nForks[left(i)]--
        nForks[right(i)]--
        return uint(0)
      }
  l := func (i uint) {
        nForks[left(i)]++
        nForks[right(i)]++
      }
  return &criticalSection { New (5, c, f, l) }
}

func (x *criticalSection) Lock (i uint) { x.Enter (i) }
func (x *criticalSection) Unlock (i uint) { x.Leave (i) }
```

However, in principle, with these solutions there is again the risk of starvation. To refine the tables in a way such that a fair synchronization results, is left as a less trivial exercise. (Hint: Study DIJKSTRA's solution!)

6.8   The Problem of the Cigarette Smokers

Even their problem "screams" for an elegant solution with universal critical sections. Here it is:

```
package smok
import "nU/cs"

type criticalSection struct {
  cs.CriticalSection
}

func newCS() Smokers {
  var avail [3]bool
  var smoking bool
  x := new(criticalSection)
  c := func (i uint) bool {
        if i < 3 { // Agent
          return ! smoking
        } else if i < 6 { // SmokerIn
          u1, u2 := others (i)
          return avail[u1] && avail[u2]
        }
        return true // SmokerOut
      }
  f := func (i uint) uint {
        u1, u2 := others (i)
        if i < 3 { // Agent
          avail[u1], avail[u2] = true, true
        } else if i < 6 { // SmokerIn
          smoking = true
          avail[u1], avail[u2] = false, false
        }
        return uint(0)
      }
  l := func (i uint) {
        smoking = false
      }
  x.CriticalSection = cs.New (6, c, f, l)
  return x
}

func (x *criticalSection) Agent (u uint) { x.Enter (u) }
func (x *criticalSection) SmokerIn (u uint) { x.Enter (3 + u) }
func (x *criticalSection) SmokerOut () { x.Leave (0) }
```

Reference

1. Tanenbaum, A. S.: Moderne Betriebssysteme. Pearson Studium, München (2003)

Fairness

7

Abstract

Fairness means, in principle, the guarantee that each of *finitely* many concurrent processes in an *infinite* execution sequence is *infinitely often* active, where there are no restrictions for the respective duration of the activity of the processes. So this is a *liveliness criterion*.

7.1   Weak Versus Strong Fairness

A typical image is the representation of an irrational number. In its infinite sequence of digits 0 and 1 after the point, both these digits are always found *again and again* (for if this were not the case, the number would at some point have the period 0 or 1, hence would be periodic, i.e., rational), without the lengths of the sequences of identical digits necessarily being bounded.

With "φ is again and again true" we mean that for any point in time, there exists a later point in time in which φ is true (even if that is again and again *not* the case), particularly that φ is *infinitely often* fulfilled.

A self-evident demand on every process management is the following property:

A process management is called

- *elementarily fair*,
  if it activates any *ready* process *eventually*.

But this notion is not sufficient if processes are *blocked* because they cannot become ready, if the condition to unblock them is not fulfilled.

For that reason we distinguish:

A process management is called

- *weakly fair,*
  if it is elementarily fair and eventually activates any blocked process provided that the condition causing it to be unblocked is not subsequentially falsified until it is unblocked, once it has become true;
- *strongly fair,*
  if it is elementarily fair and eventually activates any blocked process provided that the condition causing it to be unblocked is fulfilled, is *again and again* true.

It is immediately clear that strong fairness implies weak fairness. However, the converse is *not* true, because the truth value of a condition might change in the time in which a process waits for it to be unblocked.

The following example illustrates the differences:

```go
package main
import ("time"; "math/rand")

const pause = 1e9
var (
  ahead = true
  halt = false
  done = make (chan bool)
)

func verify() {
  for ahead {
    time.Sleep (time.Duration(rand.Int63n (pause)))
    halt = true
  }
}

func falsify() {
  for ahead {
    halt = false
  }
  done <- true
}

func stop() {
  for ! halt {
    time.Sleep (pause)
  }
  ahead = false
}

func main() {
  go verify()
  go falsify()
```

```
go stop ()
<-done
}
```

A weakly fair process management cannot guarantee that the loop exit condition `halt` in process `stop` eventually immediately after *that* point in time is checked when the statement `halt = true` has been executed and before `halt` was already again set to `false` by process `falsify`.

Consequently, it is impossible to give a definite assurance of whether—let alone when—the program terminates; this is only possible with *strong* fairness.

Program runs show that it can, indeed, take quite a while for the program to terminate; this can be easily tracked by including statements to the processes to increase counters and write them to the screen, and with variations in the length of pauses.

As a rule, process managements are weakly fair.

It may sound reasonable to demand that a process management be *strongly fair*, but to implement this *efficiently* in a *general form* is practically impossible. It is more practicable when concretely implementing a class of `await` statements, to construct the algorithms in such a way that they guarantee strong fairness. This is the case with semaphores, for example, if their waiting queues are implemented as FIFO-queues, as we have described.

On the question of the fairness of the Go scheduler, we would like to refer to IAN LANCE TAYLOR's contribution in the worldwide web

https://groups.google.com/forum/#!topic/golang-nuts/KDqeQp2jOgA

from which we quote an excerpt:

The current scheduler does not optimize for fairness. Of course, the scheduler has changed in the past and it will change in the future.

The current scheduler (approximately) associates goroutines with threads. When a thread has to choose a new goroutine to run, it will preferentially choose one of its associated goroutines. If it doesn't have any ready to run, it will steal one from another thread.

For details, see the file `runtime/proc.go` in the Go library (with more than five thousand lines of code).

Deadlocks

8

Abstract

Processes that definitely got stuck in the operational sequence without regular measures for the synchronization with other processes being the cause are called jammed. "Definitely" means that any continuation of their execution is impossible, particularly, they cannot be unblocked. A state in which processes are jammed in this way is called a *deadlock*. In this chapter, such states are characterized and illustrated by simple examples. Measures for their prevention and for their detection and recovery are discussed; and to avoid them, the banker's algorithm of DIJKSTRA is presented. Finally, the blocking probabilities are calculated, and all countermeasures are evaluated.

8.1 Characterization

By "operating resources" we mean all resources needed by any processes such as shared variables, conditions, memory, files, and input and output devices. A deadlock can roughly be defined as a situation, in which processes require such resources that are held by other processes and are, therefore, blocked, whereby these blockings occur alternately.

We will not consider "determined deadlocks", i.e., those that—as simple programming errors—*also* occur at any *other* execution sequence with the same input values.

An exact characterization of deadlocks in the form of the following necessary and sufficient conditions was given by COFFMAN, ELPHICK, and SHOSHAN in [1]:

© Springer Fachmedien Wiesbaden GmbH, part of Springer Nature 2021

C. Maurer, *Nonsequential and Distributed Programming with Go*,

https://doi.org/10.1007/978-3-658-29782-4_8

1. *"mutual exclusion condition"*:
   At least two processes are involved, which principally use the requested resources only under mutual exclusion.
2. *"hold and wait condition"*:
   Requested operating resources are also allocated in parts, and processes hold resources or parts of them already allocated while requesting additional resources.
3. *"no preemption condition"*:
   Resources are only released by the processes themselves after having used them, but they cannot be withdrawn.
4. *"circular wait condition"*:
   The resource requests and allocations between the processes involved form a *cycle*, i.e., each process holds a resource that is requested by the next process in that cycle.

The details of these conditions are explained in Sects. (8.2.1), (8.2.2), and (8.2.3).

It does not matter whether there are only one or more types of operating resources and whether only one or more copies of this type are available. It is clear that deadlocks represent an error situation that can seriously affect the functionality of a system. Therefore, it is necessary to examine appropriate measures to prevent them.

8.1.1 A Simple Examples

The first example is a cross road with the right of way rule due to the "right before left" principle, where at each junction a car that wants to go straight ahead is waiting (see Fig. 8.1).

Each driver waits for the car to his right to go ahead, thereby releasing the "resource" it is holding—the quadrant of the intersection immediately in front of him.

Fig. 8.1 Cross road with four quadrants

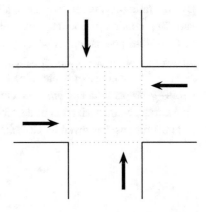

Under the rigid conditions that

- worried about a collision, nobody just drives into the intersection,
- each driver insists on his right of way while respecting that of the car to his right,
- the right of way is not regulated in another way, e.g., by the traffic police or by an agreement between the drivers, and
- nobody abandons his intention to cross the intersection,

definitely *none* of the drivers can go ahead, i.e., the cars are jammed.

The simplest example of a deadlock is that of two processes, each of which is allocated an exclusively usable resource and which also request a resource held by the other process.

If the use of resources is secured by binary semaphores A and B, it can be described paradigmatically by the sequence shown in Table 8.1, in which they are requested by two processes in reverse order.

A standard example of this situation is the following:

Student 1 borrowed the second volume B of a textbook, and student 2 the first volume A, of which the university library has only one copy each. Both students also need the other volume and order it in advance. The result is that both are waiting for GODOT (who never came, as we know from BECKETT) unless

- the library buys at least another copy,
- one of the two students returns the borrowed book, or
- the library reclaims a volume due to advance order and exceeded loan period.

This example is prototypical in the sense that it can be easily transferred to several processes and other resources.

Table 8.1 Deadlock between two processes

Process	Statement	A	B	Comment
		true	true	
1	A.P()	false		
2	B.P()		false	
1	B.P()			1 is blocied
2	A.P()			2 is also blocked

8.2   Countermeasures

In order to counteract the occurrence of deadlocks, there are basically the following possibilities:

- to *prevent* them right from the beginning,
- to *detect* them when they have occurred and then to *resolve* them (in data bank systems this is called *recovery*), or
- to *avoid* them by means of an anticipatory analysis of the resource requests and not to admit states that could lead to deadlocks.

8.2.1   Prevention

According to the characterization of deadlocks, their occurrence is prevented, if with each operating resource request by several processes, at least *one* of the following conditions is fulfilled:

(a) It is *not* insisted on the principle that the requested operating resources are used only under mutual exclusion.

(b) Processes preclaim their complete requests of operating resources at the beginning, before they start working, and are blocked, if necessary, until it is ensured that their requests can be *entirely* fulfilled, *or* processes to which certain resources are allocated, but to which further requests cannot be fulfilled are, in principle, willing to return already acquired resources and to request them later on anew—together with the additional requirements.

(c) Resources can be withdrawn from processes.

(d) The resource requests and allocations between the processes are at any time *linearly ordered* (cycles are, therefore, impossible, because $x_1 \leq x_2 \leq \cdots \leq x_n \leq x_1$ in an ordered set implies $x_1 = x_2 = \cdots = x_n$).

Using the example of the four cars with equal rights at the intersection, this means that a deadlock can be ruled out by one of the following events:

1. the crossing area is large enough to allow all vehicles to pass each other without collision,
2. a traffic policeman waves the cars individually through or one of the drivers relinquishes his right of way and lets the neighbour to his left pass,
3. a traffic policeman detains individual cars, or
4. one of the drivers despairs of the stubbornness of the others and drives back, so that the other drivers have clear right of way rules.

Condition 1. is out of the question for obvious reasons, and, therefore, strategies to rule out any deadlock must be based on the fulfilment of one of the other conditions in each case. If each of these points can be only partially fulfilled, suitable hybrid forms may, of course, also be considered.

8.2.2 Detection and Recovery

In order to resolve existing deadlocks, the cyclic resource requests and allocations mentioned in point 4. of their characterization in Sect. 8.1 must first be recognized as such.

To clarify this concept, we consider the *resource graph*—a directed graph defined as follows. Its nodes are resources and processes—edges are there only between resources and processes. If an edge points from a resource to a process, this means that the resource is allocated to the process, and vice versa that the process requests a resource (but does not yet hold it). One can also consider the subgraph consisting only of resources as nodes; an edge from node A to node B is represented by a process that requests B, while A is allocated to it.

An alternative is the *waiting graph*. Its nodes are processes, its directed edges are the waiting relations between them, and an edge pointing from P to Q means that P is waiting for Q.

The simplest deadlock example for two processes P and Q and resources A allocated to P and B to Q has the graph shown in Fig. 8.2 as a resource graph and the graph shown in Fig. 8.3 as a waiting graph.

Common to all models is the fact that the condition 4. is fulfilled, iff one of the graphs contains *cycles*, which can be decided by *depth first search* in linear time with the number of nodes.

As a representation of resource graphs, it is possible to keep for each resource allocated to a process a list of processes with this process as head and the processes requesting it as tail, and, additionally, the list of all processes with references to the resources requested by them. From this, the waiting graph can easily be determined.

If an examination of the graphs has found a cycle, it is possible to

Fig. 8.2 Resource graph

Fig. 8.3 Waiting graph

- terminate the processes involved in the deadlock, so that their resources are available again, or
- to withdraw the resources allocated to them until the deadlock is resolved.

An important question is the frequency with which these analyses are carried out. In addition to estimates of the probability of the occurrence of deadlocks, also heuristics in the concrete operation scheduling are necessary in order to weigh up whether the acceptance of occasional deadlocks may result in a lower load of the operation scheduling than its creeping delay due to continuous monitoring. The first case does not principally rule out the risk of further deadlocks after restarting the processes.

There are no general rules for the selection of processes that have to be terminated or from which resources are withdrawn, because only the context of the application can play a role in that, for example,

- the priorities of the processes involved, taking into account any time requirements placed on them,
- their execution duration prior to the deadlock or the expected execution duration until their termination, and
- the quantity and type of resources requested.

8.2.3   Avoidance

Just like the exclusion of deadlocks, also their *avoidance* (under the obvious assumption that not only *one* process is involved) is based on the fulfillment of at least *one* of the conditions mentioned above.

Since mutual exclusion is at the fore of our considerations with regard to the use of resources, it is out of the question to avoid deadlocks by (a). To avoid deadlocks by (c) is absurd in so far as that basically amounts to withdrawing already allocated resources from processes or enforcing their release *after* the occurrence of deadlocks.

Consequently, deadlocks can only be avoided if conditions (b) or (d) are fulfilled. An approach to the solution is the idea of anticipating whether the requesting process can become jammed with other processes when allocating resources, in order not to allocate resources to it in this case but to block it.

However, it is not enough to simply refuse the allocation only in *those* cases that would *immediately* lead to a deadlock, but it must also be ruled out that the allocation of operating resources does not lead *later* to a situation in which a deadlock cannot be avoided.

Such a procedure was presented by DIJKSTRA in his paper [2] cited in the previous chapter as a solution to the problem of the "*deadly embrace*". We will stick to his example in the following.

8.2.4 The Bankers' Algorithm

A bank grants loans to customers. Loan contracts with new customers are only concluded if they announce their maximum credit request, which, of course, must not exceed the bank's capital. They can then at any time request partial loans up to the agreed upon amount, which they will eventually be granted. They repay all their loans after a finite time, at the latest after the granting of their maximum credit request.

Before any partial loan is granted, the bank must ensure that *at any time thereafter* its cash balance, i.e., its capital less the total of all partial loans granted, will be sufficient to grant at least *one* customer a loan up to his maximum credit request; because only in this way is it always in the position to satisfy other customers.

A situation in which this is no longer possible can lead to a deadlock: If no customer repays his partial loan, but all insist on the allocation of their maximum credit request, all wait in vain, because the bank is then no longer able to grant any loan.

States that cannot lead to such deadlocks are denoted *safe*. In other words, a state is safe if no customer has any more requests or if a customer's request can be satisfied, and the subsequent state after repayment of his credit and termination of his contract is also safe.

Let us consider the following example: The bank has a capital of 10 units; it has three customers with maximum credit requests of 8, 3, and 9 units, who want partial credits of 4, 2, and 2 units.

The corresponding state, shown in Table 8.2, is *safe:*

Customer 1 can be granted his highest possible credit, and if he repays it afterwards, the state shown in Table 8.3 results, in which the remaining credit request of customer 0 can be fulfilled.

If customer 0 also repays his credit, we have the situation shown in Table 8.4, which is immediately recognizable as safe, because now customer 2 can finally be satisfied.

With an increase of the loan of customer 2 to 3 units, on the other hand, the first situation would lead to the state shown in Table 8.5.

Table 8.2 Safe state

	Customer 0	Customer 1	Customer 2	Bank
Maximal credit requests	8	3	9	
Partial credits/cash balance	4	2	2	2
Remaining credit requests	4	1	7	

Table 8.3 Remaining credit request of 0 can be granted

	Customer 0	Customer 1	Customer 2	Bank
Maximal credit requests	8	0	9	
Partial credits/cash balance	4	0	2	4
Remaining credit requests	4	0	7	

Table 8.4 Customer 2 can be satisfied

	Customer 0	Customer 1	Customer 2	Bank
Maximal credit requests	0	0	9	
Partial credits/cash balance	0	0	2	8
Remaining credit requests	0	0	7	

Table 8.5 Unsafe state

	Customer 0	Customer 1	Customer 2	Bank
Maximal credit requests	8	3	9	
Partial credits/cash balance	4	2	3	1
Remaining credit requests	4	1	6	

This situation is no longer safe: Customer 1 can still be granted his maximum credit, but after its repayment a situation arises as shown in Table 8.6, in which the cash balance is too small for all maximum credits.

The definition of the problem directly provides the appropriate algorithm. As global data we hold for each customer his maximum credit request need and his partial credit loan, as well as the cash balance cash of the bank as the difference between its capital and the sum of all partial loans granted, furthermore a copy n of need for a purpose to be explained below:

Table 8.6 Cash balance too small

	Customer 0	Customer 1	Customer 2	Bank
Maximal credit requests	8	0	9	
Partial credits/cash balance	4	0	3	3
Remaining credit requests	4	0	6	

```
const (
  capital = ...
  C = ... // number of customers
)
var (
  need, loan, n [C]uint
  cash uint
)
```

The invariants are

$$0 <= loan[i] <= need[i] <= capital$$

and

$$loan[0] + ... + loan[C-1] + cash = capital$$

In order to avoid any deadlocks, before granting or increasing a partial loan the bank examines whether the resultant subsequent condition is *safe*. The following recursive function serves this purpose, although it does not operate on the array need because it resets its values, but rather on a copy n of this (as an efficient alternative to passing need to each recursive call):

```
func safe (amount uint) bool {
  var s uint
  for i := 0; i < K; i++ {
    s += n[i]
  }
  if s == 0 {
    return true // all customers satisfied
  }
  for i := 0; i < K; i++ {
    if n[i] > 0 && n[i] - loan[i] <= amount {
```

```
      n[i] = 0
      return safe (amount + loan[i])
    }
  }
  return false
}
```

From the conceptual end recursivity of `safe`, we easily get the iterative original version of this function of DIJKSTRA (for readers of this paper: with `doubtful[i] = M[i] > 0`).

The complexity of `safe` is obviously at best linear, at worst quadratic in the number of customers.

Each time a (partial) loan is requested, the banker decides whether to grant it according to the value of the function

```
func possible (k /* number of client */, claim uint) bool {
  for i := 0; i < K; i++ { // copy for "safe"
    n[i] = need[i]
  }
  loan[k] += claim // simulation ...
  e := false
  if loan[k] <= need[k] {
    e = safe (cash - claim)
  }
  loan[k] -= claim // ... back to the old value
  return e
}
```

which determines by simulating the allocation, whether a safe situation will result again afterwards.

As an exercise it is suggested to generalize the algorithm to units of different kind.

8.3   Probability of Deadlocks

The assumption that deadlocks occur quite rarely is supported by practical experience but can only be confirmed by quantitative statements. For a rough estimation of the risk of deadlocks, we present the mathematical model in [3]:

A system with $n + 1$ processes and b only exclusively usable resources, whereby each process again and again in single steps requests k operating resources and then returns them, i.e., on average has approximately $\frac{k}{2}$ operating resources.

The probability that a process has a certain resource is, therefore, $\frac{k}{2b}$; the probability that a process will be blocked because it requests a *particular* resource owned by one of the others n processes, is, therefore,

$$p_1 = \frac{nk}{2b} \qquad\qquad (8.1)$$

and the probability that all of his k requests are fulfilled, is

$$(1 - p_1)^k = \sum_{i=0}^{k} \binom{k}{i}(-1)^i {p_1}^i$$

$$= 1 - kp_1 + \binom{k}{2}p_1^2 - \binom{k}{3}p_1^3 + - \dots. \tag{8.2}$$

We assume that the number of available resources is very large in comparison to the total number of their requests, which implies $b \gg nk$ and—in conjunction with (8.1)

$$p_1 = \frac{nk}{2b} \ll 1 \tag{8.3}$$

Here the terms of higher order in (8.2) can be neglected, and we get

$$(1 - p_1)^k \approx 1 - kp_1.$$

Therefore, when a process requests a resource allocated to another process, it is blocked with the *waiting probability*

$$p_W = 1 - (1 - p_1)^k \approx kp_1 = \frac{nk^2}{2b}. \tag{8.4}$$

Because the probability that the other process requests a resource that is allocated to the first one, is $\frac{1}{n}$ of that, we get

$$p_W \cdot \frac{p_W}{n} = \frac{1}{n}\left(\frac{nk^2}{2b}\right)^2 = \frac{nk^4}{4b^2}$$

as an approximation of the probability of a deadlock between a certain process and another one, and

$$p_V = (n+1)p_W\frac{p_W}{n} = \frac{(n+1)nk^4}{4b^2} \approx p_W^2 = \frac{n^2k^4}{4b^2}, \tag{8.5}$$

as probability for a *deadlock between two processes* that alternately wait for a resource occupied by the other, because there is a total of $n + 1$ processes.

The probability of deadlock cycles of length l is proportional to the l-th power of p_V; if the probability p_W for blocking of processes is $\ll 1$, the probability of deadlocks with longer cycles is significantly lower than with two cycles.

Although this model, due to its simplicity, does not sufficiently capture real processes quantitatively, it allows two conclusions to be drawn under condition (8.3). Due to (8.5), the deadlock probability increases proportionally to the fourth power of the number k of the requested operating resources; and in the case of a reduction of k, it decreases accordingly. The deadlock probability p_V is approximately the square of the waiting probability p_W.

So we can state the assumption made at the beginning more precisely:

▶   If *waiting* occurs *rarely* (which is an important requirement for a usable system), *deadlocks* occur *very rarely*.

8.4   Evaluation of the Countermeasures

It is not generally possible to decide which of the measures presented is to be preferred. All procedures have advantages and disadvantages, which have to be carefully balanced in each individual case with regard to the respective application.

The different variants of the *prevention* of deadlocks subject to one of the points (b) or (d) mentioned above have a number of disadvantages. Announcing overall requirements is generally difficult; it may even be impossible, if the requests are not predictable because they only emerge in the course of interaction with users.

A process must inevitably make unfavourable assumptions when estimating its scope of requests, if for each case it wants to be provided with sufficiently many resources. If it turns out in the course of its execution that its actual requests are lower than initially claimed (which should be the rule), existing resources will not be used. But this blatantly contradicts a basic idea of nonsequentiality.

A demand-oriented *dynamic* request of operating resources, however, is not compatible with the principle of preventing deadlocks. This is complicated because it is highly dependent on the specific application, hence by *general* procedures not achievable at all. To cancel processes that have to wait for requests suitable fallback points have to be found at which their state can be archived, so that they can be restarted after their restoration.

In addition, even in a specific case, it would hardly be possible to guarantee the fairness of such a procedure, even to the slightest extent: Processes can be constantly ousted by others when they announce their requests.

Even point (d) is not easily achievable: It is unrealistic to expect that a proper order can always be found on the set of operating resources. Therefore, it can happen that processes deprive other processes of a considerable amount of resources without actually needing them, only because they request them in order to obtain—in the sense of the order—"larger" resources. As with (b), this amounts to an absurd waste of resources.

Also the *detection* of deadlocks is not unproblematic. The adjustment of the resource graph whenever a request is made to determine the associated waiting graph and then to search for cycles in it, can significantly slow down the system throughput despite linear complexity. It is more justifiable to carry out these examinations periodically at certain intervals.

Since in larger systems it is out of the question to refuse all requests while these analyses are performed, they must be executed concurrently. But there is a risk of *phantom deadlocks*: For example, it may have been found that P is waiting for Q, and a moment later, after Q

has returned the requested resources, that Q is waiting directly or indirectly for P, triggering an erroneous deadlock alarm.

In distributed systems, the detection of deadlocks by graph algorithms presumes that the graph representations in the various systems are known to all participants. For these reasons, a different, extremely restrictive measure is often used to detect deadlocks: "*timeout*". This procedure is based on the fact that each process receives a certain amount of time in advance for any request for resources, after which it is terminated by the process management. However, this hard measure is sometimes completely unavoidable, e.g., if an input is expected, and the input device is defective, a line is interrupted, or the user has fallen asleep.

Apparently, it is only conditionally suitable for detecting deadlocks. A reasonable compromise is, therefore, if any waiting time beyond the granted advance is interpreted as deadlock, to wait for the time lapse and then to search for cycles in the waiting graph, if necessary.

When *recovering* deadlocks, principally, the question arises as to *which one* of the processes involved should be terminated in order to disturb the program progress as little as possible. As a rule, this can only be decided in the context of the individual case; a *general* strategy is hardly conceivable.

Also the *avoidance* of deadlocks by using the banker's algorithm reaches its limits very quickly. If the demand for the requested resources cannot be reasonably accurately estimated at the beginning, its application makes little sense, and if for each resource request, all maximum subsequent variants are recalculated, the system performance suffers massively from its (usually) quadratic complexity.

The considerations of the previous section legitimate a widespread practice in large systems. With a low waiting probability, it may be more efficient to accept blockages in order to resolve them if necessary instead of preventing them from the beginning, to recognize them immediately after they occur or anticipatorily avoid them. Another trivial reason is that the disadvantages of all the procedures to prevent, detect, and avoid them are obvious, while their resolution is usually much simpler than programming the complicated algorithms taking into account all these aspects.

References

1. Coffman, E.G., Elphick, M.J., Shoshan, A.: System deadlocks. ACM Comput. Surv. **3**, 67–78 (1971). https://doi.org/10.1145/356586.356588
2. Dijkstra, E.W.: Cooperating sequential processes. Technical Report EWD-123, Technological University, Eindhoven (1965). https://www.cs.utexas.edu/users/EWD/ewd01xx/EWD123.PDF
3. Gray, J., Reuter, A.: Transaction Processing. Concepts and Techniques. Morgan Kaufmann, San Francisco (1992)

Monitors

9

Abstract

All examples shown so far illustrate some disadvantages of the implementation of locks, which cannot be eliminated even with the use of semaphores. We have to thank HOARE for the appropriate answer to this problem. He introduced the package-like concept of *monitors*. In this chapter, HOARE's idea is introduced, the necessary terms are clarified, condition variables are introduced as language tool for synchronization, and it is shown how they are applied to the synchronization of various classical problems such as the bounded buffer and the readers–writers problem. The detailed discussion of signal semantics is dedicated to the competition problems of different approaches to the realization of monitors. This is followed by the broadcast concept and monitor solutions for barrier synchronization, the problem of the sleeping barber, HOARE's alarm clock, and prioritizing the shortest jobs. The final part is a short presentation of the problem of nested monitor calls.

9.1 Characterization of Monitors

The disadvantages 3), 4), and 5) presented in Sect. 4.1 show very clearly that the synchronization of cooperating and competing processes by means of locks or semaphores is not yet the non plus ultra.

It is clear that these constructions are quite error-prone. Forgotten P-operations allow, for example, access to shared data without mutual exclusion, forgotten V-operations result in deadlocks. Both types of errors are completely unacceptable because they can lead to data corruption or destruction or to the crash of the whole system.

However, semaphores provide indeed very efficient synchronization measures by allowing processes to be blocked on them, until certain conditions have occurred, which are the prerequisite for their further execution. Consequently, in the search for a language construct

© Springer Fachmedien Wiesbaden GmbH, part of Springer Nature 2021
C. Maurer, *Nonsequential and Distributed Programming with Go*,
https://doi.org/10.1007/978-3-658-29782-4_9

to eliminate their deficits, it can only be a matter of abstracting from the concrete semaphore operations without abandoning their fundamental mechanisms.

The following demands are by no means intended to introduce a much more efficient procedure but merely to postulate a higher level of language:

- The synchronization aspects of the algorithms are concentrated in a suitable local construction, in which the shared data and the accesses to them are encapsulated.
- Accesses are carried out only by using the functions defined in an interface, but not necessarily with a textual separation between its specification and implementation.
- The protocols for the mutual exclusion of the access operations are provided by the *compiler* and are executed without any action on the part of the client.
- The construction provides a method for condition synchronization that is as general as possible.

9.1.1 Hoare's Approach

Such considerations make HOARE's concept of a *monitor* in [3] seem almost natural. It is characterized by the following features:

- It is a *language* and not an operating system construct.
- A monitor is not a *process* but a passive construct that must not contain any processes; it keeps *own data* that are not visible from the outside, i.e., in particular it does not export variables, but it may export constants if necessary.
- It is not an abstract data type, i.e., it does not export any types and methods, but only an *abstract data object*, which exports the access functions to the data (the *monitor functions*) that can be called concurrently by processes.
- It allows only *one* execution of a monitor function at a time and, thus, ensures the *mutual exclusion* of the processes that use its functions, consequently *blocks* other processes that call a monitor function for the time in which a process executes a monitor function until this function is finished, and unblocks the processes blocked on it, i.e., those waiting for the "*entry*" into it according to the FIFO principle: as next always *that* process can enter that has waited the longest.
- It allows its data to be initialized in a—nonexported—statement sequence before monitor functions are called.
- It provides an efficient mechanism for the implementation of monitor functions to block and unblock processes on conditions that are externally only available implicitly, i.e., by *using* these functions, where it allows *another* process to (further) execute its function, if a process has been blocked on a particular condition while executing a monitor function.

- It has a clearly defined semantics to distinguish the processes that are blocked on it as long as they have to wait for the execution of a monitor function from those that are blocked on a condition during the execution of a monitor function.

The principle of mutual exclusion in a monitor can be realized by checking for each process that calls a monitor function whether the monitor is *free*, i.e., whether another process is not currently executing a monitor function; if this is not the case, the calling process is blocked.

This is why behind the scenes of each monitor there is a waiting queue into which all processes are inserted that have to wait for it, the *monitor entry queue*.

When a process has *left the monitor*, i.e., if it has executed its monitor function to the end, unless this monitor entry queue is empty, the first process in it will be unblocked, so that now *this process*—again in exclusive possession of the monitor—can execute its function. The basic idea of this construction of HOARE is very similar to the implementation of semaphores; in Sect. 9.10 it will be shown that monitor functions can indeed be emulated by semaphores. However, HOARE's monitor concept in its *pure* form is only implemented in a few programming languages, e.g., in Modula-2, Pascal-FC, and SR. In C, Java, and Go its essential basic constructs are provided by libraries; we will go into the details in Sect. 9.3.

9.1.2 Virtual Monitors in Go

For the simple presentation of the concept and some applications to classical synchronization problems, for the time being we adhere—closely following the language conventions of Go—to the HOARE construct.

For this, the following agreement is obvious:

By *monitors* we understand a special form of *packages*, i.e., on the one hand we use the keyword `monitor` syntactically as well as semantically similar to `package`:

- The keyword must be followed by an identifier.
- A monitor exports exactly those constants and functions which names begin with an uppercase letter.
- Within a monitor internal data can be initialized in the implementation of the `init()` function.

On the other hand, there are some serious differences to packages that have to be realized by the compiler and the runtime system.

- The compiler generates code that ensures that all functions exported by a monitor are always executed under *mutual* exclusion.
- The following attempts lead to syntax errors at compile time:
  - the export of *variables* or *types* by a monitor and

- the *creation of processes* or the *start of a program* within a monitor by calling `go` or `main`. (An indirect call to `go` in an imported function must, of course, lead to a runtime error.)

With this "virtual" construction (the Go developers should add this concept to their language), the first three postulates of the characterization of monitors are fulfilled.

As a first example we take up our introductory problem and show how easy its solution is with the help of a monitor:

```
monitor counter

var c uint

func Inc (n uint) { c += n }

func Value() uint { return c }
```

In this example, it is not necessary to block processes because incrementing of the counter is not dependent on conditions.

9.2   Condition Variables

A simple generalization of this problem is an account that several processes can concurrently dispose of as long as it can have any debit. On the other hand, without it a loan a condition is needed; only as much may be withdrawn as is available as credit. Otherwise the withdrawing process has to be blocked until a deposit has been made—if necessary, repeatedly—to allow it to withdraw if the balance is sufficient thereafter.

This brings us to the realization of the last postulates of the characterization of monitors. Semaphores offer a limited condition synchronization, where the conditions *implicitly* are given by Boolean expressions of type $n \geq k$ for natural numbers n and k. In monitors, the value of Boolean expressions is *explicitly* used to decide whether processes may keep working or must be blocked.

In order to be able to capture several conditions, for the implementation of the functions *inside the monitor*, we postulate an abstract data type `Condition` which—according to the following specification—allows processes to be blocked or deblocked, depending on the value of the Boolean expressions associated with them:

```
package cond

type Condition interface {

// The calling process is (unconditionally) blocked on x,
// the monitor is free.
  Wait()

// The first process blocked on x is unblocked, if such exists
```

```
// (when it in competition to other processes can   continue its work
// in the monitor depends on the implemented signal semantics);
// otherwise nothing has happened.
  Signal()

// Pre: The function was called within the implementation
//      of a monitor function of x (see remark).
// Returns true, iff (at least) one process is blocked on x.
  Awaited() bool
// Remark: The value can have changed immediately after the call;
//         consequently it can only be used, if the indivisibility
//         between the call and later operations is secured.
//         This is the case if the precondition is fulfilled.
}

// Returns a new condition.
func New() Condition { return new_() }
```

Condition variables (i.e., variables of type `Condition`) can only be declared *within* monitors, they are only usable as objects that provide these methods and have *no state* that can be altered in any other way. The conditions that allow a process to continue its work are formulated as Boolean expressions using only variables that are declared globally in the monitor. These variables must not be visible from the outside, because otherwise the conditions could be changed by bypassing the monitor functions, which would violate the monitor invariants and would not even guarantee the mutual exclusion of the changes.

Each condition has its own condition variable with the typical code fragments

```
if ! ... /* condition */ {
  c.Wait()
}
```

or

```
... // fulfill the condition
c.Signal()
```

Behind the scenes of a condition variable, one has to imagine an (initially empty) waiting queue of those processes that must be blocked as long as the corresponding condition is not fulfilled, the *condition waiting queue*.

It is clear that a process that is blocked on a condition variable must release the exclusive ownership of the monitor to avoid deadlocks. On the other hand, the answer to the question of *when* it can continue its interrupted work in the monitor is not uniquely clear.

HOARE demanded that it reenter the monitor immediately after a `Signal` operation of another process without being interrupted by a third process. But there are also other possibilities. For example, in [1], ANDREWS favours that the process that has executed the `Signal` operation can finish its work in the monitor first, and that the unblocked process is inserted again into the monitor entry queue.

The diversity of these approaches, which can, of course, also be evaluated differently from the point of view of fairness, is a consequence of the guarantee of the mutual exclusion of all monitor functions from each other.

An unblocked process competes for the monitor with *those* processes that are waiting to enter the monitor and also with the deblocking process, if deblocking by Signal was not the *last statement* in its monitor function. For this reason, there is the risk that other processes may change the condition again, *after* it has led to unblocking of a process, *before* the unblocked process can continue its interrupted monitor function. Therefore, either the deblocking process has to transfer the control of the monitor *directly* to the deblocked process and must *itself* be blocked immediately afterwards, or the deblocked process must check the corresponding condition each time it reenters the monitor to ensure the monitor invariant, which is achieved by replacing the case distinction

```
if ! ... {
   B.Wait ()
}
```

by a loop

```
for ! ... {
   B.Wait ()
}
```

Before we define the different *signal semantics* and examine their consequences more closely in Sect. 9.6, we will present applications in which the deblocking Signal operations only occur as the last statements in monitor functions, thus avoiding the dilemma because the problem described above does not arise due to the lack of competition. Otherwise, we consider HOARE's approach as to be agreed , which was also implemented by BURNS/DAVIES in Pascal-FC:

▶   All processes unblocked in a monitor by Signal have priority over all others who want to enter the monitor.

Using a condition variable, a monitor for the above account example is rudimentarily easy to implement:

```
monitor account
import . "condition"

var (
   balance uint
   cond Condition
)

func Deposit (a uint) uint {
   balance += a
   cond.Signal ()
   return a
}

func Draw (a uint) uint {
```

```
  for balance < a {
    cond.Wait()
  }
  balance -= a
  cond.Signal()
  return a
}

func init() { cond = New() }
```

Since a depositing process does not know whether its amount is sufficient to permit the withdrawal of a process blocked on `cond`, such a process must recheck its condition each time it is resumed, even if the underlying signal semantics does not necessarily require that.

In addition, if several processes were blocked during withdrawal, when some process deposits, not only *one* of them must be given the opportunity to check whether it can now make its withdrawal, but *all* blocked processes. This can be achieved by calling `Signal` also after the withdrawal; an alternative to this is the *broadcast* that we will introduce in Sect. 9.7

A modification of the identifiers of this example

$$\text{Deposit} \rightsquigarrow \text{V}$$

$$\text{Draw} \rightsquigarrow \text{P}$$

shows that this is an (albeit inefficient) implementation of an *additive semaphore* and without the parameters at `Deposit` and `Draw` (with `b == 1` in the function bodies) of a *general* semaphore!

This makes it clear to some extent that the linguistic expressiveness of the monitor concept is at least equal to that of semaphores. We will state that more precisely in Sect. 9.10 and show that both synchronization methods are equivalent.

Despite this *fundamental* equivalence of both concepts there are *clear differences* in details when using their functions for synchronization, which will be summarized here once again:

- A variable of type `Semaphore` can be declared at *any* places in a nonsequential program; the functions `P` and `V` as methods of such a variable can be called *anywhere* in their validity area.
- Whether or not a call of `s.P()` blocks the calling process on the semaphore `s`, depends on the value of the semaphore `s`, and
- a call to `s.V()` in *any* case has an effect—also depending on the value of `s`.

With *conditions* the situation is quite different:

- A variable of type `Condition` can only be declared *within a monitor*; the functions `Wait`, `Signal`, and `Awaited` as methods of such a variable can only be called in *this monitor*.
- A call to `c.Wait()` blocks the calling process *categorically*—i.e., without any further check of any prerequisite—on the condition variable `c`.
- A call to `c.Signal()` is *effect free* if no process is blocked on `c`.

9.3   Monitors in C, Java, and Go

In the following, we will briefly explain to what extent and in what form the monitor concept is supported in these three languages. It turns out that *none* of these three languages fully implements HOARE's ideas. This observation gives rise to the development of another universal synchronization class in the next chapter.

9.3.1   Monitors in C

Since the monitor construct in the narrow sense does not exist in C, the mutual exclusion of the monitor functions must be ensured with a variable `mutex` of type `pthread_mutex_t`.
The `pthread` library supplies for condition synchronization the type

$$pthread\_cond\_t$$

for condition variables, including the routine `pthread_cond_init` to initialize these variables. Here is the specification from the *manpage*:

NAME
    pthread_cond_init – initialize condition variables
SYNOPSIS
    #include <pthread.h>
    int pthread_cond_init(pthread_cond_t *restrict cond,
        const pthread_condattr_t *restrict attr);
DESCRIPTION
    The pthread_cond_init() function shall initialize the condition variable referenced
    by cond with attributes referenced by attr. If attr is NULL, the default condition
    variable attributes shall be used; the effect is the same as passing the address of a default
    condition variable attributes object. Upon successful initialization, the state of the condition
    variable shall become initialized.
    ...
    Attempting to initialize an already initialized condition variable results in undefined beha-
    viour.
RETURN VALUE
    If successful, the pthread_cond_init() function shall return zero; ...

and that of the functions

`pthread_cond_wait` and `pthread_cond_signal`

to block and unblock:

NAME
  `pthread_cond_wait` – wait on a condition
SYNOPSIS
  `#include <pthread.h>`
  `int pthread_cond_wait(pthread_cond_t *restrict cond,`
  `    pthread_cond_wait(pthread_mutex_t *restrict mutex);`
DESCRIPTION
  The `pthread_cond_wait()` functions shall block on a condition variable. It shall be
  called with mutex locked by the calling thread.
  This function atomically releases mutex and causes the calling thread to block on the con-
  dition variable `cond`.
  Upon successful return, the mutex shall have been locked and shall be owned by the calling
  thread.
  When using condition variables there is always a Boolean predicate involving shared varia-
  bles associated with each condition wait that is true if the thread should proceed. Since the
  return from `pthread_cond_wait()` does not imply anything about the value of this
  predicate, the predicate should be re-evaluated upon such return.
RETURN VALUE
  Upon successful completion, a value of zero shall be returned; …

NAME
  pthread_cond_signal – signal a condition
SYNOPSIS
  `#include <pthread.h>`
  `pthread_cond_signal(pthread_cond_t *cond);`
DESCRIPTION
  This function shall unblock threads blocked on a condition variable.
  The `pthread_cond_signal()` function shall unblock at least one of the threads that
  are blocked on the specified condition variable `cond` (if any threads are blocked on `cond`).
  If more than one thread is blocked on a condition variable, the scheduling policy shall
  determine the order in which threads are unblocked. When each thread unblocked as a result
  of a `pthread_cond_signal()` returns from its call to `pthread_cond_wait()` or
  `pthread_cond_timedwait()`, the thread shall own the mutex with which it called
  `pthread_cond_wait()` or `pthread_cond_timedwait()`. The thread(s) that are
  unblocked shall contend for the mutex according to the scheduling policy (if applicable),
  and as if each had called `pthread_mutex_lock()`.
  The `pthread_cond_signal()` function shall have no effect if there are no threads
  currently blocked on `cond`.
RETURN VALUE
  If successful, the `pthread_cond_signal()` function shall return zero; …

Therefore, `mutex` has to be passed as parameter to calls of these functions, so that the release or acquisition of the exclusion secured by `mutex` is possible. This can be used to implement a "monitor" for our account example; the interface would be a `header`-file `account.h`:

```
void deposit(unsigned int b);
void draw(unsigned int b);
unsigned int Balance();
```

The implementation is then

```
#include <pthread.h>
#include "account.h"

unsigned int balance = 0;
pthread_mutex_t mutex = PTHREAD_MUTEX_INITIALIZER;
pthread_cond_t cond = PTHREAD_COND_INITIALIZER;

void deposit(unsigned int b) {
  pthread_mutex_lock(&mutex);
  balance += b;
  pthread_cond_signal(&cond);
  pthread_mutex_unlock(&mutex);
}

void draw(unsigned int b) {
  pthread_mutex_lock(&mutex);
  while (balance < b) {
    pthread_cond_wait(&cond, &mutex);
  }
  balance -= b;
  pthread_cond_signal(&cond);
  pthread_mutex_unlock(&mutex);
}
```

9.3.2 Monitors in Java

The monitor concept is supported by Java to the extent that the modifier `synchronized` allows the execution of methods under *mutual exclusion*.

In addition, the class `java.lang.Object` provides the methods `wait()` and `notify()`, which can be considered as operations to block and unblock on a—for any synchronized object *implicitly* existing, even if syntactically invisible—"condition variable". Here is an excerpt from this class:

```
package java.lang;
public class Object {
  /**
```

```
     * Wakes up a single thread that is waiting on this object's
     * monitor. If any threads are waiting on this object, one
     * of them is chosen to be awakened. The choice is arbitrary
     * and occurs at the discretion of the implementation.
     * A thread waits on an object's monitor by calling one of
     * the wait methods.
     * The awakened thread will not be able to proceed until
     * the current thread relinquishes the lock on this object.
     * The awakened thread will compete in the usual manner
     * with any other threads that might be actively competing
     * to synchronize on this object.
     */
    public final native void notify();
    /**
     * Causes the current thread to wait until another thread
     * invokes the notify() method or the notifyAll() method
     * for this object.  ... should always be used in a loop:
     *     synchronized (obj) {
     *         while (<condition does not hold>)
     *             obj.wait();
     *         ... // Perform action appropriate to condition
     *     }
     */
    public final void wait() throws InterruptedException {
      wait(0);
    }
}
```

Using this, the implementation of the account example is as follows:

```
public class Account
{
   private int balance;
   public Account() { balance = 0; }

   public synchronized void deposit(int b) {
     balance += b;
     notify();
   }

   public synchronized void draw(int b) {
     while (balance < b) {
       try { wait(); } catch (InterruptedException e) {}
     }
     balance -= b;
     notify();
   }
}
```

Since 1.5, in the package `java.util.concurrent.locks` there is the interface
`Condition.java`, which now also provides *explicit* condition variables (the detailed
comments on the specification are not reproduced here):

```
package java.util.concurrent.locks;
import java.util.concurrent.*;
import java.util.Date;

public interface Condition {
  /**
   * Causes the current thread to wait until it is signaled
   * or interrupted.
   * The lock associated with this Condition is atomically
   * released and the current thread becomes disabled for
   * thread scheduling purposes and lies dormant until ...
   * - Some other thread invokes the signal method for this
   *   Condition, and the current thread happens to be chosen
   *   as the thread to be awakened; or
   * - Some other thread invokes the signalAll method for this
   *   Condition;
   * - ...
   * In all cases, before this method can return, the current
   * thread must reacquire the lock associated with this
   * condition. When the thread returns it is guaranteed
   * to hold this lock.
   */
  void await() throws InterruptedException;
  /**
   * Wakes up one waiting thread.
   * If any threads are waiting on this condition then one
   * is selected for waking up. That thread must then
   * reacquire the lock before returning from await.
   */
  void signal();
}
```

This means that finer granulated monitors can now also be constructed in Java—in principle
just as in C or Go.

9.3.3   Monitors in Go

For Go, the package `sync` provides—in complete analogy to the `pthread` library—a
type `Cond` for condition variables with the functions `Wait` and `Signal` (see `cond.go`
in the package `sync`), shown here in an excerpt:

```
package sync

import "runtime"
```

```
// Cond implements a condition variable, a rendezvous point
// for goroutines waiting for or announcing the occurrence
// of an event. Each Cond has an associated Locker L (...),
// which must be held when changing the condition and
// when calling the Wait method.

type Cond struct {
  L Locker // held while observing or changing the condition
  m Mutex  // held to avoid internal races
  ...

// NewCond returns a new Cond with Locker l.
func NewCond(l Locker) *Cond { ...

// Wait atomically unlocks c.L and suspends execution
// of the calling goroutine. After later resuming execution,
// Wait locks c.L before returning.
func (c *Cond) Wait() { ...

// Signal wakes one goroutine waiting on c, if there is any.
func (c *Cond) Signal() { ...
```

With this, in Go monitors can be implemented similarly as in C. We show this with the account example:

With the specification

```
package macc

type MAccount interface {

// The balance is incremented by a. Returns the deposited amount
  Deposit (a uint) uint

// The balance is decremented by a.
// The calling process was delayed, if necessary, until that was
possible.
// Returns the withdrawn amount.
  Draw (a uint) uint
}

func New() MAccount { return new_() }
```

the implementation is

```
package macc
import . "sync"

type maccount struct {
  uint "balance"
  Mutex
  *Cond
}

func new_() MAccount {
  x := new(maccount)
  x.Cond = NewCond(&x.Mutex)
  return x
}
```

```
func (x *maccount) Deposit (a uint) uint {
  x.Mutex.Lock()
  defer x.Mutex.Unlock()
  x.uint += a
  x.Cond.Signal()
  return a
}

func (x *maccount) Draw (a uint) uint {
  x.Mutex.Lock()
  defer x.Mutex.Unlock()
  for x.uint < a {
    x.Cond.Wait()
  }
  x.uint -= a
  x.Cond.Signal()
  return a
}
```

For these reasons, all the solutions presented lack the elegance of HOARE's approach—none of the three languages really has a clean monitor concept. But, as has already been indicated, this can be "repaired" at a higher level of abstraction. In Chap. 10 on *universal monitors*, we will present a corresponding really cool synchronization class—in analogy to our universal critical sections.

9.4   The Bounded Buffer

As the first of our meanwhile well-known standard examples we show an example of a monitor with more than one condition variable. Here we do not give the conceptual implementation of a bounded buffer according to our postulate for a `monitor` construct, but the implementation in Go as a package:

```
package mbuf
import (. "sync"; . "nU/buf")

type mbuffer struct {
  buf.Buffer
  notFull, notEmpty *Cond
  Mutex
}

func newC (n uint) MBuffer {
  x := new(condition)
  x.Buffer = buf.New(n)
  x.notFull, x.notEmpty = NewCond (&x.Mutex), NewCond (&x.Mutex)
  return x
}

func (x *condition) Ins (b byte) {
  x.Mutex.Lock()
  defer x.Mutex.Unlock()
```

```
for x.Buffer.Full() {
  x.notFull.Wait()
}
x.Buffer.Ins (b)
x.notEmpty.Signal()
}

func (x *condition) Get() byte {
  x.Mutex.Lock()
  defer x.Mutex.Unlock()
  for x.Buffer.Num() == 0 {
    x.notEmpty.Wait()
  }
  x.notFull.Signal()
  return x.Buffer.Get()
}
```

To use this implementation, the specification of `Buf` from Sect. 4.4 has to be extended by the line

```
func NewCondition (n uint) Buffer { return newC(n) }
```

Due to the forced mutual exclusion of the monitor functions by means of the lock `Mutex` it is irrelevant, in this case, whether only one or more producers and consumers have access.

9.5   The Readers–Writers Problem

An application that is well suited for analyzing the competition problem of unblocking processes within a monitor is the readers–writers problem. As with the semaphore solution, we will not isolate in a monitor the data on which readers and writers work, but the entry and exit protocols.

The monitor invariant

$$(n_R = 0) \wedge (n_W = 1) \vee (n_W = 0)$$

is equal to the semaphore invariant of the problem; it must be created when the monitor is initialized and preserved by each monitor function.

With each of the two entry conditions ($n_W = 0$ for the readers and ($n_R = 0) \wedge (n_W = 0)$ for the writers) a condition variable is associated: `okR` for the readers and `okW` for the writers. This makes the entry protocols very easy to implement.

It is a little more difficult with the exit protocols. When a last reader or a writer has finished, the entry conditions for *both* process classes are fulfilled, i.e., actually a `Signal` on both condition variables is due.

Therefore, if the obvious solution is chosen, to call one after the other `Signal` operations on both condition variables, the problem of the dependence of the implementation on the underlying signal semantics immediately arises. But one can easily get around this by deciding with a call of `Awaited` whether readers or writers should be unblocked.

With this, the extremely elegant monitor solution of HOARE in [3]

```
monitor rw

var (
  nR, nW uint
  okR, okW Condition
)

func ReaderIn() {
  if nW > 0 {
    okR.Wait()
  }
  nR++
  okR.Signal()
}

func ReaderOut() {
  nR--
  if nR == 0 {
    okW.Signal()
  }
}

func WriterIn() {
  if nR > 0 || nW > 0 {
    okW.Wait()
  }
  nW = 1
}

func WriterOut() {
  nW = 0
  if okR.Awaited() {
    okR.Signal()
  } else {
    okW.Signal()
  }
}
```

can be constructed, which has the obvious advantage that the question of the priority of readers or writers can be settled with small variations. For example, it can be immediately achieved that a first reader is not only blocked when a writer is active, but also—as in HOARE's paper—if writers apply for entrance to the critical section:

```
func ReaderIn() {
  if nW > 0 || okW.Awaited() {
    okR.Wait()
  }
  nR++
```

```
   okR.Signal()
}
```

An advantage of this solution is its independence from the signal semantics, since in the monitor functions after the call of `Signal` no further statements are executed. The translation of this "virtual" solution on the basis of our postulated `monitor` extension of Go into a syntactically sound Go program is unfortunately not possible, because the type `Cond` in the package `sync` does not contain a method with the semantics of `Awaited`. We will "crack that nut" in the next chapter.

9.6   Signal Semantics

We will now classify the *signal semantics* i.e., the methods for the resolution of the competition of the signaling, i.e., deblocking, functions.

9.6.1   Signal and Continue

In this semantics—briefly called *SC semantics* ("*Signal and Continue*")—the calling process continues executing its function in the monitor to the end, but at least until it is itself blocked on a condition variable; the deblocked process is then appended to the monitor queue. For this reason, the unblocked process can be overtaken by other processes that entered the monitor after it.

9.6.1.1 Signal and Exit
As the name indicates, in this semantics with the short name *SX semantics* ("*Signal and eXit*") the calling process immediately stops its monitor function; the unblocked process directly gains control of the monitor and continues the execution of its interrupted function. As a result of this effect, `Signal` is a last statement of the calling function; further statements are blunders because they are not reachable.

9.6.2   Signal and Wait

The *SW semantics* ("*Signal and Wait*") is somewhat contrary to the SC semantics. If there is no blocked process, the call is effect free, and the calling process continues without interruption. Otherwise, the calling process immediately transfers the control of the monitor to the unblocked process; it is blocked itself and appended to the monitor entry queue. This procedure is not fair either, because it allows the signaling process to be overtaken by other processes that called their monitor functions later than it did.

9.6.3   Signal and Urgent Wait

Exactly this unfairness of the SW semantics is avoided by the semantics with the abbreviation
SU ("*Signal and Urgent wait*"): In principle, the procedure is the same as for SW, but the
overtaking phenomenon is eliminated by introducing a further waiting queue, the "*urgent
queue*", which contains the processes that have called a `Signal` operation until they were
unblocked. After a process leaves the monitor, the processes in the urgent queue gain priority
over those waiting to enter the monitor (i.e., those in the monitor entry queue).

9.6.4   Preemptive Versus Nonpreemptive Semantics

The SX, SW, and SU semantics are summarized under the term "*preemptive*" semantics.
SX semantics can be achieved by a rigid programming discipline by not allowing any more
statements after a `Signal` call in a monitor function which, however, unduly restricts the
freedom to formulate algorithms.

But even with such restrictive programming, a careful distinction between preemptive
and nonpreemptive semantics is necessary. In SC semantics, an unblocked process must
always again check the condition on which it was blocked, since it may have been changed
by other processes in the meantime. For this, the `Wait` operation has to be surrounded by
a loop, because a case distinction is only sufficient, if it is ensured that a process blocked on
a condition variable immediately resumes its interrupted monitor function if it is unblocked
before another process can change its condition.

An alternative in the writers' exit protocol is to unblock blocked readers as well as blocked
writers:

```
func WriterOut() {
  nW = 0
  okR.Signal()
  okW.Signal()
}
```

With SX semantics, this variant is, of course, pointless, because the second `Signal` statement is not executed; with SC semantics, the entry protocols must be modified as follows:

```
func ReaderIn() {
  for nW > 0 {
    okR.Wait()
  }
  ...

func WriterIn() {
  for nR > 0 || nW > 0 {
    okW.Wait()
  }
  ...
```

9.6.5   Comparing Evaluation of the Signal Semantics

In principle, the signal semantics are equivalent; with a little effort, any desired effect can be achieved in any semantics. Details can be found in [1].

In the preemptive case, compliance with the monitor invariant is usually more difficult to prove, because when interrupted by a signal operation, the code fragments to be checked are scattered over several monitor functions. The nonpreemptive semantics offers the advantage that the monitor functions can be developed independently of each other.

With SW/SU semantics, a signal operation as a last statement in a monitor function causes a reentry into the monitor—just to state that it can be left. This is annoying because of the useless effort for the process scheduling management. On the other hand, there is the additional expense of running time due to the continuous rechecking of the conditions with SC semantics.

Since SX restricts very strongly in programming, and SC can be implemented with less effort than SW or SU, ANDREWS propagates in [1]—contrary to HOARE's original suggestion—the nonpreemptive semantics as the method of choice for implementing the monitor concept in a programming language. These questions do not play a role in the programming of monitors; more important are fundamental considerations of portability.

The program text of a monitor is independent of whether the programming language used provides preemptive or nonpreemptive semantics, if it fulfills the following conditions:

- The monitor invariant is the only interface between the functions for blocking and unblocking on a condition variable, i.e., it is true before any `Signal` operation, and the blocked processes, when unblocked, make—apart from the monitor invariant—no assumptions about the values of any variables in the monitor.
- A condition that caused the unblocking of a process does not change, even if the unblocking process continues, i.e., immediately after a `Signal` operation only statements to block follow, but never value assignments to variables of the monitor.
- No *broadcast signal* is used (see Sect. 9.7).

9.6.6   A Semaphore as Monitor

An example where the signal semantics affects the order in which processes blocked on condition variables are unblocked is the following monitor construction of a *semaphore*:

```
monitor semaphore

var (
  val int
  greaterZero Condition
)
```

```
func New (n uint) {
  val = int(n)
}

func P() {
  for val == 0 {
    greaterZero.Wait()
  }
  val--
}

func V() {
  val++
  greaterZero.Signal()
}
```

In the case of preemptive semantics, the semaphore is fair if the condition waiting queues in the monitor are implemented strictly according to the FIFO principle, which we have postulated.

This is not the case with nonpreemptive semantics. If, at the time when a process blocked on greaterZero in its P-operation is unblocked, already other processes with a P-operation hang in the monitor entry queue, and the first of them may execute its P-operation prior to it without being blocked, and has, therefore, overtaken it at the entrance to the critical section.

By a clever modification it can be achieved that this monitor is also fair with SC semantics: A process must not change the value of the semaphore before the signal operation in the call of V if there are blocked processes; appropriately, a process blocked on greaterZero in its P-operation must immediately return from the monitor if it is deblocked, without decrementing the value of the semaphore:

```
func P() {
  if val > 0 {
    val--
  } else {
    greaterZero.Wait()
  }
}

func V() {
  if greaterZero.Awaited() {
    greaterZero.Signal()
  } else {
    val++
  }
}
```

But in this case val is no longer the difference $n_V - n_P$ of the completed V and P-operations but has the value $n_V - n_P - w$, where w is the number of processes that are unblocked by greaterZero.Signal but not yet have completed their P-operation.

The example shows that portability by no means has to be bought at the price of illegibility, but can be compatible with the demand for a clear and self-documenting programming style.

In particular, it shows that general semaphores can be implemented with monitors, i.e.:

▶   The synchronization concept of the monitors is at least as expressive as that of the semaphores.

9.6.7   Barrier Synchronization

Another example of an algorithm whose correctness depends on the signal semantics is the following monitor variant of the barrier synchronization:

```
monitor barr

const m = ... // Anzahl der beteiligten
Prozesse
var (n uint; c Condition)

func Wait() {
  n++
  if n < m {
    c.Wait()
  } else {
    for n > 0 {
      n--
      if n > 0 {
        c.Signal()
      }
    }
  }
}
```

In contrast to the semaphore solution presented in Sect. 4.10, in this case, the process that reaches the barrier as the last one must unblock *all* processes that encountered the barrier before. However, this requires SC or SU semantics: It must be avoided that deblocked processes reinitialize the barrier or have to wait for it before *all* waiting processes are unblocked. This technique—deblocking simultaneously *all* blocked processes—can also be useful in other contexts. It, therefore, gives rise to a generalization in the next section.

This abstract formulation can be used in Go by means of the conditions `Cond` from the package `sync` in an implementation of the interface `Barrier` in Sect. 4.10:

```
package barr
import . "sync"

type gobarrier struct {
  uint "number of processes involved"
  waiting uint
```

```
  *Cond
  Mutex "to block"
}

func newG(m uint) Barrier {
  x := new(gobarrier)
  x.uint = m
  x.Cond = NewCond(&x.Mutex)
  return x
}

func (x *gobarrier) Wait() {
  x.Mutex.Lock()
  x.waiting++
  if x.waiting < x.uint {
    x.Cond.Wait()
  } else {
    for x.waiting > 0 {
      x.waiting--
      if x.waiting > 0 {
        x.Cond.Signal()
      }
    }
  }
  x.Mutex.Unlock()
}
```

9.7   Broadcast in C, Java, and Go

Another function on condition variables—only with nonpreemptive semantics—is a *broadcast signal* with the same effect as

```
for c.Awaited() {
  c.Signal()
}
```

for a condition variable var c Condition.

Our postulated package Condition is extended with it:

```
// All processes blocked on c are unblocked, if such exist,
// otherwise nothing has happened.
  SignalAll()
```

A simple application is a modification of the solution of the readers–writers problem (of course, only in connection with the necessary rechecking of the conditions in the entry protocol of the writers):

```
func ReaderIn() {
  for nW > 0 {
    okR.Wait()
  }
  nR++
}

func WriterOut() {
```

```
nW = 0
okR.SignalAll()
okW.Signal()
}
```

However, this example clearly violates the portability requirement of the penultimate section.

9.7.1 Broadcast in C

In C, this is realized with the function `pthread_cond_broadcast`:

NAME
    `pthread_cond_broadcast` – broadcast a condition
SYNOPSIS
    `#include <pthread.h>`
    `int pthread_cond_broadcast(pthread_cond_t *cond);`
DESCRIPTION
    This functions shall unblock threads blocked on a condition variable.
    The `pthread_cond_broadcast()` function shall unblock all threads currently blocked on the specified condition variable cond.
    If more than one thread is blocked on a condition variable, the scheduling policy shall determine the order in which threads are unblocked.
    The `pthread_cond_broadcast()` function shall have no effect if there are no threads currently blocked on cond.
RETURN VALUE
    If successful, the `pthread_cond_broadcast()` function shall return zero; ...

9.7.2 Broadcast in Java

For its original monitor concept, with the function `notifyAll` in the class `java.long.Object`, Java offers the following:

```
/**
 * Wakes up all threads that are waiting on this object's
 * monitor. A thread waits on an object's monitor by calling
 * one of the wait methods.
 */
public final native void notifyAll();
```

and in the interface `Condition` something that is comparable to the construct in C:

```
/**
 * Wakes up all waiting threads.
 * If any threads are waiting on this condition then they
 * are all woken up. Each thread must reacquire the lock
 * before it can return from await.
```

```
*/
void signalAll();
```

9.7.3 Broadcast in Go

The package `sync` from the Go library contains the function `Broadcast`:

```
// Broadcast wakes all goroutines waiting on c.
func (c *Cond) Broadcast() {
  c.signalImpl(true)
}
```

9.8   The Sleeping Barber: Haircut as a Rendezvous

If a buffer is not bounded in size, Sect. 4.5 of the semaphore chapter, in principle, provides the approach of a monitor solution for an unbounded buffer. However, we do not pursue this further here, because the implementation—conveniently with a linked list as its representation—is a simple exercise. Instead, we once again take up DIJKSTRA's approach of the *sleeping barber* and respond to the remark about the synchronization of the participants.

First, we show the implementation of the barber using a monitor:

```
monitor barber

var (
  n uint
  customer Condition
)

func wait() {
  takeSeatInWaitingRoom()
  n++
  customer.Signal()
}

func barber() {
  sleepInBarbersChair()
  for n == 0 {
    customer.Wait()
  }
  n--
  haveSeatInBarbersChair()
}
```

The subtle problems of the corresponding algorithm only using binary semaphores do not arise in this case. A simple dualization of the application of the condition variable customer in conjunction with the number n of waiting customers extends the algorithm by a *synchronization point* in which the "customers get haircuts from the barber".

This goes beyond the actual function of the buffer to the extent that not only the customers "take a seat in the waiting room" (i.e., insert their data into the buffer) and the barber "invites" them one after the other "to sit on the barber's chair" (i.e., get data from the buffer), but also the "haircut" is synchronized—in the form of a "rendezvous" between barber and customer for the handing over of ~~hair~~ data:

```
monitor barber

var (
   customerWaiting, barberFree, barberFinished bool
   customer, barber, finished Condition
)

func wait() {
   takeSeatInWaitingRoom()
   for ! barberFree {
     barber.Wait()
   }
   barberFree = false
   customerWaiting = true
   customer.Signal()
   getBarbed() // Synchronisationspunkt
   for ! barberFinished {
     finished.Wait()
   }
   barberFinished = false
}

func barber() {
   barberFree = true
   barber.Signal()
   sleepInBarbersChair()
   for !customerWaiting {
     customer.Wait()
   }
   customerWaiting = false
   haveSeatInBarbersChair()
   barbeTheCustomer() // Synchronisationspunkt
   barberFinished = true
   finished.Signal()
}
```

The synchronisation pattern indicated by this solution will as a *client-server-paradigm* play a central role in the chapter on *message passing*: the barber as a "server" and each of his customers as a "client".

9.9   Priority Rules

In order to obtain more finely granulated control options to unblock certain processes, an extension of the condition variables by a priority rule is conceivable. Processes during blocking are given a number as rank; at each signal operation, the lowest ranked process is unblocked (i.e., the condition variables are conceptually equipped with priority queues):

```
// The calling process is (categorically) blocked on c
// with the rank r, ...
  Wait(r uint)

// The process blocked on C with the smallest rank
// is unblocked, if such exists,
// otherwise nothing has happened.
  Signal()

// Returns the minimum of the ranks of all processes,
// that are blocked on c, if such exists; returns otherwise -1.
  MinRank() int
```

9.9.1   Hoare's Alarm Clock

Here is the classic example of HOARE's alarm clock from [3]:

```
monitor alarm

var (
  time uint
  alarmclock Condition
)

// Simulation of the system's time impulse:
func tick() {
  time++
  alarmclock.Signal()
}

// The calling process is blocked for a duration
// of t time units from with the call.
func sleep (t uint) {
  alarmtime := time + t
  for time < alarmtime {
```

```
        alarmclock.Wait()
    }
    alarmclock.Signal()
}
```

This avoids the costly alternative of assigning each process its own condition variable. An unblocked process awakens the next one, if one is still asleep, to give it the opportunity to see if its rest period has expired; this process awakens the next one, and so on. (Of course, with SC semantics, the cascade-like wake up could also be replaced by a `SignalAll`.)

But with a view to efficiency, this solution leaves something to be desired. Imagine your alarm clock ringing again and again at short intervals, so that you can see whether you have to get up or can go on sleeping ... (You would probably throw it out of the window.)

With a priority rule, the construction becomes much more elegant:

```
func tick() {
    time++
    for alarmclock.Awaited() &&
        alarmclock.MinRank() <= time {
        alarmclock.Signal()
    }
}

func sleep (t int) {
    alarmtime := time + t
    if alarmtime > time {
        alarmclock.Wait (alarmtime)
    }
}
```

9.9.2 Shortest Job next

Condition variables with priorities also make it much easier to solve the problem of resource allocation by prioritizing the shortest requirements presented in Sect. 4.11. A process requesting the resource is blocked if it is occupied by another process. The release after its use has the consequence that—if processes are waiting for it—the process with the request of the shortest needed time is unblocked, and the resource is allocated to him:

```
monitor resourceAllocation

var (free = true; turn Condition)

func Request() (time uint) {
    if free {
        free = false
    } else {
        turn.Wait (time)
```

```
    }
}

func Release() {
  if turn.Awaited() {
    turn.Signal()
  } else {
    free = true
  }
}
```

9.10 Equivalence of the Semaphore and the Monitor Concepts

We now show that monitor functions can be emulated using *locks*. In order to ensure the mutual exclusion in the monitor, an (initially open) lock `mutex` is sufficient, which must be part of the monitor. The compiler must supply the monitor functions with the corresponding `Lock` and `Unlock` operations for entry and exit:

```
func enter (m *Monitor) {
  m.mutex.Lock()
}

func leave (m *Monitor) {
  m.mutex.Unlock()
}
```

More detailed considerations regarding the parameterization of all functions by the respective monitor are not yet necessary for these basic considerations; we will catch up on this in the next section.

A lock is sufficient to block processes on a condition variable. Because locks (like semaphores) do not provide the ability to enquire how many processes are blocked on them, their number must be recorded in order to make the necessary case distinctions. Therefore,

```
type condition struct {
  s sync.Mutex "condition waiting queue"
  ns uint "number of the processes in this queue"
}
```

is a suitable data structure, wherein the two components of the struct, when declaring a condition variable in accordance with the specification of Go, are set to their "*zero values*", which means that in the beginning, `s` is open and `ns == 0`.

In principle, you can construct the functions on the condition variables as follows (where `mutex` is the semaphore that manages the monitor's entry queue):

```
func (c *condition) Wait() {
  c.nx++
  mutex.Unlock()
// *
  c.s.Lock()
```

```
    mutex.Lock()
    c.ns--
}

func (c *condition) Signal() {
    if c.ns > 0 {
        c.s.Unlock()
    }
}
```

An interruption at the point * is harmless:

A process that is overtaken there by other processes with a call for unblocking is, indeed, not blocked by `c.s.Lock()` if the preceding U-operations have opened the lock `c.s`, but at the time of its activation, the signal operations have also fulfilled the condition that it can continue.

The additional functions are also easily implemented:

```
func (c *condition) SignalAll() {
    for i := 0; i < c.ns; i++ {
        c.s.Unlock()
    }
    c.ns = 0
}

func (c *condition) Blocked() uint {
    return c.ns
}

func (c *condition) Awaited() bool {
    return c.ns > 0
}
```

This implementation variant provides SC semantics and, therefore, requires the use of `for` loops around the function to block.

However, the FIFO property of all waiting queues of the monitor is only guaranteed if the locks used unblock according to FIFO.

If `Signal` only occurs as a last call, SX semantics can also be achieved with a small modification.

A blocked process does not have to reapply for entry into the monitor after it has been unblocked, that is, the call to the corresponding `Lock` operation when blocking is omitted,

```
func (c *condition) Wait() {
    c.ns++
    mutex.Unlock()
    c.s.Lock()
    c.ns--
}
```

which amounts to the direct transfer of control over the monitor to the unblocked process.

To compensate for this, the monitor exit is not integrated into the calling monitor function; the mutual exclusion in the monitor is, instead, abandoned by the deblocking process when there are no more blocked processes:

```
func (c *condition) Signal() {
  if c.ns > 0 {
    c.s.Unlock()
  } else {
    me.Unlock()
  }
}
```

If more statements are admitted after the call of Signal in a monitor function, a similar
measure also provides SW semantics—also in this case, the call of mutex.Lock() during
blocking is omitted, and the deblocking process passes the mutual exclusion in the monitor
directly to the deblocked process, whereby it is blocked itself by the call of mutex.Lock:

```
func (c *condition) Signal() {
  if c.ns > 0 {
    c.s.Unlock()
    mutex.Lock()
  }
}
```

If in the monitor also a semaphore for the urgent queue and a counter for the processes saved
in it

```
var (
  u sync.Mutex
  nu uint
)
```

are held—whereby at the beginning u is closed and nu == 0, this approach can also be
extended to SU semantics. When leaving the monitor, the processes from the urgent queue
are preferred to those from the monitor entry queue, that is, those that are blocked on the
semaphore for mutual exclusion in the monitor, by giving control directly to one of them:

```
func leave() {
  if nu > 0 {
    u.Unlock()
  } else {
    mutex.Unlock()
  }
}
```

The blocking procedure is analogous:

```
func (c *condition) Wait() {
  c.ns++
  if nu > 0 {
    u.Unlock()
  } else {
    mutex.Unlock()
  }
  c.s.Lock()
  c.ns--
}
```

After a signal operation, the calling process is blocked, leaves the monitor, and ends up in
the urgent queue, if it has unblocked another one:

```
func (c *condition) Signal() {
  if c.ns > 0 {
    nu++
    c.s.Unlock()
    u.Lock()
    nu--
  }
}

func (c *condition) SignalAll() {
  for c.ns > 0 {
    nu++
    c.s.Unlock()
    u.Lock()
    nu--
  }
}
```

In Sect. 9.6.6, we have shown that general (and, therefore, also binary) *semaphores* can be implemented by recourse to monitors. In conjunction with the consequence of Sect. 4.7.3 on the construction of general semaphores from binary ones, we achieved the aim of this section:

▶   Monitors and semaphores are basically equivalent synchronization concepts.

9.11   Implementation of the Monitor Concept

The protocols of monitors and the functions on condition variables can also be implemented directly in a process management using the routines of the process core, which were introduced in the corresponding section and used for the implementation of semaphores.

One approach can be found in the specification of the process state *blocked*, which here covers three cases:

- *blocked* on the *monitor entry queue*,
- *blocked* on the queue of a condition variables or
- —only for SU semantics—*blocked* on the *urgent queue* of the monitor.

We can use this to refine our process model from Sect. 1.9 on the process states:

Between *these* three states and the states *active* and *ready* there are the following transitions, which are shown in Fig. 9.1.

- Process remains in the state *active*
  by entering the monitor if it is *not locked*,

- *active → blocked on the monitor entry queue*
  by entering the monitor when it is *locked* or—in the case of SW semantic—by the call of a `Signal` operation,
- *blocked on the monitor entry queue → ready*
  by the exit of another process from the monitor,
- *active → blocked on a condition variable*
  by a call of `Wait` on one of the condition variables,
- *blocked on a condition variable → blocked on the monitor entry queue*
  or *blocked on a condition variable → ready*
  —depending on the semantics—by a `Signal` operation of another process,
- *active → blocked on the urgent queue*
  —for SU semantics—by the call of a `Signal` operation,
- *blocked on the urgent queue → ready*
  by the exit of another process from the monitor, or by a call of `Wait` of another process.

The considerations from the previous section provide exact instructions for the implementation of all signal semantics. Thereby one can orient oneself to the realization of the semaphore functions:

- `enter` and `Wait` are in essence related to the P-operation,
- `leave` and `Signal` to the V-operation and are, therefore, constructed quite analogously.

This aspect is taken up in the following chapter in the construction of a further universal synchronization class.

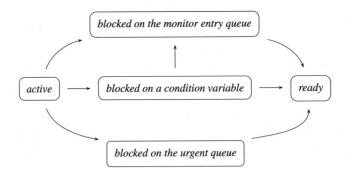

Fig. 9.1 State transitions for monitors

9.12   The Problem of Nested Monitor Calls

LISTER recognized in [4] the problems that arise when in a monitor functions of another monitor are called.

An example of this is read-write operations in the file system on disks: a readers–writers monitor exports routines for managing the data; below it is a layer for buffering data blocks; at the bottom is the layer for physical access to the disk, in which, among other things, the movements of the read-write head are optimized to counteract the negative influence of the inertia of moving masses on the throughput of the system.

The construction of a monitor is also suitable for the lowest layer, which collects several requests and, if necessary, rearranges them in order to be able to perform as many operations as possible with a head movement from the inside to the outside or vice versa; which is very similar to the operation of an elevator.

There are the following basic procedures, the advantages and disadvantages of which must be balanced:

- *Closed calls*:
  The outer monitors from which others are called are *not released*; if necessary only the inner monitor, if the process is blocked in it. While this ensures that the calling process can immediately return to any outer monitor during unblocking, it is associated with disadvantages for the liveliness of the system and the risk of deadlocks.
- *Open calls*, due to HADDON in [2]:
  A monitor will *always* be released at a descent. This increases the concurrency and eliminates deadlocks. In this case, however, a process can only descend to the next one if the monitor variant is valid, because the variables of the outer monitor can meanwhile be changed by other processes; this also leads to a somewhat more complicated semantics of open calls and to a higher system load, because a process has to apply again and again for entry to the outer monitors when it ascends.
- A *hybrid form* due to WETTSTEIN in [6]:
  Closed calls are used, but all outer monitors are released, if the calling process is blocked in the inner monitor.
- Nested monitor calls are *forbidden*, whereby, however, the advantages of the modular monitor concept for a hierarchical system architecture are lost.

—unless you share the opinion of PARNAS in [5].

References

1. Andrews, G.R.: Concurrent Programming, Principles and Practice. Addison-Wesley, Menlo Park (1991)
2. Haddon, B.K.: Nested monitor calls. ACM SIGOPS Oper. Syst. Rev. **11**, 18–23 (1977). https://doi.org/10.1145/850648.850650

3. Hoare, C.A.R.: Monitors: an operating systems structuring concept. Commun. ACM **17**, 549–557 (1974). https://doi.org/10.1145/355620.361161
4. Lister, A.: The problem of nested monitor calls. ACM SIGOPS Oper. Syst. Rev. **11**, 5–7 (1977). https://doi.org/10.1145/850644.850645
5. Parnas, D.L.: The non-problem of nested monitor calls. ACM SIGOPS Oper. Syst. Rev. **12**, 12–14 (1978). https://doi.org/10.1145/775323.775324
6. Wettstein, H.: The problem of nested monitor calls revisited. ACM SIGOPS Oper. Syst. Rev. **12**, 19–23 (1978). https://doi.org/10.1145/775323.775325

Universal Monitors

10

Abstract

The proof of the equivalence of the semaphore and monitor concept, as well as the details on the implementation of the monitor concept in the previous chapter can be used—like the baton algorithm—as a template for the construction of a universal synchronization class, the *universal monitors* developed in this chapter. However, it is not about the protocols to protect critical sections but about ensuring the mutual exclusion of concurrent processes in their operations on shared data. It should be possible that the functions can only be executed if certain conditions are fulfilled, which—like the statements—may depend on the data.

Thus, even in C, Java, and Go, which—strictly speaking—do not support the monitor concept, monitor solutions are possible in a very simple way, for which many already known examples are given here: semaphores, the account, bounded buffers and the sleeping barber, barrier synchronization, the readers–writers and the left–right problems, the dining philosophers, and the cigarette smokers.

10.1 The Basic Idea

The approach of the following construction is similar to that of the universal critical sections, but it is conceptually different:

Universal monitors are used to ensure *mutual exclusion* between functions and for condition synchronization with SU as the underlying semantics of the signal operations (*signaling and urgent waiting*, see Sect. 9.6.3).

The *monitor functions* are identified by consecutive numbers starting from 0; they are bundled in a function spectrum parameterized by these numbers, which has to be constructed by clients and passed by them to a monitor when they generated it. The "number of functions" of a monitor is, therefore, one of its parameters. With each function, implicitly a condition

© Springer Fachmedien Wiesbaden GmbH, part of Springer Nature 2021
C. Maurer, *Nonsequential and Distributed Programming with Go*,
https://doi.org/10.1007/978-3-658-29782-4_10

variable with the same number is linked, on which a calling process is blocked during its execution, if necessary, until the condition is fulfilled, and then unblocked again.

The abstract data type *Monitor* provides the methods `Wait`, `Signal`, `SignalAll`, `Blocked`, and `Awaited` that clients need to synchronize when constructing their monitor functions, which they pass to a monitor as function spectra when it is generated. To do this, they have to connect the implicit condition variables semantically fitting to their conditions in the form of Boolean expressions. With this they do not construct conditions, but they are themselves responsible for the correctness of their synchronization—exactly as is the case with the conventional monitor concept.

10.1.1 Specification

First, we extend the package `nU/obj` by the required function spectra:

```
type FuncSpectrum func (Any, uint) Any
```

Here is the specification:

```
package mon
import . "nU/obj"

type Monitor interface {

// Pre: i < number of functions of x.
// The calling process was blocked in x on i, if necessary,
// until sufficiently many other processes have called Signal(i).
   Wait (i uint)

// Pre: i < number of functions of x.
// If there are processes blocked in x on i,
// exactly one of them is unblocked.
   Signal (i uint)

// Pre: i < number of functions of x.
// All processes blocked in x on i are unblocked.
   SignalAll (i uint)

// Pre: i < number of functions of x.
// Returns true, iff at the moment of the call
// there are processes, that are blocked in x on i.
// Remark: See Remark at the function Awaited
//         in the specification of monitors.
   Awaited (i uint) bool

// Pre: i < number of functions of x.
// Returns the number of processes, that at
// the moment of the call are blocked in x on i.
// Remark: See Remark above.
   Blocked (i uint) uint

// Pre: i < number of functions of x.
```

```
//       a == nil or a is the object to be operated on.
// Returns the value of the i-th function for the argument a
// after the calling process correspondingly to the calls
// of Wait(i) and Signal(i) or SignalAll(i) was blocked in
// the functions of x (where f is the monitor function of x).
// The function cannot be interrupted by monitor functions.
  F (a Any, i uint) Any
}
```

```
// Pre: n > 0. f is defined for all i < n.
// Returns a new Monitor with n as number of its
// functions and the functions f(--, i) for all i < n.
// Clients are themselves responsible for the
// condition synchronization with appropriate
// calls of Wait, Signal and SignalAll
  func New (n uint, f FuncSpectrum) Monitor { return new_(n,f) }
```

10.1.2 Implementation

The basis for the implementation are the constructions from Sect. 9.10 on the equivalence of the semaphore and the monitor concept.

The synchronization functions Wait, Signal, etc., are just the straightforward takeovers of the corresponding functions developed at the end of this section for SU semantics with an urgent queue. The monitor functions F (-, i) call at their exit from the monitor the i-th function of the passed spectrum and proceed as described for the function leave. For the used package perm, we refer to Sect. 6.1.2.

Hence, the following implements SU semantics:

```
package mon
import ("sync"; . "nU/obj"; "nU/perm")

type monitor struct {
  uint "number of monitor functions"
  sync.Mutex "monitor entry queue"
  s []sync.Mutex "condition waiting queues"
  ns []uint "number of processes blocked on them"
  u sync.Mutex "urgent queue"
  nu uint "number of processes blocked on it"
  FuncSpectrum "monitor functions"
  perm.Permutation "indeterminism"
}

func new_(n uint, f FuncSpectrum) Monitor {
  x := new(monitor)
  x.uint = n
  x.s = make([]sync.Mutex, x.uint)
  for i := uint(0); i < x.uint; i++ {
    x.s[i].Lock()
  }
  x.ns = make([]uint, x.uint)
  x.u.Lock()
  x.FuncSpectrum = f
```

```
   x.Permutation = perm.New (x.uint)
   return x
}

func (x *monitor) Wait (i uint) {
  x.ns[i]++
  if x.nu > 0 {
    x.u.Unlock()
  } else {
    x.Mutex.Unlock()
  }
  x.s[i].Lock()
  x.ns[i]-- --
}

func (x *monitor) Blocked (i uint) uint {
  return x.ns[i]
}

func (x *monitor) Awaited (i uint) bool {
  return x.ns[i] > 0
}

func (x *monitor) Signal (i uint) {
  if x.ns[i] > 0 {
    x.nu++
    x.s[i].Unlock()
    x.u.Lock()
    x.nu-- --
  }
}

func (x *monitor) SignalAll (i uint) {
  for x.ns[i] > 0 {
    x.nu++
    x.s[i].Unlock()
    x.u.Lock()
    x.nu-- --
  }
}

func (x *monitor) F (a Any, i uint) Any {
  x.Mutex.Lock()
  y := x.FuncSpectrum (a, i)
  if x.nu > 0 {
    x.u.Unlock()
  } else {
    x.Mutex.Unlock()
  }
  return y
}
```

It makes absolutely no sense, if monitors would export *types*, because the objects of such types created outside the monitor would not be subject to its synchronization methods, and a client could completely circumvent these methods, thus completely counteracting the actual purpose of using a monitor.

Here, we can see another clear advantage of universal monitors: When used, this limitation is meaningless, because the methods of instances of the abstract data types constructed with them are fully covered by the synchronization of the monitors and are consequently *monitor functions* in the original sense.

Finally, the following fact—common to the universal critical sections–is expressly pointed out:

▶   The concept of the universal monitors is *by no means* bound to Go.

For example, they can be implemented in C, Modulà-2, or Java (which the author has been doing, teaching, and using in various projects in Modula-2 and Java for years)!

10.2   Conditioned Universal Monitors

Standard cases in which each processing depends on at most one condition can be handled with the following type of monitors: Using a monitor in these cases is easy, as clients construct the condition spectrum that defines the conditions for the execution of monitor functions and pass it to the monitor when it is generated. For this, Signal and Wait from the previous section are not used in the monitor functions, because this is done in the monitor function "behind the scenes" (see the implementation of the method F in 10.2.2).

10.2.1 Specification

For the above/mentioned reason, the specification of the conditioned monitors does not include Wait- and Signal operations. It also differs from the "nonconditioned" monitors in so far as the monitor functions no longer have a parameter for passing further information.

```
package cmon
import . "nU/obj"

type Monitor interface {

  Blocked (i uint) uint

  Awaited (i uint) bool

  F (i uint) Any
}

// Returns a conditioned monitor with function spectrum f
// and condition spectrum with SU-semantics.
func New (n uint, f NFuncSpectrum, c CondSpectrum) Monitor {
  return new_(n,f,c) }
```

10.2.2 Implementation

The implementation differs from the nonconditioned monitors by the following changes: In the representation, i.e., the struct that defines the monitor, the monitor function
FuncSpectrum is replaced by NFuncSpectrum, and the component CondSpectrum
for the conditions is added.

The signature of the constructor is adjusted:

```
func new_(n uint, f NFuncSpectrum, c CondSpectrum) Monitor {
  ... // wie vorher\query{Should this read "As before"?}
  x.NFuncSpectrum, x.CondSpectrum = f, c
}
```

and the line

```
  x.FuncSpectrum = f
```

is replaced by

```
  x.NFuncSpectrum, x.CondSpectrum = f, c
```

The implementations of the functions Wait and Signal are identical; only their names
start with a *lower case* letter to document that they are not exported, but only used in the
package. The function SignalAll is missing because it is not needed. The functions
Blocked and Awaited are identical.

Only F is more complex, because the synchronization is done with wait and signal:

```
func (x *monitor) F (i uint) Any {
  x.Mutex.Lock()
  if ! x.CondSpectrum (i) {
    x.wait (i)
  }
  y := x.NFuncSpectrum (i)
  x.Permutation.Permute()
  for j := uint(0); j < x.uint; j++ {
    n := x.Permutation.F(j)
    if x.CondSpectrum (n) {
      x.signal (n)
    }
  }
  if x.nu > 0 {
    x.u.Unlock()
  } else {
    x.Mutex.Unlock()
  }
  return y
}
```

Table 10.1 Synchronization of semaphores

Function	Condition	Statement
P	val > 0	val- -
V	true	val++

10.3   Semaphores

A particularly simple example of the use of universal monitors is the construction of general semaphores. Their synchronization is described in Table 10.1.

The implementation with a universal monitor realizes the construction from Sect. 9.6.6:

```
package sem
import (. "nU/obj"; "nU/mon")

const (
  p = iota
  v
)

type monitor struct {
  mon.Monitor
}

func newM (n uint) Semaphore {
  val := n
  x  := new(monitor)
  f  := func (a Any, i uint) Any {
          if i == p {
            if val == 0 {
              x.Monitor.Wait (v)
            }
            val-- --
          } else { // i == v
            val++
            x.Monitor.Signal (v)
          }
          return val
        }
  x.Monitor = mon.New (2, f)
  return x
}

func (x *monitor) P() { x.F (nil, p) }
func (x *monitor) V() { x.F (nil, v) }
```

A touch more elegant is the implementation with a conditioned monitor:

```
package sem
import "nU/cmon"
```

```
type conditionedMonitor {
  cmon.Monitor
}

func newCM (n uint) Semaphore {
  val := n
  x := new(conditionedMonitor)
  c := func (i uint) bool {
        if i == p {
           return val > 0
        }
        return true // i == v
      }
  f := func (i uint) uint {
        if i == p {
          val-- --
        } else { // i == v
          val++
        }
        return val
      }
  x.Monitor = cmon.New (2, f, c)
  return x
}

func (x *conditionedMonitor) P() { x.F (p) }
func (x *conditionedMonitor) V() { x.F (v) }
```

10.4   Account

Our standard problem of an account without debit is a simple generalization of the semaphores (P and V are simply special cases of Draw or Deposit of the amount 1).
The situation is completely described in the synchronization table in Table 10.2 with var
balance uint.

The corresponding universal monitor results immediately from this table; with the specification from Sect 9.3.3, the implementation is as follows:

```
package acc
import (. "nU/obj"; "nU/mon")

type monitor struct {
```

Table 10.2 Account monitor

Function	Condition	Statement
Deposit (a uint)	true	balance += a
Draw (a uint)	balance >= a	balance -= a

```
    mon.Monitor
}

func newM() Account {
  balance := uint(0)
  x := new(monitor)
  f := func (a Any, i uint) Any {
        if i == deposit {
           x.Monitor.Signal (deposit)
           balance += a.(uint)
        } else { // draw
           if balance < a.(uint) {
             x.Monitor.Wait (deposit)
           }
           balance -= a.(uint)
        }
        return balance
     }
  x.Monitor = mon.New (2, f)
  return x
}

func (x *monitor) Deposit (a uint) uint {
  return x.Monitor.F (a, deposit).(uint)
}

func (x *monitor) Draw (a uint) uint {
  return x.Monitor.F (a, draw).(uint)
}
```

10.5   Bounded Buffers

Also this classical problem can be solved very elegantly with a universal monitor:

```
package mbuf
import (. "nU/obj"; "nU/bbuf", "nU/mon")

type monitor struct {
  mon.Monitor
}

func newM (a Any, n uint) MBuffer {
  buffer := bbuf.New (a, n)
  x := new(monitor)
  f := func (a Any, i uint) Any {
        if i == ins {
           buffer.Ins (a)
           x.Monitor.Signal (ins)
           return nil
        }
        if buffer.Num() == 0 {
           x.Monitor.Wait (ins)
        }
```

Table 10.3 Barber monitor

Function	Condition	Statement
Customer	true	n++
Barber	n > 0	n- -

```
        return buffer.Get ()
    }
  x.Monitor = mon.New (2, f)
  return x
}

func (x *monitor) Ins (a Any) { x.Monitor.F (a, ins) }
func (x *monitor) Get () Any { return x.Monitor.F (nil, get) }
```

10.6   The Sleeping Barber

The problem of the sleeping barber in its simple form can also be solved with this method. For this purpose, only Table 10.3 must be implemented in a conditioned universal monitor.

The translation into source code is trivial; instead, we show the slightly more elaborate source code for an unconditioned monitor:

```
package barb
import (. "nU/obj"; "nU/mon")

const (customer = iota; barber)

type monitor struct {
  mon.Monitor
}

func newM () Barber {
  var n uint
  var m mon.Monitor
  f := func (a Any, i uint) Any {
        if i == customer {
          n++
          m.Signal (customer)
        } else { // barber
          for n == 0 {
            m.Wait (customer)
          }
          n-- --
        }
        return n
      }
  m = mon.New (2, f)
  x := new(monitor)
```

```
   x.Monitor = m
   return x
}


func (x *monitor) Customer() { x.F (nil, customer) }
func (x *monitor) Barber() { x.F (nil, barber) }
```

10.7 Barrier Synchronization

This problem can also be easily solved with a universal monitor:

```
package barr
import (. "nU/obj"; "nU/mon" )

type monitor struct {
  mon.Monitor
}

func newM (n uint) Barrier {
  involved := n
  waiting := uint(0)
  x := new(monitor)

  f := func (a Any, i uint) Any {
         waiting++
         if waiting < involved {
           x.Monitor.Wait (0)
         } else {
           for waiting > 0 {
             waiting-- --
             if waiting > 0 {
               x.Monitor.Signal (0)
             }
           }
         }
         return waiting
       }
  x.Monitor = mon.New (1, f)
  return x
}

func (x *monitor) Wait() { x.F (nil, 0) }
```

10.8 The Readers–Writers Problem

A modification of the synchronization table, which led to the solution of the first readers–writers problem with a universal critical section, also provides a solution with a universal monitor (see Table 10.4), if the interface from Sect. 4.12.6 is extended by the respective constructors.

Table 10.4 Readers–writers monitor

Function	Condition	Statement
ReaderIn	nW == 0	nR++
ReaderOut	true	nR- -
WriterIn	nR == 0 && nW == 0	nW = 1
WriterOut	true	nW = 0

In the resulting translation into the following source code of a (nonconditioned) monitor

```
package rw
import (. "nU/obj"; "nU/mon")

type monitor1 struct {
  mon.Monitor
}

func newM1() ReaderWriter {
  x := new(monitor1)
  var nR, nW uint
  f := func (a Any, k uint) Any {
        switch k {
        case readerIn:
          for nW > 0 {
            x.Wait (readerIn)
          }
          nR++
          x.Signal (readerIn)
        case readerOut:
          nR-- --
          if nR == 0 {
            x.Signal (writerIn)
          }
        case writerIn:
          for nR > 0 || nW > 0 {
            x.Wait (writerIn)
          }
          nW = 1
        case writerOut:
          nW = 0
          if x.Awaited (readerIn) {
            x.Signal (readerIn)
          } else {
            x.Signal (writerIn)
          }
        }
        return nil
      }
  x.Monitor = mon.New (4, f)
  return x
}
```

```
func (x *monitor1) ReaderIn()  { x.F (nil, readerIn)  }
func (x *monitor1) ReaderOut() { x.F (nil, readerOut) }
func (x *monitor1) WriterIn()  { x.F (nil, writerIn)  }
func (x *monitor1) WriterOut() { x.F (nil, writerOut) }
```

two superfluous condition variables for the exit protocols are created, and redundant Signal operations are inserted for them; however, this does not affect the execution sequence significantly, since the associated Wait operations are not called,

The priority of the processes after a Signal operation is given by the order in the for loop within the function F—i.e., its numbering; by this order reader versus writer priority can be determined.

As an—in general probably optimal—alternative, a "stochastic" fairness is given by the installation of a random permutation around the loop in the function F exactly as in the function val1 in the universal critical sections (see Sect. 6.1.2).

The constructor for a conditioned monitor is, of course, much more elegant; we will show this in the next example.

10.9   The Left–Right Problem

The first left–right problem is quite simple, so we will limit ourselves here to the more interesting case of the second problem. Its synchronization table is given in Sect. 6.5 (Table 6.3).

Here, is the corresponding constructor for a conditioned monitor:

```
package lr
import "nU/cmon"

type conditionedMonitor2 struct {
  cmon.Monitor
}

func newCM2() LeftRight {
  x := new(conditionedMonitor2)
  var nL, nR uint
  c := func (i uint) bool {
        switch i {
        case leftIn:
          return nR == 0 && (x.Blocked (rightIn) == 0 || nL == 0)
        case rightIn:
          return nL == 0 && (x.Blocked (leftIn) == 0 || nR == 0)
        }
        return true
      }
  f := func (i uint) uint {
        switch i {
        case leftIn:
          nL++
          return nL
        case leftOut:
          nL-- --
```

```
                return nL
          case rightIn:
            nR++
          case rightOut:
            nR-- --
        }
        return nR
      }
  x.Monitor = cmon.New (4, f, c)
  return x
}
```

10.10 The Dining Philosophers

This problem can, of course, be solved with universal monitors—by adding the respective
constructors to the interface from Sect. 4.14. We present two solutions with the denotations
in that section.

Here is a simple approach:

```
package phil
import (. "nU/obj"; "nU/mon")

type monitorUnfair struct {
  mon.Monitor
}

func newMU() Philos {
  var m mon.Monitor
  f := func (a Any, i uint) Any {
          p := a.(uint)
          if i == lock {
            status[p] = starving
            for status[left(p)] == dining || status[right(p)] ==
  dining {
              m.Wait (p)
            }
          } else { // unlock
            m.Signal (left(p))
            m.Signal (right(p))
          }
          return nil
        }
  m = mon.New (NPhilos, f, nil)
  x := new(monitorUnfair)
  x.Monitor = m
  return x
}

func (x *monitorUnfair) Lock (p uint) {
  status[p] = hungry
  x.F (p, lock)
  status[p] = dining
```

```
}

func (x *monitorUnfair) Unlock (p uint) {
  status[p] = thinking
  x.F (p, unlock)
}
```

However, this solution is just as unfair as DIJKSTRA's semaphore solution: two philosophers can *starve* the colleague sitting between them.

And here is the solution with a conditioned universal monitor based on the semaphore approach at the end of Sect. 4.14, where the simultaneous pickup of *both* forks is the decisive action:

```
package phil
import "nU/cmon"

type conditionedMonitor struct {
  cmon.Monitor
}

func newCM() Philos {
  nForks := make([]uint, 5)
  for i := uint(0); i < 5; i++ {
    nForks[i] = 2
  }
  c := func (i uint) bool {
        if i < 5 { // Lock
          return nForks[i] == 2
        }
        return true // Unlock
      }
  f := func (i uint) uint {
        if i < 5 {
          nForks[left(i)]--
          nForks[right(i)]--
          return i
        }
        i -= 5
        nForks[left(i)]++
        nForks[right(i)]++
        return i
      }
  x := new (conditionedMonitor)
  x.Monitor = cmon.New (5, f, c)
  return x
}

func (x *conditionedMonitor) Lock (i uint) {
  status[i] = hungry
  x.F (lock + i)
  status[i] = dining
}

func (x *conditionedMonitor) Unlock (i uint) {
  status[i] = thinking
```

```
x.F (5 + i)
}
```

Of course, the fair solution of DIJKSTRA can be implemented *also* in this form, but we leave that as an exercise.

10.11 The Cigarette Smokers

It is obvious that also *this* problem can be solved very elegantly with a universal monitor. Also in this example, the implementation is very similar to the one with a universal critical section; the difference consists essentially of a modified parameterization in order to use the Wait and Signal operations optimally:

```
package smok
import (. "nU/obj"; "nU/mon")

type monitor struct {
  mon.Monitor
}

func others (u uint) (uint, uint) {
  return (u + 1)
}

func newM() Smokers {
  var avail [3]bool
  smoking := false
  x := new(monitor)
  f := func (a Any, i uint) Any {
          u := a.(uint)
          u1, u2 := others (u)
          switch i {
          case agent:
            if smoking {
              x.Wait (3)
            }
            avail[u1], avail[u2] = true, true
            x.Signal (u)
          case smokerOut:
            smoking = false
            x.Signal (3)
            return uint(3)
          case smokerIn:
            if ! (avail[u1] && avail[u2]) {
              x.Wait (u)
            }
            smoking = true
            avail[u1], avail[u2] = false, false
          }
          return u
        }
  x.Monitor = mon.New (4, f)
```

```
   return x
}

func (x *monitor) Agent (u uint) { x.F (u, agent) }
func (x *monitor) SmokerIn (u uint) { x.F (u, smokerIn) }
func (x *monitor) SmokerOut () { x.F (u, smokerOut) }
```

Of course, this is also possible with a conditioned universal monitor:

```
package smok
import "nU/cmon"

type condMonitor struct {
  cmon.Monitor
}

func newCM () Smokers {
  var avail [3]bool
  x := new (condMonitor)
  var smoking bool
  p := func (i uint) bool {
        if i < 3 { // Agent
          return ! smoking
        }
        if i == 6 { // SmokerOut
          return true
        }
        u1, u2 := others (i - 3) // SmokerIn
        return avail[u1] && avail[u2]
      }
  f := func (i uint) uint {
        if i < 3 { // Agent
          u1, u2 := others (i)
          avail[u1], avail[u2] = true, true
        } else if i == 6 { // SmokerOut
          smoking = false
        } else { // SmokerIn
          smoking = true
          u1, u2 := others (i - 3)
          avail[u1], avail[u2] = false, false
        }
        return 0
      }
  x.Monitor = cmon.New (7, f, p)
  return x
}

func (x *condMonitor) Agent (u uint) { x.F (u) }
func (x *condMonitor) SmokerIn (u uint) { x.F (3 + u) }
func (x *condMonitor) SmokerOut () { x.F (uint(6)) }
```

Message Passing

11

Abstract

All previously introduced programming language constructions synchronize processes by accessing shared variables, i.e., they require shared memory. For distributed applications, however, a paradigm is needed in which processes are not dependent on that: communication by *message passing*.

The chapter begins with the introduction of channels and the definition of *synchronous* and *asynchronous* message passing, and simple examples and elegant applications of these concepts: The construction of semaphores, bounded buffers, and networks of filters. Then, "selective waiting" is introduced, which gives message passing the expressiveness of all other synchronization constructs and enables the introduction of the client–server paradigm. In Go, "guarded selective waiting" can also be realized, which contributes greatly to the clarity of algorithms. Both concepts are again illustrated by many examples known from the previous chapters. The chapter concludes with the proof of the equivalence of the expressiveness of the semaphore concept and message passing and a concise comparison of the language means of the monitor concept and the client–server paradigm.

11.1   Channels and Messages

As was already indicated in the Introduction (in the Go part of Sect. 1.9.1), this chapter is strongly influenced by the recommendation of Go developers, that not *synchronization of accesses to shared data* should be the essential aspect of nonsequential programming, but rather to *access shared data by means of communication*. This can, indeed, be considered as a certain shift in the focus of the NSP paradigms.

Processes could communicate directly with each other via their process numbers or the like, but—significantly influenced by HOARE's groundbreaking work [5]—another approach has prevailed, which models the connections of computers in a network: An abstract data

© Springer Fachmedien Wiesbaden GmbH, part of Springer Nature 2021
C. Maurer, *Nonsequential and Distributed Programming with Go*,
https://doi.org/10.1007/978-3-658-29782-4_11

type for *channels* with atomic operations to *send* and *receive*, so that processes can exchange messages. In principle, channels are tied to a type, i.e., only messages of *that* type can be sent on a channel for which they are declared.

This, however, is "annulled" if the messages are of type `Any ( interface{})`— so quasi *everything* can be transmitted over the corresponding channels. We need this in Sect. 11.7 on *guarded selective waiting* and will also make extensive use of it in Chaps. 13 on *network-wide message passing* and 14 on *universal far monitors*.

Processes in a call to *receive* a message from a channel are principally blocked, as long as the channel does not yet contain a message.

For the *sending* of a message two concepts are distinguished:

- *synchronous* message passing,
  message passing, where a channel cannot buffer messages, i.e., the sender is blocked until another process is ready to receive and has got the message, and
- *asynchronous* message passing,
  where a channel is a *queue of finite capacity* > 0, so that a process can continue immediately after sending unless the channel—i.e., the queue—is not full.
  In this case, sending and receiving is done according to the FIFO principle, i.e., the messages are received exactly in the order in which they were sent.

In Sects. 11.7.1 on the equivalence of message passing and the semaphore concept and 11.6.2 on bounded buffers, we will show that both concepts can be transferred to each other and, therefore, are principally equivalent as programming tools.

With asynchronous message passing—apart from the fact that the senders can go ahead of the receivers in time—situations can occur that are not compatible with the idea of an *infinite* capacity of channels, because a sending process must be blocked *in any case*:

- *until receipt of an answer*, if it is dependent on a process having received its message, or
- *for an undetermined time* if the (de facto *finite!*) capacity of the channel buffer is filled up by messages that have not been received.

This problem does not arise with synchronous message passing; messages do not have to be buffered in the channels because they are transmitted when a sending process continues. This form of synchronization of sender and receiver is also called *rendezvous*, because the processes involved communicate synchronously.

The following analogy fits this: *Asynchronous message passing* corresponds to the transmission of messages by letter or E-mail, and *synchronous message passing* corresponds to personal conversation or by telephone.

In the literature, there are different opinions on the question as to which of these two methods should be preferred: The *advantages* of synchronous message passing, in which a sender can rely on the fact that its message has arrived, a receiver has up-to-date information from the sender, and no buffer memory is required for the channels, are countered by its *disadvantages*: a certain restriction of liveliness, since *principally* one of the two communication partners is blocked until the other is ready to communicate, and has as a higher susceptibility to deadlocks.

But much more important is a decisive advantage of *both* methods: Since no shared memory is required, it is not a matter of synchronizing concurrent accesses to shared data. Solutions to problems by means of the exchange of messages are rather, in principle, *distributed algorithms*—independent of whether the processes involved run on *one* computer or on *several*—even if this chapter only deals with message passing between concurrent lightweight processes within an operating system process.

This chapter presents many examples of the construction of algorithms for lock and condition synchronization using message passing techniques. We limit ourselves to Go, because this is one of the strengths of this programming language. In Go, channels are "first class objects"—see https://golang.org/doc/faq#csp.

11.1.1 Syntax of Message Passing in Go

The developers of Go decided to follow the concept of HOARE. The syntax of their language closely leans on the formalism of his paper [5]; the syntactic proximity to Occam cannot be overlooked. (HOARE was involved in the development of this language).

Go supports synchronous message passing to an extent that only a few languages do (e.g., Occam, Pascal-FC, and SR and its successor MPD), as well as asynchronous (SR/MPD).

As a constructor for channel types, the identifier `chan` is used:

- For each type `T`, `chan T` is the type of channels for messages of type `T`.

Channels are *reference types*; therefore, each channel must be initialized with the `make` function. With the second parameter, its capacity—and, thus, its transmission behaviour—can be determined: For an expression `a` of type `int` or `uint` with a value `>= 0`

```
make(chan T, a)
```

provides a channel for messages of type `T` with a buffer size of the value of `a`. If there is no `a` (or if `a == 0`) the channel realizes *synchronous* message passing, otherwise *asynchronous* message passing. (However, the value for the buffer size must not be too large, because otherwise the runtime error " `out of memory`" occurs.)

The syntax for the communication operations is very short—similar to that of Occam:

- For a channel `c` of type `chan T` and an expression `a` of type `T`, `c <- a` is the statement to send `a` on `c`.
- For a channel `c` of type `chan T`, `<-c` is an expression of type `T` for a message received on `c`.

Typical statements of a *receiver* are, therefore, x = <-c for a declared variable var
x T or x := <-c.

Here for comparison the corresponding syntax in Occam:

- For a channel c of type chan T and an expression a of type T, c ! a is the statement
  to send a on c.
- For a channel c of type chan T, ? c is an expression of type T for a message received
  on c.
  A typical statement of a *receiver* is c ? x for a variable x of type T.

Communication by message passing can be accurately interpreted as a *distributed value
assignment*: The sender evaluates an expression, and the receiver assigns it to a variable or
a parameter of a function call.

The example

```
func order (c, r chan int, d chan bool) {
  c <- 1
  c <- 2
  println (<-r)
  d <- true
}

func add (c, r chan int) {
  r <- <-c + <-c
}

func main () {
  c, r := make (chan int), make (chan int)
  done := make (chan bool)
  go order (c, r, done) // Auftraggeber
  go add (c, r) // Addierer
  <-done
}
```

shows all aspects mentioned so far.

It also indicates another paradigm that goes beyond simple synchronous message passing:
The *remote procedure calls* or *extended rendezvous*, with which a sender expects a response
to its message and is blocked until it has received it.

Even our old counting problem from Sect. 1.6 can be easily solved by message passing:
At each of the two entrance gates to the zoo in Berlin, we set up a transmitter that sends
its identity to the administration each time a person enters. The administration receives this
information, increases the corresponding visitor counter and is, thus, continuously informed
about the number of its visitors:

```
package main
import (. "time"; "math/rand")

var (
  counter [2]int // lion- and elephant-gate
  c chan int
)

func gate (t int) {
  for {
    Sleep(Duration(rand.Int63n(1e9))) // person through gate
    c <- t
  }
}

func main() { // administration of the zoo
  c = make(chan int)
  for t := 0; t < 2; t++ {
    go gate(t)
  }
  for {
    counter[<-c]++
    println("lion-gate ", counter[0],
            " / elephant-gate ", counter[1])
  }
}
```

The concept of message passing also makes sense if the content of the messages is irrelevant: It can also be used as pure means of synchronization. We will get to know many more examples of this.

11.1.2 Synchronous Message Passing with Asynchronous

A *synchronous* send statement

```
c <- a
```

can be combined with an *asynchronous* Send/Recv and a channel ok of type chan int through the sequence

```
Send(c, a)
Recv(ok)
```

where the reception of the message must be acknowledged by

```
Send(ok, 0)
```

11.2   Asynchronous Communication

First, we show that the expressive power of asynchronous message passing is sufficient to reproduce *semaphores* and *bounded buffers*.

11.2.1 Semaphores

Binary semaphores can be constructed with synchronous message passing on two channels `var p, v chan bool` by generating a central *server* with a `go` statement:

```
func binSemServer() {
  p, v := make(chan int), make(chan int)
  for {
    <-p
    <-v
  }
}
```

where the `P` and `V`-operations are simply transmissions of irrelevant values on the corresponding channel:

```
func P() { p <- 0 }
func V() { v <- 0 }
```

However, asynchronous message passing offers a simpler alternative: It does not require a central process and only *one* channel

```
  c := make(chan int, 1)
```

initially filled with a message by `c <- 0`:

```
func P() { <-c }
func V() { c <- 0 }
```

According to this example, the construction of *general semaphores* with the help of asynchronous send and receive operations "lies on the hand"; for this, only as many send statements have to be executed in advance until the initial value of the semaphore is reached:

```
package sem

type semaphore struct {
  c chan int
}

func new_(n uint) Semaphore {
  x := new(semaphore)
  x.c = make(chan int, n)
  for i := uint(0); i < n; i++ {
    x.c <- 0
  }
```

```
    return x
}

func (x *semaphore) P() { <-x.c }
func (x *semaphore) V() { x.c <- 0 }
```

This implementation is also correct in the case of `n == 0`. (Proof: Exercise! Hint: Synchronous message passing.)

So we have proved:

▶   The concept of asynchronous message passing is at least as expressive as the semaphore concept.

11.2.2 Bounded Buffers

In a very similar style to the semaphores, also bounded buffers can be implemented:

```
package mbbuf
import . "nU/obj"

type channel struct {
  c chan Any
}

func newCh (a Any, n uint) MBuffer {
  x := new(channel)
  x.c = make(chan Any, n)
  return x
}

func (x *channel) Ins (a Any) { x.c <- a }
func (x *channel) Get() Any { return Clone (<-x.c) }
```

The brevity and elegance of this version compared to the implementations presented in the previous chapters is, of course, not surprising, because behind the scenes of asynchronous sending and receiving *that* is found that is expressed here. You should carefully consider these examples—even if they are trivial: They are really predestinated as an "*abstract*" for a short and concise characterization of the asynchronous message passing.

11.2.3 The Cigarette Smokers

Another example for the use of asynchronous communication is the solution of a problem with asynchronous message passing, which cannot be surpassed in elegance:

```
package smok
```

```
type channel struct {
  ch []chan uint
}

func newCh() Smokers {
  x := new(channel)
  x.ch = make([]chan uint, 4)
  for i := 0; i < 3; i++ {
    x.ch[i] = make(chan uint, 1)
  }
  x.ch[3] = make(chan uint, 1)
  x.ch[3] <- 0 // A
  return x
}

func (x *channel) Agent (u uint) {
  <-x.ch[3]
  x.ch[u] <- 0
}

func (x *channel) SmokerIn (u uint) {
  <-x.ch[u]
}

func (x *channel) SmokerOut () {
  x.ch[3] <- 0
}
```

In the beginning, the landlady puts two randomly selected utensils on the table (program line A), otherwise only when called by a smoker who has finished smoking.

11.3   Networks of Filters

Before we address the problem, to transfer the results of the previous section to the *synchronous* case, we will show with some other examples that synchronous message passing is suitable to construct *filters* for processing data, known, e.g., as "*pipes*" on the Unix command level.

11.3.1 Caesar's Secret Messages

As an introductory example, we reproduce the encryption method of CAESAR, who dictated his messages to one of his officers, who moved each letter by three positions in order to deliver the encrypted message to a messenger on horseback:

```
package main
import ("os"; "bufio")
```

```
const lf = 10
var input = bufio.NewReader(os.Stdin)

func cap (b byte) byte {
  if b >= 'a' {
    return b - 'a' + 'A'
  }
  return b
}

func accepted (b byte) bool {
  B := cap(b)
  if 'A' <= B && B <= 'Z' || b == ' ' || b == lf {
    return true
  }
  return false
}

func dictate (t chan byte) {
  for {
    b, _ := input.ReadByte()
    if accepted (b) {
      t <- b
    }
  }
}

func encrypt (t, c chan byte) {
  for {
    b := <-t
    if b == ' ' || b == lf {
      c <- b
    } else if cap(b) < 'X' {
      c <- b + 3
    } else {
      c <- b - 23
    }
  }
}

func send (c, m chan byte) {
  b := byte(0)
  for b != lf {
    b = <-c
    print(string(b))
  }

  println()
  m <- 0
}
```

```
func main () {
  textchan := make(chan byte)
  cryptchan := make(chan byte)
  messengerchan := make(chan byte)
  go dictate (textchan)                    // Caesar
  go encrypt (textchan, cryptchan)         // officer
  go send (cryptchan, messengerchan)       // messenger
  <-messengerchan
}
```

11.3.2 The Sieve of Eratosthenes

Such filters can also be connected in series several times. An example of this is the sieve of ERATOSTHENES for the output of the first prime numbers, where in a given ordered list of numbers, the first is split off as a prime number, and its multiples are "sieved" before the list is passed on. The channel architecture shown in Fig. 11.1 results directly from the procedure.

Here are the details:

```
package main // Eratosthenes

const N = 313

func start (out chan uint) {
  a := uint(2)
  out <- a
  a++
  for {
    out <- a
    a += 2
  }
}

func sieve (in, out, off chan uint) {
  primenumber := <-in
  off <- primenumber
  for {
```

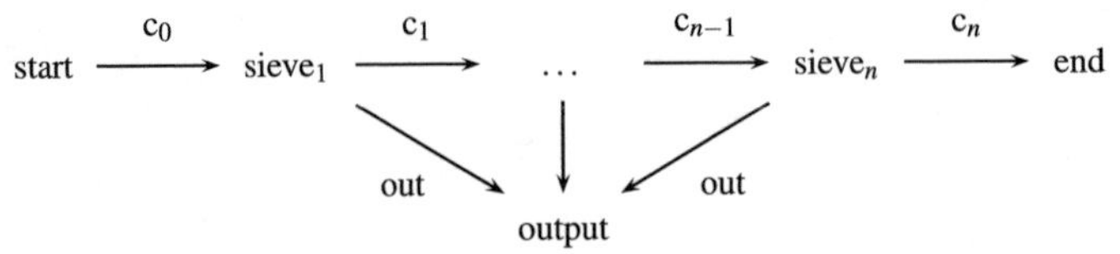

Fig. 11.1 Channel architecture of the sieve of ERATOSTHENES

```
    a := <-in
    if (a % primenumber) != 0 { out <- a }
  }
}

func stop (in chan uint) {
  for { <-in }
}

func write (in chan uint, d chan bool) {
  for i := 1; i < N; i++ {
    print (<-in, " ")
  }
  println ()
  d <- true
}

func main () {
  var c [N] chan uint
  for i := 0; i < N; i++ {
    c[i] = make (chan uint)
  }
  out := make (chan uint)
  done := make (chan bool)
  go start (c[0]) // Start
  for i := 1; i < N; i++ {
    go sieve (c[i-1], c[i], out) // sieve[i]
  }
  go stop (c[N - 1]) // end
  go write (out, done) // output
  <-done
}
```

Remarkable is that for the output *one* channel is sufficient.

11.3.3 Mergesort

An example with a completely different architecture in which the filters are nested into each other is mergesort—if you follow the paths of the messages, you will notice that also in this case the channel architecture hits a core idea of the algorithm—it is a binary tree:

```
package main // mergesort
import "math/rand"

const (
  N = 128 // Potenz von 2!
  max = 2 * N - 2
)
var (
```

```
  c [max+1] chan int
  done chan bool
)

func generate() {
  for s := 0; s < N; s++ {
    n := rand.Intn(1000)
    c[max] <- n // unsortiert an die Ausgabe
    c[s] <- n // und zu den Sortierern
  }
}

func nAwaitedNumbers (i int) int {
  e, d, m := N / 2, 1, N - 2
  for m > i {
    d *= 2; m -= d; e /= 2
  }
  return e
}

func sort (i int) { // i = number of sorting processes
  rL, rR := 2 * i, 2 * i + 1 // number of the left and
  t := N + i // right channels to receive and send
  e := nAwaitedNumbers(i) // number of the expected
  e0 := 1 // and the messages received on the left
  nL := <-c[rL]
  e1 := 1 // and on the right
  nR := <-c[rR]
  for e0 <= e && e1 <= e {
    if nL <= nR {
      c[t] <- nL
      e0++
      if e0 <= e {
        nL = <-c[rL]
      }
    } else {
      c[t] <- nR
      e1++
      if e1 <= e {
        nR = <-c[rR]
      }

    }
  }
  for e0 <= e {
    c[t] <- nL
    e0++; if e0 <= e {
      nL = <-c[rL]
    }
  }
  for e1 <= e {
```

```
      c[t] <- nR
      e1++
      if e1 <= e {
        nR = <-c[rR]
      }
    }
  }
}

func write() {
  println("randomly generated:")
  for i := 0; i < N; i++ {
    print(<-c[max], " ")
  }
  println(); println("sorted:")
  for i := 0; i < N; i++ {
    print(<-c[max], " ")
  }
  println(); done <- true
}

func main() {
  for i := 0; i <= max; i++ {
    c[i] = make(chan int)
  }
  done = make(chan bool)
  go generate()
  for i := 0; i <= N - 2; i++ {
    go sort(i)
  }
  go write()
  <-done
}
```

11.3.4 The Dining Philosophers

This section has nothing to do with *filtering* but it fits here, because it uses also *synchronous* message passing. The most elegant solution of the problem of the dining philosophers with message passing is that of BEN-ARI in [2]. We extend the interface of the package phil from Sect. 4.14 by the constructor newCh and add the translation of this solution to Go to the package equipped with asymmetry to prevent deadlocks:

```
package phil
import . "nU/lockn"

type channel struct {
  ch []chan int
}
```

```
func newCh() Philos {
  x := new(channel)
  x.ch = make([]chan int, 5)
  for p := uint(0); p < 5; p++ {
    x.ch[p] = make(chan int)
  }
  for p := uint(0); p < 5; p++ {
    go func (i uint) {
      x.fork (i)
    }(p)
  }
  return x
}

func (x *channel) fork (p uint) {
  for {
    x.ch[p] <- 0
    <-x.ch[p]
  }
}

func (x *channel) Lock (p uint) {
  status[p] = hungry
  if p % 2 == 0 {
    <-x.ch[left (p)]
    <-x.ch[p]
  } else {
    <-x.ch[p]
    <-x.ch[left (p)]
  }
}

func (x *channel) Unlock (p uint) {
  x.ch[p] <- 0
  x.ch[left (p)] <- 0
}
```

BEN- ARI explains his implementation, in principle, as follows: Each `fork` process branched off in the constructor is connected through a channel with "its" philosopher. Hungry philosophers wait for the two `fork` processes from their neighbours that eventually send messages (with irrelevant values). When a `fork` process has sent a message, it is blocked until it receives a message from its philosopher, who has finished eating. As an exercise, we recommended to program the asymmetrical solution from Sect. 4.14 with message passing (for the solution, see package `nU/phil`).

11.4 Selective Waiting

To transfer the results of Sect. 11.2 on asynchronous communication to the *synchronous* case, we turn to the problem of constructing semaphores with *synchronous message passing*. However, the simple generalization of the server for binary semaphores is not sufficient, because the sequence `<-cP; <-cV` in the function

```
func semServer(n uint) {
  cP, cV = make(chan bool), make(chan bool)
  val := n
  for {
    if val == 0 {
      <-cV
      val = 1
    } else { // val > 0
      <-cP
      val--
      <-cV
      val++
    }
  }
}
```

leads to the fact that a P-operation, a sending to the channel cP, blocks all further processes—no matter how large val is—at their P-operations, until a V-operation, a sending to the channel cV has happened. The server should, therefore, be able to "listen" concurrently on *both* channels.

So, we have not taken a step further but are facing a disaster of strict alternation, i.e., the approach is *also* only suitable as a protocol for mutual exclusion; the application to a bounded buffer would principally give the capacity 1 to it.

A comparable dilemma also arises with the readers–writers problem: If we establish four channels inR, outR, inW, and outW—one for each of the four protocols—the procedure is only clearly regulated in the case nW > 0, because then the exit of an active writer via a message to the channel outW is the only protocol that can be executed:

```
if nW == 1 {
  <-outW
  nW = 0
}
```

The alternative nW == 0 does not help us, neither in the case of nR > 0 because readers may enter as well as exit, i.e., messages could be received on inR as well as on outR, nor in the case of nR == 0, because then entries of readers as well as of writers are possible, i.e., also in this case messages can arrive from two channels, inR and inW.

Consequently, for the solution of these problems, it does not suffice to only send and receive messages over channels. Even simple approaches to solve classical problems fail, if a process can always receive messages only from *one* channel. Rather—as the above examples suggest—a process must be able to wait concurrently for messages from *several* channels to receive one of them.

Like other languages that support message passing, Go provides a construct for *selective* receiving and sending, i.e., for a nondeterministic selection from *those* channels where processes are ready for reception and/or transmission.

The syntax is very similar and uses the same keyword as other languages in which semantically related constructs exist (all of which are basically based on the corresponding construct in Ada):

```
select {
case a: // communication operation
    ...     // further statements
case b: // communication operation
    ...     // further statements
    ...     // further "cases", if necessary
}
```

whereby the communication operations a, b, ..., are statements for sending an expression or for assignments of the values of expressions received to variables, which usually use *pairwise disjoint* channels. This construct is semantically reminiscent of the Unix system call select for synchronous I/O multiplexing (see /usr/include/sys/select.h and *manpage* of select).

The select statement has the following semantics (see https://golang.org/ref/spec# Select_statements): Among the channels where there is a communication partner ready to exchange messages (in the case of a send statement a process waiting for a message, in the case of an expression to receive, a process that has sent a message) exactly *one* of the alternatives is selected *nondetermistically* from the runtime system, and the message is received and sent, respectively; then, if necessary, the statements following the send or receive operation are executed under mutual exclusion. If there is no communication partner in the above sense, the process that executes the select statement is blocked, until this is the case.

In order to avoid this, Go provides the default alternative. It is subordinated to the communication statements in select; the following statements are, therefore, only executed if message passing due to a lack of communication-ready partners does not happen at the time of the call. If the default branch is empty, i.e., if it does not contain any statements, this, of course, causes the select statement to be effect free, especially that it does not block the calling process, which is desirable in certain situations.

A select statement, in which all channels involved have the value nil definitely blocks; this fact is fundamental, because it permits *guarded selective waiting* (see Sect. 11.7).

If only *receive statements* may occur in the select statements, this is called *selective receiving*. This is sufficient for many tasks; Occam, for example, does not know any *selective sending*.

The so-called *symmetric selection* whose alternatives contain both receive and send statements, in the synchronous case is highly prone to deadlocks, as the following example with two channels c and d shows:

```
func A() {
   select {
   case c <- a:
      . . .
   case x := <-d:
      . . .
   }
}

func B() {
   select {
   case y := <-c:
      . . .
   case d <- b:
      . . .
   }
}
```

—in all branches there are partners ready for communication, but a nondeterministic selection can lead to the first branch being selected in one function and the second branch being selected in the other …The synchronous case, therefore, requires corresponding care in the development of algorithms. In the asynchronous case, this is unproblematic, as long as there are no blockages due to a lack of buffer capacity of a participating channel.

11.5   The Client–Server Paradigm

With the select construct, many distributed problems can be solved that can be summarized under the paradigm of the *client–server principle*: A *server* provides services to *clients*; the clients send requests to the server and wait for its response—in both cases with synchronous operations.

A systematic method for developing the algorithms is simply the transfer of the tasks of a monitor to a server process, whereby the number of established channels is determined by the number of the monitor functions. So, the channels are virtually equipped with a semantics in the following sense: The server process can decide—depending on internal conditions— whether or not it wants to receive messages from certain channels, i.e., whether it allows the corresponding sending processes to continue or blocks them. For the server, this poses the problem of being able to react concurrently to messages from different channels, which is possible with the selective reception construct.

11.6   Synchronous Communication

Using the methods from the last two sections, we are now able to apply the algorithms from Sect. 11.2 on asynchronous communication to the *synchronous* case.

11.6.1 Semaphores

As a first example for such a construction we show how general (and, therefore, also binary) semaphores can be implemented with synchronous message passing:

```go
package sem

type channel struct {
  p, v chan int
}

func newCh (n uint) Semaphore {
  x := new(channel)
  x.p, x.v = make(chan int), make(chan int)
  go func() {
    val := n
    for {
      if val == 0 {
        <-x.v
        val = 1
      } else { // val > 0
        select {
        case <-x.p:
          val--
        case <-x.v:
          val++
        }
      }
    }
  }()
  return x
}

func (x *channel) P() { x.p <- 0 }
func (x *channel) V() { x.v <- 0 }
```

11.6.2 Bounded Buffers

Bounded buffers can be implemented according to the same principle; consequently with two channels to differentiate the requests for inserting and getting:

```
package mbbuf
import . "nU/obj"

type channel1 struct {
  cIns, cGet chan Any
}

func newCh1 (n uint) MBuffer {
  x := new(channel1)
  x.cIns = make(chan Any)
  x.cGet = make(chan Any)
  go func() {
    buffer := make([]Any, n)
    var count, in, out uint
    for {
      if count == 0 {
        buffer[in] = <-x.cIns
        in = (in + 1) % n; count = 1
      } else if count == n {
        x.cGet <- buffer[out]
        out = (out + 1) % n; count = n - 1
      } else { // 0 < count < n
        select {
        case buffer[in] = <-x.cIns:
          in = (in + 1) % n; count++
        case x.cGet <- buffer[out]:
          out = (out + 1) % n; count--
        }
      }
    }
  }()
  return x
}

func (x *channel1) Ins (a Any) { x.cIns <- a }
func (x *channel1) Get() Any { return <-x.cGet }
```

11.6.3 Equivalence of Synchronous and Asynchronous Message Passing

If the sender is preceded by a (FIFO) queue, the effect of *asynchronous message passing* can be achieved with *synchronous* exchange of messages. The details are left as a simple exercise. Try to implement the interface

```
package achan
import . "nU/obj"

type AsynchronousChannel interface {
  Send (a Any)
```

```
  Recv() Any
}
```

```
func New (a Any) AsynchronousChannel { return new_(a) }
```

without looking into the following solution:

```
package achan
import ("sync"; . "nU/obj"; "nU/buf")
```

```
type asynchronousChannel struct {
  Any
  buf.Buffer
  ch chan Any
  sync.Mutex
}
```

```
func new_(a Any) AsynchronousChannel {
  x := new(asynchronousChannel)
  x.Buffer = buf.New(a)
  x.ch = make(chan Any) // synchronous !
  return x
}
```

```
func (x *asynchronousChannel) Send (a Any) {
  x.Mutex.Lock()
  x.Buffer.Ins (a)
  x.Mutex.Unlock()
}
```

```
func (x *asynchronousChannel) Recv() Any {
  x.Mutex.Lock()
  defer x.Mutex.Unlock()
  a := x.Buffer.Get()
  if a == x.Any { panic("fatal error: all goroutines are asleep" +
                        " - deadlock!") }
  return a
}
```

In conjunction with the insight from Sect. 11.1.2 that synchronous send statements can easily be simulated with asynchronous ones, we have verified that:

▶   The concepts of synchronous and asynchronous message passing are equivalent.

11.6.4 The Readers–Writers Problem

Another example is the client–server solution of the readers–writers problem:

```go
package rw

type channel struct {
  inR, outR, inW, outW chan int
}

func newCh() ReaderWriter {
  x := new(channel)
  x.inR, x.outR = make(chan int), make(chan int)
  x.inW, x.outW = make(chan int), make(chan int)
  x.done = make(chan int)
  go func() {
    var nR, nW uint
    for {
      if nW == 0 {
        if nR == 0 {
          select {
          case <-x.inR:
            nR++
          case <-x.inW:
            nW = 1
          }
        } else { // nR > 0
          select {
          case <-x.inR:
            nR++
          case <-x.outR:
            nR--
          }
        }
      } else { // nW == 1
        select {
        case <-x.outW:
          nW = 0
        }
      }
    }
  }()
  return x
}

func (x *channel) ReaderIn() { x.inR <- 0 }
func (x *channel) ReaderOut() { x.outR <- 0 }
func (x *channel) WriterIn() { x.inW <- 0 }
func (x *channel) WriterOut() { x.outW <- 0 }
```

We have rejected the idea of establishing for each reader and writer an own channel to which Boolean values are sent to distinguish entry from exit (as well as the ability to identify these two cases by their strict alternation in the access rule) and have used the method propagated above to establish different channels for the entry and exit protocols.

11.6.5 The Left–Right Problem

Here is an excerpt of the corresponding solution of the first left–right problem with channels for the entry and exit of processes moving to the left and the right, respectively:

```
package lr
import . "nU/obj"

type channel struct {
  inL, outL, inR, outR chan int
}

func newCh() LeftRight {
  x := new(channel)
  x.inL, x.outL = make(chan int), make(chan int)
  x.inR, x.outR = make(chan int), make(chan int)
  go func() {
    var nL, nR uint
    for {
      if nL == 0 {
        if nR == 0 {
          select {
          case <-x.inL:
            nL++
          case <-x.inR:
            nR++
          }
        } else { // nL == 0 && nR > 0
          select {
          case <-x.inR:
            nR++
          case <-x.outR:
            nR--
          }
        }
      } else { // nL > 0
        select {
        case <-x.inL:
          nL++
        case <-x.outL:
          nL--
        }
      }
    }
```

```
      }
   } ()
   return x
}

func (x *channel) LeftIn ()   { x.inL <- 0 }
func (x *channel) LeftOut ()  { x.outL <- 0 }
func (x *channel) RightIn ()  { x.inR <- 0 }
func (x *channel) RightOut () { x.outR <- 0 }
```

However, these solutions are considerably lacking in elegance. Because a one-to-one relationship between the entry conditions and the communication operations is not possible,
some communication operations occur more than once. Furthermore, with the case distinctions it has to be ensured that, on the one hand, they are disjoint and, on the other, that they
completely cover all entry conditions. Solving more complex problems such as the bounded
left–right problem in this way would probably lead to a very confusing implementation. So,
what is missing, is the ability to allow the reception for each entry condition on precisely
those channels where the requests are sent, for which these conditions are fulfilled. In order
to achieve this, a more far-reaching concept is necessary, which we present in the following
section.

11.7   Guarded Selective Waiting

SR offers *guarded selective waiting* as an extension of selective waiting, to enable a process—
depending on its internal state—to "suppress" listening to certain channels from which it
does not want to receive messages, again following such a construct in Ada.

Go does not provide this construction *directly*, but with a little trick, we can also "rebuild"
this very useful concept in Go. With respect to the aspect of the specification of the select
statement, that all those branches whose channel has the value nil, are "not present" in it,
i.e., are ignored, we use the following function, which is placed in the package nU/obj:

```
func When (b bool, c chan Any) chan Any {
   if b {
      return c
   }
   return nil
}
```

Its name is chosen according to the syntax in the above-mentioned languages, where in
the select statement, a Boolean expression—a so-called *guard*—is placed, before a
communication operation is initiated with the keyword when. This concept extends that of
selective waiting.

A branch is called

- *open* if the associated guard—in our case the value of the first parameter in the call to the When function—is *true*; therefore, the When function returns the second parameter as a value, and
- otherwise *closed*.

The fact described above, therefore, implies that—just like in the other languages mentioned—only the *open* branches (which also include communication operations without guards) are used for selective receiving or sending.

The receipt or sending of a further message from or to one of the channels, however, causes *no* reevaluation of the guards; consequently, a process that executes a select statement is blocked, if necessary.

The implementation of guarded selective waiting is generally very complex; the explanations in the appendix of [3] show, using the example of Pascal-FC, that this construct represents the most complex mechanism for communication between processes.

A realization for distributed systems requires additional measures. Either a central process (with the obvious drawbacks that such a "bottleneck" represents) is used to coordinate all sending and receiving statements, or the processes that want to exchange messages communicate directly with all other participants.

The very extensive details can be found in [4] or [1]. They are—especially in the decentralized case—extremely complex; they are far outside the scope of this book, which only deals with the presentation of the main features of nonsequential and distributed programming.

Because of the far-sighted decision on blocking of the select statement on channels with the value nil (see Sect. 11.4), this complexity is circumnavigated with our When construct (as long as it is not about *network-wide* message passing).

11.7.1 Semaphores

We will now use some of our standard examples to show how understandable and extremely elegant the solutions can be formulated with this concept. Here is our first example:

```
package sem
import . "nU/obj"

type guardedSelect struct {
  p, v chan Any
}

func newGS (n uint) Semaphore {
  x := new(guardedSelect)
  x.p, x.v = make(chan Any), make(chan Any)
  go func() {
```

```
      val := n
      for {
        select {
        case <-When (val > 0, x.p):
          val--
        case <-x.v:
          val++
        }
      }
    }()
  return x
}


func (x *guardedSelect) P() { x.p <- 0 }
func (x *guardedSelect) V() { x.v <- 0 }
```

11.7.2 Bounded Buffers

With guards also the algorithms to manage buffers becomes a bit nicer:

```
package mbuf
import . "nU/obj"

type guardedSelect struct {
  cIns, cGet chan Any
}

func newGS (n uint) MBuffer {
  x := new(guardedSelect)
  x.cIns, x.cGet = make(chan Any), make(chan Any)
  go func() {
    buffer := make ([]Any, n)
    var in, out, num uint
    for {
      select {
      case buffer [in] = <-When (num < n, x.cIns):
        in = (in + 1) % n
        num++
      case When (num > 0, x.cGet) <- buffer [out]:
        out = (out + 1) % n
        num--
      }
    }
  }()
  return x
}


func (x *guardedSelect) Ins (a Any) { x.cIns <- a }
func (x *guardedSelect) Get() Any { return Clone (<-x.cGet) }
```

11.7.3 The Readers–Writers Problem

The following solution of the readers–writers problem also shows very clearly—in comparison to the variant with selective reception—*without* guard the superiority of guarded waiting:

```
package rw
import . "nU/obj"

type guardedSelect struct {
  inR, outR, inW, outW chan Any
}

func newGS() ReaderWriter {
  x := new(guardedSelect)
  x.inR, x.outR = make(chan Any), make(chan Any)
  x.inW, x.outW = make(chan Any), make(chan Any)
  go func() {
    var nR, nW uint // active readers, writers
    for {
      select {
      case <-When (nW == 0, x.inR):
        nR++
      case <-When (nR > 0, x.outR):
        nR--
      case <-When (nR == 0 && nW == 0, x.inW):
        nW = 1
      case <-When (nW == 1, x.outW):
        nW = 0
      }
    }
  }()
  return x
}

func (x *guardedSelect) ReaderIn() { x.inR <- 0 }
func (x *guardedSelect) ReaderOut() { x.outR <- 0 }
func (x *guardedSelect) WriterIn() { x.inW <- 0 }
func (x *guardedSelect) WriterOut() { x.outW <- 0 }
```

11.7.4 The Left–Right Problem

Accordingly, we also have a similar solution of the left–right problem:

```
package lr
import . "nU/obj"

type guardedSelect struct {
```

```
  inL, outL, inR, outR chan Any
}

func newGS() LeftRight {
  x := new(guardedSelect)
  x.inL, x.outL = make(chan Any), make(chan Any)
  x.inR, x.outR = make(chan Any), make(chan Any)
  go func() {
    var nL, nR uint
    for {
      select {
      case <-When (nR == 0, x.inL):
        nL++
      case <-When (nL > 0, x.outL):
        nL--
      case <-When (nL == 0, x.inR):
        nR++
      case <-When (nR > 0, x.outR):
        nR--
      }
    }
  }()
  return x
}

func (x *guardedSelect) LeftIn()  { x.inL <- 0 }
func (x *guardedSelect) LeftOut() { x.outL <- 0 }
func (x *guardedSelect) RightIn()  { x.inR <- 0 }
func (x *guardedSelect) RightOut() { x.outR <- 0 }
```

11.8   Equivalence of Message Passing and the Semaphore Concept

Semaphores can also be used to simulate the synchronous exchange of messages, as demonstrated by the previous implementations of semaphores by means of message passing in Sects. 11.2.1 on semaphores via asynchronous communication and 11.6.1 on general semaphores:

▶   Message passing and the semaphore concept have structurally the same expressive power.

For this, we show a slightly extended simulation of BURNS/DAVIES from [3].

They describe a channel by the message contained in it, a Boolean variable to distinguish which was the first partner to reach the rendezvous (the sender or the receiver), a binary semaphore to protect access to it, and a binary semaphore to synchronize the rendezvous.

Since message passing in Pascal-FC is only constructed for 1:1-channels, the simulation in [3] does not correspond to the channel concept of Go. For this reason, in our implementation, we have made concurrent calls of Send or Recv indivisible with additional locks s and r.

The function of the send and receive operations is easy to understand by playing through the possible execution sequences of such a pair.

```
package schan
import ("sync"; . "nU/obj")

type synchronousChannel struct {
  pattern Any
  Any "object in channel"
  bool "first at rendezvous"
  mutex, s, r, rendezvous sync.Mutex
}

func new_(a Any) SynchronousChannel {
  x := new(synchronousChannel)
  x.pattern = Clone(a)
  x.Any = nil // Clone(a)
  x.bool = true
  x.rendezvous.Lock()
  return x
}

func (x *synchronousChannel) Send (a Any) {
  x.s.Lock()
  x.mutex.Lock()
  x.Any = Clone(a)
  if x.bool {
    x.bool = false
    x.mutex.Unlock()
    x.rendezvous.Lock()
    x.mutex.Unlock()
  } else {
    x.bool = true
    x.rendezvous.Unlock()
  }
  x.s.Unlock()
}

func (x *synchronousChannel) Recv() Any {
  var a Any
  x.r.Lock()
  x.mutex.Lock()
  if x.bool {
    x.bool = false
    x.mutex.Unlock()
    x.rendezvous.Lock()
```

```
    a = Clone(x.Any)
    x.Any = x.pattern
    x.mutex.Unlock()
  } else {
    x.bool = true

    a = Clone (x.Any)
    x.Any = x.pattern
    x.mutex.Unlock()
    x.rendezvous.Unlock()
  }
  x.r.Unlock()
  return a
}
```

Table 11.1 Duality between the procedure-orientated and the message-oriented approach

Procedure-oriented	Message-oriented
Monitor (passive construct)	Server (active process)
Dynamically variable number of many small processes	Static number of few processes
Function identifier	Channel to the server
Monitor variables	Variables of the server
Function call	Sending of a request with subsequent blocking
Monitor entry queue	select construct
Monitor entry	Receipt of a request from a channel in one of the select branches
function body	Statements after the reception in the corresponding select branch
Monitor exit	Termination of the statements of a select branch if necessary, sending of the result
Return from the function	Unblocking after the receipt of the request, if necessary, receipt of the result
Condition variables	Guards of the branches in the select statement
Wait statement	Guarded receiving; if necessary registering with reference to the corresponding channel
Signal statement	With guarded receiving not necessary; otherwise execution of the registered request and sending of the result

11.9 Duality Between Monitors and Servers

The many examples in this chapter have shown a way to implement monitor functions in the client–server paradigm with message passing. Table 11.1 shows the systematic translation mechanism that LAUER and NEEDHAM called "duality between two categories of operating system design" in [6].

References

1. Andrews, G.R.: Concurrent Programming. Principles and Practice. Addison-Wesley, Menlo Park (1991)
2. Ben-Ari, M.: Grundlagen der Parallelprogrammierung. Hanser, München (1984)
3. Burns, A., Davies, G.: Concurrent Programming. Addison-Wesley, Harlow (1993)
4. Buckley, G.N., Silberschatz, A.: An effective implementation for the generalized input-output construct of CSP. ACM Trans. Program. Lang. Syst. **5**, 223–235 (1983). https://doi.org/10.1145/69624.357208
5. Hoare, C.A.R.: Communicating sequential processes. Commun. ACM **21**, 666–677 (1978). https://doi.org/10.1145/359576.359585
6. Lauer, H. C., Needham, R. M.: On the duality of operating system structures. Proc. Second International Symposium, IRIA: reprinted. ACM SIGOPS Oper. Syst. Rev. **13**(1979), 3–19 (1978). https://doi.org/10.1145/850656.850658

Comparison of the Previous Language Constructs 12

Abstract

The detailed treatment of the basic synchronization techniques with the use of *locks*, *semaphores*, *monitors*, and *message passing* enables a good assessment of the respective strengths and weaknesses of these language concepts. Here, the essential points of the previous chapters are briefly described once more.

12.1 Locks

They represent the lowest level language concept that can be used for the efficient implementation of services of lower operating system layers but is—apart from that—only of historical or academic interest. An exception are locks of the type `sync.Mutex` in Go, which are excellently suited for use as binary semaphores.

12.2 Semaphores

They are a basic construct for all layers of an operating system that require shared memory. They are extremely efficient to implement and are a very useful —if not indispensable—tool to implement higher constructs.

As a construct for the construction of concurrent programs, however, they are only suitable to a very limited extent due to their susceptibility to errors; they do not have any abstraction mechanisms, because all measures for synchronization with them must be explicitly programmed. They are, in a way, the `GOTO` of nonsequential programming.

© Springer Fachmedien Wiesbaden GmbH, part of Springer Nature 2021
C. Maurer, *Nonsequential and Distributed Programming with Go*,
https://doi.org/10.1007/978-3-658-29782-4_12

12.3   Monitors

This modular concept provides a quite comfortably usable higher level of abstraction: Monitors offer the advantage of local aggregation of concurrent accesses to data by encapsulating them with the guarantee of mutual exclusion and also allow a quite clear programming of condition synchronization. As *passive* constructs, they have the advantage of minimizing the load on the runtime system. However, to implement them, it is necessary to explicitly program the logical relationship between the conditions and the operations on condition variables.

12.4   Message Passing

This language tool provides the appropriate level of abstraction for communication and synchronization between processes, if access to shared variables is not possible, because the processes involved do not have shared memory—for example, if they run on different computers or in different operating system processes.

The disadvantage that the server processes come into play as *active* components is in opposition to the expressiveness of the guards with selective waiting (and thus a good maintainability of the program texts): This eliminates the need to explicitly program complex mechanisms for monitoring Boolean expressions, i.e., the compliance with the associated synchronization conditions disappears completely behind the scenes.

A certain disadvantage is the inherently static channel architecture of the programs, which are constructed with message exchange.

Netwide Message Passing

13

Abstract

As efficient as the exchange of messages presented is so far for many tasks, its concept basically contradicts the concept of *distributed* programming that does not require shared memory. The communication between different goroutines, which—in contrast to operating system processes—are lightweight processes with a shared address space, runs in Go via channels that are already shared variables themselves. Distributed message passing in the *strict* sense is the communication between different computers or different operating system processes on one or more computers. After a short sketch of aspects of network communication based on TCP/IP, this chapter presents a channel concept by developing a package that permits the exchange of messages in networks and the construction of distributed programs on this basis. As an example of a distributed program, the algorithm of RICART and AGRAWALA for decentralized mutual exclusion is explained.

13.1   Channels in the Network

The connection points between computers are *network addresses*. They consist of two parts:

- the *IP number* or the *name of the computer*
  resolvable either by an entry in /etc./hosts or by the directory service *DNS* ("*Domain Name System*") of the namespace for the worldwide network, and
- the number of a *port* ,
  a natural number $< 2^{16} = 65536$.

A connection between two computers is worldwide uniquely identified by their two network addresses.

© Springer Fachmedien Wiesbaden GmbH, part of Springer Nature 2021
C. Maurer, *Nonsequential and Distributed Programming with Go*,
https://doi.org/10.1007/978-3-658-29782-4_13

Many port numbers are reserved for specific tasks in network communication and identify the associated protocols. For this purpose, the IANA ("*Internet Assigned Numbers Authority*") assigns

- the reserved ("*system-*") ports (< 1024) for popular protocols such as, e.g.,
  - 21 for ftp ("*File Transfer Protocol*"),
  - 22 for ssh ("*Secure Shell*"),
  - 25 for smtp ("*Simple Mail Transfer Protocol*"),
  - 80 for http ("*Hypertext Transfer Protocol*"),
  - 123 for ntp ("*Network Time Protocol*") and
  - 161 for snmp ("*Simple Network Management Protocol*"

and

- the registered ("*users*") ports (from 1024 to $3 \cdot 2^{14} - 1 = 49151$) for certain services (usually defined by companies),

and registers them with the participation of the IETF ("*Internet Engineering Task Force*") (https://www.iana.org/assignments/service-names-port-numbers/).

The reserved ports can only be used by processes with `root` rights; the private ("*dynamic*") ports from `49152` on are at free disposal.

13.1.1 Technical Aspects (in C)

The most suitable foundation for reliable message passing is the connection-oriented TCP/IP protocol, which is derived from the protocol for the worldwide IP ("*Internet Protocol*") and the transmission control protocol TCP in the overlying layer.

For details on this, we refer to previous knowledge on technical computer science or the relevant literature, as well as to the header files `netinet/tcp.h` and `sys/socket.h` in the directory `/usr/include`.

Each connection is set up *asymmetrically*: One of the two computers involved is the *server*, the other the *client*. The server executes the following operations (for details, see the corresponding *manpages*):

`socket`

to select the communication protocol (`TCP` versus `UDP`, `IP4` versus `IP6`, `raw socket` for `ICMP` or not) with the return of a *socket* as a parameter for the following calls, then

`bind`

to assign a local protocol address, and finally

`listen`

to change the state of the socket in order to be ready to receive messages. Then it blocks at the call of the operation

accept

for the return of a descriptor which, like a file descriptor, is used as a parameter for the send and receive operations `write` and `read` until a client who has called

socket

for the same purpose as the server, contacts the server by calling

connect

with the return of a descriptor as with the `accept` of the server, which leads to the connection by a *"three-way handshake"*.

13.1.2 Remarks on the Realization in Java

The server defines with the call of a constructor

```
ServerSocket sS = new ServerSocket(port);
```

at first a server-socket for a specific port of type `int` and then blocks with the statement

```
Socket s = sS.accept()
```

to the return of a socket until a client's message is received at the port. (These statements must be included in `try/ catch` statements). When a messages arrives, for example, it fetches, e.g., with

```
InputStreamReader i = new InputStreamReader(s.getInputStream());
BufferedReader r = new BufferedReader(i);
```

a buffered `Reader`, on which it receives with the statement

```
String r = b.ReadLine();
```

the string sent by a client and can assign it to the variable `r`.

It then sends a reply with a `PrintWriter` to this client, which it has defined with the call of a constructor

```
PrintWriter p = new PrintWriter(s.getOutputStream, true);
```

and then with

```
p.println(r);
```

a string `r` constructed by it back to the client.

In principle, a client processes in a very similar way; it must, of course, specify the server whose service it wants to use. To do this, it parameterizes the call of the `socket` constructor with its name (or IP address)

```
String host = "..."; // ... = hostname or IP-address
int port = 50000;
Socket s = new Socket(host, port);
```

It gets the `Reader` and `Writer` with the same statements as given above for the server. A (server)-socket `s` is closed with the statement `s.close()`.

Details on the calls used can be found in the classes `java.net.Socket`, `java.net.ServerSocket`, `java.io.BufferedReader`, `java.io.InputStream-Reader`, and `java.io.PrintWriter`.

13.2   Realization in Go

In Go the calls of `socket` and `bind` for the server are realized with the function `Listen`, and the calls of `socket` and `connect` for the client by `Dial`. The functions `Accept` and `Dial` return the descriptors of type `Conn` for the send and receive functions `Write` and `Read`. The details of `Listen` and `Accept` can be found in the file `tcpsock.go` and those of `Dial` in `dial.go` in the package `net` of the Go library.

13.3   1:1-Network Channels Between Processes on Arbitrary Computers

For the following, we need a package to exchange messages over the network between processes on two computers (or between different operating system processes on one computer). Since, for obvious reasons, instances of abstract data objects cannot be sent over a network, but only streams (i.e., byte sequences), the following must be assumed for the objects to be transported over the network:

▶   The types of the objects to be transported over the network implement the interface `Coder` or are handled in its functions.

For the term " `Coder`" we refer to Sect. 2.3.2.4.

This is a task that for *remote procedure calls* classically is handled by "*stubs*". For the network-wide message passing between two communication partners, we supply a drastically reduced version of an old package of the Go authors that is no longer included in Go 1 (it was denoted as "*deprecated*" some time ago).

To determine *which* one of two computers involved has to play the role of the server, the processes involved in message passing are supplied with *identities* in form of consecutive natural numbers—beginning with 0. This is also done in many textbooks, e.g., in [1–3] and [4].

For this—apart from the pattern object to determine the channel type and the number of the port—the following parameters are required for the constructor:

- the identity of the calling process,
- the (different!) identity of his communication partner, and
- the name of the host on which its process is running.

Here is the specification of the package nchan (for the term "stream" Sect. 2.3.2.4):

```
package nchan
import . "nU/obj"
const Port0 = 49152 // first "private" port (== 1<<16 - 1<<14)

type NetChannel interface { // Channels for the net-wide exchange
                            // of objects between processes

// Pre: a is of type of x with Codelen(a) < 65536.
// The object a is sent on x to the communication partner
// of the calling process.
  Send (a Any)

// Returns a stream which is not bound to a type.
// In this case, the receiver has to decode that stream
// into an object of the appropriate type.
// Returns otherwise the object of the type of x,
// that was sent on x by the communication partner.
// The calling process was blocked on x, if necessary,
// until an object was received.
  Recv () Any

// All channels used by x are closed.
  Fin ()
}


// Pre: me is the identity of the calling process and
//      i != me the identity of the process that runs
//      on the host with the name h (h is an entry
//      in /etc/hosts or is resolvable via DNS).
//      Port0 + p < 65536 is not occupied by a network
//      service on one of the participating computers.
//      The communication partner calls New with an object
//      of the same type as the type of a and with the same port
//      but with exchanged values of me and i and with the
//      name of the host on which the calling process is running.
// Returns an asynchronous channel for the exchange of messages
// of the type of the pattern object a between the host on which
// the calling process is running and a process running on h,
// as communication partner of the calling  process.
```

```
// Port0 + p is now occupied by a network service
// on these two hosts.
// For a == nil objects of a different size can be exchanged.
// In this case, calls of Recv() return streams that have to be
// decoded by the receiver, which assumes that both partners
// use the channel for the exchange of messages of the same type.
func New (a Any, me, i uint, h string, p uint16) NetChannel {
  return new_(a,me,i,h,p) }
```

Here is the representation of the network channels and the implementation of the constructor:

```
package nchan
import ("time"; "strconv"; "net"; . "nU/obj")

const (network = "tcp"; maxWidth = uint(1<<12))

type netChannel struct {
  Any "pattern object"
  uint "capacity of the channel"
  Stream "buffer for transmission of data"
  net.Conn "communication channel"
}

func new_(a Any, me, i uint, n string, p uint16) NetChannel {
  if me == i { panic("me == i") }
  x := new(netChannel)
  if a == nil {
    x.Any, x.uint = nil, maxWidth
  } else {
    x.Any, x.uint = Clone(a), Codelen(a)
  }
  x.in, x.out = make(chan Any), make(chan Any)
  x.Stream = make(Stream, x.uint)
  x.oneOne = true
  x.isServer = me < i
  ps := ":" + strconv.Itoa(int(Port0 + p))
  if x.isServer {
    x.Listener, x.error = net.Listen (network, n + ps)
    x.Conn, x.error = x.Listener.Accept()
  } else { // client
    for {
      if x.Conn, x.error =
        net.Dial (network, n + ps); x.error == nil {
        break
      }
      time.Sleep (500 * 1e6)
    }
  }
  return x
}
```

If a pattern object != nil has been to the constructor, the value of the size of this object (i.e., its code length) is assigned to the channel width, otherwise the maximum size of the objects to be sent.

The decision as to which of the two computers works as a server and which as a client is made by comparing the identities of the two processes: The computer on which the process with the smaller identity is running plays the role of server. This avoids the unpleasant problem of making visible in the specification the asymmetry of the role of the participating computers caused by the TCP protocol while transporting data over the network; instead, we *hide* that completely in the implementation.

The reason for this is obvious: In the message passing in Chap. 11, there are also no different roles of sender and receiver—both communication partners have equal rights.

The server starts with the operations Listen and Accept described in the previous section, which establishes the contact to its communication partner, the client, when it leaves its initial loop by a successful selection of the server with the operation Dial.

And here is the implementation of the send and receive functions:

```
var c0 = C0()

func (x *netChannel) Send (a Any) {
  if x.Any == nil { // objects of different sizes are
transported,
                  // therefore, the object must be preceded by
its size
     x.Conn.Write (append (Encode (Codelen(a), Encode(a)...))
  } else { // all objects have the size of the pattern object
     x.Conn.Write (Encode(a))
  }
}


func (x *netChannel) Recv () Any {
  if x.Any == nil { // for the exchange of objects of different
size
                  // at first the size of the sent object is
determined
     x.Conn.Read(x.Stream[:c0])
     x.uint = Decode (uint(0), x.Stream[:c0]).(uint) // to read
     x.Conn.Read (x.Stream[c0:c0+x.uint]) // correspondingly many
bytes
     return x.Stream[c0:c0+x.uint]         // from the buffer
  x.Conn.Read (x.Stream) // with fixed channel width this problem
  return Decode(Clone(x.Any), x.Stream) // does not arise
}
```

The code length C0() comes from the package nU/obj (see Sect. 2.3.2.4). We implicitly assume that all computers involved have the same architecture; otherwise, either more effort is required or the use of uint has to be replaced by uint32 or uint64, according to the address width of the computers.

The calls of Read and Write return as first value the number of bytes read or written, the second value of these calls and the return value of Listen, and Accept is an error of type error (see net.go and tcpsock.go in the package net in the Go library).

For serious applications, these data should be evaluated for exception handling if something "has gone wrong", because the first value is less than the number of bytes to be read or written or the error is different from nil.

We rely on the fact that no errors occur during the call and ignore these values, because an appropriate error handling does not contribute anything to the basic procedures explained here.

In any case, the objects to be sent are encoded within the send operations. In case x.Any == nil the sent streams can be of different size, therefore the encoded object must be preceded by its code length in the send operation, so that in the receive operation, the correct number of bytes representing the encoded sent object is read. This allows the receiver to restore this object by decoding the received stream of the correct length.

Otherwise—i.e., if the pattern object is different from nil—the sent streams always have the same size determined by the code length of the type of the exchanged objects. In this case, the decoding is already performed in the receive operation, and the receiver only has to apply the corresponding "*type assertion*" (see the example in Sect. 13.3.1).

All in all, our network channels are thus bound to a data type and enable the exchange of arbitrary objects of this type, provided that it fulfils the above-mentioned prerequisite, i.e., that these objects can be coded uniquely reversibly as streams.

We will make extensive use of the second possibility in Chaps. 16 on *heartbeat algorithms* and 17 on *traversing algorithms*, because there *graphs* increase in size as the algorithms run are transmitted.

13.3.1 A Simple Example

As a small application of nU/nchan we show the "ping-pong" between two processes on the same computer or on two different computers. The two processes use the following program with objects of type string of length 4:

```
package main
import ("time"; "nU/env"; "nU/nchan")

func main() {
  me := uint(env.Arg1()) - '0'
  c := nchan.New ("word", me, 1 - me, host, 123)
  for i := uint(0); i < 3; i++ {
    if me == 1 {
      println (c.Recv().(string)); time.Sleep(3e9)
      c.Send ("pong"); time.Sleep(3e9)
    } else {
      c.Send ("ping"); time.Sleep(3e9)
```

```
    println (c.Recv().(string)); time.Sleep(3e9)
  }
}
```

In the second program line of `main`, for `host` the name of the host on which the communication partner's process is running must be applied i.e., the program text is the same for
both processes if they are running on the same host. One of them calls the program with the
argument `0`, the other with `1`. The argument is evaluated with the function

```
// Returns the first byte of the first argument of the program
call,
// if that was given, otherwise 0.
func Arg1() byte { return arg1() }
```

from the package `nU/env`; this then in the second program line leads to the (different!)
identities `1` and `0` of the two processes. The break with `time.Sleep` serves only to
simulate a longer duration of message transmission.

The type assertion after `c.Recv()` is indispensable; if it is forgotten, the compiler
reports the error "…: cannot use c.Recv() (type obj.Any) as type string in assignment: need
type assertion".

13.4   Distributed Locks Due to Ricart/Agrawala

If processes in different operating system processes—especially on different computers—
want to access shared data, none of the methods developed so far can be used to guarantee
mutual exclusion. For this we need a "distributed synchronization", i.e., all computers involved must communicate with each other with the aim of negotiating access rights.

With our construction of the network channels, we are able to present the solution of this
problem by RICART and AGRAWALA in [5]. Their basic idea is the following:

When a process wants to enter the critical section, it sends a message with its time to all
other participants. If a process receives such a message, there are three cases:

(a) It is in the critical section,
(b) it has no interest in it, or
(c) it wants to enter it, too.

In case (a), it does not reply to the sender, but first registers it as interested in a queue. In case
(b), it replies to the sender with an "ok"-message. In case (c), it compares the time received
with the time it sent to the other with the request. The older process is prioritized—i.e., if
the received time is before its own, it sends an "ok" to the sender, otherwise it proceeds as
in case (a). If the times are the same, the computer numbers are used for the decision. The
entry into the critical section is possible for a process, iff it has received the "ok" from all
others.

The global time is always the maximum of all times of the participating processes; each process sets its own time in the entry protocol to the time following the global time. In the exit protocol, a process sends "ok" to all participants in its queue and deletes the queue.

The specification of the package for distributed locks is based on the package nU/lock of the locks because it implements their interface:

```
package dlock
import  .  "nU/lock"

type DistributedLock interface {

  Locker
}

// Pre: h is the sequence of the names of the participating
hosts.
//      me is the identity of the calling process (me < len(h)).
//      The process with the identity i runs on host h[i].
//      The ports p..p+n*n are not occupied by a network service.
// Returns a new distributed lock.
func New (me uint, h []string, p uint16) DistributedLock {
  return new_(me,h,p)  }
```

The bookkeeping described above, of course, has be outsourced to concurrent processes for each participant, which implies that the implementation of the constructor is quite complex:

```
package dlock
import ("sync"; "nU/nchan")

const ok = uint(0)

type distributedLock struct {
  uint "number of participating hosts"
  host []string // their names
  me uint // identity of the calling process
  request, reply [][]nchan.NetChannel
  mutex, cs sync.Mutex
  time, ownTime, nReplies uint
  interested bool
  deferred []bool
}

func new_(me uint, hs []string, p uint16) DistributedLock {
  x := new(distributedLock)
  x.uint = uint(len(hs))
  x.deferred = make([]bool, x.uint)
  x.me = me
  x.host = make([]string, x.uint)
  for i := uint(0); i < x.uint; i++ {
```

```
    x.host[i] = hs[i]
  }
  x.cs.Lock()
  x.request = make([][]nchan.NetChannel, x.uint)
  x.reply = make([][]nchan.NetChannel, x.uint)
  for i := uint(0); i < x.uint; i++ {
    x.request[i] = make([]nchan.NetChannel, x.uint)
    x.reply[i] = make([]nchan.NetChannel, x.uint)
  }
  var other string
  for i := uint(0); i < x.uint; i++ {
    for j := uint(0); j < x.uint; j++ {
      if i != j && (x.me == i || x.me == j) {
        if x.me == i {
          other = x.host[j]
        } else { // me == j
          other = x.host[i]
        }
        k := i * x.uint + j
        x.request[i][j] = nchan.New(x.ownTime, other,
                                    uint(k), true)
        x.reply[i][j] = nchan.New(x.ownTime, other,
                                  uint(k + x.uint * x.uint),
                                  true)
      }
    }
  }
  for i := uint(0); i < x.uint; i++ {
    if i != x.me {
      go func (j uint) { // bookkeeping of the requests
        for {
          otherTime := x.request[j][x.me].Recv().(int)
          x.mutex.Lock()                                        // 1
          if otherTime > x.time {
            x.time = otherTime
          }
          if x.interested && (x.ownTime < otherTime ||
                              x.ownTime == otherTime &&
                              x.me < j) {
            x.deferred[j] = true
          } else {
            x.reply[x.me][j].Send(ok)
          }
          x.mutex.Unlock()                                      // 1
        }
      }(i)
      go func (j uint) { // bookkeeping of the requests
        for {
          _ = x.reply[j][x.me].Recv().(int)
```

```
              x.mutex.Lock()
              x.nReplies++
              if x.nReplies == x.uint - 1 {
                x.cs.Unlock()
              }
              x.mutex.Unlock()
          }
       }(i)
     }
  }
  return x
}
```

The implementation of the protocols is, therefore, quite simple:

```
func (x *distributedLock) Lock() {
  x.mutex.Lock()              // 2
  x.interested = true
  x.ownTime = x.time + 1
  x.nReplies = uint(0)
  x.mutex.Unlock()            // 2
  for i := uint(0); i < x.uint; i++ {
    if i != x.me {
      x.request[x.me][i].Send (x.ownTime)
    }
  }
  x.cs.Lock()
}
```

```
func (x *distributedLock) Unlock() {
  x.mutex.Lock()
  x.interested = false
  x.mutex.Unlock()
  for i := uint(0); i < x.uint; i++ {
    if x.deferred[i] {
      x.deferred[i] = false
      x.reply[x.me][i].Send (ok)
    }
  }
}
```

In order to illustrate how the algorithm works, we will play through—essentially as a pla-giarism of the example from [5]—a sequence in which three processes A, B, and C want to access shared data on the computers with the numbers 1, 2, and 3, which makes it necessary to protect the accesses by lock synchronization.

In the following, we will use—as in the source code above—the time "0" as content of the "ok" message. While A on computer 1 has no interest in the critical section, the processes B and C on computers 2 and 3 want to enter it approximately simultaneously and send their own initial time "1" to the other two (see Fig. 13.1).

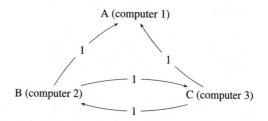

Fig. 13.1 B and C send their start time to the others

This implies that A acknowledges both requests with "ok", and the competition between B and C is resolved in favour of B, because 2 < 3, i.e., B retains the reply to computer 3 and registers the request, and C replies to the request of B by sending "ok" to computer 2 (see Fig. 13.2).

A short time later, A also wants to enter the critical section and—after updating its time after receiving the times "1" from B and C—sends the time "2" to computers 2 and 3 (see Fig. 13.3).

Regardless of which of the two messages from A arrive first at computer 2, now process B on computer 2 is in exclusive possession of the critical section, because even if "2" arrives before "0", B "wins", so its "ok" to A is delayed. Because 1 < 2, C wins the competition against A; hence A sends "ok" to computer 3, and C retains his reply to computer 1. When B leaves the critical section, it sends its two retained replies (see Fig. 13.4).

Thus, C is now in possession of the critical section, because the replies from A and B have arrived. In its exit protocol, it sends the retained message to computer 1. A has now received both "ok" replies and will be in the possession of the critical section (see Fig. 13.5).

Fig. 13.2 A and C send their "ok"

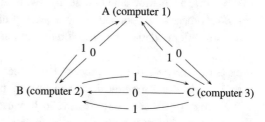

Fig. 13.3 The third step

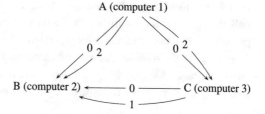

Fig. 13.4 The fourth step

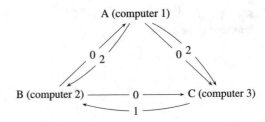

Fig. 13.5 A has received both "ok" replies

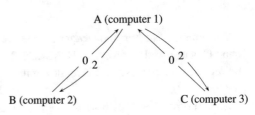

We show the guarantee of the *mutual exclusion*—as in on [5]— with a proof by contradiction:

Suppose two processes, 1 and 2, were in the critical section at the same time. Then both have previously sent their own time to all other processes and received the "ok" reply from all others. Now, for the execution sequence of the sections secured by the lock `mutex` in the concurrent bookkeeping of the requests and in the function `Lock` —confined in the source text by the selections 1 and 2—there are three cases:

(a) Process 1 sent the "ok" reply, *before* it updated its own time, i.e., the section 1 for it was executed *before* its section 2.
(b) We have a situation dual to case (a)—with interchanged roles of processes 1 and 2.
(c) *Both* processes responded to the request of the other *after* the execution of its section 2 so—after updating their own time—answered with "ok".

In case (a), the own time of process 1 was then later than that of process 2. Since process 2 received a later time in the request of process 1, for it—in contrast to process 1— `interested == true` was valid, because the corresponding assignment happened *before* the sending of the requests, and process 1 received this request before sending its own. Consequently, process 2 delays the request due to the comparison and acknowledges it only in its exit protocol with the "ok" answer. However, in contradiction to the assumption, process 1 could not enter the critical section. The same is true in case (b).

In case (c), for *both* processes `interested == true` holds when they receive each other's requests. Consequently, at the request, *both* compare the other's time and computer number with their own data. However, the comparisons now return the opposite result for both processes, which leads to the result that exactly *one* of them retains the reply to the request until the critical section is left. Thus, also *this* case results in a contradiction to the assumption. In all cases, therefore, both processes are prevented from concurrently entering the critical section, i.e., mutual exclusion is guaranteed.

The reason for a *deadlock* would be that several requesting processes cannot enter the critical section, because they are waiting for reciprocal "ok" replies, which would have to be sent by other processes involved in the deadlock, which, in turn, are waiting for a reply and are, therefore, blocked.

Consequently, there must be a cycle of processes, each of which has sent a request to the next one in that cycle, but has not yet received a reply from the previous one. Since each process in this cycle delays the request, it must have requested the critical section itself and determined that the comparison has given priority to it. However, this is impossible for all processes in the cycle due to the temporal order. This prevents deadlocks.

The algorithm is also *fair*, because with a starving process, we would have the following situation: Processes answer requests in finite time because the concurrent processes for the bookkeeping of the requests—apart from mutual exclusion to protect access to some shared variables—do not block but run in endless loops.

After a request from the starving process, the recipient cannot send in *its* requests at the same or an earlier time. With that the starving process eventually has the *earliest* time of all enquiring processes, which is why it retains all replies, and, therefore, no other process can enter the critical section.

Since we have seen above that the algorithm is free of deadlocks, eventually *some* process *must* gain access to the critical section, because that cannot be any other process, it can only be the starving one. Consequently, he does *not* starve. Thus fairness is also proved.

The algorithm requires one channel for the request and one for the reply between each two processes; for n participating processes, the number of channels needed is, therefore, a total of

$$2\sum_{i=1}^{n-1} i = 2\frac{(n-1)n}{2} = (n-1)n \ .$$

For each entry into a critical section, there is one request and one reply to and from each other process, so a total of $2(n-1)$ messages is required; for each exit again up to $n-1$ messages are sent.

The source texts of this book contain the file `distributedMutex.go`—a program to animate the distributed mutual exclusion.

RICART and AGRAWALA showed that this number cannot be undercut if the processes work independently from each other and concurrently, i.e., their algorithm is optimal in this respect.

Finally, it should be noted that their algorithm can thus be modified in such a manner that it also solves the readers–writers problem. For this, readers must not retain the answers to requests, but principally have to acknowledge them immediately with the sending of "ok".

References

1. Andrews, G. R.: Concurrent Programming, Principles and Practice. Addison-Wesley, Menlo Park (1991) https://www.cs.arizona.edu/people/greg
2. Ben-Ari, M.: Principles of Concurrent and Distributed Programming, 2nd ed. Addison-Wesley, Harlow (2006)
3. Erciyes, K.: Distributed Graph Algorithms for Computer Networks. Springer, London (2013)
4. Raynal, M.: Distributed Algorithms and Protocols. John Wiley & Sons, Chichester (1988)
5. Ricart, G., Agrawala, A.K.: An optimal algorithm for mutual exclusion in computer networks. Commun. ACM **24**, 9–17 (1981). https://doi.org/10.1145/358527.358537

Universal Far Monitors

14

Abstract

In this chapter, at first our construction of the network channels is extended in such a way that it can also be used for 1:n-connections. Therefore, the realization of the client–server paradigm is possible *network-wide*. In addition, this allows the development of another universal synchronization class, the *far monitors*. Their significance lies in their similarity to the conditioned universal monitors. They have a number of advantages over procedure remote calls: the quite simple completion of tasks that are otherwise only possible with RPCs. The power of this concept is evident in many applications: The construction of distributed semaphores, waiting queues and bounded buffers and the implementation of the distributed readers–writers and left–right problems. In the last three chapters on network topology, distributed depth and breadth search, and the election of a leader in the local network, this construction is used intensively.

14.1 Extension of Net Channels to the Case 1:n

First, we extend the package `nU/nchan` with the aim to provide network channels not only for 1:1-connections between processes on two computers, but also for 1:n-connections between a server and *several* clients. The most important application, then, is the network-wide realization of the *client-server paradigm* (see Sect. 11.5).

The main difference between this and a simple case is that a server must be able to listen to *several* computers in order to receive their requests in the form of messages and send his reply to *exactly that* client who sent the request to it.

For this purpose, we extend the representation of the network channels by two local channels `in, out chan Any`, which we use for the communication within the server. Thus, it looks like this:

© Springer Fachmedien Wiesbaden GmbH, part of Springer Nature 2021
C. Maurer, *Nonsequential and Distributed Programming with Go*,
https://doi.org/10.1007/978-3-658-29782-4_14

```
type netChannel struct {
  Any "pattern object"
  uint "capacity of the channel"
  in, out chan Any
  Stream "buffer to transmit data"
  net.Conn "communication channel"
}
```

The advantage of using the channels is, inter alia, that guarded selective waiting can be used in an application, which is an essential part of the performance of the concept. To be able to use them, a method for exporting them must, of course, be provided and included in the specification.

In the parameter for the host name, the name of the communication partner is no longer passed to the constructor as in the 1:1-case, but that of the server. A Boolean parameter is used to determine whether the calling process shall play the role of the server or that of a client. As a consequence, the identities that made this distinction possible in Sect. 13.3 via 1:1-network channels have become superfluous and are no longer handed over. This extends the specification of the interface NetChannel in this section by the method for exporting the two local channels and a constructor for 1:n-connections:

```
type NetChannel interface {
  ...

// Returns the input- and the output-channel,
// which allow an user, to communicate with
// server-processes that are branched off.
  Chan() (chan Any, chan Any)
}

// ...
// h is the name of the server.
// If s has the value true, the calling process
// plays the role of the server, otherwise that of a client.
// ...
func NewN (a Any, h string, port uint16, s bool) NetChannel {
  return newf(a,h,port,s) }
```

In the case of a server, the function Accept now no longer returns the descriptor for the send and receive operations of "the" 1:1-partner, but that of *any* client. Its operation is outsourced to a concurrent process to which this descriptor is passed, whereby the role of the additional channels is clearly shown:

```
var c0 = C0()

func (x *netChannel) serve (c net.Conn) {
  var r int
  for {
    r, x.error = c.Read (x.Stream)
```

```
    if r == 0 {
      break
    }
    if x.Any == nil {
      x.uint = uint(Decode (uint(0), x.Stream[:c0]).(uint))
      x.in <- x.Stream[c0:c0+x.uint]
      a := <-x.out
      x.uint = Codelen(a)
      _, x.error = c.Write(append(Encode(x.uint),
Encode(a)...))
    } else {
      x.in <- Decode (Clone (x.Any), x.Stream[:r])
      _, x.error = c.Write (Encode(<-x.out))
    }
  }
  c.Close()
}
```

If NewN is called successively, the correct pairing must be observed in both programs in order to avoid deadlocks.

Altogether we have the following extension of the implementation from 1:1-network channels (see Sect. 13.3) to 1:*n* network channels:

```
func (x *netChannel) Chan() (chan Any, chan Any) {
  return x.in, x.out
}

func newn (a Any, h string, port uint16, s bool) NetChannel {
  x := new(netChannel)
  x.Any = Clone(a)
  x.uint = Codelen(a)
  if a == nil {
    x.uint = maxWidth
  }
  x.Stream = make([]byte, x.uint)
  x.in, x.out = make(chan Any), make(chan Any)
  x.isServer = s
  ps := ":" + strconv.Itoa(int(port))
  if x.isServer {
    x.Listener, x.error = net.Listen (network, ps)
    go func() {
      for {
        if c, e := x.Listener.Accept(); e == nil { // NOT
x.Conn, x.error !
          go x.serve (c) // see above remark
        }
      }
    }()
  } else { // client
```

```
    for {
      if x.Conn, x.error = net.Dial (network, h + ps);
x.error == nil {
          break
      }
      time.Sleep(500 * 1e6)
    }
  }
  return x
}
```

14.2   Construction of the Far Monitors

We now extend the concept of universal conditioned monitors to that of the *far monitors*, which, beyond their functionality offer *distribution*. The server runs in an operating system process on *one* computer, and clients call the monitor functions within operating system processes on *this* or on *other* computers. A major advantage of our construct in comparison with remote procedure calls is that servers and clients use the same source code, thus eliminating the need for a separate— quite costly—compilation. To my knowledge, this concept has not been found in the literature so far —nor has our concept of universal critical sections and universal monitors.

14.2.1 Specification

For the parameters in the constructor New the same preconditions apply as for monitors. Furthermore, it is presumed,, that

- h is the name of a computer accessible in the network,
- the values of p do not exceed the number $16384 = 1 \ll 16 -$ nchan.Port0,
- the ports used are not occupied by other network services, and
- a process on the computer h also starts a far monitor and, thus, adopts the role of the server by calling New with the same values, except for the last one that must contain the value true.

This is the specification of the far monitors:

```
package fmon
import (. "nU/obj")

type FarMonitor interface {

// Pre: i < number of the monitor functions of x.
```

```
// The value of a is sent with the call to the server.
// The monitor function fs(_, i) is executed on the server;
// until the i-th predicate ps(-, i) was true.
// Returns the value, that was sent back by the server.
   F (a Any, i uint) Any

// All network-channels occupied by x are closed.
   Fin()
}


// Pre: fs and ps are defined in their second argument
//       for all i < n. h is the name of a computer, that
//       is contained in /etc/hosts or accessible via DNS.
//       The ports p..p+n-1 are not used by a network service.
//       In case s == true New is called by a process
//       on the computer h.
// Returns a far monitor with n monitor functions.
// For all i < n fs(_,i) is the i-th monitor function
// and ps(_, i) the corresponding predicate, with which it
// is decided, whether the monitor function can be executed.
// h is the name of the server, that executes the monitor
// and p..p+n-1 are the ports, that are used by the
// TCP-IP-connections between server and clients.
// The needed network channels are open.
// The far monitor runs as server, iff s == true,
// otherwise as client.
// For a == nil objects of different sizes with
// a codelength <= 4096 can be sent or received.
// In this case the server as value of a monitor call
// returns a byte sequence of type Stream and
// the caller has to decode that sequence himself;
// otherwise this is done by the receive operations
// of the used network channels.
func New (a Any, n uint, fs FuncSpectrum, ps PredSpectrum,
            h string, p uint16, s bool) FarMonitor {
   return new_(a,n,fs,ps,h,port,s)
}
```

14.2.2 Implementation

The basic idea behind the implementation of the constructor is very close to that of the conditioned universal monitors:

```
package fmon
import ("time"; . "nU/obj"; "nU/nchan")

type farMonitor struct {
```

```
    Any "pattern object"
    uint "number of the monitor functions"
    ch []nchan.NetChannel
    FuncSpectrum; PredSpectrum
    bool "true iff the monitor is the server"
}

func new_(a Any, n uint, fs FuncSpectrum, ps PredSpectrum,
         h string, p uint16, s bool) FarMonitor {
  x := new(farMonitor)
  x.Any = Clone(a)
  x.uint = n
  x.ch = make([]nchan.NetChannel, x.uint)
  x.bool = s
  in := make([]chan Any, x.uint)
  out := make([]chan Any, x.uint)
  any := make([]Any, x.uint)
  for i := uint(0); i < x.uint; i++ {
    x.ch[i] = nchan.NewN (x.Any, h, p + uint16(i), s)
    in[i], out[i] = x.ch[i].Chan()
  }
  if ! x.bool {
    return x // x is a client
  }
  x.FuncSpectrum = fs
  x.PredSpectrum = ps
  for i := uint(0); i < x.uint; i++ {
    go func (j uint) {
      for {
        select {
        case any[j] = <-When (x.PredSpectrum (x.Any, j),
in[j]):
            if x.PredSpectrum (any[j], j) {
              out[j] <- x.FuncSpectrum (any[j], j)
            } else {
              out[j] <- x.FuncSpectrum (x.Any, j)
            }
        default:
        }
        time.Sleep(1e9)
      }
    }(i)
  }
  return x
}

func (x *farMonitor) F (a Any, i uint) Any {
  x.ch[i].Send (a)
  return x.ch[i].Recv()
```

```
}

func (x *farMonitor) Fin() {
  for i := uint(0); i < x.uint; i++ {
    x.ch[i].Fin()
  }
}
```

The clients with their function calls are now served by the server, i.e., the server receives objects from them and sends them back to them after processing. For this purpose, at the creation of the server a goroutine is branched off for each of the n monitor functions. Of course, clients must not get to this point, because they would otherwise also have to work as a server; this is secured by the program line commented by "x is a client".

The goroutines of the server do this as follows. For each j < n, they always enquire within an infinite loop by guarded selective waiting (with a combination of select statement and When) the input channel provided by the network channel used to determine whether a request has been received from a client (see Sect. 11.7).

That cannot be done without default branch in the select statement, because otherwise, if the predicate is not fulfilled, which happens all the time in between, the process according to the description of select would remain blocked and would, therefore, no longer be able to react to further calls (see 11.4).

With When only a "preliminary check" is carried out with the pattern object x.Any, which was passed to the constructor of the far monitor.

Then it is checked whether the received object any[j] *also* fulfills this predicate. Although this second check is obsolete in *those* cases in which no objects other than the pattern object are sent in the monitor calls, which is the case in many examples in the next sections. However, this is necessary in applications such as account management, where each monitor call sends the amount to be deposited or withdrawn.

If this "precheck" already returns a negative result, the calling process remains blocked, because the channel in[j] has the value nil, and, therefore, no reception is possible (see the specification of When in Sect. 11.7).

Otherwise, if also the second check is positive, i.e., the j-th predicate from the predicate spectrum returns true, the object any[j] from the j-th function from the function spectrum is processed and sent back via the output channel of the network channel. Otherwise, the far monitor must return a special value that shows a client—e.g., in the case of an intended withdrawal from an account—that this request could not be served.

14.3 Correctness

The semantics of this procedure is exactly the same as for conditioned monitors (see Sect. 10.2.2). Not accepting the message on the channel in[i] by virtue of the When construct (see Sect. 11.7 in the chapter on message exchange) corresponds to the call of wait if

!x.PredSpectrum(pattern, j); and the processing of the value of the message in the statement x.FuncSpectrum(any[j], j) and the subsequent return of the result on the channel out[j] correspond to the call of y = x.NFuncSpectrum(i) and the return of the result with return.

For this reason, it is clear that in applications, the constructions of the function and condition spectra NFuncSpectrum and CondSpectrum, as well as the calls of the monitor functions F at the far monitors are *nearly identical* with the corresponding constructions of the function and predicate spectra FuncSpectrum and PredSpectrum in applications of conditioned monitors.

For example, compare the source text of the constructor of the conditioned monitor for semaphores in Sect. 10.3 with that of the constructor in the following section.

Since our implementation of the constructor of a universal monitor in Sect. 10.2.2 is only a straightforward translation of the simulation of the monitor concept by semaphores in Sect. 9.10 of the chapter on monitors, which is admittedly recognized as correct (see [4] Sect. 2, [2] Sect. 5.4, [1] Sect. 6.6 (implementations), and [5] Sect. 3.3.4), the procedure is correct.

14.4   Distributed Semaphores

As first simple application we show a distributed implementation of the interface of semaphores in Sect. 4.5.1—in contrast to Sect. 13.4 a *centralized* solution of *distributed* mutual exclusion.

In these examples—as in all subsequent sections— the respective constructor, of course, has to be included in the specification in the form of an appropriate function call.

```
package sem
import (. "nU/obj", "nU/fmon")

type farMonitor struct {
  fmon.FarMonitor
}

func newFM (n uint, h string, port uint16, s bool) Semaphore {
  x := new(farMonitor)
  val := n
  ps := func (a Any, i uint) bool {
        if i == p {
          return val > 0
        }
        return true
      }
  f := func (a Any, i uint) Any {
        if i == p {
          val--
```

```
            } else {
                val++
            }
            return true
        }
    x.FarMonitor = fmon.New (false, 2, f, ps, h, port, s)
    return x
}


func (x *farMonitor) P() { x.F (true, p) }
func (x *farMonitor) V() { x.F (true, v) }
```

14.5   Distributed Queues and Bounded Buffers

The following examples are also so simple that it is hardly necessary to explain them (“*the source is the doc*”). The only point worth mentioning is that the pattern object is indispensable to avoid a type error when returning the values of the monitor functions. The object passed in the call of Get of the monitor function F as first parameter must have the same type as the one passed as first parameter to the constructor of the far monitor.

```
package mbuf
import (. "nU/obj"; "nU/buf", "nU/fmon")

const (ins = uint(iota), get)

type farMonitor struct {
  Any "Musterobjekt"
  buf.Buffer
  fmon.FarMonitor
}

func newFM (a Any, h string, port uint16, s bool) MBuffer {
  x := new(farMonitor)
  x.Any = Clone (a)
  x.Buffer = buf.New (a)
  p := func (a Any, i uint) bool {
          if i == get {
              return x.Buffer.Num() > 0
          }
          return true
      }
  f := func (a Any, i uint) Any {
          if i == get {
              return x.Buffer.Get()
          }
          x.Buffer.Ins (a)
```

```
            return a
         }
  x.FarMonitor = fmon.New (a, 2, f, p, h, port, s)
  return x
}


func (x *farMonitor) Fin() { x.FarMonitor.Fin() }


func (x *farMonitor) Ins (a Any) { x.F(a, ins) }
func (x *farMonitor) Get() Any { return x.F(x.Any, get) }
```

The distributed solution of *bounded* buffers is a trivial modification of the previous ones; the capacity of the buffer must also be passed to the constructor, and `Buffer` is replaced by `BoundedBuffer` and the package `buf` by `bbuf`.

14.6   Distributed Readers–Writers and Left–Right Problems

The distributed solutions to these problems are the straightforward translations of the solutions with a conditioned monitor, whereby the first parameter in the monitor functions is irrelevant. It only has to be ensured that—as in the previous section—their types are the same and that they match the type of the object that is given to the constructor of the far monitor as first parameter.

Here is the implementation for the readers–writers problem:

```
package rw
import (. "nU/obj"; "nU/fmon")

type farMonitor struct {
  fmon.FarMonitor
}


func newFM (h string, port uint16, s bool) ReaderWriter {
  var nR, nW uint
  x := new(farMonitor)
  p := func (a Any, i uint) bool {
        switch i {
        case readerIn:
          return nW == 0
        case writerIn:
          return nR == 0 && nW == 0
        }
        return true // readerOut, writerOut
      }
  f := func (a Any, i uint) Any {
        switch i {
        case readerIn:
```

```
                 nR++
                 return nR
             case readerOut:
                 nR--
                 return nR
             case writerIn:
                 nW = 1
             case writerOut:
                 nW = 0
                 }
             return nW
           }
    x.FarMonitor = fmon.New (uint(0), 4, f, p, h, port, s)
    return x
}


func (x *farMonitor) ReaderIn() { x.F (0, readerIn) }
func (x *farMonitor) ReaderOut() { x.F (0, readerOut) }
func (x *farMonitor) WriterIn() { x.F (0, writerIn) }
func (x *farMonitor) WriterOut() { x.F (0, writerOut) }
```

and here is the implementation for the left–right problem:

```
package lr
import (. "nU/obj"; "nU/fmon")

type farMonitor struct {
  fmon.FarMonitor
}

func newFM (h string, port uint16, s bool) LeftRight {
  var nL, nR uint
  x := new(farMonitor)
  p := func (a Any, i uint) bool {
         switch i {
         case leftIn:
           return nR == 0
         case rightIn:
           return nL == 0
         }
         return true // leftOut, rightOut
       }
    f := func (a Any, i uint) Any {
         switch i {
         case leftIn:
           nL++
         case leftOut:
           nL--
         case rightIn:
           nR++
```

```
         case rightOut:
           nR--
         }
         return 0
     }
  x.FarMonitor = fmon.New (0, 4, f, p, h, port, s)
  return x
}

func (x *farMonitor) LeftIn () { x.F (0, leftIn) }
func (x *farMonitor) LeftOut () { x.F (0, leftOut) }
func (x *farMonitor) RightIn () { x.F (0, rightIn) }
func (x *farMonitor) RightOut () { x.F (0, rightOut) }
```

The source texts for this book contain the file farlr.go—a program to animate the
left–right problem with far monitors.

It is a very simple exercise to extend these two solutions in such a way that their inherent
unfairness is eliminated (see, e.g., the second readers–writers problem or the bounded left–
right problem).

14.7   Account

Here is the example mentioned above, in which in the call of a monitor function, an object
is sent to the monitor, and after is has been processed is returned with another value. A
client can deposit money without restriction; the return value of the request is the deposited
amount, correspondingly, with a request to withdraw if the account balance is sufficient for
the requested amount with the withdrawn amount as return value.

Otherwise, the client cannot be blocked because the far monitor cannot perform the check
if it does not know the amount requested. Consequently, it has to receive the message sent
to it on the input channel in the When clause to evaluate the predicate ps (any[draw],
draw) in the following line. If the account balance is not sufficient, the pattern object is
returned —in this case 0—from which the client recognizes without doubt that the payout
is not possible.

The implementation is also immediately understandable here:

```
package macc
import (. "nU/obj"; "nU/mon")

const (deposit = uint(iota), draw)

type farMonitor struct {
  fmon.FarMonitor
}

func newFM (h string, port uint16, s bool) MAccount {
```

```
balance := uint (0)
x := new (farMonitor)
p := func (a Any, i uint) bool {
      if i == deposit {
        return true
      }
      return balance >= a.(uint) // draw
   }
f := func (a Any, i uint) Any {
      if i == deposit {
        balance += a.(uint)
      } else {
        balance -= a.(uint)
      }
      return a
   }
x.FarMonitor = fmon.New (balance, 2, f, p, h, port, s)
return x
}

func (x *farMonitor) Deposit (a uint) uint {
  return x.FarMonitor.F (a, deposit).(uint)
}

func (x *farMonitor) Draw (a uint) uint {
  return x.FarMonitor.F (a, draw).(uint)
}
```

14.8   Remote Procedure Calls

In the package `net/rpc`, the Go library offers a construction of servers and clients for remote procedure calls. It is, however, quite tricky and in relation to the possibilities of its use in abstract layers with respect to the principle of *information hiding*, it is, in my opinion, suboptimal.

The simplest general form of a remote procedure call is a function with a single argument, which in the general case is of the type `func (a Any) Any`. (This type is called `Func` and is contained in the package `nU/obj`.)

The realization is given by the client–server paradigm: The possibility of a remote procedure call is provided by a server, which can be used by clients.

In details the following happens:

1. The rpc-server starts the RPC with the function in question.
2. A client does the following:

a) He calls the far function with an argument.
b) A "*stub*" encodes the argument as stream,
c) sends this stream to the server process, and
d) waits for the receipt of the result.

3. This stream is transmitted over the network to the server.
4. The server does the following:

a) He receives the stream and
b) his stub decodes from that the received argument.
c) He calls the function with this argument and
d) executes it.
e) His stub encodes the function result as a stream and
f) sends this stream back.

5. The stream is transported over the network to the client.
6. The client now does the following:

a) He receives the stream,
b) its stub decodes the result from that, and
c) he, thus, has the result of the remote call.

The procedure is schematically represented in Fig. 14.1, (taken from Fig. 1 on page. 44 in [3]).

Because this is the same basic idea as for far monitors, the specification of a corresponding package `rpc` looks almost the same as that of the far monitors. This is why we show only the syntax:

```
package rpc
import . "nU/obj"

type RPC interface {
  F (a Any, i Any) Any
  Fin ()
}
```

It is left as an exercise to formulate the comments to this specification. (Hint: Specification of the far monitors—solution in the nUniverse.)

Far monitors operate on objects of *one* type, whereas, here, the type of the result is usually different from the type of the argument. Therefore, the constructor must be extended by a parameter of the result type in which an object of the result type is passed. Apart from this, no predicate spectrum is needed; therefore, clients have to make sure themselves that all assumptions for the execution of the far function are fulfilled. The last parameter passed is the function defined by the client that is to be executed on the far server.

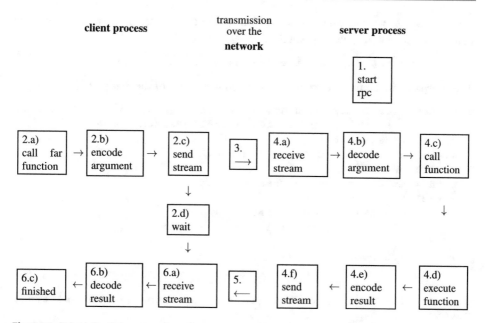

Fig. 14.1 Principle of the execution of remote procedure calls

```
func New (a, b Any, h string, p uint16, s bool, fs
FuncSpectrum) RPC {
             return new_(a,b,h,p,s,fs) }
```

However, for the implementation, we need an extension of the far monitors that takes into account the second parameter of the constructor being of another type, i.e., a second constructor

```
func New2 (a, b Any, n uint, fs FuncSpectrum, ps PredSpectrum,
           h string, p uint16, s bool) FarMonitor {
    return new2(a,n,fs,ps,h,p,s) }
```

The second type must, of course, be included in the representation:

```
package fmon
import ("time"; . "nU/obj"; "nU/nchan")

type farMonitor struct {
  Any "pattern object for the argument"
  result Any // pattern object for the result
  ... // rest as in the above implementation
}
```

The implementation of the constructor New2 is very similar to that of new_. Since the sizes of the objects can be different, as first parameter nil is passed to the constructors for the required network channels (see the specification of the constructor New in Sect. 13.3).

The predicate spectrum, which is not needed for the constructor of the remote procedure call, is replaced by `AllTrueSp` in the package `nU/obj`:

```
func AllTrueSp (a Any, i uint) Any { return true }
```

The rear part—in the method `common`—is identical to that of the rear part of `new_`:

```
func new2 (a, b Any, n uint, fs FuncSpectrum, ps PredSpectrum,
          h string, p uint16, s bool) FarMonitor {
  x := new (farMonitor)
  x.Any, x.result = Clone (a), Clone (b)
  x.uint = n
  x.ch = make ([]nchan.NetChannel, x.uint)
  x.bool = s
  for i := uint (0); i < x.uint; i++ {
    x.ch[i] = nchan.NewN (nil, h, p + uint16 (i), s)
  }
  return x.common (fs, ps)
}

func (x *farMonitor) common (fs FuncSpectrum, ps PredSpectrum)
FarMonitor {
  in, out := make ([]chan Any, x.uint), make ([]chan Any, x.uint)
  for i := uint (0); i < x.uint; i++ {
    in[i], out[i] = x.ch[i].Chan ()
  }
  if ! x.bool {
    return x // x ist ein Kunde
  }
  x.FuncSpectrum, x.PredSpectrum = fs, ps // x is the server
  any := make ([]Any, x.uint)
  for i := uint (0); i < x.uint; i++ {
    ... // rest as in the implementation of new_
```

The implementation of our remote procedure call package with a far monitor is, therefore, absolutely trivial:

```
package rpc
import (. "nU/obj"; "nU/fmon")

type rpc struct {
  fmon.FarMonitor
}

func new_ (a, b Any, n uint, h string, p uint16, s bool,
           fs FuncSpectrum) RPC {
  return &rpc { fmon.New2 (a, b, n, f, AllTrueSp, h, p, fs,
Nothing) }
}
```

The functions F and Fin from the interface do not have to be implemented, because they are taken directly from the "inherited" far monitor.

14.8.1 Example of a Remote Procedure Call

With the type Intstream = []Int in the package obj and appropriate enhancements of the implementations of the functions obj/equaler.go and obj/coder.go (see Sects. 2.3.2.1 and 2.3.2.4), we can realize the example given in the file net/rpc/server. go by the Go authors, in which the product of 7 and 8 is calculated remotely, as follows:

```go
package main
import (. "nU/obj"; "nU/ego"; "nU/rpc")

func f (a Any, i uint) Any {
  p := IntStream{0, 0}.Decode (p, a.(Stream)).(IntStream)
  return p[0] * p[1]
}

func main() {
  serving := ego.Me() == 0
  input, c := IntStream{7, 8}, 0
  server, port := ..., ...
  r := rpc.New (input, c, server, port, serving, f)
  if serving { // rpc-server is called
    for { }
  } else { // Kunde
    output = Decode (c, r.F (input, 0).(Stream)).(int)
    println ("7 * 8 =", c)
  }
}
```

If in the call 0 is passed as an argument, the server is started, otherwise it is a call of a client (which, of course, assumes the start of the server). Strictly speaking, the explicit declaration of the construction of the return value of the remote procedure call in the function f—i.e., in the implementation of this function—contradicts the reasonable requirement that this source code is actually only implemented on the computer on which the server process is running. However, this can easily be achieved by outsourcing the function f into a separate package f with the specification

```go
package f
import "nU/obj"

func f (a Any) Any { return f(a) }
```

and by implementing f on the server computer as follows:

```go
func f (a Any) Any {
```

```
if ego.Me() == 0 {
  p := IntStream{0, 0}
  p = Decode (p, a.(Stream)).(IntStream)
  return p[0] * p[1]
}
return 0
}
```

On all other computers on which f can be called, it is simply implemented in such a way that it only returns a meaningless value—e.g., the corresponding *zero value*:

```
func f (a Any, i uint) Any {
  return 0
}
```

So, the example is as follows:

```
package main
import (". nU/obj; "nU/ego"; "nU/rpc"; "f")

func main() {
  ... // the first three source code lines as above
  r := rpc.New (input, c, server, port, serving, f.F)
  ... // as above
}
```

References

1. Andrews, G.R.: Foundations of Multithreaded, Parallel and Distributed Programming. Addison-Wesley, Reading (2000)
2. Ben-Ari, M.: Principles of Concurrent and Distributed Programming. Prentice Hall, Hemel Hempstead (1990)
3. Birrell, A.D., Nelson, B.J.: Implementing remote procedure calls. ACM Trans. Comput. Syst. **2**, 39–59 (1984). https://doi.org/10.1145/2080.357392
4. Hoare, C.A.R.: Monitors: an operating systems structuring concept. Commun. ACM **17**, 549–557 (1974). https://doi.org/10.1145/355620.361161
5. Raynal, M.: Concurrent Programming: Algorithms, Principles and Foundations. Springer, Berlin Heidelberg (2013)

Networks as Graphs

15

Abstract

In this chapter, the concept of *graphs* is taken up and formalized. For this purpose, an abstract data type is presented as an interface that describes graphs and is extended to an interface for distributed graphs. The reason for this is obvious: A network conceptually represents an undirected graph. The processes on the participating computers, uniquely defined by their name or IP address, form its vertices and the communication paths between them—realized by network lines, e.g., Ethernet cables, and the programs that enable the network traffic—the transport of messages over the network, e.g., by TCP/IP, form its edges. The following chapters will show that many distributed algorithms fit exactly into this framework.

15.1 Graphs

To avoid misunderstandings, we define a few basic terms:

A *relation* R on a set S is a subset $R \subset S \times S$ of pairs of elements from S. R is called

- *reflexive*, if $(x, x) \in R$ for all $x \in S$,
- *irreflexive*, if there is no $x \in S$ with $(x, x) \in R$,
- *strict*, if for all $x, y \in S$, $(x, y) \in R$ implies $(y, x) \notin R$, and
- *symmetric*, if for all $x, y \in S$, $(x, y) \in R$ implies that also $(y, x) \in R$.

For $(x, y) \in R$, usually only $x R y$ is written.

© Springer Fachmedien Wiesbaden GmbH, part of Springer Nature 2021
C. Maurer, *Nonsequential and Distributed Programming with Go*,
https://doi.org/10.1007/978-3-658-29782-4_15

15.1.1 Definition of the Graph Concept

This allows us to clearly define the term "graph". A *graph* is a pair (G, R) of a set G and an *irreflexive* relation $R \subset G \times G$ on G. The elements of G are called *vertices* (sometimes also denoted as *nodes*). Two vertices $v, v_1 \in G$ with $(v, v_1) \in R$ form an "*edge*" from v to v_1. In this case, the vertices v and v_1 are *connected* by this edge—v is a *neighbour*(-vertex) of v_1 and vice versa, wherein the edge seen from v is an *outgoing* edge and seen from v_1, it is an *incoming* one; R is, therefore, also often called a "*neighbourhood relation*". The *irreflexiveness* of R means that no vertex in the graph is connected by an edge to itself.

If the neighbourhood relation R is *strict*, the graph is called "*directed*", i.e., each edge (v, v_1) has a *direction*—"from v to v_1"; if R is symmetric, it is called *undirected*, i.e., *no* edge (v, v_1) has a direction.

The *star* of a vertex v of a graph (G, R) is the graph (G', R') with $G' = \{v' \in G \mid (v, v') \in R\}$ and $R' = R \cap (\{v\} \times G)$, i.e., with v and the neighbours of v as vertices and all edges $(v, v') \in R$ of the neighbours (but not with the edges *between* these neighbours!).

A *path* in a graph (G, R) from a vertex $v_1 \in G$ to a vertex $v \in G$ is a sequence of edges $(v_1, v_2), (v_2, v_3), \ldots, (v_{n_1}, v) \in R$ ($v_i \in G$) with vertices $v_i \in G$ ($1 \leq i < n$), i.e., from each of these vertices v_i—with the exception of the last one—an edge goes out to the next vertex v_{i+1}.

A *simple path* is a path made up of pairwise different vertices.

The *length of a path* is the sum of the values of all its edges—for unvalued graphs, this is their number. A *shortest path* between two vertices v_1 and v in a graph is the minimum of the lengths of all paths from v_1 to v.

A *circle* is a path with $(v_{n-1}, v_0 \in R$, so with an extra edge from the last vertex v_{n-1} of the path to v_0, the first one. The *diameter* of a graph is the maximum of the lengths of all shortest paths between any two vertices in it.

An *undirected* graph (G, R) is called *connected*, when between any two vertices v, $v_1 \in G$, there is a path in G from v to v_1 or vice versa. A *directed* graph is called *strongly connected* if between any two vertices $v, v_1 \in G$, there is a path from v to v_1, as well as one from v_1 to v.

▶   In this book, only (strongly) connected graphs are considered.

15.2   Realization in Go

The interface presented in the next section requires some explanations. We consider only graphs whose vertices are "reasonable" objects, i.e., either variables of an elementary data type or objects that implement our interface `Object` (see Sects. 2.3 and 2.3.3 in Chap. 2 about packages, etc.).

The outgoing edges from a vertex are numbered consecutively, beginning with 0; the vertex with which a vertex is connected by its n-th outgoing edge is denoted as its n-th (outgoing or incoming, if necessary) neighbour vertex.

In addition, we restrict ourselves to *valued* graphs, those whose edges have a natural number as a *value*. (Sometimes they are called *weighted* graphs, and integer or real numbers are allowed as values.) For this, we need the following interface, which is included in the package obj:

```
package obj

type Valuator interface {

// Returns the value of x.
  Val() uint

// Returns true, iff x can be given a value.
// In this case x.Val() == n.
// Returns otherwise false.
  SetVal (n uint) bool
}

func Val (a Any) uint { return val(a) }
func SetVal (x *Any, n uint) { setVal(x,n) }
```

For valued graphs, we demand that:

- either all edges have the value 1, or
- their value is determined by the function val.

So, they have to be of a uint-compatible type (uint{8|16|32|64}) or implement the interface Valuator.

The following terms prove to be very useful when describing algorithms, especially when manipulating individual vertices or edges of a graph, such as connecting vertices by edges or searching for vertices, edges, or neighbours. In every nonempty graph, exactly one vertex is marked as the *colocal* vertex, and one as the *local* vertex. Furthermore, we allow vertices and edges in a graph to be *marked*.

15.2.1 Specification

The interface of the package gra begins with the clause Object, i.e., it implements *that* interface. Consequently, our graphs also implement the interfaces Equaler, Comparer, Clearer, and Coder (see Sects.2.3.2, etc. and 2.3.3). This is important because coding and decoding graphs as streams is used in all our distributed algorithms where graphs are transported over the net.

The specification is

```
package gra
import . "nU/obj"

type Graph interface {

  Object

// Returns true, iff x is directed.
  Directed() bool

// Returns the number of vertices of x.
  Num() uint

// Returns the number of edges of x.
  Num1() uint

// Returns the number of marked vertices of x.
  NumMarked() uint

// Returns the number of marked edges of x.
  NumMarked1() uint

// If v is not of the vertex-type of x
// or if v is already contained in x,
// nothing has happened. Otherwise:
// v is inserted as vertex in x.
// If x was empty, then v is now the colocal and local
// vertex of x, otherwise, v is now the local vertex and
// the former local vertex is now the colocal vertex of x.
  Ins (v Any)

// If x was empty or if the colocal vertex of x coincides
// with the local vertex of x, or if e is not of the edge-type
// of x, nothing has happened. Otherwise:
// e is inserted into x as edge from the colocal to the
// local vertex of x (if these two vertices were already
// connected by an edge, that edge is replaced by e).
// For e == nil e is replaced by uint(1).
  Edge (e Any)

// Returns true, iff the colocal vertex of x does not
// coincide with the local vertex of x and there is
// no edge in x from the colocal to the local vertex.
  Edged() bool

// Returns true, iff v is contained as vertex in x.
// In this case v is now the local vertex of x.
```

```
// The colocal vertex of x is the same as before.
  Ex (v Any) bool

// Returns true, iff v and v1 are contained as vertices
// in x and do not coincide. In this case now
// v is the colocal vertex in x and v1 the local.
  Ex2 (v, v1 Any) bool

// Pre: p is defined on vertices.
// Returns true, iff there is a vertex in x, for which
// p returns true. In this case now some such vertex
// is the local vertex of x.
// The colocal vertex of x is the same as before.
  ExPred (p Pred) bool

// Returns the pattern vertex of x, if x is empty.
// Returns otherwise a clone of the local vertex of x.
  Get () Any

// Returns a clone of the pattern edge of x, if x is empty
// or if there is no edge from the colocal vertex to the
// local vertex in x or if these two vertices coincide.
// Returns otherwise a clone of the edge from the
// colocal vertex of x to the local vertex of x.
  Get1 () Any

// Returns (nil, nil), if x is empty.
// Returns otherwise a pair, consisting of clones
// of the colocal and of the local vertices of x.
  Get2 () (Any, Any)

// If x is empty or if v is not of the vertex-type of x
// or if v is not contained in x, nothing has happened.
// Otherwise, v is now the local vertex of x and is marked.
// The colocal vertex of x is the same as before.
  Mark (v Any)

// If x is empty of if v or v1 are not of the vertex-type
// of x or if v or v1 is not contained in x or
// if v and v1 coincide, nothing has happened.
// Otherwise, v is now the colocal and v1 the
// local vertex of x and these two vertices and
// the edge between them are now marked.
  Mark2 (v, v1 Any)

// Returns true, if all vertices
// and all edges of x are marked.
  AllMarked () bool
```

```
// If x is empty, nothing has happened. Otherwise:
// The colocal vertex of x coincides with the

// local vertex of x, where for f == true that
// was the former local vertex and for f == false
// the vertex that was the former colocal vertex of x.
// The only marked vertex is this vertex;
// no edges are marked.
   Locate (f bool)


// Returns 0, if x is empty. Returns otherwise the
// number of all incoming and outgoing edges to
// resp. from the local vertex of x.
   NumNeighbours() uint


// Returns false, if x is empty or if
// i >= NumNeighbourOut(); returns otherwise true,
// iff the edge to the i-th neighbour
// of the local vertex is an outgoing edge.
   Outgoing (i uint) bool


// Returns nil, if x is empty or if
// i >= NumNeighbours(); returns otherwise
// a clone of the i-th neighbour vertex
// of the local vertex of x.
   Neighbour (i uint) Any


// Pre: o is defined on vertices.
// o is applied to all vertices of x.
// The colocal and the local vertex of x
// are the same as before;
// the marked vertices and edges are unaffected.
   Trav (o Op)


// Returns nil, if x is empty.
// Returns otherwise the graph consisting of the
// local vertex of x, all its neighbour vertices and
// of all edges outgoing from it and incoming to it.
// The local vertex of x is the local vertex
// of the star. It is the only marked vertex
// in the star; all edges in the star are marked.
   Star() Graph


// Pre: x is directed, iff all graphs y are directed.
// x consists of all vertices and edges of x before
// and of all graphs y.
// Thereby all marks of y are overtaken.
   Add (y ...Graph)
```

```
// Pre: w is defined on vertices and w2 on edges.
// w and w2 are the actual write functions
// for the vertices and the edges of x.

  SetWrite (w CondOp, w2 CondOp2)

// The values of the vertices of x and all edges
// of x are written to the screen in simple lines.
  Write()
}


// Pre: v is atomic or implements Object.
//      e == nil or e is of a uint-type
//      or implements Valuator.
// Returns an empty graph, which is directed,
// iff d == true (otherwise undirected).
// v is the pattern vertex of x defining the type
// of the vertices of x.
// For e == nil e is replaced by uint(1) and
// all edges have the value 1; otherwise
// e is the pattern edge of x, which
// defines the type of the edges of x.
func New (d bool, v, e Any) Graph { return new_(d,v,e) }
```

15.2.2 Implementation

Since the specification of the package is absolutely sufficient to understand the distributed algorithms in the next chapters, we will not reproduce the implementation here. Exactly *that* is one of the advantages of our postulate of the strict separation of specification and implementation—see Sect. 2.1 on the role of packages. Only the representation of the objects occurring in it is sketched here.

Vertices, edges, and the relationships between them are represented by structs that are contained in doubly-linked ring lists with an "anchor node". The representation of a vertex or edge consists of the following components:

- a value of type Any for the pattern vertex/edge,
- for vertices one, for edges two pointers to the vertex-edge relationships,
- a Boolean value, whether or not it is marked, and
- pointers to the next and previous vertex/edge in the vertex/edge list;

and that of a vertex or edge of

- a pointer to its edge,
- two pointers to its two vertices,
- a Boolean value, whether it is an outgoing edge or not, and
- pointers to the next and previous vertex in the relationship list.

The representation of a graph consists essentially of

- its name to store the graph in a file,
- the Boolean value, whether or not it is directed,
- the number of its vertices and edges,
- pointers to the anchors of its vertex and edge list, and
- pointers to his colocal and his local vertex.

In addition, there are some other components in the representations that are useful for some algorithms—but they are irrelevant here.

As a prototypical example the implementation of the method is shown, which returns the star-shaped graph of the local vertex of the graph:

```go
func (x *graph) Star() Graph {
   y := new_(x.bool, x.vAnchor.Any, x.eAnchor.Any).(*graph)
   y.Ins (x.local.Any)
   y.local.bool = true
   local := y.local // saving the local vertex of y
   if ! x.bool {
      for n, i := x.local.nbPtr.nextNb, uint(0);
         n != x.local.nbPtr; n, i = n.nextNb, i + 1 {
         y.Ins (Clone(n.to.Any)) // a now colocal
         y.edgeMarked (Clone(n.edgePtr.Any), true) // edge
                     // from a to the local inserted vertex
                     // with the same content as in x
         y.local = local // a now again local vertex in y
      }
   } else { // x.bool
      for n, i := x.local.nbPtr.nextNb, uint(0);
         n != x.local.nbPtr; n, i = n.nextNb, i + 1 {
         y.Ins (Clone(n.to.Any)) // a is now again the colocal
   // vertex and the inserted vertex is the local vertex in y
         if n.outgoing { // we need an edge from a
                     // to the inserted vertex
         } else { // ! n.outgoing: we need an edge
                     // from the inserted vertex to a
            y.local, y.colocal = y.colocal, y.local
         }
         y.edgeMarked (Clone(n.edgePtr.Any), true) // edge in y
                     // from the colocal to the local vertex
         y.local = local
```

```
      }
    }
  return y
}
```

15.2.2.1 Writing Graphs to the Screen

The construction of the method `Write` in the `nU/gra` package is based on the nUniverse versions of the colour and screen packages that are drastically reduced versions of the corresponding packages in the μUniverse ([1]), which consist of several thousand lines of code.

The functions from these packages can be used to write texts (also in colour) and primitive lines between two screen positions to the screen, which consist only of the minus sign, the vertical line, and the two slashes. Thus, it is possible to write the figures of graphs contained in Chaps. 13, 16, 17, and 18—even if only somewhat roughly. If after each change, the statement for the output of a graph is inserted, this leads to the visualization of the algorithms during their execution.

The implementations of the two packages are not shown here; they are contained in the source texts of this book.

Here, is the specification of the *colour package*:

```
package col
import . "nU/obj"

type colour interface {
  Object

// Returns the red/green/blue-part of x.
  R() byte; G() byte; B() byte

// x has the part b for red/green/blue.
  SetR (b byte); SetG (b byte); SetB (b byte)
}

func New() colour { return new_() } // Black
func New3 (r, g, b byte) colour { return new3(r,g,b) }

func Black() colour    { return new3 (  0, 0, 0) }
func DarkRed() colour  { return new3 ( 85, 0, 0) }
func Red() colour      { return new3 (170, 0, 0) }
... etc.
```

and here is the specification of the *screen* package:

```
package scr
import "nU/col"
```

```
// character width/-height of the standard font
const (Wd1 = uint(8); Ht1 = uint(16)) // to be adjusted if
necessary

type Screen interface {

// Returns the pixelwidth/height of x.
  Wd() uint; Ht() uint

// Returns the number of text lines/columns of x.
  NLines() uint; NColumns() uint

// x is cleared. The cursor of x has the position (0, 0).
  Cls()

// f and b is the actual fore and background colour
// for writing operations.
  colours (f, b col.colour)
  ColourF (f col.colour); ColourB (b col.colour)

// The cursor of x is visible, iff on == true.
  Switch (on bool)

// Pre: 1 < NLines, c < NColumns.
// The cursor of x has the position (line, column) == (1, c).
// (0, 0) is the left top corner of x.
  Warp (1, c uint)

// The cursor of x has the position (1, 0), whereby 1 is
// the first line, that was not used be outputs of x.
  Fin()

// Pre: 32 <= b < 127, 1 < NLines, c + 1 < NColumns.
// b is written to x starting at position (1, c).
  Write1 (b byte, 1, c uint)

// Pre: 1 < NLines, c + len(s) < NColumns.
// s is written to x starting at position (1, c).
  Write (s string, 1, c uint)

// Pre: c + number of digits of n < NColumns, 1 < NLines.
// n is written to x starting at position (1, c).
  WriteNat (n, 1, c uint)

// Pre: 1, 11 < NLines, c, c1 < NColumns.
// A line consisting of the characters "-", "|", "/"
// and "\" is written to x from position (1,c) to (11,c1).
  Line (1, c, 11, c1 uint)
```

```
// Pre: l, c >= r, l + r < NLines, c + r < NColumns
// A circle consisting of the character "*" with the
// center (l, c) and the radius r is written to x.
   Circle (l, c, r uint)

// Guarantee the mutual exclusion
// for concurrent writing operations
   Lock(); Unlock()
}


// Returns a new screen.
func New() Screen { return new_() }
```

15.3   Adjacency Matrices

An alternative way to describe graphs is their representation as *adjacency matrices*. Usually, a square matrix $(m_{ik})_{n,n}$ with n rows and columns ($n > 0$) is called an *adjacency matrix*, if its entries m_{ik} are of truth values—realized by the numbers 0 and 1 for false and true, respectively. From this, it is possible to reversible uniquely construct a graph with the following properties. It has exactly n vertices with the contents 0, 1, ..., $n - 1$, and from a vertex i there is an edge to the vertex k, iff $m_{ik} = 1$. In this model, a graph is directed, iff its adjacency matrix is symmetric, i.e., iff $m_{ik} = m_{ki}$ for all $i, k < n$. But that is not enough for our needs.

With this definition, we can neither model graphs that have vertices with contents other than just consecutive pairwise different natural numbers, nor valued graphs.

So we expand it. An adjacency matrix is a matrix whose entries contain pairs of the form (v, e), where

- v is any object (where all these objects must be of the same type), and
- e is a natural number.

In Go, for the elements of these pairs, we allow—more generally—objects that are permitted as vertices or as edges in the package gra, Therefore, the corresponding data type is realized in this way:

```
type pair struct {
   vertex,   // vertex is atomic or implements Object
   edge Any // edge has a uint-type or implements Valuator
}
```

We also need a relation between adjacency matrices and graphs. The following additional methods in our package gra serve this purpose:

```
// Returns the representation of x as adjacency matrix.
```

```
Matrix() adj.AdjacencyMatrix

// Pre: a is symmetric, iff x is ordered.
// x is the graph with the vertices a.Vertex(i) and edges
// from a.Vertex(i) to a.Vertex(k),
// if a.Val(i,k) > 0 for all i, k < a.Num()).
  SetMatrix (a adj.AdjacencyMatrix)
```

Thus, an adjacency matrix is equivalent to a graph with its entries as vertices and edges, which are given by the position of the entries (vertices). Any such matrix $(a_{ij})_{n,n}$ defines a graph in the following way:

$a_{ik} = (v, e)$ means for

$i = k$: v is a vertex in the graph (in this case, e is the pattern vertex of x).

$i \neq k$: There is an edge from the i-th to the k-th vertex of the graph with the value of e, if e is not the "pattern edge" of the matrix with the value 0. In this case, v is the pattern vertex of x.

Thus, it is clear that in the algorithms, the information contained in an adjacency matrix can also be encoded in graphs that can be transported over the network—provided that the graph package—like our package `gra`—provides the necessary operations for this.

15.3.1 Specification

We now show the specification of the package `adj` that defines the abstract data type *adjacency matrix*, whose interface—as with the graphs—also implements the interface `Object`:

```
package adj
import . "nU/obj"

type AdjacencyMatrix interface {

  Object

// Returns the number of lines/columns of x.
  Num() uint

// Returns true, iff x and y have the same number of lines,
// the same pattern vertices and the same pattern edges.
  Equiv (y AdjacencyMatrix) bool

// Pre: e has the type of the pattern-vertex of x.
// If i or k >= x.Num(), nothing has happened. Otherwise:
// x(i,k) is the pair (v, e) with v = pattern vertex of x,
```

```
// i.e., in the corresponding graph there is an edge with
// the value of e from its i-the vertex to its k-th vertex,
// iff x.Val(i,k) > 0.
  Edge (i, k uint, e Any)


// Returns the first element of the pair x(i,i), a vertex.
  Vertex (i uint) Any


// Pre: i, k < x.Num().
// Return 0, if e in x(i,k) = (v, e) is the pattern edge
// of x; returns otherwise the value of e.
  Val (i, k uint) uint


// Pre: v has the type of the pattern-vertex of x and
//      e has the type of the pattern-edge of x.
// If i or k >= x.Num(), nothing has happened.
// Otherwise now x(i,k) == (v, e).
  Set (i, k uint, v, e Any)


// Returns true, iff x(i,k) == x(k,i) for all i, k < x.Num(),
// i.e., the corresponding graph is undirected.
  Symmetric() bool


// Pre: x and y are equivalent.
// x contains all entries of x and additionally
// all entries of y, but only edges with a value > 0.
// Entries of x occurring at the same places in y
// are overwritten by the entries in x.
  Add (y AdjacencyMatrix)


// Returns true, if each line of x contains
// at least one entry (v, e) with x.Val(e) > 0,
// i.e., if each vertex in the corresponding graph
// has at least one outgoing edge.
  Full () bool
}


// Pre: The entries of x are of type uint
//      or implement Valuator.
// x is written to the screen.
  Write()


// Pre: n > 0. v is atomic of implements Object and
//      e has a uint-type or implements Valuator.
// v is the pattern vertex and e the pattern edge of x.
// Returns a n*n-matrix only with the entries (v, e).
func New (n uint, v, e Any) AdjacencyMatrix {
  return new_(n,v,e) }
```

15.3.2 Implementation

The representation of the adjacency matrices and the constructor are implemented as follows:

```
package adj
import . "nU/obj"

type pair struct {
  vertex, edge Any
}

type adjacencyMatrix struct {
  uint "number of rows/columns"
  v, e Any // pattern-vertex and -edge
  entry [][]pair
}

func new_(n uint, v, e Any) AdjacencyMatrix {
  CheckAtomicOrObject (v)
  CheckUintOrValuator (e)
  x := new(adjacencyMatrix)
  x.uint = n
  x.v, x.e = Clone(v), Clone(e)
  x.entry = make ([][]pair, n)
  for i := uint(0); i < n; i++ {
    x.entry[i] = make ([]pair, n)
    for k := uint(0); k < n; k++ {
      x.entry[i][k] = pair { x.v, x.e }
    }
  }
  return x
}
```

The implementation could actually—for the same reason as with the graph package gra—
be omitted. It is reproduced here, so that at least *once* in this book it is shown how the
methods of Object can be implemented in a package that extends this interface. In this
example—in contrast to the graphs—the effort for this is limited.

First of all, we limit ourselves to exactly these methods:

```
func (x *adjacencyMatrix) Eq (Y Any) bool {
  y := Y.(*adjacencyMatrix)
  if x.Empty() {
    return y.Empty()
  }
  for i := uint(0); i < x.uint; i++ {
    if ! Eq (x.Vertex(i), y.Vertex(i)) {
      return false
    }
    for k := uint(0); k < x.uint; k++ {
```

```
      if ! Eq (x.entry[i][k].edge, y.entry[i][k].edge) ||
         ! Eq (x.entry[i][k].vertex, y.entry[i][k].vertex) {
        return false
      }
    }
  }
  return true
}

func (x *adjacencyMatrix) Copy (Y Any) {
  y := Y.(*adjacencyMatrix)
  x.uint = y.uint
  x.e, x.v = Clone(y.e), Clone(y.v)
  for i := uint(0); i < x.uint; i++ {
    for k := uint(0); k < x.uint; k++ {
      x.entry[i][k].vertex = Clone (y.entry[i][k].vertex)
      x.entry[i][k].edge = Clone (y.entry[i][k].edge)
    }
  }
}

func (x *adjacencyMatrix) Clone() Any {
  y := new_(x.uint, x.v, x.e)
  y.Copy (x)
  return y
}

func (x *adjacencyMatrix) Less (Y Any) bool {
  return false
}

func (x *adjacencyMatrix) Empty() bool {
  for i := uint(0); i < x.uint; i++ {
    for k := uint(0); k < x.uint; k++ {
      if ! Eq (x.entry[i][k].edge, x.e) {
        return false
      }
    }
  }
  return true
}

func (x *adjacencyMatrix) Clr() {
  for i := uint(0); i < x.uint; i++ {
    for k := uint(0); k < x.uint; k++ {
      x.entry[i][k] = pair { x.v, x.e }
    }
  }
}
```

```
func (x *adjacencyMatrix) Codelen() uint {
  v, e := Codelen(x.v), Codelen(x.e)
  return 4 + (1 + x.uint * x.uint) * (v + e)
}

func (x *adjacencyMatrix) Encode() Stream {
  bs := make (Stream, x.Codelen())
  v, e := Codelen(x.v), Codelen(x.e)
  copy (bs[:4], Encode (uint32(x.uint)))
  i := uint(4)
  copy (bs[i:i+v], Encode (x.v))
  i += v
  copy (bs[i:i+e], Encode (x.e))
  i += e
  for j := uint(0); j < x.uint; j++ {
    for k := uint(0); k < x.uint; k++ {
      copy (bs[i:i+v], Encode (x.entry[j][k].vertex))
      i += v
      copy (bs[i:i+e], Encode (x.entry[j][k].edge))
      i += e
    }
  }
  return bs
}

func (x *adjacencyMatrix) Decode (bs Stream) {
  v, e := Codelen(x.v), Codelen(x.e)
  x.uint = uint(Decode (uint32(0), bs[:4]).(uint32))
  i := uint(4)
  x.v = Decode (x.v, bs[i:i+v])
  i += v
  x.e = Decode (x.e, bs[i:i+e])
  i += e
  for j := uint(0); j < x.uint; j++ {
    for k := uint(0); k < x.uint; k++ {
      x.entry[j][k].vertex = Decode (x.v, bs[i:i+v])
      i += v
      x.entry[j][k].edge = Decode (x.e, bs[i:i+e])
      i += e
    }
  }
}
```

The rest of the implementation is not shown here; it is included in the source texts of this book (in the package nU/adj).

15.4 Distributed Graphs

As described in the abstract, each network represents a graph. Each process has an identity that is needed to construct the 1:1-network channels to its neighbours (see the comment on the constructor New in Sect. 13.3 on 1:1 network channels in the chapter on network-wide message passing). To do this, clearly distributed graphs are modeled as extensions of graphs, i.e., they are constructed as an abstract data type—i.e., a package—based on graphs.

15.4.1 Specification

Here, a small but very important part of the interface of this package, which—depending on the point of view—inherits or expands the interface of the graph package gra:

```
package dgra
import "nU/gra"

type DistributedGraph interface {
  gra.Graph
}

// Pre: The values of the edges of g, incremented by
nchan.Port0,
//       are the ports of the 1:1-net channels between the
vertices
//       connected by them.
// Returns a distributed graph with the underlying graph g.
func New (g gra.Graph) DistributedGraph { return new_(g) }
```

Further parts will follow in the course of the next chapters when they are needed.

15.4.2 Implementation

The representation of the distributed graphs is, for obvious reasons, quite complex.

To write its vertices to the screen, not only their identity is needed, but also their position on the screen. A separate package with the following specification is provided for this purpose:

```
package vtx
import . "nU/obj"

type Vertex interface {
  Object
  Valuator
```

```
// x has the position (x, y).
   Set (x, y uint)

// Returns the position of x.
   Pos () (uint, uint)

// x is written to the screen at its position.
   Write ()
}

// Returns a new actual vertex.
func New (n uint) Vertex { return new_(n) }

// Pre: v implements Vertex.
// v is written to the screen at its position.
func W (v Any) { w(v) }

// Pre: v and v1 implement Vertex.
// The positions of v and v1 are connected by a line.
func W2 (v, v1 Any) { w2(v,v1) }
```

(The implementation of nU/vtx is included in the source texts of this book.)

Thus, the representation essentially consists of the following components:

- the neighbourhood graph of the calling process, i.e., it, its neighbours, and the network channels to them (this graph must be preserved, i.e., it must not be changed by the algorithms)
- and a temporary copy of this graph for the use of the algorithms that are allowed to modify it,
- the Boolean information whether the graph is directed or not,
- the calling process as the current vertex in the graph,
- the identity of the calling process ("me"),
- the name of the host on which it is running,
- and the number of his neighbourhood processes,
- their vertices in the graph
- and their identities,
- the names of the computers they are running on,
- and the 1:1-network channels to them
- with their ports.

In addition, there are some other components that are needed to execute algorithms. They are introduced at the appropriate places.

Here is the corresponding excerpt from the representation:

```
package dgra
import ("nU/gra"; "nU/nchan")

type distributedGraph struct {
  gra.Graph,
  tmpGraph gra.Graph
  bool "gra.Graph directed"
  actVertex vtx.Vertex
  me uint
  actHost string
  n uint
  nb []vtx.Vertex
  nr []uint
  host []string
  ch []nchan.NetChannel
  port []uint16
}
```

and here are the corresponding parts of the constructor:

```
package dgra
import (. "nU/obj"; "nU/env"; "nU/nchan"; "nU/gra")
const p0 = nchan.Port0

func new_(g gra.Graph) DistributedGraph {
  x := new(distributedGraph)
  x.Graph = g
  x.tmpGraph = Clone(x.Graph).(gra.Graph)
  x.bool = x.Graph.Directed()
  x.actVertex = x.Graph.Get().(vtx.Vertex)
  x.me = x.actVertex.Val()
  x.actHost = env.Localhost()
  x.n = x.Graph.Num() - 1
  x.nb = make([]vtx.Vertex, x.n)
  x.nr = make([]uint, x.n)
  x.host = make([]string, x.n)
  x.ch = make([]nchan.NetChannel, x.n)
  x.port = make([]uint16, x.n)
  for i := uint(0); i < x.n; i++ {
    g.Ex (x.actVertex)
    x.nb[i] = g.Neighbour(i).(vtx.Vertex)
    x.nr[i] = x.nb[i].Val()
    x.Graph.Ex2 (x.actVertex, x.nb[i])
    x.port[i] = p0 + x.Graph.Get1().(uint16)
  }
  return x
}
```

Fig. 15.1 Undirected graph
with 8 vertices and 10 edges

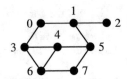

15.5   Examples

The standard example in the next three chapters is the Graph G8 from Fig. 15.1.

To create such graphs in the package dgra an additional constructor is needed internally:

```
// Pre: len(l) = len(c) = len(e) = len(e[i]) = n for all
// i < n.
//      The values of the edges of g, incremented by
// nchan.Port0,
//      are the ports of the 1:1-net channels
//      between the vertices connected by them.
// Returns the star of the vertex id of the graph with the
// vertices
// 0..n-1 at the screen positions (line,column) = (l[i],c[i]),
// the edges defined by e with appropriate ports for the net
// channels
// between the hosts defined by h as values and with the
// diameter m.
func newg (dir bool, l, c []uint, e [][]uint,
           h []string, m, id uint) DistributedGraph {
  g := gra.New (dir, vtx.New(uint(0)), uint16(1)) // g is a
new
    // graph with vertex-type uint and edges of the type of
ports
  g.SetWrite (vtx.W, vtx.W2)
  n := uint(len(e))
  v := make([]vtx.Vertex, n)       // create vertices of all
processes
  for i := uint(0); i < n; i++ { // and fill them for all
i < n
    v[i] = vtx.New(i)                // with i as value, give them
    v[i].Set (l[i], c[i])           // the position (l[i],c[i])
    g.Ins(v[i])                     // and insert them into g
  }
  for i := uint(0); i < n; i++ {
    for _, j := range e[i] {
      g.Ex2 (v[i], v[j])       // i is now the colocal and
                               // j the local vertex in g
      if ! g.Edged(){ // if there is no edge yet from i to j ,
        p := nchan.Port (n, i, j, 0)
        g.Edge (p)       // connect i with j by an edge
```

```
                                        // with the value of the above port
        }
      }
   }

   g.Ex (v[id])     // v[id] is now the local vertex in g
   g.SetWrite (vtx.W, vtx.W2)
   g = g.Star()     // g is now only the star of v[id]
   d := new_(g).(*distributedGraph) // d is the distributed
                    // graph with g as underlying graph
   d.setSize (n)    // line-/column number of the adjacency
matrix
                    // = number of the vertices of g
   if h == nil {    // such that examples.go is more simple
     h = make([]string, n)
     for i := uint(0); i < n; i++ {
       h[i] = env.Localhost()
     }
   }
   for i := uint(0); i < d.n; i++ { // the names of the hosts,
     d.host[i] = h[d.nr[i]] // on which the neighbour processes
   } // run, are overtaken (or see above)
   d.diameter = m // diameter of g
   return d
}
```

The thereby used function

```
func Localhost() string {
  return localhost()
}
```

returns the name of the host on which the calling process was started; it comes from the package nU/env already mentioned in Sect. 13.3.1. Thus, constructions of arbitrary graphs in the package dgra are possible, from which each of the processes involved receives its star (see Sect. 15.1.1). They should be stored in their own file—e.g., examples.go.

Examples of this is our "standard graph" G8:

```
package dgra

func G8 (i uint) DistributedGraph {
/*
          0 --- 1 --- 2
         /        \
        /          \
      3 --- 4 --- 5
        \  /      /
         \ /     /
          6 --- 7
*/
```

```
  l := []uint { 0, 0, 0, 3, 3, 3, 6, 6 }
  c := []uint { 4,10,16, 1, 7,13, 4,10 }
  return newg (false, l, c, e, nil, 4, i)
}
```

as well as the slightly larger graph G12:

```
func G12 (i uint) DistributedGraph {
 g12 (i uint) DistributedGraph {
/*
      0-----1----2
     /|\   / \      \
    / | \ /   \      \
   3  4  5   6--7----8
    \ |   \ | /
     \|    \|/
      9----10----11
*/
  l := []uint { 0, 0, 0, 3, 3, 3, 3, 3, 3, 6, 6, 6 }
  c := []uint { 5,11,17, 2, 5, 8,11,14,20, 5,11,17 }
  e := [][]uint { []uint { 1, 3, 4, 5 },
                  []uint { 2, 5, 7 },
                  []uint { 8 },
                  []uint { 9 },
                  []uint { 9 },
                  []uint { 10 },
                  []uint { 7, 10 },
                  []uint { 8, 10 },
                  []uint { },
                  []uint { 10 },
                  []uint { 11 },
                  []uint { } }
    return newg (false, l, c, e, nil, 4, i)
}
```

If the parameter nil is passed, according to the implementation of the constructor newg, all processes run on the local host. If, on the other hand, the processes are to be executed on different computers, their names must be passed to the constructor. If, for example, in the graph G8 process 1 shall run on Venus, processes 4 and 5 on Mars, process 7 on Jupiter, and the others on Terra, the last line must be replaced by

```
  v, m, t, j := "Venus", "Mars", "Terra", "Jupiter"
  h := []string { t, v, t, t, m, m, t, j }
  return newg (false, l, c, e, h, 4, i)
```

For this, to each program call on the computers involved, of course, the *appropriate process identity* has to be passed as an argument, i.e., on venus 1, on mars 4 and 5, on terra 0, 2, 3, and 6, and on jupiter 7!

15.5.1 Output to the Screen

The following program writes for each vertex of G8 its star to the screen:

```
package main
import ("nU/scr"; "nU/ego"; "nU/dgra")

func main() {
  scr.New(); defer scr.Fin()
  me := ego.Me()
  g := dgra.G8(me)
  g.Write()
}
```

Each of the eight processes that start this program must pass its identity—a natural number < 8—as an argument. To avoid the creation of eight different program texts, this is done by the use of an argument in the form of one of these numbers, which is passed to the program call as an argument and is evaluated in the program.

To do this, the following function from the small package nU/ego is used:

```
package ego

// Pre: The first argument of the program call
//      is a natural number.
// Returns this number.
func Me() uint {
  return me()
}
```

with the simple implementation

```
package ego
import ("strconv"; "nU/env")

func me() uint {
  if i, err := strconv.Atoi(env.Arg(1)); err == nil {
    return uint(i)
  }
  return uint(1<<16)
}
```

After its compilation, the program is executed by opening eight small windows on a graphical user interface and calling the program in each of them with one of the numbers from 0 to 7 (in each window with another one!) as an argument. What has to be considered if the processes run on different computers was described at the end of the previous section. We will also apply this principle to all test runs in the next three chapters.

Reference

1. Maurer, C.: The μUniversum. https://maurer-berlin.eu/mU

Heartbeat Algorithms

16

Abstract

This chapter shows that for any process in a network that initially only knows its neighbours, it is possible to get to know the entire network graph by network-wide message
passing. For this purpose, the concept of *heartbeat algorithms* is developed.
A simple solution to this problem works with a representation of graphs in the form of
adjacency matrices. This assumes that each process has as the number of processes in
it (to determine the size of this matrix) and the diameter of the network graph as global
information about the network. This limitation leads to the development of a graph-based
algorithm that is able to do this without this global knowledge.

16.1 The Basic Idea

Heartbeat algorithms proceed according to the following principle (see e.g., [1, p. 373], [2,
p. 450], or [3, p. 7]). Each of the processes involved begins by sending a message with certain
information about its status to all its neighbours via a network channel. When a process has
received such a message, it links the received information with its own and then sends it
back to the sender, which now also has the status information of the neighbours in question.
We call these two steps a *heartbeat*. The heartbeats are repeated until all processes in the
network have the status information of all other processes.

We adopt this name of ANDREWS from his books [1] and [2] (*"...first expand, sending
information out; then contract, gathering new information in"*). For this, RAYNAL and
HÉLARY in [4] use the term *"wave algorithm"*. This class of these algorithms is related with
the class used for *breadth search:* With the n-th heartbeat, *those* vertices in the graph are
reached, to which there is a path of length n. We will come back to this in the next chapter.

16.2   Getting to Know the Network

The central problem of this chapter is the following: How does every process in a network that initially only knows its star (see Sect. 15.1.1)—i.e., those processes to which it is connected via a network channel—discover the entire graph of the network?

Heartbeat algorithms are well suited to solve this problem. We explain this using the example of the graph G8 (see Fig. 15.5) from Sect. 15.5 in the previous chapter itself.

Initially we have the situation shown in Fig. 16.1: Each process knows only itself.

In this figure and the following, *those* vertices of the graph are filled with *black*, whose neighbours the respective process already knows. Each process begins by creating the network channels to its neighbours and preparing the closure of the channels at the end. For this, the following methods from the `dgra` package are needed:

```
func (x *distributedGraph) connect (a Any) {
    for i := uint(0); i < x.n; i++ {
        x.ch[i] = nchan.New (a, x.me, x.nr[i], x.host[i],
x.port[i])
    }
}

func (x *distributedGraph) fin() {
    for i := uint(0); i < x.n; i++ {
        x.ch[i].Fin()
    }
}
```

It then sends the star of his neighbourhood relationships in the network as a message to his neighbours via these network channels and waits for the corresponding messages from them. When he has received them all, he knows the neighbourhood relationships of his neighbours.

In our example, this results in the situation shown in Fig. 16.2.

After the second heartbeat, in which each process has again sent the part of the network graph known to it to all its neighbours and has received the corresponding messages from all of them, everyone knows the neighbourhood relations of the *neighbours* of its neighbours. In our example, this leads to the situation shown in Fig. 16.3.

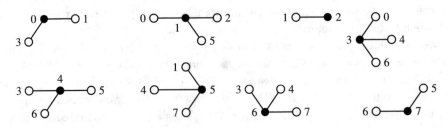

Fig. 16.1 Situation at the beginning of the algorithms

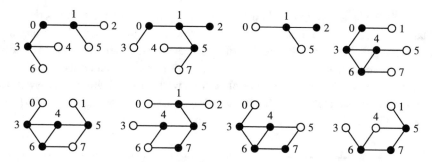

Fig. 16.2 Situation after the first heartbeat

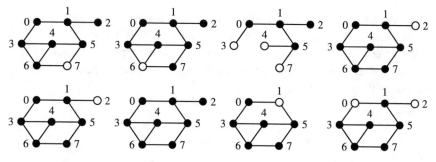

Fig. 16.3 Situation after the second heartbeat

After the third heartbeat, all processes except those with identities 2 and 6 know the entire network. The situation for these two processes is, then, the one shown in Fig. 16.4.

Now, they know all vertices but not yet the possible neighbours behind the "diametrically opposite" nodes 6 or 2. For this, they need a fourth heartbeat.

In general, this procedure will be repeated *so many times* until each process is fully familiar with the network graph. Our example suggests the assumption that this is the case after at most d heartbeats, where d is the *diameter* of the graph (in our example 4).

It is easy to see that this is actually true. From the definition of the diameter of a graph (see Sect. 15.1.1 in the previous chapter), it is immediately clear that each process P after $d - 1$ heartbeats knows all processes in the network up to those with a maximum distance from it—thus, *all*. In the d-th heartbeat it can, therefore, only find *edges* in the network graph that are not known to it at this time. If e is an arbitrary edge between two vertices in the network graph different from P, i.e., a connection between any two processes P_1 and P_2, it

Fig. 16.4 Situation after the third heartbeat for processes 2 and 6

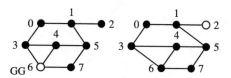

can reach both via at most of $d - 1$ connections. So it finds the connection e between them not later than at the d-th heartbeat, because they are adjacent to this edge. Therefore, we get $2ned$ as an upper bound for the number of messages necessary to determine the network, wherein n is the number of its vertices, e the number of its edges, and d its diameter.

Since some processes in our example already know the network graph after fewer heartbeats, it remains to analyze to what extent message passing can be reduced. This question is treated in Sect. 16.5 on the graph-based solution.

16.3   Preconditions for the Realization in Go

To program this we need further methods from the interface of the package `dgra` on distributed graphs. The heartbeat algorithms for calculating the network are included—for the sake of clarity of the specification and to preserve the principle of information hiding—-by means of an enumeration type in the package `dgra` and the methods for selecting and calling one of these algorithms:

```
package dgra

type HeartbeatAlg byte
const (
   HeartbeatMatrix = HeartbeatAlg(iota)
   HeartbeatGraph; HeartbeatGraph1
)

type Distributed Graph interface {

   ...

// a is the actual Pulsschlag\query{Do you mean
"Heartbeat"?} algorithm.
   SetHeartbeatAlgorithm (a HeartbeatAlg)

// Returns the actual Pulsschlag\query{Do you mean
"Heartbeat"?} algorithm.
   HeartbeatAlgorithm() HeartbeatAlg

// The actual Pulsschlag\query{Do you mean
"Heartbeat"?} algorithm is started.
   Heartbeat()
}
```

16.4   **Matrix-Based Solution**

The basic functionality is known from Sect. 16.2. The neighbourhood relations are coded as an adjacency matrix with the number of participating processes as the number of lines, which assumes that this number is known to all participating processes. This is the first place where the knowledge of each process goes beyond the information about its immediate neighbours. The entries in this matrix at the corresponding positions are the values of the edges between the processes.

First, for each process its initial adjacency matrix must be determined. This is done in the implementation of the constructor `NewG` of a distributed graph by calling the following method:

```
func (x *distributedGraph) setSize (n uint) {
  x.size = n
  x.matrix = adj.New (n, uint(0), uint(0))
  for i := uint(0); i < x.n; i++ {
    x.matrix.Set (x.me, x.nr[i], uint(0), uint(1))
    x.matrix.Set (x.nr[i], x.me, uint(0), uint(1))
  }
```

Provided that each process also knows the diameter of the network graph—the second ugly place in the algorithm—the heartbeats are executed as often as the diameter specifies:

```
package dgra
import "nU/adj"

func (x *distributedGraph) heartbeatmatrix() {
  x.connect (x.matrix)
  defer x.fin()
  x.matrix.Write()
  pause()
  for p:= uint(1); p <= x.diameter; p++ {
    for i := uint(0); i < x.n; i++ {
      x.ch[i].Send (x.matrix)
    }
    for i := uint(0); i < x.n; i++ {
      a := x.ch[i].Recv().(adj.AdjacencyMatrix)
      x.matrix.Add (a)
      x.matrix.Write()
      pause()
    }
  }
}
```

To execute this algorithm for our standard example `G8` we use the following program:

```
package main
import ("nU/ego"; "nU/col"; "nU/scr"; "nU/dgra")
```

```
func main() {
  me := ego.Me()
  g := dgra.G8 (me)
  g.SetRoot (4)
  g.SetHeartbeatAlgorithm (dgra.HeartbeatMatrix)
  g.Heartbeat()
  switch g.HeartbeatAlgorithm() {
  case dgra.HeartbeatMatrix:
    scr.ColourF (col.Red())
    scr.Write ("complete adjacency matrix", 8, 0)
    scr.ColourF (col.White())
    scr.Warp (9, 0, true)
  case dgra.HeartbeatGraph, dgra.HeartbeatGraph1:
    scr.Warp (7, 0, true)
  }
}
```

It is executed as described in Sect. 15.5.1 of the previous chapter—in eight small windows on a graphical user interface, where to the program call in each window one of the numbers 0 to 7 is passed as an argument. For all processes, the calls return the matrix from Fig. 16.5 which, of course, exactly corresponds to the edges in G8.

The "improved" solution by ANDREWS on p. 375 in [1] no longer requires the diameter of the network, so that *one* of the two restrictions is removed, but the criterion used by him to leave the for !done loop is wrong. He claims that the entire network graph is known if in every line of the adjacency matrix *at least one* 1 occurs. But that is not true. (In [2] this algorithm is also no longer included.)

The execution of his algorithm (which we do not reproduce here in Go because that would not lead us further) returns as a counterexample the same situation as for process with the identity 5 in Fig. 16.3:

After the first heartbeat, the adjacency matrix $(a_{ik})_{n,n}$ of this process looks like in Fig. 16.6, i.e., it contains a 1 in each line, but $a_{03} = a_{30} = 0$ and $a_{36} = a_{63} = 0$, so both edges between the processes 0 and 3 and between 3 and 6 are missing.

Fig. 16.5 Adjacency matrix
after four heartbeats

$$
\begin{pmatrix}
* & 1 & 0 & 1 & 0 & 0 & 0 & 0 \\
1 & * & 1 & 0 & 0 & 1 & 0 & 0 \\
0 & 1 & * & 0 & 0 & 0 & 0 & 0 \\
1 & 0 & 0 & * & 1 & 0 & 1 & 0 \\
0 & 0 & 0 & 1 & * & 1 & 1 & 0 \\
0 & 1 & 0 & 0 & 1 & * & 0 & 1 \\
0 & 0 & 0 & 1 & 1 & 0 & * & 1 \\
0 & 0 & 0 & 0 & 0 & 1 & 1 & *
\end{pmatrix}
$$

16.5   Graph-Based Solutions

A "clean" solution of the problem is offered by our ability to transport objects of different sizes through the network—by sending *graphs* instead of adjacency matrices over the net. To do this, the graph sent must be restored (see Sect. 13.3 in the chapter on network-wide message passing) from a received stream (see Sect. 2.3.2.4 in the section on packets etc.).

So, our first solution has the advantage that the knowledge about the number of processes in the network is no longer needed.

16.5.1 With Knowledge of the Diameter of the Network Graph

First, we show an implementation of the heartbeat algorithm by using the diameter of the network graph—analogously to the implementation in the previous section:

```
package dgra
import . "nU/obj"

func (x *distributedGraph) heartbeatgraph() {
  x.connect (nil)
  defer x.fin()
  x.tmpGraph.Copy (x.Graph)
  x.tmpGraph.Ex (x.actVertex)
  x.tmpGraph.Write()
  pause()
  for r := uint(1); r <= x.diameter; r++ {
    for i := uint(0); i < x.n; i++ {
      x.ch[i].Send (x.tmpGraph)
    }
    for i := uint(0); i < x.n; i++ {
      g := x.emptyGraph()
      g.Decode (x.ch[i].Recv().(Stream))
      x.tmpGraph.Add (g)
      x.tmpGraph.Write()
      pause()
    }
  }
}
```

Fig. 16.6 Adjacency matrix of process 5 after the first heartbeat

$$\begin{pmatrix} * & 1 & 0 & 0 & 0 & 0 & 0 & 0 \\ 1 & * & 1 & 0 & 0 & 1 & 0 & 0 \\ 0 & 1 & * & 0 & 0 & 0 & 0 & 0 \\ 0 & 0 & 0 & * & 1 & 0 & 0 & 0 \\ 0 & 0 & 0 & 1 & * & 1 & 1 & 0 \\ 0 & 1 & 0 & 0 & 1 & * & 0 & 1 \\ 0 & 0 & 0 & 0 & 1 & 0 & * & 1 \\ 0 & 0 & 0 & 0 & 0 & 1 & 1 & * \end{pmatrix}$$

16.5.2 Without Global Knowledge

But that can actually be done much better—namely *without* the knowledge of the diameter of the network graph; i.e., such that there is *no* global knowledge *at all* needed about the network.

The *trick* is to *mark* vertices and edges. By doing that exactly *that* is grasped, which is represented in the figures in Sect. 16.2. The difference between the knowledge about the existence of vertices whose neighbours are known—precisely *these* are marked—and those where it is still uncertain whether they have neighbours.

Unlike the previous solution, each process manages not only the temporary graph that grows from heartbeat to heartbeat, but also these markings. Initially, in the star of a process, the edges to its neighbours are marked, but not the neighbours. This reflects the fact that although it knows it neighbours, it does not know whether its neighbours have neighbours other than itself. After each heartbeat—as before—all vertices and edges from the received graph are inserted into the temporary graph, whereby the marks from the received graph are taken over; in addition, all edges to the senders are marked.

Consequently, `tmpGraph` is exactly *then* the *whole* network graph when all its vertices and edges are marked. The proof for this a direct result from the considerations on termination at the end of Sect. 16.2.

Because for a clean termination of such a sequence of heartbeats, also those processes that already know the entire network graph must send this graph, which has changed after the last heartbeat, to those processes that have not come so far, a little more effort is necessary.

Processes are denoted so long as *not ready* as they have not yet got to know the whole network graph. With each message they also send the information that they are not yet ready; therefore, with each receipt of a graph they also receive the information whether the sender is ready.

After the heartbeat with which they have obtained the knowledge of the whole network graph, they no longer execute, but only send their graph to their neighbours, together with the message that they are now ready.

```
package dgra
import . "nU/obj"

func (x *distributedGraph) heartbeatgraph1() {
  x.connect (nil)
  defer x.fin()
  ready := make([]bool, x.n)
  x.tmpGraph.Copy (x.Graph)
  x.tmpGraph.Write()
  pause()
  for r := uint(1); true; r++ {
    bs := x.tmpGraph.Encode()
    for i := uint(0); i < x.n; i++ {
      x.ch[i].Send(append(Encode(false), bs...)) // not ready
```

```
  }
  for i := uint(0); i < x.n; i++ {
    bs = x.ch[i].Recv().(Stream)
    if Decode (false, bs[:1]).(bool) {
      ready[i] = true
    }
    g := x.emptyGraph()
    g.Decode (bs[1:])
    x.tmpGraph.Add (g)
    x.tmpGraph.Mark2 (x.actVertex, x.nb[i])
    x.tmpGraph.Write()
    pause()
  }
  if x.tmpGraph.AllMarked() {
    break
  }
}
for i := uint(0); i < x.n; i++ {
  if ! ready[i] {
    x.ch[i].Send(append(Encode(true), x.tmpGraph.
Encode()...))
  }
}
}
```

The execution of this algorithm provides exactly the sequence of situations described in Sect. 16.2 on getting to know the network.

References

1. Andrews, G.R.: Concurrent Programming. Principles and Practice. Addison-Wesley, Menlo Park (1991)
2. Andrews, G.R.: Foundations of Multithreaded. Parallel and Distributed Programming. Addison-Wesley, Reading (2000)
3. Raynal, M.: Distributed Algorithms for Message-Passing Sytems. Springer, Berlin (2013)
4. Raynal, M., Hélary, J.M.: Synchronization and Control of Distributed Sytems and Programs. Wiley, New York (1990)

Traversing Algorithms

17

Abstract

Depth-first and breadth-first searches—the standard procedures to traverse graphs—are the basis for many graph algorithms, such as the construction of spanning trees and rings and the search for shortest paths. Because of their importance, in this chapter, techniques for the construction of algorithms for depth-first and breadth-first searches in distributed graphs are developed. They supply the corresponding spanning trees, and depth-first search also makes it possible to find circles. In many textbooks on distributed programming, only the principles of the algorithms are presented, without going into concrete realizations. The considerable effort for this in this chapter shows that this is by no means negligible.

17.1 Preconditions for the Realization in Go

Our algorithms to traverse a distributed graph are—analogously to heartbeat algorithms—contained as enumeration type in the package of distributed graphs, as well as the methods to select one of these algorithms and to call it:

```go
package dgra
import . "nU/obj"

type TravAlg byte
const (DFS = TravAlg(iota); DFS1; DFSfm1; Awerbuch; Awerbuch1;
       HelaryRaynal; Ring; Ring1; BFS; BFSfm; BFSfm1)

type DistributedGraph interface {
...
// a is the actual traversing algorithm.
  SetTravAlgorithm (a TravAlg)
```

© Springer Fachmedien Wiesbaden GmbH, part of Springer Nature 2021
C. Maurer, *Nonsequential and Distributed Programming with Go*,
https://doi.org/10.1007/978-3-658-29782-4_17

```
// Returns the actual traversing algorithm.
  TravAlgorithm() TravAlg {
}
```

The call `Trav(o Op)` is not contained in the interface of `dgra` because it can be accessed
through the graph package `gra`, whose interface is extended by `dgra`. For this, we refer
to the explanations on inheritability of interfaces at the end of Sect. 2.3.4 in the chapter on
packages.

As announced in Sect. 15.4.2, further components of the representation of distributed
graphs are required for programming:

- a tree and a circle of type `gra.graph`,
- the identity of the `root` process,
- a temporary vertex and a temporary edge for use in the algorithms,
- the father of every vertex and its children,
- the information from which vertex messages have already been received or which vertices
  have already been visited,
- the discovery times and the finishing times of visits of a vertex, and
- another natural number for different purposes.

They are realized by

```
package dgra
import ("nU/vtx"; "nU/gra"; "nU/nchan")

type distributedGraph struct {
   ...
  tmpVertex vtx.Vertex
  tree, cycle gra.Graph
  root uint
  tmpEdge uint16
  labeled bool
  parent uint
  child []uint
  visited []bool
  time, time1 uint
  distance uint
}
```

and are initialized in the constructor as follows:

```
const inf = uint(1<<16)

func new_(g gra.Graph) DistributedGraph {
   ...
  x.tmpVertex = vtx.New(x.actVertex.Content())
  v0 := g.Neighbour(0).(vtx.Vertex)
  g.Ex2(x.actVertex, v0)
  if g.Edged() {
    x.tmpEdge = g.Get1().(uint16)
```

```
  } else {
    g.Ex2 (v0, x.actVertex)
    x.tmpEdge = g.Get1 ().(uint16)
  }
  x.tree = gra.New (true, x.tmpVertex, x.tmpEdge)
  x.tree.SetWrite (vtx.W, vtx.W2)
  x.cycle = gra.New (true, x.tmpVertex, x.tmpEdge)
  x.cycle.SetWrite (vtx.W, vtx.W2)
  x.visited = make([]bool, x.n)
  x.parent = inf
  x.child = make([]bool, x.n)
```

We also need an internal channel for the clean termination of the algorithm

```
  var done = make(chan int, 1)
```

and the code length of uint(0)

```
  var c0 = C0()
```

from the package nU/obj and two other methods of a distributed graph:

```
// Returns the identity of the neighbour, with which the calling
// process is connected by the j-th network channel (j < x.n);
// for all j < x.n iff x.channel(i) == j,
// if x.nr[j] == i.
func (x *distributedGraph) channel (id uint) uint {
  j := x.n
  for i := uint(0); i < x.n; i++ {
    if x.nr[i] == id {
      j = i
      break
    }
  }
  return j
}


// Returns the number of a network channel, on which
// not yet was sent a message, if such exists;
// otherwise the number of neighbours:
func (x *distributedGraph) next (i uint) uint {
  for u := uint(0); u < x.n; u++ {
    if u != i && ! x.visited[u] {
      return u
    }
  }
  return x.n
}
```

17.2   Distributed Depth-First Search

We are guided by the algorithm in Sect. 23.3 *Depth-first search* in the book by CORMEN, LEISERSON, and RIVEST ([3]). The basic principle of the *distributed* depth-first search is the same as the recursive function for depth-first search in graphs:

```
func dfs (v Vertex) {
  marked[v] = true
  for all Neighbours n of v {
    if ! marked[n]
      dfs (n)
    }
  }
}
```

The call to dvs (v) for a vertex v corresponds to the sending of a message to this vertex; the start of the execution of the function corresponds to the receipt and the return from the recursion to the sending of a message.

The only difference worth mentioning is that vertices do not "know" whether a neighbour has already been visited, because the *discovery* and *finishing* times, the *marking* of vertices (in [3] with "colours") and the test on whether they are already marked or not yet, are manipulations of *shared data*. Therefore, the number of messages sent is in the order of the sum of the number of vertices and edges of the network graph (see [3, p. 479]).

We denote the sent object, with which a process progresses in the search, as *probe* and the answer to that as *echo*. The messages sent in this algorithm are times of type uint.

At the beginning, each process at first sets up the network channels of this type to its neighbours. If it is the root process—case (a) in Table 17.1—it starts the search by sending the discovery time x.time—initialized with 0—as probe to its neighbour nr[0], who, therefore, is its child and marks the 0-th channel as visited[0].

For any process, visited[i] has the value true, iff it already has received a time from the vertex nr[i], with which it is connected by its i-th network channel. When root starts the algorithm, this has the consequence that root must no longer send an echo after a response from this process, which leads to its termination. It then initializes distance with the number n of its neighbours and diameter with inf.

When a process receives a time on its j-th network channel, it first checks whether this is an echo with the same time (diameter == t) as reaction to a probe that it has sent on this network channel (distance == j). If this is the case, on the sending of this probe, it rejects its preliminary assumption that the receiver is one of its children. Then it calls next(j) and assigns the value of the result of this call to the variable u, which is the number of its neighbours iff it already has received a time from all of them, otherwise to the number of a network channel from which the sendings are still pending. Now it assigns this value to the number k of the net channel, to which it later sends its response.

Table 17.1 The cases for the sendings in the depth-first search

Case	Received	k	Time t	Kind of sending and addressee
(a)	–	0	`x.time == 0`	probe to `x.nr[0]`
(b)	echo	v	`x.time1`	echo to father
(c)	echo	u	unchanged	probe to `x.nr[u]`
(d)	probe	j	unchanged	echo to sender `x.nr[j]`
(e)	probe	u	`x.time`	probe to `x.nr[u]`
(f)	probe	j	`x.time1`	echo to sender (father)

Now it has to distinguish between two cases: Either it has already marked the `j`-th network channel, because it has already received a probe from it or not. In the first case, the sending was an echo, in the second a probe.

If in the *first case*, `u` is equal to the number of its neighbours, i.e., if it has already marked all its network channels, it increments the received time `t` by 1 and assigns to this value its finishing time `time1`. If it is `root`, it sends a message (with irrelevant content) to the channel `done` and terminates. In the other case (b), it replaces the value of `k` by the number of the network channel to its father. Otherwise there is still an unmarked network channel number `u`.

In the *second case*—i.e., when it has got a probe—it marks its `j`-th network channel. If it already knows its father, it replaces—-case (d)—the channel number `k` by `j`. If its father is still undefined, the sender—the process with the identity `nr[j]`— is its father. In this case, it increments the received time by 1 and assigns its discovery time to this value. If its network channels are all marked—case (f)—, it increments the received time once again by 1, assigns its finishing time to this value; if not, we have the case (e).

Cases (a) to (f) are—for the sake of clarity—summarized again with the value `k` of the network channel number for the later transmission, the time to be sent, and the type of the message (probe or echo) in Table 17.1 (whereby `v` is the number of the network channel to the father).

It then marks the `k`-th network channel. In the case `k == u`, it "saves" the values of `k` and `t` for the purpose of the check described above in the temporary variables `distance` and `diameter` (misused for this purpose) and considers the neighbour `nr[k]` accessible by channel `k` temporarily as one of its children. (Since the case `u == n` was already intercepted above, `u < n` is ensured, i.e., there is another such neighbour.) At the end it sends the time t to the k-th network channel as probe or back as echo and sends a message to the internal channel done.

In this procedure, each process receives on each network channel *exactly one* message and then sends one. Therefore, it makes sense to outsource its routines for the receipt of messages for each of its network channels to a goroutine. The waiting for the end of these goroutines is ensured by the fact that only the corresponding number of messages must have been received from done.

These goroutines do not work concurrently, because the reception on a network channel other than that one on which the first probe has arrived is only possible after a message has been sent on it beforehand, and these transmissions take place in the order of ascending network channel numbers. For this reason, the mutual exclusion of the goroutines is secured.

This gives us the depth-search algorithm with the logging of discovery and finishing times for each visited vertex:

```go
package dgra
import . "nU/obj"

func (x *distributedGraph) dfs (o Op) {
  x.connect (x.time) // network channels have the type uint
  defer x.fin()
  x.Op = o
  if x.me == x.root {
    x.parent = x.root
    x.time = 0
    x.child[0] = true
    x.visited[0] = true
    x.ch[0].Send(x.time) // (a) root sends as first
  }
  x.distance, x.diameter = x.n, inf
  for i := uint(0); i < x.n; i++ { // (x.n == number of the neighbours!)
    go func (j uint) {
      t := x.ch[j].Recv().(uint)
      mutex.Lock()
      if x.distance == j && x.diameter == t { // t unchanged back from
                                // j-th network channel, so reject assumption
        x.child[j] = false // that x.nr[j] is child of x.me
      }
      u := x.next(j) // == x.n, iff all network
                     // channels != j are already marked
      k := u // channel for the next sending
      if x.visited[j] { // i.e. echo
        if u == x.n { // no network channel is unmarked any more
          t++
          x.time1 = t
          if x.me == x.root { // root must not send an echo any more
            mutex.Unlock()
            done <- 0
            return
          }
          k = x.channel(x.parent) // (b) echo to father
        } else {
```

```
                // (c) k == u < x.n, t unchanged as probe to x.nr[u]
             }
          } else { // ! x.visited[j], i.e. probe
            x.visited[j] = true
            if x.parent < inf { // father already defined
              k = j // (d) t unchanged as echo to sender
            } else { // x.parent == inf, i.e. father still
                    // undefined (not for root!)
              x.parent = x.nr[j]
              t++
              x.time = t // if u < x.n:
                         //   (e) k == u, probe x.time to x.nr[u]

              if u == x.n { // all network channels marked
                t++
                x.time1 = t // (f) echo to sender (father)
                k = j // == x.channel(x.parent)
              }
            }
          }
          x.visited[k] = true
          if k == u {
            x.distance = k // save k and
            x.diameter = t // t for above check
            x.child[k] = true // preliminary assumption
          }
          x.ch[k].Send(t) // for k == u probe, otherwise echo
          mutex.Unlock()
          done <- 0
        }(i)
      }
  for i := uint(0); i < x.n; i++ { // wait for the end
    <-done                        // of all goroutines
  }
  x.Op (x.me) // executed passed operation
}
```

To execute this algorithm for our standard example G8 with process 4 as `root`, we use a similar program to the one used to execute the heartbeat algorithms in Sect. 16.4 from the previous chapter on the matrix-based solution.

It is given here in full—with a view to later applications—although we need a only a part of it for the time being:

```
package main
import (. "nU/obj"; "nU/ego"; "nU/col"; "nU/scr"; "nU/dgra")

func main() {
  scr.New(); defer scr.Fin()
  me := ego.Me()
  g  := dgra.G8(me)
  g.SetRoot(4)
/*
  g.SetTravAlgorithm (dgra.DFS)
  g.SetTravAlgorithm (dgra.DFS1)
```

```
    g.SetTravAlgorithm (dgra.DFSfm1)
    g.SetTravAlgorithm (dgra.Awerbuch)
    g.SetTravAlgorithm (dgra.Awerbuch1)
    g.SetTravAlgorithm (dgra.HelaryRaynal)
    g.SetTravAlgorithm (dgra.Ring)
    g.SetTravAlgorithm (dgra.Ring1)
    g.SetTravAlgorithm (dgra.BFS)
    g.SetTravAlgorithm (dgra.BFSfm)
    g.SetTravAlgorithm (dgra.BFSfm1)
*/
    g.SetTravAlgorithm (dgra.DFS)
    g.Trav (Ignore)
    switch g.TravAlgorithm() {
    case dgra.DFS, dgra.Awerbuch, dgra.HelaryRaynal,
         dgra.BFS, dgra.BFSfm:
      scr.Write ("father:        child[ren]:", 0, 0)
      scr.ColourF (col.LightBlue())
      scr.WriteNat (g.Parent(), 0, 8)
      scr.ColourF (col.Orange())
      scr.Write (g.Children(), 0, 24)
      if g.TravAlgorithm() == dgra.DFS {
        scr.ColourF (col.White())
        scr.Write ("arrival     / departure", 1, 0)
        scr.ColourF (col.Green())
        scr.WriteNat (g.Time(), 1, 8)
        scr.ColourF (col.Red())
        scr.WriteNat (g.Time1(), 1, 23)
      }
    case dgra.Ring:
      scr.ColourF (col.Yellow())
      scr.Write ("  is number    in the ring.", 0, 0)
      scr.WriteNat (g.Me(), 0, 0)
      scr.ColourF (col.Green())
      scr.WriteNat (g.Time(), 0, 13)
    }
}
```

The methods `Parent()`, `Children()`, `Time()`, and `Time1()` from the package `nU/dgra` supply the corresponding components:

```
func (x *distributedGraph) Parent() uint { return x.parent }
func (x *distributedGraph) Children() string {
  s, n := "", uint(0)
  for i := uint(0); i < x.n; i++ {
    if x.child[i] {
      n++; if n > 1 { s += ", " }
      s += strconv.Itoa(int(x.nr[i]))
    }
  }
  if n == 0 { s = "-" }
  return s
}
func (x *distributedGraph) Time() uint { return x.time }
func (x *distributedGraph) Time1() uint { return x.time1 }
```

Table 17.2 Father and child[ren] of processes 0 to 7 at depth first search

Process	Father	Child[ren]
0	3	1
1	0	2, 5
2	1	
3	4	0
4	4	3
5	1	7
6	7	
7	5	6

Table 17.3 Discovering and finishing times of processes 0 to 7

Process	Discovering time	Finishing time
0	2	13
1	3	12
2	4	5
3	1	14
4	0	15
5	6	11
6	8	9
7	7	10

Because nothing has to happen during traversing, the function

```
func Ignore (a Any) { }
```

from the nU/obj is given to the graph that does not perform an operation.

For processes 0 to 7, the program provides the information on fathers and children from Table 17.2 and the discovering and finishing times from Table 17.3 to record the distance traveled during the depth-first search.

This allows anyone who receives this information after a program run for all processes to determine the spanning tree generated: It looks like Fig. 17.1.

Fig. 17.1 Spanning tree of the depth-first search in G8 with process 4 as root

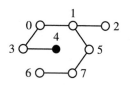

However, this spanning tree remains hidden to the individual processes, because each of them only determines its own father–child relationships. In the next section, this disadvantage is eliminated by an extension of the algorithm.

If the program is executed with process 1 instead of 4 as root, the depth-first search returns the spanning tree from Fig. 17.2 by interpreting the outputs in the tables.

Finally, in Fig. 17.3, we show the details of the individual steps of the depth-first search in order to be able to follow them closely: In each vertex, their discovering and finishing times are entered. Solid arcs denote probes and dashed arcs denote echoes; besides the entries there is the number of the message, and at the arcs, the time it was sent and the case involved.

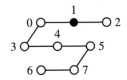

Fig. 17.2 Spanning tree of the depth-first search in G8 with process 1 as root

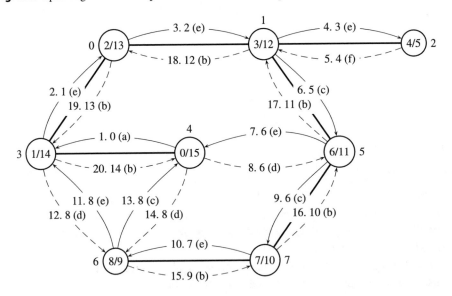

Fig. 17.3 Order of the steps at depth-first search in G8 with process 4 as root

17.2.1 Transfer of the Spanning Tree to All Processes

Basically, it is quite simple to give the knowledge of the entire spanning tree to *all* processes: We omit the logging of times and use instead the continuously updated spanning trees as content of the messages.

In the source text, the following is changed in detail: All program lines that manipulate times are omitted without replacement. The initialization of the network channels is configured for objects of different code length:

```
x.connect (nil)
```

The current spanning tree is initially empty:

```
x.tree.Clr()
```

The `root` process sends as first message the spanning tree, which consists only of a (marked) vertex.

```
x.tree.Ins (x.actVertex)
x.tree.Mark (x.actVertex)
x.ch[0].Send (x.tree)
```

After each reception, the sent spanning tree is decoded from the received stream, and the initial check as to whether the assumption about the child must be rejected takes place not by time comparison but by comparison of the received spanning tree with the saved one:

```
bs := x.ch[j].Recv().(Stream)
x.tree = x.decodedGraph(bs)
if x.distance == j && x.tree.Eq (x.tmpGraph) { // spanning tree
               // is unchanged back from the j-th network channel,
  x.child[j] = false // hence x.nr[j] is no child of x.me
}
```

If it is a probe, and the receiver is not yet included in the spanning tree, it is inserted and connected to the sender by an edge:

```
if ! x.tree.Ex (x.actVertex) {
  x.tree.Ex (x.nb[j]) // x.nb[j] local in x.tree
  x.tree.Ins (x.actVertex) // x.actVertex local und
                          // x.nb[j] colocal, both
  x.tree.Edge (x.edge(x.nb[j], x.actVertex)) // connect
}
```

When temporarily setting `x.child`, the spanning tree is saved instead of the time:

```
x.tmpGraph.Copy (x.tree)
```

Sendings consist of the actual spanning tree:

```
x.ch[k].Send (x.tree)
```

Only at the end is a little more effort necessary than just the execution of the operation: A second round of messages of reception and transmission.

The `root` process now fully knows the spanning tree by the return from the depth-first search and sends it to its children; every other process receives it from its father and also sends it to its children:

```
x.tree.Ex (x.actVertex)
var bs Stream
if x.me == x.root {
  bs = x.tree.Encode()
} else {
  bs = x.ch[x.channel(x.parent)].Recv().(Stream)
  x.tree = x.decodedGraph (bs)
}
x.tree.Ex (x.actVertex)
for k := uint(0); k < x.n; k++ {
  if x.child[k] {
    x.ch[k].Send(bs)
  }
}
x.Op (x.me)
x.tree.Write()
```

Consequently, after this round it is known to all processes.

With our example graph, `G8`, the last statement to output the spanning tree yields the (expected) result from Fig. 17.1. If after each line in the source code at which `x.tree` is updated, the statement for the output `x.tree.Write()`—followed by a short break `x.time.Sleep(1e9)`—is inserted, the algorithm can be followed step-by-step in the windows.

17.2.2 Realization with Far Monitors and Transfer of the Spanning Tree

Of course, the whole thing also works with far monitors—which is, in my opinion, more elegant. To use them for algorithms in the `dgra` package, a slice of far monitors

```
mon [] fmon.FarMonitor
```

is added to the representation of the distributed graphs, which in the constructor `new_` is initialized with

```
x.mon = make([]fmon.FarMonitor, x.n)
```

in addition, there is the method

```
func (x *distributedGraph) finMon() {
  for i := uint(0); i < x.n; i++ {
    x.mon[i].Fin()
  }
}
```

for the clean termination of all monitors and the method

```
func (x *distributedGraph) awaitAllMonitors() {
  for k := uint(0); k < x.n; k++ {
    for x.mon[k] == nil {
      time.Sleep (100 * 1e6)
    }
  }
}
```

such that each process as a client of the far monitors of its neighbour processes keeps waiting until they have all started their monitor as a server. The actual spanning tree—initially for all processes only consisting of their identity—is passed as a parameter to the monitor functions:

Two monitor operations are required for the depth-first search:

- `search` for the recursive progression in the depth-first search, and
- `deliver` to recursively pass on the spanning tree from each process to its children—starting with the `root` process.

This ensures that at the end, all processes know the tree.

The functionality of the algorithm is explained in detail in the comments in the following implementation:

```
package dgra
import (. "nU/obj"; "nU/vtx"; "nU/fmon")

const (search = iota; deliver)

func (x *distributedGraph) dfsfm1 (o Op) {
  go func() {
    fmon.New (nil, 2, x.d1, AllTrueSp,
              x.actHost, p0 + uint16(2 * x.me), true)
  }()
  for i := uint(0); i < x.n; i++ {
    x.mon[i] = fmon.New (nil, 2, x.d1, AllTrueSp,
                         x.host[i], p0 + uint16(2 * x.nr[i]),
                         false)
  }
  defer x.finMon()
  x.awaitAllMonitors()
  x.Op = o
  x.tree.Clr() // in the beginning the spanning tree
  x.tree.Ins (x.actVertex) // of each process consists only of
  x.tree.Mark (x.actVertex) // its own vertex, which is marked
  if x.me == x.root {
    x.parent = x.me
    for k := uint(0); k < x.n; k++ {
      x.tree.Ex (x.actVertex) // x.actVertex is local in x.tree
      bs := x.mon[k].F(x.tree, search).(Stream) // search
      if len(bs) == 0 {          // receiver already contained
        x.vitited[k] = true      // in the spanning tree
      } else {                   // otherwise the receiver
```

```
      x.child[k] = true              // is a child of root and its
      x.tree = x.decodedGraph(bs) // spanning tree is overtaken
    }
  }
  x.tree.Ex (x.actVertex) // x.actVertex is local vertex in x.tree
  for k := uint(0); k < x.n; k++ {
    if x.child[k] {                  // pass spanning tree
      x.mon[k].F(x.tree, deliver) // to all children
    }
  }
  x.Op (x.me)
} else {
  <-done // wait, until root is ready
}
x.tree.Write()
}

func (x *distributedGraph) d1 (a Any, i uint) Any {
  x.awaitAllMonitors()
  bs := a.(Stream)

  x.tree = x.decodedGraph(bs)
  if i == search {
    if x.tree.Ex (x.me) { // receiver already contained in the
      return nil // spanning tree,, therefore, corresponding
    }            // message to sender and stop searching further
    s := x.tree.Get().(vtx.Vertex).Val() // the value of the vertex
    j := x.channel(s) // of the sender x.nr[j], j is the number of
    x.parent = x.nr[j] // the channel to it. Sender is now father.
    x.tree.Ins (x.actVertex)  // insert the vertex of the process
                   // and connect the vertex of its father
    x.tree.Edge (x.edge(x.nr[j], x.me)) // with it by an edge
    for k := uint(0); k < x.n; k++ {
      if k != j {
        if ! x.tree.Ex (x.nb[k]) {
          x.tree.Ex (x.actVertex) // x.actVertex is local vertex
          bs = x.mon[k].F(x.tree, search).(Stream) // continue
          if len(bs) == 0 {                       // searching
            return nil // see above
          } else {                            // otherwise
            x.child[k] = true              // the receiver is a child
            x.tree = x.decodedGraph (bs) // of x.me and its spanning
          }                              // tree is overtaken
        }
      }
    }
  } else { // i == deliver
    x.tree.Ex (x.actVertex) // x.actVertex is local vertex in x.tree
    for k := uint(0); k < x.n; k++ { // pass the spanning tree
      if x.child[k] {                  // to all children
        x.mon[k].F(x.tree, deliver)
      }
    }
    x.Op (x.me) // execute passed operation
    done <- 0 // send signal to dfs1fm1 to end
```

```
    }
    return x.tree.Encode()
}
```

A test run with our standard example, of course, results in the same as before.

I like this version much more than the previous one, because in its source code the *recursive character of the depth-first search* is much more clearly visible.

17.3 Algorithm of Awerbuch

AWERBUCH published another algorithm for depth search in [1]. It has four messages: `discover`, `return`, `visit`, and `ack`, and it uses for the bookkeeping for each vertex two Boolean arrays `visited` and `flag`, indexed by their neighbours. The author describes his algorithm as follows:

> Whenever a node receives a `discover` message, it means that this node is visited for the *first time*, and the sender of the message is its father in the tree. At that time, the node sends (simulaneously) a special message `visit` to all the neighbours, except for the father. Now, the search process is temporarily suspended. Upon receipt of the `visit` message, a node learns that the sender of the message was visited, and then sends back an acknowledgement `ack`. Whenever the `ack` messages have been collected from all the neighbours, the center delivers a `return` message to itself. Whenever a node receives the `return` message, it means that the search is resumed from that node. Namely, if there exists an unvbisited neighbour, the `discover` message is forwarded to it, and it is marked als *visited*; otherwise, the `return` message is sent back to the father.

According to AWERBUCH, the number of messages in his algorithm is $= O(v)$ for $v =$ number of the edges: In the course of the depth-first search, along each edge on its way, a pair of `discover` and `return` (in the opposite direction) is sent; in addition, for each `discover` step to another vertex a pair `visit` and `ack` for each edge outgoing from it.

17.3.1 Realization with Far Monitors

AWERBUCH's algorithm becomes more understandable when constructed with far monitors. This makes the messages `ack` and `return` obsolete because they are implicitly included as results of the calls of the monitor functions of the far monitors. So, there remain only the messages `discover` and `visit`, which now play the role of monitor functions.

To each call of one of these monitor functions, its own identity is passed:

```
x.mon[k].F(x.me, f)
```

for `f` = `discover` or `f` = `visit`.

When calling the monitor function `visit` a monitor only has to mark the sender as visited. The work when calling the monitor function `visit` is more extensive, because it ultimately constitutes the recursive character of the depth-first search:

At the call of `discover`

- the sender is registered as a father,
- the monitor function `visit` is called for all neighbour monitors (except the sender), then
- for every neighbour (except the sender) that is not yet marked as `visited`,
  - after its marking with `visited` and registering as a child
  - the function `discover` of its monitor is called
  - and then its answer is awaited,
- and finally the operation is executed.

The messages on the channel `done` are necessary, so that the started monitor of a process different from `root` is not immediately terminated.

At the beginning, each process starts its monitor as server by branching off its initialization (with the last parameter `true`) as a goroutine. Then it starts—dually to that—as client the far monitors of all neighbours (last parameter `false`) and prepares the termination of all monitors and waits until all neighbours have also started their monitor as a server.

As `root` process, it registers itself as its father with the sequence described above and then sets the whole thing in motion by calling the monitor function `visit` of all neighbours, and subsequently calling the monitor function `discover` for any neighbour not yet marked as `visited` ...until the operation has been executed, after which at the end a message is sent to the channel `done` to terminate the execution of the function `awerbuch`.

This results in the following implementation:

```
package dgra
import (. "nU/obj"; "nU/fmon")

const (visit = uint(iota); discover)

func (x *distributedGraph) awerbuch (o Op) {
  go func() {
    fmon.New (uint(0), 2, x.a, AllTrueSp,
              x.actHost, p0 + uint16(2 * x.me), true)
  }()
  for i := uint(0); i < x.n; i++ {
    x.mon[i] = fmon.New (uint(0), 2, x.a, AllTrueSp,
                         x.host[i], p0 + uint16(2 * x.nr[i]),
                         false)
  }
  defer x.finMon()
  x.awaitAllMonitors()
  x.Op = o
  if x.me == x.root {
    x.parent = x.me
```

```
    for k := uint(0); k < x.n; k++ {
      x.mon[k].F(x.me, visit)
    }
    for k := uint(0); k < x.n; k++ {
      if ! x.visited[k] {
        x.visited[k] = true
        x.child[k] = true
        x.mon[k].F(x.me, discover)
      }
    }
    x.Op (x.me)
  } else {
    <-done
  }
}


func (x *distributedGraph) a (a Any, i uint) Any {
  x.awaitAllMonitors()
  s := a.(uint)
  j := x.channel(s)
  switch i {
  case visit:
    x.visited[j] = true
  case discover:
    x.parent = x.nr[j]
    for k := uint(0); k < x.n; k++ {
      if k != j {
        x.mon[k].F(x.me, visit)
      }
    }

    for k := uint(0); k < x.n; k++ {
      if k != j && ! x.visited[k] {
        x.visited[k] = true
        x.child[k] = true
        x.mon[k].F(x.me, discover)
      }
    }
    x.Op (x.me)
    done <- 0
  }
  return x.me
}
```

This modified version with nested far monitors is obviously more elegant than the somewhat brittle original by AWERBUCH. Those who follow the individual steps closely will notice that the procedure does not differ significantly from the distributed depth-first search in Sect. 17.2. Therefore, it is clear that a run of the program from this section with dgra.Awerbuch on the graph G8 with process 4 as root, results with the same father–child relationships as shown in Table 17.2.

17.3.2 Transfer of the Spanning Tree to All Processes

The algorithm from the previous section has, of course, the same disadvantage as the from the first Sect. 17.2. But also in *this* case, the deficit can be remedied by transporting the spanning trees over the network.

In the previous algorithm, the identities of the processes are exchanged as messages. They are used in the function spectrum a of the far monitors to identify the caller of the second monitor function (discover) by its channel number, so that it is omitted in the monitor when calling the same function of the neighbour monitors (see program lines with if k != j).

If the content of the messages is now replaced by the respective actual spanning trees, it is still possible to identify the caller of a monitor function. For this, the statement

```
g.Get().(vtx.Vertex).Val()
```

is used; it gets the local vertex from g and returns its value. In order for this to work, before any transmission of a spanning tree, the vertex of the sender must be made to the local vertex with the statement x.Ex(x.actVertex).

The function

```
func (x *distributedGraph) awerbuch1 (o Op)
```

is constructed in close accordance with awerbuch. The beginning with the initialization of all far monitors is virtually identical; only the function spectrum a has to be replaced by a1.

At the beginning, the spanning tree is cleared; i.e., the next statement is

```
x.tree.Clr()
```

and the root process initializes it by inserting its vertex into it and marking it as described in Sect. 17.2.1

```
x.tree.Ins (x.actVertex)
x.tree.Mark (x.actVertex)
```

To each call of the monitor function F, not the identity x.me is passed as a parameter, but the respective actual spanning tree; the call in the first for loop of the root process is, therefore,

```
x.mon[k].F(x.tree, visit)
```

In order to identify the sender of the call in the function spectrum, it must be determined from the transferred spanning tree. For this, in the second for loop of the root process it is made to the local vertex. Apart from this, in this loop, the spanning tree is updated by the result of the monitor function call; after the assignment of true to x.child[k], the statements

```
x.tree.Ex (x.actVertex) // x.actVertex local vertex in x.tree
bs := x.mon[k].F(x.tree, discover).(Stream)
x.tree = x.decodedGraph(bs)
```

are inserted.

A third monitor function is needed, which ensures that the spanning tree—beginning with the `root` process—is passed recursively to all children. For this purpose, we extend the declaration of constants:

```
const (visit = uint(iota); discover; distribute)
```

Similar to the extension of the distributed search to pass on the spanning tree to all processes in Sect. 17.2.1 the `root` process outputs the spanning tree and then sends it to its children:

```
x.tree.Write()
x.tree.Ex (x.actVertex)
for k := uint(0); k < x.n; k++ {
  if x.child[k] {
    x.mon[k].F(x.tree, distribute)
  }
}
```

The function spectrum

```
func (x *distributedGraph) a1 (a Any, i uint) Any
```

is more different from the one in the previous section.

At the beginning, the spanning tree is decoded from the received stream, and the sender is determined from it:

```
x.tree = x.decodedGraph(a.(Stream))
s := x.tree.Get().(vtx.Vertex).Val()
```

At the call of the second monitor function (`discover`) at first the identity of the receiver and an edge from the sender to it is inserted:

```
x.tree.Ins (x.actVertex) // x.nb[j] colocal, x.actVertex local
x.tree.Edge (x.edge(x.nb[j], x.actVertex))
```

In the first `for` loop, the vertex of the caller—as with the `root` process—is made to the local vertex; its body is, therefore,

```
x.tree.Ex (x.actVertex)
x.mon[k].F(x.tree, visit)
```

Also in the second `for` loop the same as with the `root` process is done, i.e., the same statements are inserted. In addition, the actual spanning tree is returned as a result of the monitor call:

```
return x.tree.Encode()
```

At the call of the third monitor function (`distribute`) it is processed in the same way as for the `root` process: Every other process receives the spanning tree from its father and sends it to its children.

The function spectrum is terminated with the return statement

```
return nil
```

to ensure that the compiler is satisfied (the important return has already taken place—see the previous paragraph).

Of course, our "standard test" with G8 returns the same result from Fig. 17.1 as with the extension of the distributed search.

17.3.3 Algorithm of Hélary/Raynal

In [5], HÉLARY and RAYNAL published an alternative version of the algorithm of AWERBUCH.

They do not need to synchronize the sending of the messages discover and return with the messages visited and ack by adding the identities of all processes visited so far to each transmission. The decisive advantage is the reduction of the number of messages to a maximum of $2(e - 1)$, so to $O(e)$ with $e =$ number of the vertices. The main purpose of her work is to use the basic idea of her algorithm to construct graphs in the form of rings, which is not pursued further here.

As type for the messages we use UintStream—streams of natural numbers of different length (see 2.3.2.4). In contrast to the method used in Sect. 17.5 on distributed breadth-first search, here we use a somewhat "dirty" trick to terminate the algorithm: When attempting to receive a message any of the Read errors *"no more input available"* or *"use of closed network connection"* occurs, the termination of the major for loop is forced, and the branched goroutine is finished.

```
package dgra
import . "nU/obj"

const (DISCOVER = uint(iota); RETURN)
var chanus = make(chan UintStream)

func (x *distributedGraph) helaryRaynal (o Op) {
  x.connect (nil); defer x.fin()
  x.Op = o
  if x.me == x.root
    x.parent = x.root
    us := append(UintStream {DISCOVER}, x.me)
    x.ch[0].Send (us)
    x.child[0] = true
  }
  for i := uint(0); i < x.n; i++ {
    go func (j uint) {
      loop:
      for {
        t := x.ch[j].Recv()
        if t == nil {
          chanus <- nil
          break loop
        }
        us := Decode (UintStream{}, t.(Stream)).(UintStream)
        chanus <- append (UintStream{j}, us...)
```

```
      }
    } (i)
  }
  for {
    us := <-chanus
    if us == nil {
      break
    }
    j := us[0]
    us = us[1:]
    neighbours := us[1:]
    existUnvisitedNeighbours := false
    for i := uint(0); i < x.n; i++ {
      for _, n := range neighbours {
        if n == x.nr[i] {
          x.visited[i] = true
        }
      }
      if ! x.visited[i] {
        existUnvisitedNeighbours = true
      }
    }
    k := x.n // channel number of the smallest unvisited neighbour

    if existUnvisitedNeighbours {
      for i := uint(0); i < x.n; i++ {
        if ! x.visited[i] {
          k = i
          break
        }
      }
    }
    if us[0] == DISCOVER {
      x.parent = x.nr[j]
      us = append(us, x.me)
      if ! existUnvisitedNeighbours {
        us[0] = RETURN
        x.ch[j].Send (us)
      } else { // existUnvisitedNeighbours
        x.ch[k].Send (us) // DISCOVER
        x.child[k] = true
      }
    } else { // us[0] == RETURN
      if existUnvisitedNeighbours {
        us[0] = DISCOVER
        x.ch[k].Send (us)
        x.child[k] = true
      } else { // ! existUnvisitedNeighbours
        if x.parent == x.me {
          x.Op(x.me)
          return
        } else {
          x.ch[x.channel(x.parent)].Send (us)
        }
      }
    }
```

```
      }
    }
  x.Op(x.me)
}
```

17.4   Construction of a Ring

Since the classical algorithms for the *election of a leader* in a network (e.g., [2, 4, 7] and [6]) are limited to networks that have the form of a unidirectional or bidirectional *ring*, a method is needed for their application to order and connect the vertices of a network graph in such a way that they form a ring.

The principle of depth-first search can be excellently exploited for this purpose. We show this using the example of a modification of the algorithm of AWERBUCH from Sect. 17.3.1.

The additional effort consists only in the following: Each process records its discovery times in the component time by incrementing the time received and—combined with its identity—forwarding it to the next process, such that the receiver is able to restore the identity of the sender as well as the transmitted time from the obtained value. In this way, the processes can be ordered linearly according to their arrival times.

We get the implementation of the function

```
func (x *distributedGraph) ring()
```

with the function spectrum

```
func (x *distributedGraph) r (a Any, i uint) Any
```

by the following changes to the functions awerbuch and a: All program lines in both functions that contain x.Op, x.parent, or x.child are omitted, correspondingly also the parameter in the first function.

The root process initializes x.time with 0 before the second for loop in the first function.

For all calls of

```
  x.mon[k].F(x.me, discover)
```

in both functions x.me incremented by x.time*inf is passed; in the function spectrum r fitting to this the assignment

```
  s := a.(uint)
```

is replaced by

```
  s := a.(uint) % inf}
```

and the return by

```
  return x.me + inf * t
```

the received time is decoded by

Table 17.4 Output of processes 0 to 7 at the construction of a ring

Output
0 is number 2 in the ring
1 is number 3 in the ring
2 is number 4 in the ring
3 is number 1 in the ring
4 is number 0 in the ring
5 is number 5 in the ring
6 is number 7 in the ring
7 is number 6 in the ring

```
x.time = a.(uint) / inf + 1
```

and incremented, and in each execution of the second `for` loop, the return value of the monitor call is assigned to it:

```
t = x.mon[k].F(x.me + x.time * inf, discover).(uint) / inf
```

(The resulting file `ring.go` code is contained in the source texts of this book.)

The program for the depth-first search from the previous sections returns with

```
func (x *distributedGraph) Me() uint {
    return x.me
}
```

and the output statement

```
println (g.Me(), "ist #", g.Time())
```

in the last line with the traversing algorithm `dgra.ring` on our standard example the numbering from Table 17.4.

These numbers are, of course, identical to the "successively arranged" discovering times of the depth-first search in Table 17.3 from Sect. 17.2.

If another edge is added from vertex 6 (the one with the highest number) to vertex 4 (the one with the number 0), this sequence can be interpreted as a directed ring as in Fig. 17.4

Fig. 17.4 Ring after depth-first search in g8 with process 4 as root

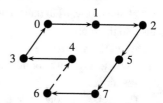

17.4.1 Transfer of the Ring to All Processes

The algorithm from the previous section suffers from an analogous disadvantage like the algorithms in Sects. 17.2 and 17.3.1. At the end, the processes do not know the ring, because each of them only knows its own number. You will certainly guess how this can be improved: by transporting the *spanning trees* over the network.

The algorithm is very similar to the extension of the algorithm of AWERBUCH to the one with the transfer of the spanning tree to all processes in Sect. 17.3.2. Instead of `x.tree` we use `x.cycle`, and all program lines in which `x.Op` or `x.parent` occurs, are omitted. Larger parts of the function `awerbuch1` can be adopted for `ring1`.

The function spectrum differs more from `a1` because with every call, not the actual ring with the identity of the caller as the local vertex is forwarded, but pairs of identities and graphs in the form of streams.

Such a pair of an identity `i` (of code length `c0`) and a graph `g` is coded as stream `bs` of type `Stream` in this way:

```
s = append(Encode(i), x.g.Encode()...)
```

and from a stream `bs` again decoded by

```
i = Decode(uint(0), b[:c0]).(uint)
g = x.decodedGraph(b[c0:])
```

With these hints, an implementation that returns the result from Fig. 17.4 will certainly not be difficult for you, so it is left as an exercise. (The solution can be found in the source texts of this book.)

17.5   Distributed Breadth-First Search

As the first algorithm for breadth-first search we present the algorithm of ZHU and CHEUNG from [8]. The basic idea of their algorithm is the following: One of the processes begins as root by sending a message to all its neighbours, that contains its identity and their distance 1 to root. The neighbours respond with an answer. This means that now all vertices in the graph with the distance 1 from root are reached.

A second round follows. Root sends a message to all neighbours with the distance 2, which they forward to their neighbours. These vertices send their response on the same way back to the root.

So, in the n-th round, all vertices with the distance n from root are reached—cascade-like. Whether or not a round reaches more vertices depends on which messages are sent with the responses.

The messages consist of triples of a constant (the authors call it " `status`") from the range

```
const (label = uint(iota); keepon; stop; end; term)
```

and the identity of the sending vertex and its distance `distance` from root (called `level` by the authors).

Because such triples with `inf = 1«16` as variable `t` of type `uint` can be coded by

```
t := status + 8 * distance + inf * id
```

and decoded by

```
status = (t % inf) % 8
distance = (t % inf) / 8
id = t / inf
```

we send messages of the type `uint`.

For the transfer of the algorithm into the package of distributed graphs, we still need the following components in their representation:

```
type distributedGraph struct {
    ...
    sendTo, echoed []bool
    labeled bool
    chan1 chan uint
```

which are initialized in the constructor `new_` by

```
sendTo = make([]bool, x.n)
labeled = false // virtually superfluous, because default-value
chan1 = make(chan uint, 1)
```

Its meaning is the following:

With `x.sendTo` a process marks those neighbours to which it has to send further `label` messages in the course of the depth-first search, and with `x.echoed` those that have already answered to a `label` message with a `keepon`, `stop`, or `end` message. With `x.labeled` it registers if it has already received a `label` message.

In order to determine the depth-first search tree, at the appropriate places, of course, the father–child relationships are registered with `x.parent` and `x.child`. For the clean termination we also again use the channel `done`. The algorithm is started by the root process by sending—after the necessary initializations—a `label` message to all the neighbours.

The essential part of the algorithm is an infinite loop, within that the processes react to the receipt of a message with the content `t`. First, each receiver determines the sender of the message using the number `j` of the receive channel, determines the remainder of `t` modulo `inf` and decodes the transmitted distance:

```
j := x.channel (t / inf)
t %= inf
x.distance = t / 8
```

Now it distinguishes—according to the kind of the message `t%8`—four cases:

1. This is a `label` message.

If this is its first received `label` message, the sender `x.nr[j]` is its father. It then assigns `true` to `labeled` and increments its distance by 1. Then it registers that further `label` messages have to be sent to all neighbours `x.nr[k]` except to its father by assigning `true` to x.sendTo[k] for them. If it has no neighbours apart from its father, it sends an end message to its father, otherwise a keepon message.

If, on the other hand, it has already received label messages (which can be seen by x.labeled), it then sends, if the sender is its father, x.nr[k] to all neighbours to which it still has to send label messages, such a message with its distance and registers that they have not yet responded; otherwise, i.e., if the sender is another neighbour, it reacts with the sending of a stop message to it.

2. It is a keepon message.
In this case, the sender is one of its children. It registers in echoed[j] that its previous message to the sender has been answered and in x.sendTo[j] that it does not have to transmit to the sender any more label messages.

3. It is a stop message.
In their paper, ZHU and CHEUNG only state that, in this case, the reaction is registered in echoed[j] and that no further label messages have to be sent. But that is not enough. The receiver has more to do.

If the sender x.nr[j] was its father, it sends a stop-message to all children, executes the operation, and sends a term message to all neighbours. If it has then received a message from done by all the neighbours, it leaves the loop with return, i.e., it terminates. If the sender was someone else, it proceeds as stated in the paper (see above).

4. An end message was received.
As in the second case, the sender x.nr[j] is one of its children. Then it does the same as in the core of the third case: It bears in mind that the sender has sent an echo and that there are no more label messages to be sent.

In *each of the four cases* the following has to be done afterwards: If there are still neighbours to which label messages have to be sent, and each one of them has already reacted to a label message, then to all these neighbours it sends as root process another label message with its own distance and assigns false to x.echoed[k]; if it is not the root process, it sends a keepon message to its father.

If there are no more neighbours to which label messages are to be sent, it sends as root process a stop message to all children, executes the passed operation, sends a term message to all neighbours and x.n messages to done, and leaves the loop with return, i.e., it terminates; otherwise, it sends an end message to its father.

Since in Go branched goroutines cannot simply be stopped "from the outside", in this case, we proceed somewhat differently than in the distributed depth-first search in Sect. 17.2:

Each process—as there—branches off a goroutine for each network channel, which receives the messages from this network channel in an endless loop. Thereby a distinction is made between as to whether or not it is a term message. In the first case, this loop is left, and a message is sent to the channel done; in the second case, the message is transmitted to the internal channel chan1, so the goroutine is cleanly terminated.

In the first case, this leads to a clean end for each process, because in the end it waits there for just as many messages from done as it has neighbours.

In the receive loop of the individual processes they receive the messages from the channel chan1. At the end each process has *exactly one* father: For the root process, this is immediately clear. To any other process that has not yet assigned true to labeled its neighbours still have to send label messages. Therefore, it eventually receives at least one such message, hence, it *has* a father; it cannot have *more* than one because of the bookkeeping in labeled.

Because each child of a process has a distance that is greater by 1 than that of its father; no circles can arise in the father–child relationship; consequently, the algorithm returns a *tree*.

From the above explanations, it follows that for every label message eventually there is a reaction with a stop or end message, i.e., that for each such message, the number of numSendTos() of the still outstanding messages is decremented by 1 and, therefore, will eventually be 0. Consequently, the algorithm *terminates*.

So we have the following implementation:

```
package dgra
import . "nU/obj"

const (label = uint(iota); keepon; stop; end; term)

// Returns the number of the neighbours, to which
// to which still label-messages have to be send.
func (x *distributedGraph) numSendTos() uint {
  v := uint(0)
  for k := uint(0); k < x.n; k++ {
    if x.sendTo[k] { v++ }
  }
  return v
}


// Returns true, iff for each neighbour either
// no more label-messages have to be sent to it
// or it has already reacted to a label-message.
func (x *distributedGraph) allSendTosEchoed() bool {
  for k := uint(0); k < x.n; k++ {
    if x.sendTo[k] && ! x.echoed[k] {
      return false
    }
  }
  return true
}


func (x *distributedGraph) bfs (o Op) {
  x.connect(uint(0)) // all messages are of type uint
  defer x.fin() // prepare closure of all channels at the end
  x.Op = o // the operation to be executed
  m := inf * x.me // to not always have to compute this product
  if x.me == x.root {
    x.parent = x.root // root is its own father, it
    x.labeled = true  // has not to wait for label-messages
    x.distance = 0    // distance to itself
```

```
  for i := uint(0); i < x.n; i++ { // to all neighbours
    x.child[i] = false // that have (not yet) a child send a
    x.ch[i].Send (label + 8 * x.distance + m) // label-message
    x.echoed[i] = false // but there is not yet a reaction
    x.sendTo[i] = true // later send more label-messages
  }
}
done = make(chan int, x.n)
for j := uint(0); j < x.n; j++ { // for each neighbour channel
  go func (i uint) { // branch off a goroutine
    loop: // that works in an endless loop
    for {
      t := x.ch[i].Recv().(uint)

      if t % 8 == term { // if a term-message was received,
        break loop       // the loop is left
      } else {           // otherwise the message
        x.chan1 <- t     // is passed on to chan1
      }
    }
    done <- 1 // send a message to terminate
  }(j)
}
for {
  t := <-x.chan1 // read message from chan1
  j := x.channel (t / inf) // channel number of the sender
  t %= inf
  x.distance = t / 8
  switch t % 8 { // kind of the message
  case label: // Fall 1
    if ! x.labeled { // this was the first label-message
      x.labeled = true
      x.parent = x.nr[j] // sender is father
      x.distance++       // time = received time + 1
      for k := uint(0); k < x.n; k++ { // to all neighbours
        x.sendTo[k] = k != j            // except the sender
      }                   // still label-messages have to be sent
      if x.n == 1 { if x.numSendTos() > 0 { panic(∃ops") }
        x.ch[j].Send (end + m) // no more neighbours
      } else {
        x.ch[j].Send (keepon + m) // keep on, father!
      }
    } else { // already previously label-messages received
      if x.parent == x.nr[j] { // sender is father
        for k := uint(0); k < x.n; k++ { // to all neighbours,
          if x.sendTo[k] { // to which still label-messages
            // have to be sent, a further message is sent
            x.ch[k].Send (label + 8 * x.distance + m)
            x.echoed[k] = false // but their reaction
          }                     // is still missing
        }
      } else { // sender someone else than father
        x.ch[j].Send (stop + m) // sender: stop!
      }
    }
```

```
case keepon: // Fall 2
  x.echoed[j] = true // sender has reacted
  x.child[j] = true  // sender is child
case stop: // Fall 3
  x.echoed[j] = true // sender has reacted
  if x.nr[j] == x.parent { // if sender is the father,
    for k := uint(0); k < x.n; k++ { // then to all
      if x.child[k] { // children send the message:

        x.ch[k].Send (stop + m) // stop
      }
    }
    x.Op (x.me) // execute passe operation
    for k := uint(0); k < x.n; k++ { // for all neighbours
      x.ch[k].Send (term) // arrange termination
    }                     // of the goroutine
    for k := uint(0); k < x.n; k++ { // wait,
      <-done // until all neighbours are ready
    } // then the calling process leaves the loop,
    return // i.e., it terminates
  } else { // sender - not the father - has reacted
    x.sendTo[j] = false // so no more labels to it
  }
case end: // Fall 4
  x.echoed[j] = true  // sender has reacted
  x.child[j] = true   // sender is child
  x.sendTo[j] = false // no more labels to it
}
if x.numSendTos() == 0 { // virtually ready
  if x.me == x.root {
    for k := uint(0); k < x.n; k++ {
      if x.child[k] {
        x.ch[k].Send (stop + m)
      }
    }
    x.Op (x.me)
    for k := uint(0); k < x.n; k++ { // see case 3
      x.ch[k].Send(term)
    }
    for k := uint(0); k < x.n; k++ {
      <-done
    }
    return // algorithm terminates for root
  } else { // the calling process is not root
    k := x.channel(x.parent) // channel to the father
    x.ch[k].Send (end + m) // message to him: end
  }
} else { // x.numSendTos() > 0: continue with depth-first
  if x.allSendTosEchoed() { // searcH; for all neighbours
    // either no more label-messages have to be sent to
    // them or they have already reacted on a label-message
    if x.me == x.root {
      for k := uint(0); k < x.n; k++ { // to all neighbours,
        if x.sendTo[k] { // to which still label-messages
                         // have to be sent, a further is sent
```

```
            x.ch[k].Send (label + 8 * x.distance + m)
            x.echoed[k] = false // no reaction until now
          }

        }
      } else { // the calling process is not root
        k := x.channel(x.parent) // channel to the father
        x.ch[k].Send (keepon + m) // message to him: keep on
      }
    }
  }
}
}
```

The execution of the main program from Sect. 17.2 with the traversing algorithm `dgra.BFS` for breadth-first search for the standard example G8 with 4 as root returns the results shown in Table 17.5. From this, the tree from Fig. 17.5 can be read.

It is left as an exercise to show that the number of messages in this algorithm is $O(v^2)$ (v = number of the vertices in the graph). (Hint: Consider the case of a graph without branches.)

Table 17.5 Father and child[ren] of processes 0 to 7 at depth-first search with root 4

Process	Father	Child[ren]
0	3	
1	5	2
2	1	
3	4	0
4	4	3, 5, 6
5	4	1
6	4	7
7	6	

Fig. 17.5 Spanning tree of the breadth-first search in G8 with process 4 as root

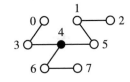

17.5.1 Realization with Far Monitors

The algorithm of ZHU and CHEUNG also suffers from the disease, which we meanwhile know well: At its end it does not provide the processes with the spanning tree but only with their father–child relationships.

We will find the solution to *this* problem also—similar to the step from Sect. 17.2.1 on transferring the spanning tree to all processes to Sect. 17.2.2 on the realization with far monitors and transfer of the spanning tree—in the next section with our "universal tool" from distributed programming: The far monitors.

But for this, first, we have transform the algorithm from the previous section into a version with far monitors while preserving its basic ideas. The basic idea of this version is, of course, the same as in the algorithm of ZHU/CHEUNG, but it will be much easier.

The reply messages keepon, etc., are omitted because what is to be communicated with them is simply the result of a monitor call; i.e., we only need *one* monitor function.

The content of the messages—here the parameters of the monitor function—are, thus, also only pairs (identity of the sender and distance), which are somewhat more simply coded and decoded as values of the type uint than in the previous section.

The far monitors involved are initialized analogously to all such algorithms introduced so far. At the beginning the root process assigns x.root to x.parent, all other processes assign inf to x.parent,

In the main program root executes a loop, in which it calls the monitor function of all those neighbours with a distance 0, for which echoed[k] still has the value false.

If the call returns inf a result, it does not make any sense to keep searching at the neighbour; it registers this by assigning false to echoed for this neighbour. Otherwise, the neighbour is one of its children. It also counts for how many neighbours this is still the case. If this counter, then, returns the value 0 it leaves its loop, otherwise it increments the distance by 1 and continues with the next round. At the end it executes the passed operation. All other processes only wait in the main program for root.

In the function spectrum at the call of the monitor function, at first—as in the previous section—the sender (by the number of the receiver channel) and the distance are determined; since the calls in far monitors only return values of the type Any, a type assertion is, of course, necessary:

```
j := x.channel(a.(uint) % inf)
x.distance = a.(uint) / inf
```

After that, true is assigned to echoed[j], so that the sender is omitted in the further breadth-first search. If the distance transmitted is 0, the end of a round of calls is reached.

There are two cases to be distinguished: Either the process that executes this function spectrum already knows its father or not. In the first case, it reacts by returning inf, which tells the caller that a further search here is pointless; otherwise the sender is its father; it then executes the operation passed and sends back its identity.

Otherwise, it continues with the breadth-first search with a distance decremented by 1 for those neighbours for which `echoed[k]` is `false` (with the exception of his father, see above). Like the root process in the main program, it sets `echoed[k]` and `x.child[k]` and counts how many neighbours do *not* send back `inf`.

If the value of the counter is greater than 0, the call to the monitor function returns the identity of the sender as a result, which tells the caller to continue searching. If is equals 0, no more children can be reached, which the function spectrum tells the caller by returning the value `inf` after it has sent a message to the `done` channel to terminate. These considerations prove that this procedure terminates and that it is correct.

So we have the implementation:

```
package dgra
import (. "nU/obj"; "nU/fmon")

func (x *distributedGraph) bfsfm (o Op) {
  go func() {
    fmon.New (uint(0), 1, x.b, AllTrueSp,
              x.actHost, p0 + uint16(x.me), true)
  }()
  for i := uint(0); i < x.n; i++ {
    x.mon[i] = fmon.New (uint(0), 1, x.b, AllTrueSp,
                         x.host[i], p0 + uint16(x.nr[i]), false)
  }
  defer x.finMon()
  x.awaitAllMonitors()
  x.Op = o
  x.parent = inf
  if x.me == x.root {
    x.parent = x.root
    for {
      c := uint(0)
      for k := uint(0); k < x.n; k++ {
        if ! x.echoed[k] {
          if x.mon[k].F(x.me + inf * x.distance, 0).(uint) == inf {
            x.echoed[k] = true
          } else {
            x.child[k] = true
            c++
          }
        }
      }
      if c == 0 { break }
      x.distance++
    }
    x.Op (x.me)
  } else {
    <-done // auf root warten
  }
}

func (x *distributedGraph) b (a Any, i uint) Any {
  x.awaitAllMonitors()
```

```
s := a.(uint) % inf
j := x.channel(s)
x.distance = a.(uint) / inf
x.echoed[j] = true
if x.distance == 0 {
  if x.parent < inf {
    return inf
  }

  x.parent = s // == x.nr[j]
  x.Op (x.me)
  return x.me
}
c := uint(0)
for k := uint(0); k < x.n; k++ {
  if k != j && ! x.echoed[k] {
    if x.mon[k].F(x.me + (x.distance - 1) * inf, 0).(uint) == inf {
      x.echoed[k] = true
    } else {
      x.child[k] = true
      c++
    }
  }
}
if c == 0 {
  done <- 0
  return inf
}
return x.me
}
```

This solution imho is more elegant than the algorithm from the previous section.

An application to our standard example G8 with process 4 as root returns the same Table 17.5 as in the previous section, i.e., the same spanning tree.

17.5.2 Realization with Far Monitors and Transfer of the Spanning Tree

We do not provide any explanation of the version in this section but leave it entirely as an exercise—again to the motto "The source is the doc".

With your previous training—especially from Sect. 17.2.2 and after your solution to the exercise in Sect. 17.4.1—it should be easy for you to understand the following implementation and to see its correctness:

```
package dgra
import (. "nU/obj"; "nU/vtx"; "nU/fmon")

func (x *distributedGraph) bfsfm1 (o Op) {
  go func() {
    fmon.New (nil, 2, x.b1, AllTrueSp,
              x.actHost, p0 + uint16(2 * x.me), true)
```

```
        } ()
    for i := uint(0); i < x.n; i++ {
        x.mon[i] = fmon.New (nil, 2, x.b1, AllTrueSp,
                              x.host[i], p0 + uint16(2 * x.nr[i]), false)
    }
    defer x.finMon()
    x.awaitAllMonitors()
    x.Op = o
    x.parent = inf
    x.tree.Clr()
    x.tree.Ins (x.actVertex)
    x.tree.Mark (x.actVertex)
    x.tree.Write()
    pause()
    if x.me == x.root {
        x.parent = x.root
        for {
            c := uint(0)
            for k := uint(0); k < x.n; k++ {
                if ! x.visited[k] {
                    x.tree.Ex (x.actVertex)
                    bs := append(Encode(x.distance), x.tree.Encode()...)
                    bs = x.mon[k].F(bs, search).(Stream)
                    if len(bs) == 0 {
                        x.visited[k] = true
                    } else {
                        x.child[k] = true
                        c++
                        x.tree = x.decodedGraph(bs[c0:])
                        x.tree.Write()
                        pause()
                    }
                }
            }

            if c == 0 {
                break
            }
            x.distance++
        }
        bs := append(Encode(uint(0)), x.tree.Encode()...)
        for k := uint(0); k < x.n; k++ {
            if x.child[k] {
                x.mon[k].F(bs, deliver)
            }
        }
        x.Op (x.me)
    } else {
        <-done // wait until root finished
    }
    x.tree.Write()
}


func (x *distributedGraph) b1 (a Any, i uint) Any {
```

```
x.awaitAllMonitors()
bs := a.(Stream)
x.distance = Decode(uint(0), bs[:c0]).(uint)
x.tree = x.decodedGraph(bs[c0:])
x.tree.Write()
pause()
s := x.tree.Get().(vtx.Vertex).Val()
j := x.channel(s)
if i == search {
  if x.distance == 0 {
    if x.parent < inf {
      return nil
    }
    x.parent = s // == x.nr[j]
    if ! x.tree.Ex (x.actVertex) {
      x.tree.Ins (x.actVertex)
    }
    x.tree.Edge (x.edge(x.nb[j], x.actVertex))
    x.tree.Ex (x.actVertex)
    x.tree.Write()
    pause()
    x.Op (x.me)
    return append(Encode(x.distance), x.tree.Encode()...)
  }

  c := uint(0) // x.distance > 0
  for k := uint(0); k < x.n; k++ {
    if k != j && ! x.visited[k] {
      x.tree.Ex (x.actVertex)
      bs = append(Encode(x.distance - 1), x.tree.Encode()...)
      bs = x.mon[k].F(bs, search).(Stream)
      if len(bs) == 0 {
        x.visited[k] = true
      } else {
        x.tree = x.decodedGraph(bs[c0:])
        x.tree.Write()
        pause()
        x.child[k] = true
        c++
      }
    }
  }
  if c == 0 {
    return nil
  }
  x.tree.Ex (x.actVertex)
  bs = append(Encode(uint(0)), x.tree.Encode()...)
} else { // i == deliver
  x.tree.Ex (x.actVertex)
  bs = append(Encode(uint(0)), x.tree.Encode()...)
  for k := uint(0); k < x.n; k++ {
    if x.child[k] {
      x.mon[k].F(bs, deliver)
    }
  }
}
```

```
    done <- 0
  }
  return bs
}
```

References

1. Awerbuch, B.: A new distributed depth-first-search algorithm. Inf. Proc. Letters **20**, 147–150 (1985). https://doi.org/10.1016/0020-0190(85)90083-3
2. Chang, E., Roberts, R.: An improved algorithm for decentralized extrema-finding in circular configurations of processes. Commun. ACM **22**, 281–283 (1979). https://doi.org/10.1145/359104.359108
3. Cormen, T.H., Leiserson, C.E., Rivest, R.L.: Introduction to Algorithms. MIT Press, Cambridge (1990)
4. Dolev, D., Klawe, M., Rodeh, M.: An O(nlog n unidirectional distributed algorithm for extrema finding in a circle. J. Algorithms **3**, 245–260 (1982)
5. Hélary, J.-M., Raynal, M.: Depth-first traversal and virtual ring construction in distributed Systems. Research Rreport RR-0704, INRIA, (1987). https://hal.inria.fr/inria-00075848
6. Hirschberg, D.S., Sinclair, J.B.: Decentralized extrema finding in circular configurations of processes. Commun. ACM **23**, 627–628 (1980). https://doi.org/10.1145/359024.359029
7. Peterson, G.L.: An nlog n unidirectional algorithm for the circular extrema finding problem. ACM Trans. Program. Lang. Syst. **4**, 758–762 (1982). https://doi.org/10.1145/69622.357194
8. Zhu, Y., Cheung, T.-Y.: A new distributed breadth-first-seach algorithm inf. Proc. Letters **25**, 329–333 (1987)

Leader Election Algorithms

18

Abstract

Many tasks in networks require server processes to offer services, mostly by providing or manipulating distributed data. In order to avoid the serious consequences of the failure of such a process, it must be possible that another process takes over the role of the server. For this, it is necessary that the processes involved agree as to which of them should play this role. So there arises the problem of *electing a leader,* for which some algorithms are presented in this chapter, which solve the problem for circular graphs, i.e., those graphs that have the form of a ring. In conjunction with our ring construction from the previous chapter, the problem can, in principle, be solved for *any* graph.

18.1 Basics

LE LANN published the first solution to this problem in [6]. After that, many other papers appeared, the aim of which was to improve the communication complexity $O(n^2)$ of his algorithm. Some of them are presented in the following sections.

In the entire chapter, we make the same assumptions as in the previous chapters:

- All processes have different natural numbers as identities.
- No one has global information in the ring; everyone only knows its two neighbours, with which it can exchange messages via the network channels.
- Everyone runs the same algorithm.

The basic principle of any algorithm is that the processes exchange their identities as messages until one of them—the one with the highest identity—is elected as leader and at the

© Springer Fachmedien Wiesbaden GmbH, part of Springer Nature 2021
C. Maurer, *Nonsequential and Distributed Programming with Go,*
https://doi.org/10.1007/978-3-658-29782-4_18

Fig. 18.1 Circular graph with
8 processes

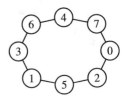

end is known to each process. Consequently, the contents of the messages are values of type
uint.

The exchange of messages can be done by either sending only in *one* direction or in *both*
directions. In the first case, we specify that the transmission is always in a mathematically
positive sense—i.e., counterclockwise. The processes "look" into the inside of the ring, i.e.,
their successor in the ring is the *right* neighbour.

Since the idea, which may initially seem obvious, of allowing the election procedure to
be carried out by only *one* process, leads to a contradiction—(Why? Think of the barber and
the Cretans from the Introduction …)— *all* processes always have to participate in it. The
example graph G8ring, on which we are working, is shown in Fig. 18.1.

18.2   Preconditions for the Realization in Go

Our algorithms for electing a leader in a ring—like the other distributed algorithms in the
dgra package—are also contained in it as enumeration type, along with the methods for
selecting an algorithm and calling it:

```
package dgra

type ElectAlg byte
const (ChangRoberts = ElectAlg(iota); HirschbergSinclair; Peterson)

type DistributedGraph interface {
   ...

// e is the actual algorithm for the leader election.
   SetElectAlgorithm (e ElectAlg)

// Returns the actual algorithm for that.
   ElectAlgorithm() ElectAlg

// Pre: The actual algorithm is started.
// It returns the identity of the elected leader.
   Leader() uint
}
```

18.3 Algorithm of Chang/Roberts

The first algorithm to solve this problem after that of LE LANN is that of CHANG and ROBERTS in [1]. It works on a *unidirectional* ring, which means that all messages will only be sent in *one* direction.

Initially, the network channels are initialized for processes of the type `uint`; their closure is prepared, and the orientation of the receive and send channels is adapted to that of the ring.

We need to distinguish whether the content of a message is the identity of the elected process or not. For this purpose, we use as "coding" that the sent identity is that of the elected process, the addition of `inf`, a number that is greater than the identities of all processes involved; a receiver decodes this with the subtraction of `inf` if necessary.

In the beginning, each process sends its identity to the right neighbour. It then enters an endless loop, the body of which begins with the reception of a message and to which it reacts as follows: First it checks whether or not the content of the message is smaller than `inf`.

In the first case, it is the identity of a process. If it is greater than its own, it forwards it; if it is smaller, it does nothing. Otherwise, it equals its own identity and it is the winner of the election. In this case, it sends the sum of `inf` and its identity to its right neighbour and then leaves the loop with `return`.

In the second case, it knows that the difference between the content and `inf` is the identity of the elected process, so it knows the winner of the election. It forwards the content and finishes its work by leaving the loop.

Due to the ring structure and the fact that messages are always sent in the same direction, each message sent is received by all other processes before returning to the sender. Therefore, the only process that receives its own identity is precisely the one with the greatest identity. Only the message with the greatest identity does not meet a greater one as it passes through the ring; therefore, the only process that receives its own identity is exactly the one with the greatest identity.

The communication complexity of the algorithm in the worst case—e.g., if the identities of the processes in the ring are ordered in descending order of the sending direction—is $O(n^2)$, as in the algorithm of LE LANN, because in this case, the identity i of the i-th process has to be passed on $i + 1$-times, i.e., the number of messages is $1 + 2 + \cdots + n = \frac{1}{2}n(n+1)$.

But the authors prove that *on average* $O(n \log n)$ messages are sufficient; if you are interested in this, you should consult their paper.

So, we have the following implementation:

```
package dgra

func (x *distributedGraph) changRoberts() {
  x.connect(uint(0))
  defer x.fin()
  out, in := uint(0), uint(1)
  if x.Graph.Outgoing(1) { in, out = out, in }
```

```
x.ch[out].Send (x.me)
for {
  id := x.ch[in].Recv().(uint)
  if id < inf {
    if id > x.me {
      x.ch[out].Send (id)
    } else if id == x.me {
      x.leader = x.me
      x.ch[out].Send (inf + x.me)
      return
    }
  } else { // n > inf
    x.leader = id - inf
    if x.leader != x.me {
      x.ch[out].Send (id)
    }
    return
  }
}
}
```

A test run of this algorithm for our example G8ring in Fig. 18.1 with a similar program as for the execution of the heartbeat and traversing algorithms from the two previous chapters

```
package main
import ("nU/ego"; "nU/dgra")

func main() {
  g := dgra.G8ringdir (ego.Me())
  g.SetElectAlgorithm(dgra.ChangRoberts)
  println ("der Leiter ist", g.Leader())
}
```

returns process 7 as leader.

18.4   Algorithm of Hirschberg/Sinclair

In [4], HIRSCHBERG and SINCLAIR published a *bidirectional* algorithm which, even in the worst case needs only $O(n \log n)$ messages. It works in a *bidirectional* ring, messages can, therefore, be sent in *both* directions.

In close reference to the original, we first reproduce the description of the authors of their algorithm and their source code.

A process can send a *both* message in both directions; it can pass a received message—possibly after changing its contents—in the ring as a *pass* message, and it can send an *echo* message as reply back to *that* direction from which it received the message.

The processes send *both* messages of certain ranges—successive powers of 2—in both directions. Processes within this range receive the message. If for a process the content of the message indicates that it cannot win the election, it forwards it and does not generate any more messages of its own. If it is clear that the original sender of the message cannot win the election, it sends back an *echo*-message informing it about that. The process at the end of the path sends back an *echo*-message informing the original sender that all processes within the range defer to the original sender.

A process that receives its *own* identity with the message has beaten all others and, thus, has won the election. It then sends a message to all other processes informing them of the completion of the election.

Their algorithm is (with slightly modified syntax):

```
const (candidate = byte(iota); lost; won
var status byte // candidate, lost or won
var maxnum uint
const (ok = true; no = false)

To run for election {
  status = candidate
  maxnum = 1
  for status == candidate {
    sendboth ("from", me, 0, maxnum)
    await both replies // but react to other messages
    if either reply == no {
      status = lost
    }
    maxnum *= 2
  }
}


On receiving message ("from", value, num, maxnum) {
  if value < me {
    sendecho (no, value)
  } else if value > me {
    status = lost
    num++
    if num < maxnum {
      sendpass ("from", value, num, maxnum)
    } else {
      sendecho (ok, value)
    }
  } else { // value == me
    status = won
  }
}


On receiving message (no, value) or (ok, value) {
  if value == me {
    this is a reply the process was awaiting
  } else {
    sendpass the message
  }
}
```

From this—quite brief—information, we now derive an implementation in Go, of course again in a method in the package `dgra` on distributed graphs. The contents of the messages are quintuples consisting of their type, the identity of a process, the number of steps taken, their maximum range, and a Boolean value. They have to be encoded into streams and decoded from them, and in the package `nchan` copies of them are needed.

For better comprehensibility, we outsource them into an internal package with the following specification:

```go
package internal
import . "nU/obj"

const (Candidate = byte(iota); Reply; Leader)

type Message interface {
  Equaler
  Coder

// Returns the kind of x.
  Kind() byte

// Returns the quadruple (id, num, maxnum, ok) of x.
  IdNumsOk() (uint, uint, uint, bool)

// x consists of kind Candidate, id i, num n, maxnum m
// und undefiniertem ok.\query{Should this read "and undefined ok"?}
  SetPass (i, n, m uint)

// x consists of kind Reply and ok b,
// the other components are unchanged.
  SetReply (b bool)

// x consists of kind Leader and id i,
// the other components are unchanged.
  SetLeader (i uint)
}

// Returns a new message, consisting
// of zero values in all components.
func New() Message { return new_() }
```

Because the implementation of `dgra/internal` is trivial, we do not include it here (of course, it is included in the source texts of this book).

First, the network channels are prepared:

```go
package dgra
import ("sync"; "nU/dgra/internal")

const (candidate = iota; lost; won)

func (x *distributedGraph) hirschbergSinclair() {
  x.connect (internal.New())
```

```
defer x.fin()
```

Then, each process assigns `candidate` to its status and 1 to the maximum range of its first message and declares the variable `replyOk`, with which it later checks whether it has received positive responses from both sides:

```
status  := candidate
maxnum  := uint(1)
var replyOk bool
```

A lock is required to protect these variables in both goroutines:

```
var mutex sync.Mutex
```

To check whether a response has arrived from *both* sides (`x.n == 2`), and for a clean termination of the algorithm, it generates two internal channels

```
gotReply := make(chan uint, x.n)
done     := make(chan uint, x.n)
```

It then outsources the message passing with its two neighbours in two endless loops, which it starts as concurrent goroutines:

```
for i := uint(0); i < x.n; i++ {
  go func (j uint) {
    loop:
    for {
```

The body of this loop begins with the reception of a message, the contents of which it stores in the variable `msg`. Then, mutual exclusion is secured:

```
      msg := x.ch[j].Recv().(internal.Message)
      mutex.Lock()
```

From `msg` it extracts the sent identity, the number of steps of the sending, its maximum range, and —in case it is an answer—the `ok` of that. Then it branches—depending on the type of message—into the three possible different cases:

```
      id, num, maxnum, ok := msg.IdNumsOk()
      switch msg.Type() {
```

As the first case, we deal with the reception of the message of another candidate.

```
      case internal.Candidate:
```

The process compares the received identity `id` with its own `x.me`, whereby there are three possibilities. If its identity is greater,

```
        if id < x.me {
```

it returns a negative response,

```
          msg.SetReply (false)
          x.ch[j].Send (msg)
```

conversely

```
} else if id > x.me {
```

it has lost, sets its status accordingly, and increments the number of steps of the message by
1.

```
status = lost
num++
```

If the number of steps is still below the maximum range,

```
if num < maxnum {
```

it transmits the message with its own identity and the new step number (j<2 !),

```
msg.SetPass (id, num, maxnum)
x.ch[1 - j].Send (msg)
```

otherwise

```
} else { // num >= maxnum
```

The message has reached the last process in its maximum range. In this case, it sends back
a positive answer because it has lost:

```
msg.SetReply (true)
x.ch[j].Send (msg)
}
```

The third possibility is the reception of its own identity,

```
} else { // id == x.me
```

which leads to the fact that is has won the election. It changes its status to won and sends
an appropriate response back to the process from which it received the message:

```
x.leader = x.me
status = won
msg.SetLeader (x.me)
x.ch[1 - j].Send (msg)
}
```

The second case is the receipt of an answer.

```
case internal.Reply:
```

If thereby the received identity equals its own,

```
if id == x.me {
```

it registers this in the variable `replyOk` and acknowledges it with a sending to the channel
`gotReply`,

```
replyOk = replyOk && ok
gotReply <- j
```

otherwise

```
} else { // id != x.me
```

it passes the message unfiltered to the next neighbour:

```
x.ch[1 - j].Send (msg)
}
```

The third case is that it receives the message that the winner of the election has been determined:

```
case internal.Leader:
```

If that is itself,

```
if id == x.me {
```

It sends a message on both internal channels and leaves the endless loop after opening the lock,

```
gotReply <- j
done <- 0
mutex.Unlock()
break loop
```

otherwise

```
} else { // id != x.me
```

it has lost the election, sends the received identity of the winner back to the process from which it received the message, assigns the winner to x.leader, sends a message to terminate on the channel done, unlocks the lock, and leaves the loop.

```
status = lost
msg.SetLeader (id)
x.ch[1 - j].Send (msg)
x.leader = id
done <- 0
mutex.Unlock()
break loop
}
```

If mutex is still closed because none of the cases resulting in a break loop has occurred, it is now opened again, so that again the body of the loop can be restarted:

```
}
mutex.Unlock()
}
```

After the end of the branching of the goroutines

```
}(i)
}
```

the process initializes the variable replyOk variable with true.

```
replyOk = true
```

Then it continuously sends—again in a loop until the end of its candidacy—

```
for status == candidate {
```

messages with its identity, the number of steps 0, and the maximum range maxnum to its
two neighbours

```
msg := internal.New()
msg.SetPass (x.me, 0, maxnum)
x.ch[0].Send (msg)
x.ch[1].Send (msg)
```

and awaits their response:

```
<-gotReply; <-gotReply // await 2 responses
```

If the two answers have arrived and both were negative, it lost:

```
if ! replyOk {
    status = lost
}
```

If it is no longer a candidate, it terminates the loop and, thus, its algorithm,

```
if status != candidate {
    break
}
```

otherwise it repeats the loop as a candidate with messages of doubled maximum range:

```
        maxnum *= 2
    }
```

To finish the program cleanly, it waits at the end for two messages from the channel done:

```
    <-done; <-done
}
```

A test run with our example G8ring naturally returns the expected result.

We conclude this section with an analysis of the communication complexity of the authors.
A process only generates messages with a range of 2^i, if it was not beaten by a process within
the range 2^{i-1} (in both directions). Within each group of $2^{i-1} + 1$ successive processes, at
most one can generate messages with the range 2^i. All n processes can generate messages
with a range of 1, but only at most $\lceil n/2 \rceil$ processes, as with the range 2, at most $\lceil n/3 \rceil$ with
a range 4, not exceeding $\lceil n/5 \rceil$ with a range 8, and so on.

When creating a message with the range 2^i at most $4 \cdot 2^i$ messages are sent. The total
number of all messages sent is, therefore, at most $4 \cdot (1 \cdot n + 2 \cdot \lceil n/2 \rceil + 4 \cdot \lceil n/3 \rceil + 8 \cdot
\lceil n/5 \rceil + \cdots + 2 \cdot \lceil n/(2^{i-1} + 1) \rceil + \ldots)$.

Anyone of the at most $1 + \lceil \log n \rceil$ terms within the brackets is less than $2n$. (No process
sends messages with a range of $2n$ or more, because if a process has generated a message
with a range of at least n, and this is accepted all the way through the ring, it is elected
and stops generating further messages.) Therefore, the total sum of all messages is less than
$8n + 8 \lceil n \log n \rceil = O(n \log n)$.

18.5   Algorithm of Peterson

In [7], PETERSON developed two *unidirectional* algorithms for the election of a leader in rings with communication complexity $O(n \log n)$, of which we present here only the first. In his algorithms, all processes run through two infinite loops, which PETERSON calls *active* and *relay*.

Processes in *active*-loop work in phases, whereby the number of these processes is halved in each phase. Each process begins with its own identity as a temporary identity `tid`. In each phase, each process receives the temporary identity of its left neighbour in `ntid` and that of the left neighbour of that left neighbour in `nntid`. If `ntid` is the largest of these three temporary identities, it assigns this value to `tid` and starts the next phase in the *active*-loop; otherwise, it jumps into the *relay*-loop. Processes in this second loop only forward all received messages.

However, PETERSON treats the case that a process is the elected one by the receipt of a message with the content of its own identity somewhat casually; he only writes *"then an exception occurs and that process will consider itself elected and will perform whatever action it is required to do."* We do this as in the algorithm of CHANG/ROBERTS by encoding the identity of the elected process by `inf`, thus achieving a clean termination.

The algorithm is integrated into the function

```
func (x *distributedGraph) peterson() {
```

and starts with the same initialization as in the algorithm of CHANG/ROBERTS:

```
x.connect(uint(0))
defer x.fin()
out, in := uint(0), uint(1)
if x.Graph.Outgoing(1) { in, out = out, in }
```

At the beginning, each process assigns its identity to the variable `tid`, enters into the *active* loop, and sends `tid` to its right neighbour:

```
tid := x.me
for { // active
  x.ch[out].Send(tid)
```

When receiving the first message in this phase, it assigns its contents to the variable `ntid`. If this value is equal to its own identity, it is elected; it then sends the sum of its identity and `inf` to its right neighbour and finishes its work with `return`:

```
ntid := x.ch[in].Recv().(uint)
if ntid == x.me {
  x.ch[out].Send(ntid + inf)
  x.leader = x.me
  return
}
```

If the value of `ntid` is greater than or equal to `inf`, it knows that the difference between `ntid` and `inf` is the identity of the elected process, so it knows the winner of the election. It then forwards `ntid` and finishes its work with `return`:

```
if ntid >= inf {
  x.leader = ntid - inf
  x.ch[out].Send (ntid)
  return
}
```

Otherwise, the value of ntid is smaller than inf, i.e., it represents an identity. If the value of tid is greater than that of ntid, it sends tid, otherwise ntid:

```
if tid > ntid {
  x.ch[out].Send (tid)
} else {
  x.ch[out].Send (ntid)
}
```

So it reaches the next phase exactly when its successor does not succeed; thus, each phase halves the number of processes that remain in the first loop. In particular, it is clear that the algorithm terminates.

It assigns the content of the second received message in this phase to the variable nntid

```
nntid := x.ch[in].Recv().(uint)
```

and does with nntid exactly the same as with the reception of ntid before:

```
if nntid == x.me {
  x.ch[out].Send (nntid + inf)
  x.leader = x.me
  return
}
if nntid >= inf {
  x.leader = nntid - inf
  x.ch[out].Send (nntid)
  return
}
```

Otherwise, it checks whether ntid is the largest of the three temporary identities considered. If that is the case, it replaces the value of tid with the value of ntid

```
if ntid >= tid && ntid >= nntid {
  tid = ntid
```

and goes to the next phase, hence again goes through the loop; otherwise, it leaves the loop with break and enters the *relay*-loop:

```
} else {
  break
}
}
```

The body of the *relay* loop begins with the reception of a message, the contents of which it assigns to the variable n:

```
for { // relay
  n := x.ch[in].Recv().(uint)
```

If the value of n equals its identity, it is the elected process:

```
if  n  ==  x.me  {
    x.leader = x.me
```

and sends the sum of x.me and inf to its successor. After receiving the next message, it terminates the algorithm with return:

```
    x.ch[out].Send (x.leader + inf)
    x.ch[in].Recv ()
    return
```

The reception of this last message is necessary for the elected process, because it still has to receive the message of its predecessor, which contains the greatest identity, in order to clear the network channel of it; therefore, the evaluation is also no longer necessary.

If the value of n otherwise is at least as large as inf, it knows that it will get the identity of the elected process after subtracting inf, so it knows it and terminates the whole thing with return:

```
if  n  >=  inf  {
    x.ch[out].Send (n)
    x.leader = n - inf
    return
    }
```

Otherwise, the value received is the identity of a process, which it forwards to its right neighbour

```
    x.ch[out].Send (n)
    }
}
```

and with that finishes its work.

Since none of the processes, except the one with the greatest identity, can ever receive a message with the content of its own identity again, because it is not forwarded in one of the phases in the first loop, it is clear that in the algorithm, exactly *that* process with the greatest identity is elected as leader.

Because each phase halves the number of processes remaining in the first loop, and in each of them each process sends two messages (as the elected process, a third), the number of messages sent is bounded by $O(n \log n)$ and, therefore, also in the worst case much better than the algorithm of CHANG/ROBERTS.

For his second version of this algorithm, PETERSON proved that at most $c \cdot n \log n + O(n)$ messages with constants $c \approx 1,440$ are necessary, where $c = 1/\log_2 \Phi$ with $\Phi = \frac{1}{2}(1 + \sqrt{5})$. This constant was—at about the same time—by DOLEV, KLAWE, and RODEH in [2] brought down to $c \approx 1,356$. Thus, the assumption of HIRSCHBERG/SINCLAIR in [4] was refuted in that a *unidirectional* election algorithm in a ring with n processes has at least the communication complexity $O(n^2)$.

18.6   Election with Depth-First Search

If we drop the requirement that all processes participate in the election procedure in the same way and mark a process as `root`, the election can also be done with algorithms for depth-first search from Chap. 17.

Although this contradicts the basic idea of the election, it is nevertheless left as an exercise, because it is a pretty application of the depth-first search. (A solution can be found in the source texts of the book.)

Here are some hints: The distributed depth-first search algorithm in Sect. 17.2 or the Awerbuch algorithm in Sect. 17.3 need only be extended in *such a way* that they forward the respective actual maximum of the identities of the processes involved. Each process compares its identity with the received value and transmits the maximum of the two. At the end—as in Sect. 17.2.1—the result of the election must be passed on via the spanning tree of the depth-first search.

The messages not only consist of the time but of the combination of time and actually determined leader in the form `t + inf * x.leader`. After the receipt of a number n, the pair `(t,1)` is determined by `t, 1 = n%inf, n/inf`, and if `1` is greater than `x.leader`, the value of `x.leader` is replaced by that of `1`. In this way, the election of a leader is possible for *any* connected graph, not just for circular ones.

Compared to the publications that deal with this topic and—partly with certain limitations—present algorithms for its solution (e.g., [3, 5] and [8]), this is, of course, much easier, because all these algorithms are quite complicated, and it is difficult to see their correctness and to implement them. To the algorithm from [5] a quotation from Peterson in [8]: "...the algorithm is extremely long and complicated and it is very difficult to determine its correctness."

References

1. Chang, E., Roberts, R.: An improved algorithm for decentralized extrema-finding in circular configurations of processes. Commun. ACM **22**, 281–283 (1979). https://doi.org/10.1145/359104. 359108
2. Dolev, D., Klawe, M., Rodeh, M.: An O(nlog n) unidirectional distributed algorithm for extrema finding in a circle. J. Algorithms **3**, 245–260 (1982)
3. Gafni, E., Afek, Y.: Election and Traversal in Unidirectional Networks. Proc. ACM SympPrinciples of Dist. Comp. 190–198 (1984). https://doi.org/10.1145/800222.806746
4. Hirschberg, D.S., Sinclair, J.B.: Decentralized extrema finding in circular configurations of processes. Commun. ACM **23**, 627–628 (1980). https://doi.org/10.1145/359024.359029
5. Korach, E., Moran, S., Zaks, S.: Tight Lower and Upper Bounds for Some Distributed Algorithms for a Complete Network of Processors. PODC '84, ACM symposion 199–207 (1984). https://doi. org/10.1145/800222.806747
6. Le Lann, G.: Distributed Systems—Towards a formal Approach. IFIP Congress Toronto (1977) 155–160 https://www.rocq.inria.fr/novaltis/publications/IFIPCongress1977.pdf

7. Peterson, G.L.: An nlog n unidirectional algorithm for the circular extrema finding problem. ACM Trans. Program. Lang. Syst. **4**, 758–762 (1982). https://doi.org/10.1145/69622.357194
8. Peterson, G. L.: Efficient Algorithms for Elections in Meshes and Complete Graphs. TR 140, Dept. of Comp. Sci., University of Rochester (1985)

Further Literature

1. Abdallah, A.E., Jones, C.B., Sanders, J.W. (eds.): Communicating Sequential Processes, The First 25 Years. Springer (2005). https://doi.org/10.1007/b136154
2. Andrews, G.R.: A Method for Solving Synchronization Problems. Science of Computer Prog. **13**, 1–21 (1989). https://doi.org/10.1016/0167-6423(89)90013-0
3. Andrews, G.R.: Paradigms for Process Interaction in Distributed Programs. ACM Comput. Surv. **23**, 49–90 (1991). https://doi.org/10.1145/103162.103164
4. Andrews, G.R., Schneider, F.B.: Concepts and Notations for Concurrent Programming. ACM Comput. Surv. **15**, 3–43 (1983). https://doi.org/10.1145/356901.356903
5. Annot, J.K., Janssens, M.D., Van de Goor, A.J.: Comments on Morris's starvation-free solution to the mutual exclusion problem. Inf. Proc. Letters **23**, 91–97 (1986)
6. Apt, K.R., de Boer, F.S., Olderog, E.-R.: Verification of Sequential and Concurrent Programs. Springer (2009). https://doi.org/10.1007/978-1-84882-745-5
7. Attiya, H., Welch, J.: Distributed Computing: Fundamentals, Simulations, and Advanced Topics. Wiley (2004). ISBN: 978-0-471-45324-6
8. Axford, T.: Concurrent Programming. Wiley (1989)
9. Bacon, J.: Concurrent Systems, 3rd edn, Operating Systems, Distributed and Database Systems. Addison-Wesley (2003)
10. Bernstein, A.J.: Output Guards and Nondeterminism in "Communicating Sequential Processes". ACM Trans. Program. Lang. Syst. **2**, 234–238 (1980). https://doi.org/10.1145/357094.357101
11. Breshears, C.: The Art of Concurrency: A Thread Monkey's Guide to Writing Parallel Applications. O'Reilly (2009). ISBN: 9780596521530
12. Block, K., Woo, T.-K.: A more efficient generalization of Peterson's mutual exclusion algorithm. Inf. Proc. Letters **35**, 219–222 (1990). https://doi.org/10.1016/0020-0190(90)90048-3
13. Brinch Hansen, P.: Java's insecure parallelism. ACM SIGPLAN Notices **34**, 38–45 (1999). https://doi.org/10.1145/312009.312034
14. Brinch Hansen, P. (ed.): The Origin of Concurrent Programming. Springer (2002). https://doi.org/10.1007/978-1-4757-3472-0
15. Carvalho, O.S.F., Roucairol, G.: On Mutual Exclusion In Computer Networks. Commun. ACM **26**, 146–147 (1983)

© Springer Fachmedien Wiesbaden GmbH, part of Springer Nature 2021
C. Maurer, *Nonsequential and Distributed Programming with Go*,
https://doi.org/10.1007/978-3-658-29782-4

16. Carvalho, O. S. F., Roucairol, G.: Further Comments on Mutual Exclusion In Computer Networks. Laboratoire de Recherche en Informatique—Université de Paris-Sud Rapport de Recherche N° 166 (1982) https://doi.org/10.13140/2.1.2085.5043

17. Chandy, K.M., Misra, J.: Parallel Program Design: A Foundation. Addison-Wesley (1988). ISBN: 978-0201058666

18. Chandy, K.M., Misra, J.: Distributed Computation on Graphs: Shortest Path Algorithms. Commun. ACM **25**, 833–837 (1982). https://doi.org/10.1145/358690.358717

19. Chang, E. J. H.: Echo Algorithms: Depth Parallel Operations On General Graphs. Softw. Eng. SE-8 (1982) 391–401 https://doi.org/10.1109/TSE.1982.235573

20. Cheung, T.-Y.: Graph Traversal Techniques and the Maximum Flow Problem in Distributed Computations. Softw. Eng. SE-9 (1983) 504–512

21. Cidon, I.: Yet Another Distributed Depth-First-Search Algorithm. Inf. Proc. Letters **26**, 301–305 (1988). https://doi.org/10.1016/0020-0190(55)

22. Downey, A. B.: The Little Book of Semaphores. http://greenteapress.com/semaphores/LittleBookOfSemaphores.pdf

23. Dowsing, R.D.: An Introduction to Concurrency Using Occam. Van Nostrand Reinhold (1988). ISBN: 978-0278000599

24. Eisenberg, M.A., McGuire, M.R.: Further comments on Dijkstra's concurrent programming control problem. Commun. ACM **11**, 999 (1972). https://doi.org/10.1145/355606.361895

25. Franklin, R.: On an Improved Algorithm for Decentralized Extrema Finding in Circular Configurations of Processors. Commun. ACM **25**, 336–337 (1982). https://doi.org/10.1145/358506.358517

26. Gallager, R.G., Humblet, P.A., Spira, P.M.: A Distributed Algorithm for Minimum-Weight Spanning Trees. ACM Trans. Program. Lang. Syst. **5**, 66–77 (1983). https://doi.org/10.1145/357195.357200

27. Garcia-Molina, H.: Elections in a Distributed Computing System. IEEE Trans. Comp. C-31 1 (1982) 48–59 https://doi.org/10.1109/TC.1982.1675885

28. Garg, V.K.: Principles of Distributed Systems. Springer (1996). https://doi.org/10.1007/978-1-4613-1321-2

29. Garg, V.K.: Elements of Distributed Computing. Wiley (2002). ISBN: 978-0471036005

30. Gehani, N., McGattrick, A. D. (eds.): Concurrent Programming. Addison-Wesley (1988). ISBN: 978-0201174359

31. Genuys, F. (ed.): Programming Languages. Academic Press (1968)

32. Gjessing, S.: Semantics and verification of monitors and systems of monitors and processes. Distributed Computing **2**, 190–200 (1988). https://doi.org/10.1007/BF01872845

33. Goetz, B., Bloch, J., Bowbeer, J., Lea, D., Holmes, D., Peierls, T.: Java Concurrency in Practice. Addison-Wesley (2006). ISBN: 978-0321349606

34. Hartley, S.J.: Operating Systems Programming: The SR Programming Language. Oxford University Press (1995). ISBN: 978-0195095791

35. Hartley, S.J.: Concurrent Programming: The Java Programming Language. Oxford University Press (1998).

36. Hemmendinger, D.: A correct implementation of general semaphores. Operating Systems Review **22**, 42–44 (1988). https://doi.org/10.1145/47671.47675

37. Hemmendinger, D.: Comments on "A correct implementation of general semaphores". Operating Systems Review **23**, 7–8 (1989). https://doi.org/10.1145/65762.65763

38. Herlihy, M.: Wait-Free Synchronization. ACM Trans. Program. Lang. Syst. **11**, 124–149 (1991). https://doi.org/10.1145/114005.102808

39. Hélary, J.-M., Plouzeau, N., Raynal, M.: A Distributed Algorithm for Mutual Exclusion in an Arbitrary Network. Comput. J. **31**, 289–295 (1988)

40. Hélary, J.-M., Raynal, M.: Distributed Evaluation: a Tool for Constructing Distributed Detection Programs. IRISA, ISTIC Université de Rennes, 184–194

41. Hesselink, W. H., Ijbema, M.: Starvation-free Mutual Exclusion with Semaphores. Formal Aspects of Computing 25 (2013) 947–969 https://doi.org/10.1007/s00165-11-0219-y https://www.rug.nl/research/portal/files/2400325/2013FormAspCompHesselink.pdf

42. Hewitt, C.: Viewing control structures as patterns of passing messages. TR 410 (1976) MIT, Artificial Intelligence Laboratory

43. Hoare, C.A.R.: An Axiomatic Basis for Computer Programming. Commun. ACM **12**, 576–580 (1969). https://doi.org/10.1145/363235.363259

44. Hull, M.E.C.: Occam - a Programming Language for Multiprocessor Systems. Comp. Lang. **12**, 27–37 (1987). https://doi.org/10.1016/0096-0551(87)90010-5

45. Johansen, K.E., Jørgensen, U.L., Nielsen, S.H., Nielsen, S.E., Skyum, S.: A Distributed Spanning Tree Algorithm. LNCS **312**, 1–12 (1987). https://doi.org/10.1007/BFb0019790

46. Kearns, P.: A correct and unrestrictive implementation of general semaphores. ACM SIGOPS Oper. Syst. Rev. **22**, 42–44 (1988). https://doi.org/10.1145/54289.54293

47. Kishon, A., Hudak, P., Consel, C.: Monitoring Semantics: A Formal Framework for Specifying, Implementing, and Reasoning about Execution Monitors. In PLDI, ACM Press (1991) 338–352 https://doi.org/10.1145/113446.113474.

48. Lakshmanan, K.B., Meenakshi, N., Thulasiraman, K.: A Time-Optimal Message-Efficient Distributed Algorithm for Depth-First-Search. Inf. Proc. Letters **25**, 103–109 (1987). https://doi.org/10.1016/0020-0190(87)90228-6

49. Lamport, L.: Proving the Correctness of Multiprocess Programs. Softw. Eng. SE-3 (1977) 125–143 https://doi.org/10.1109/TSE.1977.229904 https://research.microsoft.com/.../lamport/pubs/lamport-how-to-make.pdf

50. Lamport, L.: Fast Mutual Exclusion. ACM Trans. Comput. Syst. 5 (1987) 1–11 https://doi.org/10.1145/7351.7352 https://research.microsoft.com/.../lamport/pubs/fast-mutex.ps

51. Lamport, L.: A new Approach to Proving the Correctness of Multiprocess Programs. ACM Trans. Program. Lang. Syst. 1 (1979) 84–97 https://doi.org/10.1145/357062.357068 https://research.microsoft.com/en-us/um/people/lamport/pubs/new-approach.pdf

52. Lamport, L.: Solved Problems, Unsolved Problems and Nonproblems in Concurrency. Oper. Syst. Rev. **19**, 34–44 (1985). https://doi.org/10.1145/858336.858339

53. Lamport, L.: The mutual exclusion problem: part II—statement and solutions. J. ACM **33**, 327–348 (1986). https://doi.org/10.1145/5383.5385

54. Lamport, L.: On Interprocess Communication—Part II: Algorithms. Distributed Computing **1**, 86–101 (1986). https://doi.org/10.1007/BF01786228

55. Lavallee, I., Roucairol, G.: A Fully Distributed (Minimal) Spanning Tree Algorithm. Inf. Proc. Letters **23**, 55–62 (1986). 0020–0190(86)90043-8

56. Lea, D.: Concurrent Programming in Java (2nd ed.). Addison-Wesley (1999). ISBN: 978-0201310092

57. Lehmann, D., Rabin, M.O.: A Symmetric and Fully Distributed Solution to the Dining Philosophers Problem. ACM Symposium on Principles of Programming Languages 133–138 (1981). https://doi.org/10.1145/567532.567547

58. Lynch, N.A.: Distributed Algorithms. Morgan Kaufmann (1996). ISBN: 978-0201310092

59. Magee, J., Kramer, J.: Concurrency: State Models & Java Programs. Wiley (1999)

60. Makki, S. A. M., Havas, G.: Distributed Algorithms for Depth-First-Search. Inf. Proc. Letters 60 (1996) 7–12; https://doi.org/10.1016/S0020-190(96)00141-X

61. May, D.: Occam. ACM SIGPLAN Notices **18**, 69–79 (1983). https://doi.org/10.1145/948176.948183

62. Neilsen, M. L., Mizuno, M.: A Dag-Based Algorithm for Distributed Mutual Exclusion. IEEE 11th IntConf. on Distributed Computing Systems (1991) 354–360. https://doi.org/10.1109/ICDCS.1991.148689

63. Parnas, D.L.: The Non-Problem of Nested Monitor Calls. ACM SIGOPS Oper. Syst. Rev. **12**, 12–14 (1978). https://doi.org/10.1145/775323.775324

64. Perrott, R. H.: Parallel Programming. Addison-Wesley Publishing Company (1987). ISBN: 978-0201142310

65. Peterson, G.L.: Concurrent Reading While Writing. ACM Trans. Program. Lang. Syst. **5**, 46–55 (1983). https://doi.org/10.1145/357195/357198

66. Peterson, G. L., Fischer, M. J.: Economical solutions for the critical section problem in a distributed system. In STOC '77 Proceedings of the Ninth Annual ACM Symposium on Theory of Computing (1977) 91–97 https://doi.org/10.1145/800105.803398

67. Raynal, M.: Networks and Distributed Computation. MIT Press (1988). ISBN: 978-0946536276

68. Raynal, M.: Concurrent Programming: Algorithms, Principles and Foundations. Springer (2013). https://doi.org/10.1007/978-3-642-32027-9

69. Raynal, M.: A Simple Taxonomy for Distributed Mutual Exclusion Problems. ACM SIGOPS Oper. Syst. Rev. 25 (1991) 47–50; https://doi.org/10.1145/122120.122123

70. Raynal, M., Hélary, J.-M.: Synchronization and Control of Distributed Systems and Programs. Wiley (1990). ISBN: 978-0471924531

71. Ricart, G., Agrawala, A.K.: Author's response to 'An Optimal Algorithm for Mutual Exclusion in Computer Networks' by Carvalho and Roucairol. Commun. ACM **26**, 147–148 (1983). https://doi.org/10.1145/358699.383423

72. Roscoe, A.W.: Understanding Concurrent Systems. Springer (2010). https://doi.org/10.1007/978-1-84882-258-0

73. Roscoe, A.W., Jones, C.B., Wood, K.: Reflections on the Work of C. A. R. Hoare. Springer (2010). https://doi.org/10.1007/978-1-84882-258-0

74. Santoro, N.: Design and Analysis of Distributed Algorithms. Wiley (2006). ISBN: 978-0471719977

75. Schneider, F.B.: Synchronization in Distributed Programs. ACMTrans. Program. Lang. Syst. **4**, 179–195 (1982). https://doi.org/10.1145/357162.357163

76. Schneider, F.B.: On Concurrent Programming. Springer (1997). https://doi.org/10.1007/978-1-4612-1830-2

77. Silberschatz, A., Galvin, P.B., Gagne, G.: Operating System Concepts. Wiley (2009). ISBN: 978-1118063330

78. Suzuki, I., Kasami, T.: A Distributed Mutual Exclusion Algorithm. ACM Trans. Comput. Syst. **3**, 344–349 (1985). https://doi.org/10.1145/6110.214406

79. Tanenbaum, A. S., Van Steen, M.: Distributed Systems: Principles and Paradigms. Pearson (2007). ISBN: 978-0131972599

80. Taubenfeld, G.: Synchronization Algorithms and Concurrent Programming. Pearson Education (2006). ISBN: 978-0131972599

81. Taft, S.T., Duff, R.A. (eds.): Ada 95 Reference Manual, Language and Standard Libraries. Springer (1997). https://doi.org/10.1007/BFb0034910

82. Weber, M.: Verteilte Systeme Spektrum Akademischer Verlag (1998). ISBN: 978-0470844373

83. Wegner, P., Smolka, S, A.: Processes, Tasks and Monitors: A Comparative Study of Concurrent Programming Primitives. Softw. Eng. SE-9 (1983) 446–462 https://doi.org/10.1109/TSE.1983.234781

84. Weske, M.: Deadlocks in Computersystemen. International Thomson Publ. (1995)

85. Wellings, A.: Concurrent and Real-Time Programming in Java. Wiley (2004). ISBN: 978-0470844373

Index

© Springer Fachmedien Wiesbaden GmbH, part of Springer Nature 2021
C. Maurer, *Nonsequential and Distributed Programming with Go*,
https://doi.org/10.1007/978-3-658-29782-4

Printed in the United States
By Bookmasters